OUTLINES
PHILOSOPHY OF RIGHT

GEORG WILHELM FRIEDRICH HEGEL (1770–1831) was born in Stuttgart and is the exact contemporary of Beethoven and Wordsworth. In 1788 he entered the Theological Seminary (or *Stift*) in Tübingen, where he studied both theology and philosophy and shared a room with the future poet, Friedrich Hölderlin, and future philosopher, Friedrich Wilhelm Joseph von Schelling. After leaving Tübingen in 1793, he worked as a private tutor in Bern and Frankfurt before joining Schelling at the University of Jena in 1801. At Jena Hegel began to develop his philosophical system, lectured on natural law for the first time, and completed his monumental *Phenomenology of Spirit* (1807). After leaving Jena in 1807 he worked for a year in Bamberg as a newspaper editor, and then from 1808 to 1816 occupied the post of rector of a grammar school in Nuremberg, during which time he was married and published the three-volume *Science of Logic* (1812–16). In 1816 he was made professor at the University of Heidelberg, and in 1817 he published the first edition of his *Encyclopaedia of the Philosophical Sciences*. In 1818 he was called to a professorship in Berlin, where he would remain until his death in November 1831. During his years in the city Hegel became one of the most prominent public figures and the centre of a self-consciously 'Hegelian' school of thought. His students included Ludwig Feuerbach and David Friedrich Strauß. The *Philosophy of Right* was published in 1820, though it is dated 1821. It is one of the more widely studied of Hegel's works, and has influenced generations of philosophers and political thinkers from Karl Marx to John Rawls.

STEPHEN HOULGATE is professor of philosophy at the University of Warwick. He is the author of *Hegel, Nietzsche and the Criticism of Metaphysics* (1986), *An Introduction to Hegel: Freedom, Truth and History* (2nd edn. 2005), and *The Opening of Hegel's Logic: From Being to Infinity* (2006). He is also the editor of *Hegel and the Philosophy of Nature* (1998), *The Hegel Reader* (1998), and *Hegel and the Arts* (2007). He has served as vice-president and president of the Hegel Society of America and was editor of the *Bulletin of the Hegel Society of Great Britain* from 1998 to 2007.

OXFORD WORLD'S CLASSICS

*For over 100 years Oxford World's Classics have brought
readers closer to the world's great literature. Now with over 700
titles—from the 4,000-year-old myths of Mesopotamia to the
twentieth century's greatest novels—the series makes available
lesser-known as well as celebrated writing.*

*The pocket-sized hardbacks of the early years contained
introductions by Virginia Woolf, T. S. Eliot, Graham Greene,
and other literary figures which enriched the experience of reading.
Today the series is recognized for its fine scholarship and
reliability in texts that span world literature, drama and poetry,
religion, philosophy, and politics. Each edition includes perceptive
commentary and essential background information to meet the
changing needs of readers.*

OXFORD WORLD'S CLASSICS

G. W. F. HEGEL

Outlines of the Philosophy of Right

Translated by
T. M. KNOX

Revised, edited, and introduced by
STEPHEN HOULGATE

OXFORD
UNIVERSITY PRESS

OXFORD
UNIVERSITY PRESS

Great Clarendon Street, Oxford ox2 6DP
Oxford University Press is a department of the University of Oxford.
It furthers the University's objective of excellence in research, scholarship,
and education by publishing worldwide in

Oxford New York

Auckland Cape Town Dar es Salaam Hong Kong Karachi
Kuala Lumpur Madrid Melbourne Mexico City Nairobi
New Delhi Shanghai Taipei Toronto

With offices in

Argentina Austria Brazil Chile Czech Republic France Greece
Guatemala Hungary Italy Japan Poland Portugal Singapore
South Korea Switzerland Thailand Turkey Ukraine Vietnam

Oxford is a registered trade mark of Oxford University Press
in the UK and in certain other countries

Published in the United States
by Oxford University Press Inc., New York

Translation © Oxford University Press 1952, 2008
Editorial matter © Stephen Houlgate 2008

British Library Cataloguing in Publication Data

Data available

Library of Congress Cataloging-in-Publication Data

Hegel, Georg Wilhelm Friedrich, 1770–1831.
[Grundlinien der Philosophie des Rechts. English]
Outlines of the philosophy of right / [G.W.F. Hegel]; translated by T.M. Knox;
revised, edited, and introduced by Stephen Houlgate.
p. cm. — (Oxford world's classics)
Includes bibliographical references and index.
1. Law—Philosophy. 2. Natural law. 3. State, The. 4. Political science.
5. Ethics. I. Houlgate, Stephen. II. Title
K230.H43G7813 2008
340′.11—dc22

2008000395

Typeset by Cepha Imaging Private Ltd., Bangalore, India
Printed in Great Britain by
Clays Ltd, Elcograf S.p.A.

ISBN 978–0–19–280610–9

CONTENTS

INTRODUCTION

HEGEL'S *Outlines of the Philosophy of Right* is one of the greatest works of moral, social, and political philosophy, comparable in scope and profundity of insight to Plato's *Republic*, Aristotle's *Politics*, Rousseau's *Social Contract*, and, in the twentieth century, Rawls's *Theory of Justice*. It contains significant ideas on justice, moral responsibility, family life, economic activity, and the political structure of the state. In presenting these ideas Hegel draws on Plato, Rousseau, Montesquieu, Smith, Kant, and Fichte, and on his broad knowledge of events and conditions in Germany, France, and Britain, to produce a wide-ranging and penetrating account of modern social and political life.

Yet Hegel's political philosophy is not one with which the public, or even many professional philosophers, are intimately familiar. This is due partly to the undeniable difficulty of the *Philosophy of Right*, which has prevented Hegel's text from gaining the wider popularity enjoyed by the works of Marx or Nietzsche. (In addition to the conceptual difficulty of Hegel's thought, his text is designed to be a handbook to accompany his lectures, rather than a fully worked-out presentation of his ideas, and so is at times much more condensed than one would like.)[1] The relative obscurity in which Hegel's political philosophy still languishes is also due partly to the ill-informed but influential prejudice of philosophers such as Karl Popper. In his widely read book *The Open Society and its Enemies*, Popper accuses Hegel of churning out 'bombastic and mystifying cant', of maintaining that 'the state is everything, and the individual nothing' and of thereby being 'the missing link' between Plato and modern totalitarianism.[2] Little wonder that many who hold Popper in high regard have not felt much inclination to get to know Hegel's philosophy better. Popper's diatribe against Hegel is based, however, on a shockingly superficial and selective reading of Hegel's work, and leans heavily on the intemperate grumblings of Hegel's notoriously hostile

---

[1] See G. W. F. Hegel, *Outlines of the Philosophy of Right* [henceforth *PR*], Preface, 3–4 below.

[2] Karl Popper, *The Open Society and its Enemies*, 2 vols. (1945; London: Routledge, 1966), ii. 28, 31.

contemporary Arthur Schopenhauer, who accused Hegel of being a paid agent of the Prussian government.[3] Careful and attentive study of Hegel's *Philosophy of Right* reveals, by contrast, that Hegel's text is in fact one of the most subtle and perceptive accounts of human *freedom* that we possess. Far from being a sinister forerunner of Hitlerian fascism, Hegel emerges from the pages of his book—in the judgement of the twentieth century's greatest political philosopher, John Rawls—as a 'moderately progressive reform-minded liberal'.[4] The aim of this edition of Hegel's *Philosophy of Right* is to bring Hegel's text to a much wider audience than it has enjoyed hitherto, so that more readers can discover for themselves that Rawls's judgement on Hegel is considerably nearer the mark than that of Popper.

Hegel's Life and Political Sympathies

Georg Wilhelm Friedrich Hegel was born in Stuttgart in 1770, the same year as Beethoven and Wordsworth. In his youth Hegel read Rousseau, Lessing, Klopstock, and Wieland, and his diary, which he wrote (partly in Latin) from 1785 to 1787, indicates that he could read Greek as well as Latin, and even some Hebrew, and that at the age of 8 he had received a multi-volume translation of Shakespeare's plays (some of which he would later read in English).[5] In 1788 Hegel entered the Theological Seminary (or *Stift*) in Tübingen, where he studied both theology and philosophy. After 1790 he famously shared a room with the future poet Friedrich Hölderlin, and future philosopher Friedrich Wilhelm Joseph von Schelling, though the room was also occupied by seven other students. Hegel's 'hero' at this time was Rousseau, whose *Émile*, *Social Contract*, and *Confessions* were particular favourites. It is also likely that Hegel shared the general enthusiasm at the Seminary for the French Revolution of 1789, though the often-repeated story that Hegel, Schelling, and other friends planted a 'freedom tree' in a meadow outside Tübingen to commemorate the storming of the Bastille may well be apocryphal.[6]

---

[3] Ibid. 33.

[4] John Rawls, *Lectures on the History of Moral Philosophy* (Cambridge, Mass.: Harvard University Press, 2000), 330.

[5] Johannes Hoffmeister (ed.), *Dokumente zu Hegels Entwicklung* (1936; Stuttgart–Bad Cannstatt: Frommann-Holzboog, 1974), 12–13.

[6] Walter Jaeschke, *Hegel-Handbuch. Leben-Werk-Schule* (Stuttgart: J. B. Metzler, 2003), 6–7.

After leaving Tübingen in 1793 Hegel worked as a private tutor in Bern and Frankfurt, before joining Schelling at the University of Jena in 1801. Hegel taught at the university as a *Privatdozent* (an unsalaried lecturer paid by his students) until 1806, when he was finally offered a modest salary after the intervention of Goethe. It was at Jena that Hegel began to develop his philosophical system and first lectured on natural law. He also finished his long manuscript on 'The German Constitution', which he had started in Frankfurt, and wrote his important essay 'On the Scientific Ways of Treating Natural Law' (1802–3).[7] In October 1806 Hegel completed his monumental *Phenomenology of Spirit*,[8] and had to send his only copy of large sections of the manuscript by courier through the French lines outside Jena. On 13 October 1806—the day before the battle of Jena—the French occupied the city and Hegel saw the 'Emperor [Napoleon]—this world-soul [*Weltseele*]—riding out of the city on reconnaissance'.[9]

After leaving Jena in January 1807 Hegel worked for a year in Bamberg as a newspaper editor, and then from 1808 to 1816 occupied the post of rector of a grammar school in Nuremberg, during which time he was married and published the three-volume *Science of Logic*.[10] In 1816 Hegel was appointed to a salaried professorship at the University of Heidelberg. During his time in Heidelberg he published the first edition of his *Encyclopaedia of the Philosophical Sciences* (1817)[11] and once again lectured on natural law (1817–18). He also wrote his manuscript on the 'Proceedings of the Estates Assembly in the Kingdom of Württemberg, 1815–1816' (1817).[12]

In 1818 Hegel was called to a professorship in Berlin by the new Prussian Minister for Spiritual, Educational, and Medical Affairs, Karl Siegmund Franz vom Stein zum Altenstein. He would remain

---

[7] See Laurence Dickey and H. B. Nisbet (eds.), *G. W. F. Hegel: Political Writings* (Cambridge: Cambridge University Press, 1999), 6–180.

[8] *Hegel's Phenomenology of Spirit*, trans. A. V. Miller (Oxford: Oxford University Press, 1977).

[9] *Hegel: The Letters*, trans. Clark Butler and Christiane Seiler (Bloomington, Ind.: Indiana University Press, 1984), 114.

[10] *Hegel's Science of Logic*, trans. A. V. Miller (Amherst, NY: Humanity Books, 1999). See explanatory note to p. 4.

[11] G. W. F. Hegel, *Encyclopedia of the Philosophical Sciences in Outline* [1817] *and Critical Writings*, ed. E. Behler (New York: Continuum, 1990). See also first explanatory note to p. 3.

[12] *Hegel's Political Writings*, trans. T. M. Knox (Oxford: Clarendon Press, 1964), 246–94.

in Berlin until his death in 1831. During his years in the city Hegel
became one of the most prominent public figures and the centre of a
self-consciously 'Hegelian' school of thought. His students included
Ludwig Feuerbach and David Friedrich Strauß. Among his
acquaintances were Karl August Varnhagen von Ense and Wilhelm
von Humboldt, and his relationship with Goethe (who lived in
Weimar) became particularly close. In Berlin Hegel published his
Philosophy of Right (1820, but dated 1821) and two further editions
of his *Encyclopaedia* (1827, 1830), and he lectured on (among other
topics) logic and metaphysics, philosophy of nature, philosophy of
history, aesthetics, and philosophy of religion. He gave a full course
of lectures on 'natural law and political science or the philosophy
of right' five times: 1818–19, 1819–20, 1821–2, 1822–3, and 1824–5
(the last three lecture courses being based on the published text of
the *Philosophy of Right*).[13] After 1825 Hegel left the task of lecturing
on the philosophy of right to his student and friend Eduard Gans,
but resumed lecturing on the topic himself in the autumn of 1831.
After only a few lectures, however, he died on 14 November 1831.

As noted above, Hegel was accused by his embittered contemporary Schopenhauer—and then later by Popper—of being a paid
agent of the Prussian state. A similar charge was levelled in the 1850s
by Rudolf Haym, who asserted that Hegel's philosophy was the
'scientific home of the *spirit of the Prussian restoration*'.[14] The fact that
Hegel was called to Berlin by a Prussian minister might seem to cor-
roborate these charges. The picture is, however, somewhat more
complicated than it at first appears.

When Hegel moved to Berlin in 1818 Prussia was marked by a
tension between those who advocated civil, political, and military
reform (in the wake of the Enlightenment, the French Revolution,
and Napoleon's Civil Code) and those who wished to resist 'liberal'
ideas and restore (or rather, preserve) a patriarchal Prussian state in
which the king was responsible to God alone and supported by a
landowning, privileged aristocracy.

The high point of reform in Prussia under Freiherr vom Stein and
Karl von Hardenberg was now some years in the past. The October

---

[13] Several transcripts of Hegel's lectures have now been published and are listed
below in the Select Bibliography.

[14] Manfred Riedel (ed.), *Materialien zu Hegels Rechtsphilosophie*, 2 vols. (Frankfurt-
am-Main: Suhrkamp Verlag, 1975), i. 366.

Edict abolishing hereditary servitude had been issued in 1807; the Municipal Ordinance allowing cities and towns to establish organs of self-government had been passed in 1808; Jews had gained a measure of emancipation in 1812 under the Edict Concerning the Civil Condition of the Jews in the Prussian State; and in 1815 King Friedrich Wilhelm III had made his promise to create a seat of 'territorial representation'—a national assembly—in Berlin.[15]

After the Congress of Vienna (also in 1815), however, the prevailing concern of the ruling classes in Germany was 'to preserve rather than to change'.[16] No national assembly was established; reformers, such as Wilhelm von Humboldt, were dismissed; and the 'party of restoration' around the king and the crown prince—including the 'chief agent of reaction', the head of the Prussian police Count W. L. G. von Wittgenstein—grew in strength and power. As a consequence, universities became subject to increasingly conservative and reactionary political supervision.

In 1817, however, the new ministry for 'Spiritual, Educational and Medical Affairs' was established under the reform-minded Altenstein, who was able to remove the universities from the direct control of the party of restoration and dilute (or defer the implementation of) proposed restrictive measures. Altenstein also gave his support to Hegel throughout the latter's years in Berlin.

While it is true that Hegel was an employee of the Prussian state (since all university professors, including those hostile to Hegel, such as Friedrich Schleiermacher, were state employees), it is important to note that Hegel was called to Berlin by a *reform-minded* minister in the Prussian government. It should also be noted that Hegel was never close to the king or to the party of restoration that surrounded him. Nor did he have any special influence on the government: unlike many colleagues, Hegel was never made a privy councillor. Furthermore, though he was made rector of the university from autumn 1829 to autumn 1830, in the last year of his life he was awarded only the Red Eagle *Third Class*—a not especially high honour that indicates his distance from, rather than proximity to, the court.[17] It is clear, therefore, that Hegel was by no means as closely associated with the reactionary

[15] Christopher Clark, *Iron Kingdom: The Rise and Downfall of Prussia, 1600–1947* (London: Allen Lane, 2006), 328, 334, 337, 340.

[16] Ralph Flenley, *Modern German History* (1953; London: J. M. Dent and Sons, 1964), 137.

[17] See Jaeschke, *Hegel-Handbuch*, 45, 55.

figures in the Prussian state as Schopenhauer, Haym, and Popper would have us believe.

Hegel in fact sympathized deeply with the advocates of reform, and his distance from, indeed opposition to, the party of restoration is evident from his scathing criticism of one of the latter's chief philosophical spokesmen, Karl Ludwig von Haller.[18] Haller, Hegel tells us, maintains that it is 'the eternal, unalterable, ordinance of God, that the mightier rules, must rule, and will always rule'. In Hegel's view, however, this exhibits Haller's 'virulent hatred of all laws and legislation, of all formally and legally determined right', and so shows him to be at odds with the principles of modern freedom (note to *PR* § 258 Remark [pp. 231–2]). Popper accuses Hegel of proclaiming the 'doctrine that *might is right*'.[19] Hegel's criticism of the party of restoration, however, is precisely that *it* equates might with right by defending power and privilege against the modern insistence on the primacy of freedom, right, and law.

A similar charge is levelled by Hegel against the proponents of the new German nationalism, which had burgeoned during the wars of liberation against Napoleon and found distinctive expression in the *Burschenschaften* (or student fraternities). Hegel was no unwavering supporter of French military might—he had experienced the destructive consequences of the French occupation of Jena in 1806 at first hand—but he considered Napoleon's Civil Code to represent a significant, progressive step in the process of systematizing right and clarifying the principles of right. He regarded it as particularly 'sad', therefore, that a copy of the Civil Code had been burned by nationalists at the Wartburg festival in October 1817.[20] Hegel was also profoundly opposed to the anti-Semitism that was associated with the new nationalistic 'German freedom'. In his view, 'the fierce outcry raised against the Jews [. . .] ignores the fact that they are, above all, *human beings*; and humanity, so far from being a mere superficial, abstract quality [. . .], is on the contrary itself the basis of the fact that civil rights arouse in their possessors the *feeling of oneself* as counting in civil society as a person *with rights*' (note to *PR* § 270 Remark [p. 247]).

---

[18] See explanatory note to p. 208.

[19] Popper, *The Open Society and its Enemies*, ii. 41.

[20] Dieter Henrich (ed.), *G. W. F. Hegel. Philosophie des Rechts. Die Vorlesung von 1819/20 in einer Nachschrift* (Frankfurt-am-Main: Suhrkamp Verlag, 1983), 172.

Nationalism's 'hatred of all laws' was evident above all in the murder, in March 1819, of the playwright August von Kotzebue, by Karl Ludwig Sand, a member of the Erlangen *Burschenschaft*. After the murder Hegel's colleague, the theologian Wilhelm de Wette, wrote a letter of condolence to Sand's mother. In it he stated that the murder was carried out by a 'pure pious youth' in the belief that he was doing the right thing, and so was 'a beautiful testimonial of the time'. The fact that the law had been broken and a life taken did not seem to be of primary importance to de Wette; what mattered was that Sand had acted in the *conviction* that he was in the right: 'he held it to be right, and so he did the right thing.' When the letter became public de Wette was quickly dismissed on the orders of the king, and there ensued a heated debate among professors at the university about whether the state had the right to remove someone from his post in this way. Hegel argued that the state did have this right— provided that it continue to pay the individual's salary—and he was promptly castigated by Schleiermacher for his 'miserable' attitude. When the university refused to give de Wette his salary, however, both Hegel and Schleiermacher contributed to a secret hardship fund for him.[21]

One might be tempted to misinterpret Hegel's response to the dismissal of de Wette as evidence of his support for the suppression by the Prussian state of the rights of the individual. In fact, however, it reflects Hegel's uncompromising rejection of political violence and murder in the name of national 'freedom'. Hegel argues that genuine freedom and good action entail respect for the law and for the rights and lives of others; murdering people in the 'conviction' that one is thereby doing good by extirpating the wicked is, in Hegel's view, 'evil rather than good' (*PR* § 140 Remark [d] [p. 143]). The university and the state thus had good reason to dismiss someone who was effectively endorsing politically motivated assassination.

Prompted by the Austrian foreign minister, Metternich, the governments in Germany and the federal parliament in Frankfurt responded to the murder of Kotzebue by passing, in the autumn of 1819, the 'Karlsbad Decrees', under which universities became subject to increasingly repressive scrutiny. Censorship was increased,

---

[21] Clark, *Iron Kingdom*, 401, Jaeschke, *Hegel-Handbuch*, 43, and Johannes Hoffmeister (ed.), *Briefe von und an Hegel*, 4 vols. (1952–4; Hamburg: Felix Meiner, 1961), ii. 445.

and lecturers or professors who were suspected of promoting 'demagogical' or 'liberal' tendencies ran the real risk of losing their posts. After his death Hegel was accused by Haym of providing a 'scientifically formulated justification of the Karlsbad police system',[22] but this is far from the truth. In fact, in the period before and after the passing of the Karlsbad Decrees not only Hegel himself, but also several of his students, fell under suspicion. In July 1819, for example, one student, Leopold von Henning, was arrested on the basis of comments in letters sent to him and was held for seven weeks. (On one occasion Hegel and some of his other students rowed on the Spree river to a point by von Henning's window and assured him—in Latin, to avoid being understood by the guards—that they were working to prove his innocence.) Then, in December 1819, Hegel's choice for his teaching assistant, Friedrich Wilhelm Carové, was denounced by Count Wittgenstein as a subversive and thereupon advised by Altenstein to leave Berlin.[23] Hegel clearly felt under threat himself and in October 1819 wrote to his friend, Friedrich Creuzer: 'I am about to be fifty years old, and I have spent thirty of these fifty years in these ever-unrestful times of hope and fear. I had hoped that for once we might be done with it. Now I must confess that things continue as ever. Indeed, in one's darker hours it seems they are getting ever worse.'[24] Hegel's fears were by no means unjustified, and at the time of Carové's denunciation he was precariously close to being denounced himself.

Hegel has been charged with supporting the conservative and reactionary policies of the Prussian state, when in fact he was strongly opposed to the party of restoration that instigated those policies, and after 1819 felt (with justification) threatened by them. He has also been charged with preparing the way for twentieth-century totalitarianism, when in fact he was profoundly hostile to nationalistic political violence and deeply committed to the rule of law and respect for freedom and rights. Close attention to the *Philosophy of Right* shows that Hegel's commitment to law, freedom, and right is not merely a contingent personal preference, but a commitment rooted in his systematic philosophy of freedom.

[22] Riedel, *Materialien zu Hegels Rechtsphilosophie*, i. 371.

[23] Terry Pinkard, *Hegel: A Biography* (Cambridge: Cambridge University Press, 2000), 447–50.

[24] *Hegel: The Letters*, 451.

Hegel's Philosophical System

Hegel's philosophical system, set out in his *Encyclopaedia of the Philosophical Sciences* (as well as in his *Science of Logic* and his lectures), comprises three disciplines: logic, the philosophy of nature, and the philosophy of spirit. It is preceded by phenomenology, set out in the famous *Phenomenology of Spirit*. Hegel's philosophy proper—that is, excluding phenomenology—lays out what he understands to be the true character of *being*. It tells us what being, by virtue of its very nature, must be. The assumption underlying philosophy, for Hegel, is that thought is capable of understanding— on its own, *a priori*—the fundamental structure of being. Philosophy is thus not an empirical discipline that bases its comprehension of things on observation of nature and human society; rather, it discovers the fundamental character of being by examining the *concept* of being itself (just as Spinoza sought to disclose the nature of the world by examining the concept of substance). Philosophy certainly draws on the empirical observations of scientists and historians to flesh out and enrich its account of things, but its basic understanding of the world is developed *a priori*. As Hegel puts it in the Remark to § 2 of the *Philosophy of Right*: 'The truth is that in philosophical knowledge the *necessity* of a concept is the principal thing' (p. 19).

Hegel recognizes that ordinary, non-philosophical consciousness is likely to find the enterprise of philosophy perverse. From its perspective, thought cannot simply work out by itself what the world is like; we have to go out into the world and look. Hegel argues in his *Phenomenology*, however, that philosophy (as he understands it) is not as alien to ordinary consciousness as the latter would like to believe: for the commitments of ordinary consciousness themselves lead logically and inexorably to the standpoint of philosophy. Philosophy is thus not a perversely presumptuous undertaking, but one that is made necessary *by* ordinary consciousness. This, Hegel claims, is because the experience of ordinary consciousness itself issues in the insight that *thought* is ultimately what opens the world—or 'being'— to view.[25]

The first discipline of Hegel's philosophy proper—his science of logic—examines the most general features of being. It sets out what

[25] See Stephen Houlgate, *An Introduction to Hegel: Freedom, Truth and History* (1991; Oxford: Blackwell, 2005), 48–66.

it is to be as such, what it is to be something, to be finite and to have quantity, what it is to have form, to be substantial and to exercise causality, and what it is to be an object. In so doing, speculative logic discloses the rich variety of *ways of being* that are exemplified by things in our world, and at the same time uncovers the fundamental *categories* (such as 'finitude', 'quantity', 'substance', and 'causality') in terms of which we must think.

Logic culminates in the thought that being is the rational process of free self-determination. Hegel calls this process the '*Idea*' [*Idee*], and he contends not only that being *as a whole* is 'Idea' (since it has no transcendent creator), but also that particular forms of being, such as life, are 'Idea', too, insofar as they are self-determining and self-moving. (For further remarks on the 'Idea', and on its relation to what Hegel calls the 'concept' [*Begriff*], see the Excerpts from T. M. Knox's Foreword, below.)

Logic considers being (and the various ways of being it encompasses) without reference to space and time. In the philosophy of nature, however, Hegel discloses specifically what it is to be spatio-temporal, as well as what it is to be a material, physical object. The philosophy of nature culminates in the insight that the most complex and most freely self-determining entity in nature is the animal organism. Of all the (non-human) things in nature, therefore, it is animals that embody the 'Idea' most perfectly.

The philosophy of spirit—the largest section of Hegel's philosophical system—then considers the various forms taken by human life or 'spirit' [*Geist*]. Spirit is also an embodiment of the 'Idea', since it is implicitly or explicitly self-determining in all of its forms. In spirit, indeed, the 'Idea' emerges from nature as (more or less) *conscious* or *self-conscious* self-determination. In the philosophy of subjective spirit, Hegel argues that human life and spirit involve sensation, consciousness, self-consciousness, imagination, language, thought, drive, and freedom of the will. The philosophy of objective spirit then examines the various *objective* forms that human freedom must adopt. This is the place at which Hegel's *philosophy of right*—together with his philosophy of history—is located (though the introduction to the published text of the *Philosophy of Right*, comprising §§ 1–33, is in part a recapitulation of the later sections of the philosophy of subjective spirit). The philosophy of right, therefore, is the discipline that reveals what it is to be *free*, and, more particularly, what *objective* structures and institutions (such as civil society and the state) are made necessary by the nature of freedom. The *Philosophy of Right* is thus far from being a work that justifies political repression. It is a philosophical study of the meaning of freedom, and shows what freedom—when it is understood properly—necessarily entails. In so doing, it provides an *a priori* justification—in the name of freedom—of right, property, moral conscience, family life, civil society, and the state.

The philosophy of history then shows that freedom does not just involve moral, social, and political life in the abstract, but also entails living in history. Finally, the third section of Hegel's philosophy of spirit—his philosophy of absolute spirit—demonstrates that human freedom requires art, religion, and philosophy itself, because it is precisely in these three forms of human activity that we give the most profound expression to our developing understanding of freedom (and of the nature of being).

This brief sketch of Hegel's philosophical system does little more than hint at the richness of his thought. Yet it suffices to explain that, for Hegel, being is the process of self-determination (or 'Idea'), and that in this process being develops from being nature pure and simple to being self-conscious spirit. Such spirit is nothing mysterious or otherworldly, but is *human* self-consciousness. The world becomes 'spiritual', therefore, with the emergence of human beings. Human self-consciousness or 'spirit' is characterized above all by *freedom*—freedom of imagination, of thought, and of will. The task of Hegel's philosophy of right is thus set by the philosophical system of which it forms part: it is to lay out the various objective—judicial, moral, social, and political—forms that human freedom must take on, if it is to be true freedom. It is to show that genuine human freedom must objectify itself in rights, laws, and institutions, not just in the arbitrariness of self-will. As Hegel himself puts it in § 4 of the *Philosophy of Right*: 'the system of right is the realm of freedom made actual, the world of spirit [*Geist*] brought forth out of itself as a second nature' (p. 26).

Hegel is sometimes thought to be the quintessential historicist philosopher, for whom everything has to be understood as the product of its historical context. The *Philosophy of Right*, however, does not offer a historical account of the modern state: it does not describe the structures and institutions that just happen to be found in existing modern societies. Hegel's philosophy of right provides, rather, a *normative* account of freedom: it tells us how freedom *should* be understood and how it *should* objectify itself, if it is to be true to its own nature. This does not mean that Hegel offers us an essentially utopian vision of freedom: he does not set out merely what he believes freedom (or the state) ought to be in an ideal world (see *PR* Preface, p. 15). He shows us, rather, what freedom *is in truth*, what it is according to its own nature or *concept*. This concept, far from being an abstract utopian ideal, has been realized—albeit imperfectly—in history itself. Indeed, Hegel argues that all the essential elements of objective freedom are to be found in actual modern states—if not all together in one state—and he draws widely on his knowledge of contemporary Britain, France, and Germany in order to enrich his presentation of those elements. Nonetheless, Hegel's account of objective freedom is grounded in and made necessary by the *concept* of freedom, rather than the facts of history. His principal aim is to show what that concept requires; his secondary concern is then to indicate that that concept is best embodied and realized in modernity.

In setting out what is entailed by the concept of freedom, Hegel employs a distinctive and unusual method. He does not start with what he considers to be a rich and exhaustive definition of freedom (nor does he begin from concrete historical examples of freedom). He starts from what he takes to be the minimal concept of freedom. This concept contains the least that freedom can be understood to be and, indeed, the least that freedom can actually be. It is the thought of freedom in its most abstract and undeveloped form: freedom as the simple ability to *abstract* from all that is given to us. From this minimal starting point Hegel then derives further, more concrete conceptions—and forms—of freedom.

Hegel derives each further form of freedom by rendering *explicit* what is implicit in the form that precedes it. This is not to say that a more concrete form of freedom (the state, for example) is already present *as such* in a less concrete form (such as civil society). Rather, the state is what emerges when what is implicit in civil society has become explicit.

This activity of rendering explicit is undertaken by the philosopher. What is to be rendered explicit, however, is determined by what is implicit in a given form or conception of freedom. In that sense, the process of rendering explicit or 'unfolding' the different forms and conceptions of freedom is governed not by the philosopher, but by the nature of freedom itself. This is what Hegel means by saying that the science of right traces 'the proper immanent development of the thing itself' (*PR* § 2 [p. 18]). Subsequent forms of freedom are not introduced 'externally' by the philosopher in order to make up for deficiencies in earlier forms; rather, they are engendered by those earlier forms themselves, whose own conceptual structures implicitly point towards them. Ultimately, indeed, they are all engendered by the abstract form of freedom with which the philosopher begins. The philosophy of right, therefore, traces the process whereby abstract freedom itself makes freedom in the state necessary.

This process is not a *historical* one: Hegel is not claiming that the earliest historical form of freedom was abstract and that the other forms of freedom—right, moral action, family life, civil society, and the state—emerged in that order over the centuries. The process Hegel describes is a *logical* one, in which one form of freedom is shown to be demanded by the conceptual structure or form of the preceding one. What Hegel sets out to show in the *Philosophy of Right* is not how freedom has actually developed through history, but what forms of freedom are inherent in, and so logically required by, freedom itself. In this way he shows how freedom develops *logically* from abstraction to concreteness.

Note that this development begins from the minimal, abstract *concept* of freedom and shows how this concept renders itself concrete, or *determines itself*. In determining itself, the concept of freedom proves to be the 'Idea' (because it proves to be the very process of self-determination itself). At the start, the concept of freedom is already the *Idea* of freedom, but in an abstract, undeveloped form. The process of logical development described in the *Philosophy of Right* is thus one in which the concept or *abstract* Idea of freedom develops into the fully fledged *concrete* Idea of freedom. As Hegel himself puts it, it is 'a development through which the concept determines the *Idea, itself* at first *abstract*, until it becomes a systematized whole' (*PR* § 28 [p. 46]).

Towards the beginning of the *Philosophy of Right* Hegel describes the free will that wills itself as 'the abstract concept of the Idea of the will' (*PR* § 27 [p. 46]). Towards the end of his book he describes the state as 'the actuality of the ethical Idea' (*PR* § 257 [p. 228]). What happens in between is that the free will comes to be actually and explicitly the Idea, or free self-determination, that it is abstractly and implicitly at the start. The state is thus not something alien to freedom, but is rather the most concrete and genuinely *self-determining* manifestation of freedom. It is what true freedom proves, through its own logical development, to be.

Yet how exactly does freedom 'develop' logically, in Hegel's view? To answer this question we need to look more closely at the *Philosophy of Right* itself.

Freedom

The first and most abstract form of freedom that Hegel examines is what he calls 'negative freedom'—'my ability to free myself from everything, [. . .] abstract from everything' (*PR* § 5 Addition [p. 29]). This is my ability to set aside whatever defines and limits me— my age, sex, needs, and desires—and to think of myself as a pure 'I'. I have this ability, in Hegel's view, because I can *think*. It is thought, therefore, that enables me to free myself from all that I am given (by nature) to be.

Yet freedom also takes a more positive form: it consists in the ability to give myself a particular 'content and object', that is, to affirm a specific impulse or desire as mine (*PR* § 6 [p. 30]). In exercising this freedom, I do not consider the desire to be something that is forced upon me by nature, but know that *I myself* have affirmed or 'willed' the desire. That means that I continue to think of myself as a pure 'I' that is not bound by nature to any particular desires. That means in turn that in affirming a desire I retain the sense that I can retract my affirmation at any time and withdraw once again into the purity of my 'self'. The desire I affirm is thereby regarded not as something to which I am irrevocably tied, but as 'a mere possibility [. . .] in which it [the will] is confined only because it has put itself in it' (*PR* § 7 [pp. 31–2]). The desire is one that I *actually* affirm; but it remains a mere 'possibility' in the sense that it is no more than one option among many—one that I happen to have settled on but could just as easily give up in favour of another.

For Hegel, the act of affirming an impulse or desire, while continuing to view it as something that I did not have to affirm and that I can renounce if I so will, is the act of freely *choosing* it. At its simplest and most abstract, therefore, freedom is freedom of choice.

This, Hegel maintains, is 'the idea which people most commonly have of freedom' (*PR* § 15 Remark [p. 37]). In the popular imagination freedom consists in not being forced or constrained to do something, but in being able to choose for oneself what one does, being able to do what one pleases. Hegel calls this the freedom of 'arbitrariness' or 'caprice' [*Willkür*] (*PR* § 15 [p. 37]).

Note that Hegel shows choice to be a necessary aspect of freedom: as thinking beings, we immediately enjoy the freedom to choose. Furthermore, Hegel argues that choice itself has a necessary structure. Since it combines both the 'positive' freedom to affirm what is given and the 'negative' freedom to abstract from what is given, choice necessarily involves the consciousness that we are not bound to, and so can always abandon, whatever we affirm. Choosing always brings with it the consciousness that we could have chosen differently and could still choose differently in the future (provided, of course, that we do not choose to sacrifice the freedom of choice itself by committing suicide). Yet Hegel also goes on to argue that freedom of choice is more problematic than it first appears.

Hegel does not deny that we have genuine freedom of choice. Such freedom is not an illusion: thought gives us the real power to abstract from, settle on, and then again abstract from particular impulses and desires. Choice, however, is not quite as unconstrained as we might think, for it is in fact utterly dependent on what is given to it.

Choice, Hegel states, is grounded in the 'indeterminacy of the I', that is, the abstract thought of oneself as a pure 'I' (*PR* § 15 Addition [p. 38]). This abstract, indeterminate 'I' has no 'content' of its own—it does not have any intrinsic needs and desires—but it is simply the formal capacity to select between given desires. Moreover, the choosing 'I', or will, does not itself determine which desires are given to it. Such desires must, therefore, be given by something other than the free will itself, namely nature. *Free* choice is thus less free than it thinks it is, because it is wholly *dependent* on whatever desires nature makes available to it. This, Hegel points out, is 'the contradiction lying in arbitrariness' (*PR* § 15 Addition [p. 38])—a contradiction that is a necessary, not simply an accidental, feature of choice.

We can, indeed, freely choose to do what we please; but we do not freely determine what pleases us—nature does. (Hegel shows later in the *Philosophy of Right* that our desires and interests are also formed by those who seek to profit from their creation, namely producers

[*PR* § 191 Addition].) This, in a nutshell, is the *dialectic* at the heart of choice. Dialectic, as Hegel explains in his *Encyclopaedia Logic*, is the process whereby concepts and phenomena turn of their own accord into their opposites and thereby 'negate' themselves.[26] Choice is dialectical, for Hegel, because it is freedom which, thanks to its very structure, proves to be a form of dependence.

Hegel will go on to show that genuinely free human beings make their choices in the concrete contexts of property-ownership, moral action, family life, and economic and political activity. At the beginning of the *Philosophy of Right*, however, he focuses on choice as such and shows that it is not, as many people believe, the most complete form of freedom. This is partly because it is a dialectical form of freedom that is also a form of profound dependence. It is also because implicit within choice are the seeds of a deeper, more independent freedom. This is the freedom that consists not merely in willing what is given by nature, but in willing the free will itself.

When I choose to do something, I affirm or 'will' a given desire. I am, however, also implicitly affirming my freedom of choice itself. Implicit in every choice, therefore, is the affirmation by the free will of *itself* and its own freedom. When the free will makes itself the *explicit* object of its own affirmation, it becomes the truly free, rather than just abstractly free, will. The '*free will which wills the free will*' (*PR* § 27 [p. 46]) is truly free, because it is no longer dependent on the givens of nature for its 'content and object' but finds that content within itself. Such a free will, Hegel writes, 'is related to nothing except itself and so is released from every relation of dependence on anything else. The will is then true, or rather truth itself' (*PR* § 23 [p. 43]).

As Rawls points out, Hegel's position here reveals his closeness to Kant.[27] Hegel is led to his conception of the self-willing will, however, by the logic inherent in freedom itself: the will must will itself and so have itself as its object, for only in that way does it avoid the contradiction besetting choice. The moment of necessity here is especially important. The truly free will is not simply the will that *does actually* will itself; it is the will that *must* will itself, if it is to be free and independent. The will that wants to be truly free has no choice in the matter: as Hegel puts it, it is 'the *absolute* determination, or, if you like, the *absolute* impulse, of the free spirit [. . .] to make its freedom its object' (*PR* § 27 [p. 46], my emphasis). This moment of necessity is the key to the emergence of a new and important idea in Hegel's account of freedom: the idea of *right* [*Recht*].

All of us lay claim to various rights in our everyday lives. Some people even claim that animals, as well as humans, have rights. But what exactly is a 'right'? Hegel's answer is clear: a right is our *freedom* understood as the object of our will. Or, to put it another way, right is the objective 'existence' [*Dasein*] of our freedom (*PR* § 29 [p. 46]). As such, right is 'sacrosanct' to the free will—that which the free will must will and affirm (*PR* § 30 [p. 47]). It is thus that which commands *respect* from the free will. It should be clear why Hegel introduces this idea of right at this point in his account of freedom: for the free will that has its own freedom as its object, and that *must* will and affirm its freedom if it is to be truly free, necessarily regards its freedom as its *right*.

Hegel's argument here is subtle and important. What he shows is that the very idea of right is generated by the logical development of freedom. The will whose freedom consists solely in exercising choice has no conception of 'right'. This is because it has no (explicit) sense that it is bound by necessity. For it, freedom is all about possibility: it knows that it *can* choose this or that, but it does not feel that it *must* will anything. The truly free will, by contrast, not only wills its own freedom, but understands that it must do so if it is to be truly free. It comprehends, therefore, that there is a necessity inherent in freedom itself: the necessity that requires it to will its own freedom. It is this idea that freedom is that which *requires* affirmation and recognition from the free will that generates the idea of 'right': for 'right' is nothing but freedom-that-requires-recognition. The truly free will is thus not the one that thinks it can do as it pleases, but the one that considers freedom to constitute a realm of *right* that must be willed and affirmed by any truly free will. Accordingly, with the emergence of this truly free will, Hegel's philosophy of freedom turns into a philosophy of right.

Right

Since right is simply freedom understood as requiring respect, non-human animals that are sentient but have no awareness of being free—and so cannot make freedom their object—cannot lay claim to rights. This does not mean that we should show no concern for the welfare of non-human animals; but the only beings that can be the bearers of *rights* are those that are conscious of their freedom (or at least capable of being so conscious).

Furthermore, since right is freedom understood as requiring respect, each form of freedom that Hegel shows to be necessary in the *Philosophy of Right* constitutes a sphere of right. In Hegel's words: 'every stage in the development of the Idea of freedom has its own special right, since it is the existence of freedom in one of its own determinations' (*PR* § 30 Remark [p. 47]). All, therefore, must be willed and affirmed by the truly free will. This confirms that Hegel's account of freedom is above all a *normative* account: it does not just describe the different forms that freedom has taken in history, but sets out the different forms that are *required for true freedom* and so constitute our *right*.

The first form of right that Hegel discusses is what he calls 'abstract right'. Such right is not earned or merited through virtue or good behaviour. It belongs immediately to those who are, and know themselves to be, free beings. Abstract right is the right to be treated as a bearer of rights as such—or a *person* (*PR* § 36). More particularly, it encompasses the right to own property (*PR* § 45), the right to exchange such property with others and enter into contracts with them (*PR* § 72), and the right not to suffer personal injury or be enslaved (*PR* § 48 Remark). Note that the right, or freedom, to own and exchange property allows plenty of room for freedom of choice. Choice must, however, be exercised within the context of respect for rights and so in that sense is restricted: I may take ownership only of things that are not already the property of another (*PR* § 50).

Like choice, abstract right suffers its own dialectic, for it gives rise, in Hegel's view, to *wrong*, or *crime*. This is because, even though right commands respect, it is always a matter of contingency whether the bearers of rights will actually respect the rights of others (*PR* § 81). This contingency is grounded in the fact that all who are and know themselves to be free, immediately become the bearers of rights, whether or not they are inclined to respect rights themselves.

The criminal's violation of right, Hegel argues, requires that the authority of right be restored through punishment or 'retribution' (*PR* § 101 [p. 103]). At this stage in the *Philosophy of Right*, however, the institutions—courts of law—that are needed for properly judicial punishment have not yet been derived from the concept of freedom. Consequently, 'the annulling of crime in this sphere where right is immediate is initially *revenge*' (*PR* § 102 [p. 106]). Yet Hegel is not advocating revenge in particular. He is arguing for the *justice of punishment*; but he is also pointing out that 'in that condition of society when there are neither magistrates nor laws'—the condition produced when people see themselves as no more than bearers of rights— 'punishment always takes the form of revenge' (*PR* § 102 Addition [p. 106]).

Through the punishment of the criminal the authority of right is re-established: right is accorded clear priority over the individual will. When this priority is explicitly recognized and internalized by the individual will itself, the latter becomes a *moral* [*moralisch*] will (*PR* § 104). Moral freedom is thus the next form of freedom that we encounter in the *Philosophy of Right*.

The moral will not only accepts the primacy of right, but also considers itself to be the embodiment and actualization of right and freedom. It does not, however, equate freedom with its mere 'immediacy' as a person or bearer of rights. It equates freedom with its self-determining activity or 'subjectivity' (*PR* § 106 [p. 109]). That is to say, it equates freedom with the *actions* it undertakes to fulfil its purposes and intentions. The most basic right claimed by the moral will is the right to consider as its own action only what it has undertaken knowingly and deliberately (rather than unknowingly). In other words, the moral will insists that 'the deed can be imputed to me only if my will is responsible for it'. This, Hegel states, is 'the *right to know*' (*PR* § 117 [p. 116]).

Further rights claimed by the moral will include: the right to be held accountable only for the *kind* of action I intended (e.g. mercy-killing rather than murder) (*PR* § 120); the right to fulfil my intentions in my actions and thereby to gain *satisfaction* through those actions (*PR* § 121); the right to recognize as valid only what I judge to be good (*PR* § 132); the ('Kantian') right to recognize as binding on me only what I understand to be my duty (*PR* § 133); and the right to recognize my conscience as 'what alone has obligatory force for me' (*PR* § 136 Addition [p. 132]).

The dialectic suffered by the moral will is this: if my *own* conscience or 'conviction' is what tells me whether or not an action is right and good, then my own 'subjectivity [. . .] claims to be absolute' (*PR* § 140 [p. 138]). I do not subject myself to any genuinely independent, objective principle of action, but 'it is the subjective consciousness itself whose decision constitutes objectivity' (*PR* § 140 Remark [d] [p. 142]). This means, however, that I have the power to justify any actions I choose to undertake—including those that are self-serving and 'evil'—on the grounds that my conscience tells me they are right and good. Such a moral will does not deliberately commit acts it knows to be evil, but is firmly convinced of its own righteousness. Nonetheless, it perverts itself into an evil will precisely by insisting that it *alone* determines what counts as the good.

The moral will identifies the good with the dictates of its own subjectivity. At the same time, it does not knowingly and wilfully indulge its own desires, but wills what it takes to be genuinely *good*. In so doing, it implicitly recognizes the good to be something 'universal and objective' (*PR* § 141 [p. 151]) (even though it claims the power to determine by itself what the objective good is). The will that *explicitly* recognizes the good to be objective is the *ethical* [*sittlich*] will.

Ethical Life

The distinction between moral and ethical freedom is one of the most important in the *Philosophy of Right*. The ethical will, for Hegel, does not take the good to be simply what the inner voice of conscience tells it to do. It understands freedom and the good to be realized in the objective world around us. Specifically, it holds freedom and the good to be embodied in the *laws* and *institutions* that constitute 'ethical life' (*PR* §§ 142, 144). From the ethical point of view, therefore, we are free only when we are law-abiding participants in the institutions of civil society and the state (as well as members of a loving family).

If one reads Hegel's paragraphs on 'ethical life' very selectively and superficially, it is (just about) possible to misunderstand him as advocating unquestioning acceptance of prevailing customs and unquestioning obedience to the laws of the state, whatever those customs and laws may be. He does, after all, say that all one needs to do in an '*ethical* community' to be virtuous is to 'follow the well-known and explicit rules of his own situation' (*PR* § 150 Remark [p. 157]). Might this not suggest that, for Hegel, the 'ethical' individual just does what is done and thinks no more about it? And isn't this 'ethical' attitude precisely what allowed the Nazis to perpetrate their most heinous crimes?

What this interpretation overlooks, however, is the fact that not every social or political institution counts as *ethical* in Hegel's sense, and so not every institution deserves our respect and allegiance. Ethical life, as Hegel understands it in the *Philosophy of Right*, is 'the concept of *freedom* developed into the existing world' (*PR* § 142 [p. 154]). As such, it comprises certain specific structures and institutions that are required for, and promote, freedom. These include: family life founded on love (not violence) (*PR* § 158); civil society in which the right to own and exchange property, and the freedom to pursue the occupation of one's own choice, are guaranteed (*PR* §§ 182, 206); courts of law in which justice is upheld in public and on the basis of published laws (*PR* §§ 215, 219); a public authority and corporations that protect members of society and defend their rights (*PR* §§ 230, 252); and a state in which the monarchical, executive, and legislative powers are distinguished and assemblies (or 'Estates') responsible for legislation are established (*PR* §§ 273, 300). Such an ethical community is founded on the principle that 'a human being counts as a human being in virtue of his *humanity*, not because he is a Jew, Catholic, Protestant, German, Italian, etc.' (*PR* § 209 Remark [p. 198]); and the goal of this community is nothing less than the 'happiness of the citizens' (*PR* § 265 Addition [p. 240]). Hegelian ethical life is thus clearly a liberal community of freedom and right and is very far from the sinister 'collectivist', 'totalitarian' society attributed to Hegel by, for example, Popper.

Hegel's aim in the *Philosophy of Right* is to show that a state with these specific structures and institutions is required by the concept of freedom and so commands our allegiance (insofar as we are free beings). Such a state, it should be noted, incorporates the more abstract freedoms of choice and property-ownership. It also incorporates the moral freedom to act responsibly and pursue one's own satisfaction and welfare. The moral right to recognize as valid only what one sees as good is also incorporated into ethical life, but in the context of the latter it takes on a subtly different form.

The moral will claims for itself and its own conscience the right to decide what counts as good. The ethical will, by contrast, holds the laws and institutions of the state to be good *objectively*, that is, to have '*being in and for themselves*' (*PR* § 144 [p. 154]). The ethical will is similar to the moral will in that it, too, recognizes as valid only what it understands to be *good*. (In that sense, it remains a conscientious will.) Unlike the moral will, however, the ethical will does not *decide* by itself what counts as good, but rather *accepts* the objective goodness of the institutions in which it lives. (It is thus what Hegel calls 'true conscience', as opposed to mere formal, moral conscience [*PR* § 137 (p. 132)].) The ethical will accepts the authority of laws and institutions because (as Hegel puts it) the subject 'bears witness to them as to *its own essence*' (*PR* § 147 [p. 155]). In other words, the ethical will sees in them the embodiment of, and necessary conditions of, its own freedom. Such a will knows that the laws and institutions of the free state do not inhibit or threaten the individual, but rather provide the context within which alone individuals can flourish.

The ethical will's recognition and acceptance of laws and institutions is expressed in the *trust* it has in them (or, indeed, in the relation it enjoys with them that is 'closer to identity than even the relation of faith or trust', *PR* §§ 147, 268 [pp. 155, 240]). The moral will puts its trust in nothing but its own conscience; the ethical will, by contrast, trusts that the institutional world it inhabits is one of freedom and well-being. As such, it is much more at home in the world than the moral will and much less concerned to force the world to conform to its own demands. Precisely because it puts its trust in laws and institutions, the ethical individual is prepared to 'follow the well-known and explicit rules of his own situation' (*PR* § 150 Remark [p. 157]) in a way that the moral will is not. It must be remembered, however, that ethical individuals do not do this out of blindness: they follow such rules because they see in them the conditions of their own freedom (rather than the source of inauthenticity). Such trust is appropriate, therefore, only when the institutions are indeed *ethical* in Hegel's sense and promote freedom and right, rather than tyranny and oppression. In states that are not truly ethical and free (such as the French state during the revolutionary Terror), trust in government will be inappropriate and, indeed, impossible. In such states, Hegel notes, '*suspicion*'—rather than trust—'is in the ascendant'.[28]

---

[28] G. W. F. Hegel, *The Philosophy of History*, trans. J. Sibree (New York: Dover Publications, 1956), 450.

In Hegel's view, freedom must take the form of ethical life with its specific institutions, as well as the accompanying trust in those institutions. If the institutions in which we live are corrupt and threaten our security and well-being, not only are we denied our freedom but 'the footing of the state itself is insecure' (*PR* § 265 Addition [p. 240]). Equally, however, if we are constantly suspicious of and hostile to well-functioning institutions (and one another), there can be no freedom either: because an essential ingredient of freedom is the 'habit of feeling safe' in the institutions of public life (*PR* § 268 Addition [p. 241]).

This does not mean, by the way, that a free state is one in which nothing is debated or questioned. Far from it. Hegel sees it as the distinctive function of the legislative assemblies to provide a public space for 'knowledge, deliberations, and decisions concerning universal matters' (*PR* § 314 [p. 298]); he also acknowledges that public debates are carried on outside those assemblies and that public opinion is a 'great power' in such debates. Indeed, debate and discussion are so important in modern states that 'what is to be authoritative nowadays' derives its authority above all from 'insight and argument' (*PR* § 316 Addition [p. 299]). Hegel's point, however, is that such public discussion itself presupposes a basic trust in the institutions of the state and in one another. In other words, what makes it possible for us to live together and discuss things freely and openly with one another is 'the fundamental sense of order which everyone possesses' (*PR* § 268 Addition [p. 241]).

Does everyone today enjoy the benefits of free and orderly ethical life? No; it is obvious that not every state in our world, or Hegel's, is fully free and ethical. Hegel believed, however, that the basic elements of the ethical state were to be found in certain modern states, such as Britain, France, the Netherlands, and (to a degree) Prussia (though no single modern state mentioned by Hegel exactly matches the state of the *Philosophy of Right*). To the extent that the elements of ethical life are—or were—realized in at least some modern states, Hegel can claim that '*what is rational is actual; and what is actual is rational*' (*PR* Preface, p. 14). We should not forget, however, that many states in the post-Revolutionary world are far from rational and free, and that even rational, ethical states are not rational and ethical in every single respect: 'the state is no ideal work of art; it stands on earth and so in the sphere of caprice, chance, and error, and bad behaviour may disfigure it in many respects' (*PR* § 258 Addition [p. 234]). One should also recall that ethical life, like the other forms of freedom Hegel considers, is subject to its own dialectic.

After the family, but prior to the derivation of the state proper, Hegel examines 'civil society'. This is the sphere of economic freedom and activity in which individuals work and cooperate to produce the goods to meet their needs and satisfy their desires. Such economic freedom undermines itself dialectically because it leads to the emergence not only of great wealth, but also of poverty. This is primarily due, Hegel argues, to the fact that a society geared towards *maximizing* the free production and exchange of goods inevitably ends up producing more than it can consume. Overproduction then makes it necessary for workers to be laid off and this plunges people into poverty (*PR* § 245). Poverty, however, is not just a matter of material deprivation. Hegel's great insight is that it also involves a profound sense of alienation from society. This in turn can lead to the creation of a 'rabble' [*Pöbel*] animated by 'an inner indignation against the rich, against society, against the government, etc.' (*PR* § 244 Addition [p. 221]).

Some commentators believe that Hegel offers no solution to the problem of poverty.[29] Yet this is not in fact the case. Hegel does, indeed, think that certain courses of action—including providing charity or 'welfare' to the poor, creating new opportunities for work, exporting the excess goods, or sending people to overseas colonies— will only be partially successful. He clearly suggests, however, that the way to avoid overproduction—and, therefore, poverty—is to preserve the institutions called 'corporations'. These are not individual companies, but guild-like associations of traders and manufacturers. They were abolished in France during the Revolution, but Hegel thinks that they are essential elements in a truly free society. Their role is twofold: first, to foster an explicit concern for the welfare of others in the same trade, and second, to regulate—and, if necessary, limit—the production of goods (*PR* § 252). In this way, economic activity becomes genuinely cooperative and overproduction is avoided. Poverty thus ceases to be a *necessary* consequence of free economic activity.

---

[29] See, e.g. Shlomo Avineri, *Hegel's Theory of the Modern State* (Cambridge: Cambridge University Press, 1972), 153.

In this respect Hegel differs noticeably from Karl Marx, who is otherwise deeply indebted to him. For Marx, capitalist economic activity necessarily leads to alienation and poverty, because of the nature of *wage labour*. In capitalism goods are freely produced and exchanged for one another. Labour is also exchanged for a wage. This, however, turns human labour into a commodity that can be bought and sold like anything else. Furthermore, once a worker's labour has been sold to an employer, it can be exploited by the latter for his own, rather than the worker's, benefit. In this way, Marx argues, the system of wage labour necessarily alienates workers from their own labour and its products. This system, in Marx's view, cannot be reformed or redeemed. If human alienation is to be overcome, therefore, the only alternative is the revolutionary restructuring of the economy. The private ownership of the means of production must be abolished and factories taken into public hands. Private individuals will thus no longer be able to buy the labour of others for a wage and exploit it. Indeed, under communism not only will the exchange of labour for a wage disappear, but all exchange of goods for money will be abolished. Individuals will produce what they can, freely and generously, and take what they need, without insisting on an equal exchange of one for the other. As Marx famously puts it, the principle of communist society will be 'from each according to his ability, to each according to his needs'.[30]

Marx likes to think of himself as more of a 'materialist' and less of an 'idealist' than Hegel. As we have seen, however, Hegel understands just as well as Marx does that human freedom takes the *material* form of economic activity and labour. He is also just as aware as Marx is of the problem of poverty and alienation in civil society. The real difference between the two thinkers is this: Hegel believes that an economy based on the free production and exchange of goods and labour can be reformed so that it does not necessarily generate poverty, whereas Marx does not. For Hegel there is nothing about being a private employer that requires such employers to exploit their workers and profit excessively from the latter's labour: it all depends on their attitude of mind. The ruthless exploitation of workers can, therefore, be avoided—and with it alienation and poverty—if members of a

[30] David McLellan (ed.), *Karl Marx. Selected Writings* (1977; Oxford: Oxford University Press, 2000), 615 [*Critique of the Gotha Programme*].

trade work together towards a common end, namely, their common welfare. This happens, Hegel argues, when traders and workers are organized into corporations (and when they are informed by a sense of common citizenship as members of the state). Poverty is to be avoided, therefore, not by social and economic revolution, but by fostering an explicitly *ethical* concern for one another among producers and workers through membership of a corporation (and the state).

In his lectures Hegel is reported as saying that 'the nature of evil is that human beings may will it but need not' (*PR* § 139 Addition [p. 138]). The same is true of crime and poverty. If the sphere of freedom with which each is associated is taken by itself, then each arises necessarily; it does not arise necessarily, however, if the respective sphere is incorporated into a higher one. If abstract right is set in the context of moral freedom, moral freedom set in the context of ethical freedom, and civil society set in the context of the corporations and the rational state, then crime, evil, and poverty will no longer be structural necessities (though due to the contingencies of life—its 'caprice, chance, and error'—they will remain possibilities).

Towards the end of the *Philosophy of Right* Hegel points to one last dialectic suffered by objective freedom: the state, which is the most concrete embodiment of freedom, always faces the danger of war. In Hegel's view, no world state or federation of states would have the authority to resolve disputes between states, in the way that the state has the authority and power to resolve disputes between its citizens. Consequently, 'if states disagree and their particular wills cannot be harmonized, the matter can only be settled by *war*' (*PR* § 334 [p. 313]). This is not to say that war is absolutely inevitable (let alone desirable): through agreement, states can avoid it. War remains, however, more than just a contingent possibility (as poverty is within a genuinely free and rational state). War remains a *structural*—and therefore *necessary*—possibility, since its possibility is built into the very fabric of the unregulated relations between sovereign states. The necessary possibility of war thus reveals the essential fragility of freedom in the state—a fragility of which Hegel had been made personally aware in Jena in 1806.

In the concluding paragraphs of the *Philosophy of Right* Hegel notes that freedom and the state have a common *history*. This history of human freedom is what Hegel is referring to when he talks of the 'actualization of the universal spirit' (*PR* § 342 [p. 316]) or of the 'activity of the world-spirit' (*PR* § 344 [p. 317]). The world-spirit, therefore, is not some cosmic consciousness beyond our own that uses us for its own ends; it is simply humanity itself coming to an ever clearer understanding of its own freedom and transforming the social and political world in the process.

The stages of the historical development of freedom do not match exactly the stages in the logical development of the concept of freedom that we have been tracing: in history, for example, the state and the family both precede abstract right and morality. The history of freedom culminates, however, in a group of modern—post-Reformation, Western European—states in which the elements of true freedom described in the *Philosophy of Right* are to be found. As noted above, not every state today is a free and rational one. Nonetheless, in Hegel's view, it is in modernity (rather than ancient Greece or Rome) that true freedom in the state is—more or less imperfectly—realized. In at least parts of the modern world, therefore, the state is more or less as it should be. The *Philosophy of Right* thus provides an account of both the *free* state and the genuinely *modern* state, since the two are one and the same.

EXCERPTS FROM
T. M. KNOX'S FOREWORD

THE original edition of T. M. Knox's translation of the *Philosophy of Right* contained a Translator's Foreword in which Knox discussed the difficulties involved in translating Hegel's sometimes idiosyncratic German. Parts of that foreword are now outdated, but Knox's remarks on the meaning of certain key Hegelian terms, such as 'concept' and 'Idea', are still of great value. What follows here are edited excerpts from Knox's Foreword.

(i) The thought [*Gedanke*] of a thing.

Philosophy is thinking, the thinking of the universal. The product of thinking is a thought, and this, viewed objectively, we call the 'universal'. But we know that the universal in this sense is abstract and different from the particular. The universal is a form, and its content, the particular, stands contrasted with it.

Now if we go no further than the thought of a thing, than this abstract universal, we remain at the level of the understanding [*Verstand*], the level of reflection. The understanding is abstract or formal thinking, the thinking characteristic of the mathematical and empirical sciences or of formal logic, as well as of those philosophies which adhere to scientific method instead of abandoning it in favour of reason [*Vernunft*] and the philosophical method of the concept [*Begriff*].

(ii) The concept.

The defect of the understanding is that while it correctly distinguishes between form and content, essential and inessential, universal and particular, it fails to synthesize these opposites. Held apart from one another, however, each of these opposites becomes an abstraction, and the living whole of reality has not been explained but explained away and killed by being so analysed into its constituents. What the understanding fails to recognize is that a 'thought' is not something empty or abstract; it is a determinant, a determinant of itself. The essence of thought is its concreteness, and the concrete thought is what Hegel calls the *concept*. When the thought of a thing is handled philosophically instead of scientifically, it is seen to be inherently concrete, i.e. not a mere abstract form, but possessed of a content which it has given to itself. In a sense it is right enough to say that philosophy deals with abstractions, with thoughts abstracted from the sense-perceptions which are sometimes called 'concrete'; but in another sense this is quite false, because when the sensuous content is separated from its universal form, it also becomes an abstraction. Philosophy has to do not with these two abstractions, held apart from one another, but with their concrete synthesis, the concept. Its constituents are not self-subsistent entities, which is what the understanding takes them to be, but only 'moments' in an organic whole.

The concept is the thought in so far as the thought determines itself and gives itself a content; it is the thought in its vivacity and activity. Again, the concept is the universal which particularizes itself, the thought which actively creates and engenders itself. Hence it is not a bare form for a content; it forms itself, gives itself a content and determines itself to be the form. What is meant by 'concrete' is the thought which does not remain empty but which is self-determining and self-particularizing.

The concept is thus the inward living principle of all reality. (The background of Hegel's thought is theological, and the 'concept' is his philosophical equivalent for the wisdom and so for the creative power of God.) It follows that it is one and the same concept whose self-determining activity the philosopher studies whether in logic, or nature, or human institutions.

(iii) The Idea [*Idee*].

(This word is spelt throughout the translation with a capital letter in order to distinguish it from 'idea' [*Vorstellung*], i.e. from 'whatsoever is the object of the understanding'.)

Just as the thought of a thing, when viewed concretely, is the concept, so the concept, viewed concretely (i.e. in its truth, in its full development, and so in synthesis with the content which it gives to itself), is the Idea. The Idea is the concept in so far as the concept gives reality and existence to itself. To do this, the concept must determine itself, and the determination is nothing external, but is the concept itself, i.e. it is a self-determination. The Idea, or reason, or truth, is the concept become concrete, the unity of subject and object, of form and content.

(iv) Development.

Since the concept determines itself, it is alive and active, and its life is a development. The nature of mind [or spirit] [*Geist*] is an immanent restless process; mind is self-productive and exists in and through this self-production. Development is from implicit [*an sich, potentia*, δύναμις] to explicit [*für sich, actus*, ἐνέργεια]. To illustrate this process, Hegel frequently uses the analogy of organic growth. The tree—trunk, branches, and fruit—is present in germ in the seed. The seed is the whole life of the tree in its 'immediacy', and that life becomes explicit as its immediacy is mediated through the different stages in the tree's history. Hence as the tree grows, all that happens is that what is implicit becomes explicit; but the development is a genuine development and change, because trunk, branches, etc., do not exist *realiter* in the seed—even a microscope will not detect them there. As the seed grows, it differentiates itself into trunk, branches, leaves, etc., but when its growth is complete, it is a concrete unity (the tree as a whole) and not, as the seed was, an abstract unity, because it is now a differentiated and not an immediate, undeveloped, immature, unity.

It is a development of this sort which we study in the *Philosophy of Right*, and the process is always from immediate, undifferentiated, unity (i.e. bare abstract universality), through difference and particularization, to the concrete unity and synthesis of universal and particular, subject and object, form and content. This synthesis is individuality or concrete universality, or the concept in its truth as Idea. Since the process of its life is a single process, the determinations or particularizations which the concept gives to itself are an organically connected series, and they follow one another in stages of gradually increasing concreteness. The later stages cancel the earlier ones, and yet at the same time the earlier ones are absorbed within the later as moments or elements within them. Hence, although 'ethical life' supersedes 'abstract right' and 'morality', both of these are absorbed into ethical life as its constituents, just as family and civil society are both superseded by and incorporated in the state.

NOTE ON THE TEXT AND TRANSLATION

HEGEL'S *Outlines of the Philosophy of Right* is an immensely rich study of freedom in its various forms. Readers should keep in mind, however, that what they are studying is not a book intended for independent scrutiny, but a handbook produced to accompany Hegel's lectures. Hegel included several paragraphs on the philosophy of right in all three editions of his *Encyclopaedia*, which was published to accompany lectures on his 'encyclopaedic' system as a whole. In October 1820, however, he published the *Philosophy of Right* for use in lectures devoted specifically to that topic.

The main paragraphs and the indented 'Remarks' in the *Philosophy of Right* were written by Hegel himself. The 'Additions', on the other hand, were compiled by Hegel's student Eduard Gans, for the first posthumous edition of Hegel's works (published in 1833). Gans drew on Hegel's own notes on the philosophy of right, as well as on transcripts of Hegel's lectures by two other students, Heinrich Gustav Hotho (from Winter 1822–3) and Karl Gustav von Griesheim (from Winter 1824–5). (These transcripts are published in K.-H. Ilting (ed.), *G. W. F. Hegel. Vorlesungen über Rechtsphilosophie, 1818–1831*, 4 vols. (Stuttgart–Bad Cannstatt: Frommann-Holzboog, 1973–), vols. 3 and 4.) Since the Additions were not written by Hegel himself, they should be treated with some care. Nonetheless, they are a valuable resource for understanding Hegel's views and have been retained in this new edition for that reason.

The text reproduced here is the translation originally published in *Hegel's Philosophy of Right*, trans. T. M. Knox (Oxford: Clarendon Press, 1952). (This was reissued as a paperback by Oxford University Press in 1967.) For this new edition numerous minor alterations have been made (primarily in the interests of greater accuracy), but the substance of the translation has not been changed. The Additions have been placed immediately after the Paragraphs (abbreviated '§') or Remarks to which they apply (rather than, as in Knox's edition, at the end of the book). Indented text has been used for the Remarks (see p. 17 below). Square brackets in the text of the *Philosophy of Right* indicate an insertion by Knox or the present editor; round brackets indicate an insertion by Hegel. Asterisks in the text refer to the Explanatory Notes at the end of the book (pp. 324 ff.). Footnotes, unless specifically attributed to Hegel, are by Knox or the present editor (the latter are indicated by [S.H.]). The number of Knox's original notes has been reduced, but new notes have also been added by the present editor. Many of Knox's notes have been extensively revised.

SELECT BIBLIOGRAPHY

Collected Works of Hegel

Moldenhauer, Eva, and Michel, Karl Markus (eds.), *G. W. F. Hegel. Werke*, 20 vols. and Index (Frankfurt-am-Main: Suhrkamp Verlag, 1969–).

Translations of Hegel's Outlines of the Philosophy of Right

Dyde, S. W. (trans.), *Hegel's Philosophy of Right* (London: George Bell & Sons, 1896).

Knox, T. M. (trans.), *Hegel's Philosophy of Right* (1952; Oxford: Oxford University Press, 1967).

White, Alan, (trans.), *G. W. F. Hegel: The Philosophy of Right* (Newburyport, Mass.: Focus Publishing, 2002).

Wood, Allen W. (ed.), and Nisbet, H. B. (trans.), *G. W. F. Hegel: Elements of the Philosophy of Right* (Cambridge: Cambridge University Press, 1991).

Transcripts of Hegel's Lectures on the Philosophy of Right

Angehrn, Emil, Bondeli, Martin, and Seelman, Hoo Nam (eds.), *G. W. F. Hegel. Vorlesungen über die Philosophie des Rechts. Berlin 1819/1820. Nachgeschrieben von Johann Rudolf Ringier* (Hamburg: Felix Meiner, 2000).

Becker, C., *et al.* (eds.), *G. W. F. Hegel. Vorlesungen über Naturrecht und Staatswissenschaft. Heidelberg 1817/18 mit Nachträgen aus der Vorlesung 1818/19. Nachgeschrieben von P. Wannenmann* (Hamburg: Felix Meiner, 1983).

Henrich, Dieter (ed.), *G. W. F. Hegel. Philosophie des Rechts. Die Vorlesung von 1819/20 in einer Nachschrift* (Frankfurt-am-Main: Suhrkamp Verlag, 1983).

Hoppe, Hansgeorg (ed.), *G. W. F. Hegel. Die Philosophie des Rechts. Vorlesung von 1821/22* (Frankfurt-am-Main: Suhrkamp Verlag, 2005).

Ilting, K.-H. (ed.), *G. W. F. Hegel. Vorlesungen über Rechtsphilosophie, 1818–1831*, 4 vols. (Stuttgart-Bad Cannstatt: Frommann-Holzboog, 1973–).

Schilbach, Erich (ed.), *G. W. F. Hegel. Philosophie des Rechts. Nachschrift der Vorlesung von 1822/23 von Karl Wilhelm Ludwig Heyse* (Frankfurt-am-Main: Peter Lang, 1999).

Stewart, J. Michael, and Hodgson, Peter C. (trans.), *G. W. F. Hegel: Lectures on Natural Right and Political Science. The First Philosophy of Right.*

Heidelberg 1817–1818 with Additions from the Lectures of 1818–1819. Transcribed by Peter Wannenmann (Berkeley: University of California Press, 1995).

Letters and Other Works by Hegel

Behler, Ernst (ed.), *G. W. F. Hegel: Encyclopedia of the Philosophical Sciences in Outline* [1817] *and Critical Writings* (New York: Continuum, 1990).

Butler, Clark, and Seiler, Christiane (trans.), *Hegel: The Letters* (Bloomington, Ind.: Indiana University Press, 1984).

Dickey, Laurence, and Nisbet, H. B. (eds.), *G. W. F. Hegel: Political Writings* (Cambridge: Cambridge University Press, 1999).

Geraets, T. F., Suchting, W. A., and Harris, H. S. (trans.), *G. W. F. Hegel: The Encyclopaedia Logic. Part 1 of the Encyclopaedia of Philosophical Sciences with the Zusätze* (Indianapolis, Ind.: Hackett Publishing, 1991).

Hoffmeister, Johannes (ed.), *Briefe von und an Hegel*, 4 vols. (1952–4; Hamburg: Felix Meiner, 1961).

—— (ed.), *Dokumente zu Hegels Entwicklung* (1936; Stuttgart-Bad Cannstatt: Frommann-Holzboog, 1974).

Houlgate, Stephen (ed.), *The Hegel Reader* (Oxford: Blackwell, 1998).

Knox, T. M. (trans.), *Hegel's Political Writings* (Oxford: Clarendon Press, 1964).

Miller, A. V. (trans.), *Hegel's Philosophy of Nature: Being Part Two of the Encyclopaedia of the Philosophical Sciences (1830)* (Oxford: Clarendon Press, 1970).

—— (trans.), *Hegel's Phenomenology of Spirit* (Oxford: Oxford University Press, 1977).

—— (trans.), *Hegel's Science of Logic* (Amherst, NY: Humanity Books, 1999).

Sibree, J. (trans.), *G. W. F. Hegel: The Philosophy of History* (New York: Dover Publications, 1956).

Wallace, W., and Miller, A. V. (trans.), *Hegel's Philosophy of Mind: Being Part Three of the Encyclopaedia of the Philosophical Sciences (1830)* (Oxford: Clarendon Press, 1971).

Books on Hegel's Life and/or his Philosophy as a Whole

Beiser, Frederick, *Hegel* (London: Routledge, 2005).

Houlgate, Stephen, *An Introduction to Hegel: Freedom, Truth and History* (1991; Oxford: Blackwell, 2005).

Jaeschke, Walter, *Hegel-Handbuch. Leben-Werk-Schule* (Stuttgart: J. B. Metzler, 2003).

Pinkard, Terry, *Hegel: A Biography* (Cambridge: Cambridge University Press, 2000).

Plant, Raymond, *Hegel: An Introduction* (1972; Oxford: Blackwell, 1983).

Taylor, Charles, *Hegel* (Cambridge: Cambridge University Press, 1975).

Books on Hegel's Outlines of the Philosophy of Right

Avineri, Shlomo, *Hegel's Theory of the Modern State* (Cambridge: Cambridge University Press, 1972).

Brooks, Thom, *Hegel's Political Philosophy: A Systematic Reading of the Philosophy of Right* (Edinburgh: University of Edinburgh Press, 2007).

Hardimon, Michael O., *Hegel's Social Philosophy: The Project of Reconciliation* (Cambridge: Cambridge University Press, 1994).

Knowles, Dudley, *Hegel and the Philosophy of Right* (London: Routledge, 2002).

Neuhouser, Frederick, *Foundations of Hegel's Social Theory: Actualising Freedom* (Cambridge, Mass.: Harvard University Press, 2000).

Patten, Alan, *Hegel's Idea of Freedom* (Oxford: Oxford University Press, 1999).

Pelczynski, Z. A. (ed.), *Hegel's Political Philosophy: Problems and Perspectives* (Cambridge: Cambridge University Press, 1971).

—— (ed.), *The State and Civil Society: Studies in Hegel's Political Philosophy* (Cambridge: Cambridge University Press, 1984).

Peperzak, Adriaan T., *Modern Freedom: Hegel's Legal, Moral, and Political Philosophy* (Dordrecht and Boston: Kluwer, 2001).

Pippin, Robert B., and Höffe, Otfried (eds.), and Walker, Nicholas (trans.), *Hegel on Ethics and Politics* (Cambridge: Cambridge University Press, 2004).

Riedel, Manfred (ed.), *Materialien zu Hegels Rechtsphilosophie*, 2 vols. (Frankfurt-am-Main: Suhrkamp Verlag, 1975).

Ritter, Joachim, *Hegel und die Französische Revolution* (Frankfurt-am-Main: Suhrkamp Verlag, 1965).

Siep, Ludwig (ed.), *G. W. F. Hegel. Grundlinien der Philosophie des Rechts* (Berlin: Akademie Verlag, 1997).

Waszek, Norbert, *The Scottish Enlightenment and Hegel's Account of 'Civil Society'* (Dordrecht and Boston: Kluwer, 1988).

Wood, Allen W., *Hegel's Ethical Thought* (Cambridge: Cambridge University Press, 1990).

Williams, Robert R. (ed.), *Beyond Liberalism and Communitarianism: Studies in Hegel's Philosophy of Right* (Albany, NY: SUNY Press, 2001).

Williams, Robert R., *Hegel's Ethics of Recognition* (Berkeley: University of California Press, 1997).

Other Works

Clark, Christopher, *Iron Kingdom: The Rise and Downfall of Prussia, 1600–1947* (London: Allen Lane, 2006).

Flenley, Ralph, *Modern German History* (1953; London: J. M. Dent & Sons, 1964).

Fukuyama, Francis, *The End of History and the Last Man* (Harmondsworth: Penguin Books, 1992).

McLellan, David (ed.), *Karl Marx: Selected Writings* (1977; Oxford: Oxford University Press, 2000).

Popper, Karl, *The Open Society and its Enemies*, 2 vols. (1945; London: Routledge, 1966).

Rawls, John, *Lectures on the History of Moral Philosophy* (Cambridge, Mass.: Harvard University Press, 2000).

Sagarra, Eda, *An Introduction to Nineteenth Century Germany* (Harlow: Longman, 1980).

Further Reading in Oxford World's Classics

Burke, Edmund, *Reflections on the Revolution in France*, ed. L. G. Mitchell.

Engels, Friedrich, *The Condition of the Working Class in England*, ed. David McLellan.

Marx, Karl, *Capital*, ed. David McLellan.

—— and Engels, Friedrich, *The Communist Manifesto*, ed. David McLellan.

Mill, John Stuart, *On Liberty and Other Essays*, ed. John Gray.

Paine, Thomas, *Rights of Man, Common Sense, and other Political Writings*, ed. Mark Philp.

Rousseau, J.-J., *Discourse on Political Economy and The Social Contract*, trans. Christopher Betts.

—— *Discourse on the Origin of Inequality*, trans. Franklin Philip, ed. Patrick Coleman.

Smith, Adam, *An Inquiry into the Nature and Causes of the Wealth of Nations*, ed. Kathryn Sunderland.

A CHRONOLOGY OF G. W. F. HEGEL

1770   27 August: Georg Wilhelm Friedrich Hegel born in Stuttgart.

1776   American Declaration of Independence.

1781   Immanuel Kant's *Critique of Pure Reason* published.

1783   20 September: Hegel's mother dies.

1785   Hegel begins writing a diary, partly in Latin. Kant's *Groundwork for the Metaphysics of Morals* published.

1788   Kant's *Critique of Practical Reason* published. October: Hegel begins studies in theology and philosophy at the Tübinger Stift. He develops friendship with Friedrich Hölderlin and also with Friedrich Wilhelm Joseph von Schelling (after the latter enters the Stift in 1790).

1789   14 July: the storming of the Bastille in Paris marks the beginning of the French Revolution.

1790   Kant's *Critique of Judgement* published.

1793   Louis XVI guillotined. Hegel graduates from the Tübinger Stift. Autumn: he becomes house tutor with the family of Captain Karl Friedrich von Steiger in Bern.

1794   Fall of Robespierre.

1796   Napoleon's Italian campaign. First part of Johann Gottlieb Fichte's *Foundations of Natural Right* published.

1797   January: Hegel moves to Frankfurt-am-Main to take up a tutorship with the family Gogel. Second part of Fichte's *Foundations of Natural Right* published.

1798   Hegel works on Kant's *Metaphysics of Morals* (published the previous year). Napoleon's Egyptian campaign. Fichte's *System of Ethics* published.

1799   14 January: Hegel's father dies. Hegel completes the first draft of his manuscript on the 'German Constitution'.

1801   January: Hegel joins Schelling at the University of Jena and starts work as an unsalaried lecturer.

1802   Hegel lectures on natural law. He begins publication of the *Critical Journal of Philosophy* with Schelling. Articles by Hegel published in the journal include the essay 'On the Scientific Ways of Treating Natural Law'.

1804 12 February: Kant dies. 2 December: Napoleon crowns himself emperor.

1806 July: Hegel draws his first regular stipend at Jena. October: He completes manuscript of the *Phenomenology of Spirit*. He sees Napoleon riding out of the city on reconnaissance before the battle of Jena.

1807 *Phenomenology of Spirit* published. 5 February: Christiana Burckhardt (née Fischer), Hegel's landlady and housekeeper in Jena, gives birth to his illegitimate son, Ludwig Fischer. (Ludwig is raised in Jena by the sisters-in-law of Hegel's friend, the publisher Karl Friedrich Frommann, until he is taken into Hegel's own home in 1817.) March: Hegel moves to Bamberg to become editor of a newspaper. Autumn: period of reform begins in Prussia, initially under Freiherr vom Stein, then under Karl von Hardenberg.

1808 November: Hegel moves to Nuremberg to become rector of the Aegidiengymnasium.

1811 15 September: Hegel marries Marie von Tucher (b. 1791).

1812 Napoleon's Russian campaign. Volume 1 of the *Science of Logic* (the Doctrine of Being) published. 27 June: Hegel's daughter, Susanna, born. She dies on 8 August.

1813 7 June: Hegel's son, Karl, born. Volume 2 of the *Science of Logic* (the Doctrine of Essence) published. Søren Kierkegaard, Richard Wagner, and Giuseppe Verdi born.

1814 29 January: Fichte dies. 25 September: Hegel's son, Immanuel, born.

1815 Napoleon defeated at Waterloo.

1816 Volume 3 of the *Science of Logic* (the Doctrine of the Concept) published. Hegel becomes Professor of Philosophy at the University of Heidelberg, where he lectures on natural law in 1817–18.

1817 First edition of the *Encyclopaedia* published. Hegel writes manuscript on the 'Proceedings of the Estates Assembly in the Kingdom of Württemberg, 1815–1816'.

1818 5 May: Karl Marx born in Trier. Hegel is recruited by the reform-minded Prussian Minister, Altenstein, to become Professor of Philosophy at the University of Berlin, where he remains until his death.

1819 March: Murder of August von Kotzebue. August/September: the Karlsbad Decrees are passed authorizing press censorship and closer surveillance of universities in Germany.

1820 October: *Outlines of the Philosophy of Right* published (dated 1821).

1821 5 May: Napoleon dies.

1822 Hegel lectures for the first time on the philosophy of history.

1826 Hegel founds the *Yearbooks for Scientific Criticism*.

1827 Second edition of the *Encyclopaedia* published.

1830 Hegel is rector of the University of Berlin. Third edition of the *Encyclopaedia* published. July Revolution in France.

1831 January: Hegel awarded Red Eagle, Third Class, by Friedrich Wilhelm III of Prussia. April: he publishes first three parts of his essay 'On the English Reform Bill'. 28 August: Ludwig Fischer dies in the East Indies. 14 November: Hegel dies in Berlin (probably of a chronic gastrointestinal disease) without learning of his son's fate. 24 December: a contract is signed by Hegel's wife, students, and friends for the publication of his collected works.

1832 22 March: Goethe dies.

1835–6 David Friedrich Strauß's *Life of Jesus* is published, marking the beginning of a conscious split between Left, Right, and Middle Hegelians.

1841 Schelling called to the University of Berlin by Friedrich Wilhelm IV to counter the influence of Hegelianism. Ludwig Feuerbach's *The Essence of Christianity* published.

1848 Marx and Engels publish the *Communist Manifesto*.

1857 Rudolf Haym publishes *Hegel and his Time*, in which he accuses Hegel of embodying the spirit of the Prussian restoration.

OUTLINES OF THE
PHILOSOPHY OF RIGHT

PREFACE

THE immediate inducement to publish this manual is the need to put into the hands of my audience a textbook for the lectures on the philosophy of right which I deliver in the course of my professional duties. This compendium is an enlarged and in particular a more systematic exposition of the same fundamental concepts which, in relation to this part of philosophy, are already contained in a book of mine designed previously for my lectures—the *Encyclopaedia of the Philosophical Sciences* (Heidelberg, 1817).*

The fact, however, that this manual was to appear in print, and so to come before a wider public, induced me to amplify here a good many of the *Remarks** which were primarily meant in a brief compass to indicate ideas related to my argument or at variance with it, further inferences from it, and the like, i.e. material which would receive its requisite elucidation in my lectures. The object of amplifying them here was to clarify occasionally the more abstract parts of the text and to take a more comprehensive look at current ideas widely disseminated at the present time. Hence the result has been a number of Remarks rather more extensive than is usually consistent with the style and aim of a compendium. A proper compendium, however, has as its subject-matter what is taken to be the closed circle of a science; and what is appropriate in it, except perhaps for a small addition here and there, is principally the assembly and arrangement of the essential factors in a content which has long been familiar and accepted, just as the form in which it is arranged has its rules and conventions which have long been settled. Philosophical manuals are not now expected to conform to such a pattern, if only because it is supposed that what philosophy puts together is a work as ephemeral as Penelope's web,* one which must be begun afresh every day.

The primary difference between this manual and an ordinary compendium certainly lies in the method which constitutes its guiding principle. But in this book I presuppose that philosophy's mode of progression from one topic to another and its mode of scientific proof—this whole speculative way of knowing—is essentially distinct from any other way of knowing. It is only insight into the necessity of such a difference that can rescue philosophy from the shameful decay in which it is immersed at the present time. It is true that the forms and rules of the old logic, of definition, classification, and syllogism, which include the rules governing knowledge that is attainable by the understanding [*Verstandeserkenntnis*], have become recognized as inadequate for speculative science; or rather their inadequacy has not been recognized, it has only been felt. These rules have then been thrown off as if they were mere fetters in order to allow the heart, the imagination, and contingent intuition to say what they pleased. Yet since reflection and relations of thought must also enter the scene, people relapse unconsciously into the very method of commonplace deduction and argumentation [*Räsonnement*] that is despised.

Since I have fully expounded the nature of speculative knowing in my *Science of Logic*,* in this manual I have only added an explanatory note here and there about procedure and method. In dealing with a topic which is concrete and intrinsically of so varied a character, I have omitted to bring out and demonstrate the chain of logical argument in each and every detail. For one thing, to have done this might have been regarded as superfluous where acquaintance with philosophical method is presupposed; for another, it will be obvious from the work itself that the whole, like the formation of its parts, rests on the logical spirit [*dem logischen Geiste*]. It is also from this point of view above all that I should like my book to be taken and judged. What we have to do with here is [philosophical] *science*, and in such science content is essentially bound up with *form*.

We may of course hear from those who seem to be taking the most profound view that the form is something external and indifferent to the subject-matter, that the latter alone is important; further, the task of a writer, especially a writer on philosophy, may be said to lie in the discovery of *truths* (in the plural), the statement of *truths*, the dissemination of *truths* and sound concepts. Yet if we consider how this task is as a rule actually discharged, what we find in the first place is that the same old stew is continually warmed up again and again and served round to everybody. This task may well have the merit of educating and stimulating people's hearts; but it might better be regarded as the superfluous labour of a busybody—'for they have Moses and the Prophets; let them hear them'.[1] Above all, we have ample opportunity to marvel at the pretentious tone recognizable in these busybodies when they talk as if the world had wanted for

[1] Luke 16: 29.

nothing except their energetic dissemination of truths, or as if their reheated stew were productive of new and unheard-of truths and was to be specially taken to heart before everything else 'today' and every day. On the other hand, we find that what are given out as truths of this sort by one party are dislodged and brushed aside by truths of just the same sort purveyed by other parties. If, therefore, in this crush of truths, there is something neither new nor old but enduring, how is this to be extracted from these reflections which oscillate formlessly from this to that, how is it to be separated from them and proved, if not by [philosophical] *science*?

However we look at it, the *truth* about *right*, *ethical life*, and the *state* is as old as its recognition and formulation in public laws and in public morality and religion. What more does this truth require, insofar as the thinking mind [*Geist*] is not content to possess it in this manner that is closest to us? It requires to be *grasped in thought* as well; the content which is already rational in itself must win the *form* of rationality, so that it may appear justified to free thinking. Such thinking does not stop at the given, whether the given be supported by the external positive authority of the state or agreement among people, or by the authority of inward feeling and the heart and by the witness of the spirit which immediately concurs with it. On the contrary, thought which is free starts out from itself and thereupon demands to know itself as united in its innermost being with the truth.

The unsophisticated heart takes the simple line of adhering with trustful conviction to what is publicly accepted as true and then building on this firm foundation its conduct and its set position in life. Against this simple line of conduct there may at once be raised the alleged difficulty of how it is possible, in an infinite *variety of opinions*, to distinguish and discover what is universally recognized and valid. This perplexity may at first sight be taken for a right and genuine concern for the thing [*Sache*], but in fact those who boast of this perplexity are in the position of not being able to see the wood for the trees; the only perplexity and difficulty they are in is one of their own making. Indeed, this perplexity and difficulty of theirs is proof rather that they want something other than what is universally recognized and valid, something other than the substance of right and the ethical. If they had been serious about the latter, instead of busying themselves with the vanity and particularity of opinions and things, they would have clung to what is substantially right, namely to the commands of ethical life and the state, and would have regulated their lives in accordance with these.

A further difficulty arises, however, from the fact that human beings *think* and try to find in thinking both their freedom and the basis of ethical life. But however lofty, however divine, the right of thought may be, it is perverted into wrong if thinking counts as thinking, and thinking knows itself to be free, only when it diverges from what is *universally* recognized and valid and when it has discovered how to invent for itself something *particular*.

At the present time, the idea that freedom of thought, and of spirit [*Geist*] generally, evinces itself only in divergence from, indeed in hostility to, what is publicly recognized, might seem to be most firmly rooted in connection with the *state*; and it is for this reason that a philosophy of the state might well seem essentially to have the task of discovering and promulgating yet another *theory*, and a new and distinctive one at that. In examining this idea and the activity in conformity with it, we might suppose that no state or constitution has ever existed in the world at all or is even in being at the present time, but that *now*—and this 'now' lasts for ever—we have to start all over again from the beginning, and that the ethical world has just been waiting for such projects, investigations, and proofs as are undertaken *now*. As far as nature is concerned, people grant that philosophy must come to know it *as it is*, that the philosopher's stone lies concealed *somewhere*, somewhere *within nature itself*, that nature is inherently rational, and that what knowledge has to investigate and grasp in concepts is this actual reason present in it; not the formations and contingencies evident to the superficial observer, but nature's eternal harmony, its harmony, however, in the sense of the law and essence *immanent* within it. The *ethical world*, on the other hand, the state (i.e. reason as it actualizes itself in the element of self-consciousness), is not allowed to enjoy the good fortune which springs from the fact that reason has come to be a force and power [*Gewalt*] within that element and maintains itself and has its home there.

Addition: Laws are of two kinds—laws of nature and laws of right. The laws of nature simply are what they are and are valid as they are; they are not liable to wither away, though they can be infringed in individual cases. To know the law of nature, we must learn to know nature itself, since its laws are correct and it is only our ideas about them that can be false. The measure of these laws is outside us; knowing them adds nothing to them and does not assist their operation; our knowledge of them can expand, that is all. Knowledge of right is in one way similar, but in another way not. We learn to know its laws just as they exist; the citizen's knowledge of them is more or less of this sort, and the student of positive law [*der positive Jurist*] equally stops at what is given. But the difference in the case of laws of right is that they arouse the spirit of reflection, and their diversity at once draws attention to the fact that they are not absolute. The laws of right [*Rechtsgesetze*] are something *posited* [*Gesetztes*], something *originated* by human beings. Between what is so originated and the voice within us there may of necessity be a clash or agreement. The human being does not stop short at the existent [*Daseiendes*], but claims to have in himself the measure of what is right. He may be subjected to the compulsion and power of an external authority, though never as he is to the necessity of nature, because his inner self always tells him how things ought to be and he finds within himself the confirmation or denial of what passes as valid. In nature, the highest truth is that there *is* a law *at all*; in the laws of right, the thing is not valid simply because it exists; on the contrary, everyone demands that it should comply with his own criterion. Here then an antagonism is possible between what ought to be and what is, between right in and for itself [*an und für sich*] which stands unaltered and the arbitrary determination of what is to be recognized as right. A schism and a conflict of this sort is to be found only in the territory of spirit, and because spirit's privilege seems therefore to lead to discontent and unhappiness, people are often thrown back from the arbitrariness of life to the contemplation of nature and set themselves to take nature as an example. But it is precisely in these clashes between right in and for itself and what arbitrariness proclaims as right that there lies the need to acquire a thorough knowledge of right. In right, the human being must encounter his own reason; consequently, he must consider the rationality of right, and this is the task of our science in contrast with positive jurisprudence which often has to do only with contradictions.* The world of today has in addition a more urgent need to acquire this knowledge because, while amongst the ancients existing laws were still respected and reverenced, nowadays the civilization of the age has taken a new turn and thought has placed itself at the head of everything which is to have validity. Theories [*Theorien*] are set over against what exists and are meant to appear correct and necessary in and for themselves. From now on there is a more special need for us to become acquainted with, and understand, the thoughts of right. Since thought has risen to be the essential form, we must try to grasp right too as thought. It seems to be opening wide the door to contingent opinions to hold that thought is to be pre-eminent over right; yet true thought is not an opinion about the thing but the *concept of the thing itself*. The concept of the thing does not come our way by nature. Anyone has fingers and may take a brush and colours, but that does not make him a painter. The same is true with thinking. The thought of right is surely not the thought that everybody possesses at first hand; on the contrary, correct thinking is knowing and cognizing the thing, and our cognition should therefore be scientific.

The spiritual universe is supposed rather to be left to the mercy of contingency and caprice, to be God-forsaken, and the result is that, according to this atheistic view [*Atheismus*] of the ethical world, truth lies outside such a world, and at the same time, since even so reason is supposed to be in it as well, truth becomes nothing but a problem [*Problema*]. But it is this also that authorizes, indeed obliges, every thinker to offer his own solution—though not by *searching* for the philosopher's stone, for he is saved this search by our contemporary philosophizing,* and everyone nowadays is assured that he has this stone in his grasp just as he stands. Now admittedly it is the case that those who live within the actuality of the state and find satisfaction there for their knowledge and volition (and of these there are many, more in fact than think or know it, because ultimately this is the position of *everybody*), or those at any rate who *consciously* find their satisfaction in the state, laugh at these initiatives and assurances and regard them as an empty game, sometimes rather funny, sometimes rather serious, now delightful, now dangerous. Thus this restless activity of reflection and vanity, together with the reception and response it has encountered, would be a thing on its own [*eine Sache für sich*], developing in itself in its own way, were it not that *philosophy* as such has earned all kinds of scorn and discredit by its indulgence in this occupation. The worst of these kinds of scorn is this, that, as I said just now, everyone is convinced that he is in a position, just as he stands, to know all about philosophy in general and to condemn it. No other art or science is subjected to this last degree of scorn, to the supposition that we are all in immediate and complete possession of it.

In fact, what we have seen the philosophy of recent times* proclaiming with the maximum of pretension about the state has really justified anybody who wished to speak on such matters in this conviction that he could just as easily do the same himself and so prove to himself that he is in possession of philosophy. Besides, this self-styled 'philosophy' has expressly stated that *truth itself cannot be known*, that that only is true which each individual allows to rise out of his heart, emotion, and inspiration about ethical institutions, especially about the state, the government, and the constitution. In this connection what a lot of flattery has been talked, especially to the young! Certainly the young have listened to it willingly enough. 'He giveth to his own in sleep'* has been applied to science and hence every sleeper has numbered himself among the elect, but the concepts he has acquired in sleep are themselves of course only the wares of sleep.

A ringleader of these hosts of superficiality, of these self-styled 'philosophers', Herr Fries,*² did not blush, on a solemn public occasion* which has become notorious, to express the following ideas in a speech on 'The state and the constitution': 'In the people ruled by a genuine communal spirit, life for the discharge of all public business would come from below, from the people itself; living associations, indissolubly united by the holy chain of friendship, would be dedicated to every single project of popular education and popular service,' and so on. This is the quintessence of shallow thinking: to base philosophical science not on the development of thought and the concept but on immediate perception and contingent imagination; to take the rich inward articulation of ethical life, i.e. the state, the architectonic of its rationality—which, through determinate distinctions between the circles of public life and their rights and through the strict proportion in which every pillar, arch, and buttress is held together, produces the strength of the whole out of the harmony of the parts—to take this developed structure and let it dissolve in the broth of 'heart, friendship, and inspiration'. According to a view of this kind, the ethical world (Epicurus,* holding a similar view, would have said the 'world as such') should be given over—as in fact of course it is not—to the subjective contingency of opinion and caprice. By the simple household remedy of ascribing to *feeling* what has been produced by the labour—stretching over many thousands of years—of reason and its understanding, all the trouble of rational insight and knowledge guided by the thinking concept is of course saved. On this point, Goethe's Mephistopheles—a good authority—says something like this, a quotation I have used elsewhere* already: 'Do but despise understanding and science, the highest of all human gifts, and you have surrendered yourself to the devil and must surely perish.' The next thing is that such a view assumes even the guise of *piety*, for this activity has used any and every expedient in its endeavour to give itself authority. With godliness and the Bible, however, it

² *Hegel's note*: I have borne witness before to the superficiality of his philosophy—see *Science of Logic* (Nuremberg, 1812), Introduction, p. xvii [Miller trans., 52].

has arrogated to itself the highest of justifications for despising the ethical order and the objectivity of law: for it is piety indeed to envelop in the simpler intuition of feeling the truth which is articulated in the world into an organic realm. If it is piety of the right sort, however, it sheds the form of this [emotional] region as soon as it leaves the inner life, enters upon the daylight of the Idea's development and revealed riches, and brings with it, out of its inner worship of God, reverence for law and for a truth which is in and for itself and which has been exalted above the subjective form of feeling.*

The particular form of bad conscience revealed by the type of eloquence in which such superficiality flaunts itself may be brought to your attention here; note above all that when it is at its most *spiritless*, superficiality speaks most of spirit, when its talk is at its driest and most dead [*am totesten*], its favourite words are 'life' and 'enliven', and when it gives evidence of the pure selfishness of empty pride, the word most on its lips is 'people' [*Volk*]. But the distinctive mark which it carries on its brow is the hatred of law. Right and ethical life, and the actual world of right and ethical life, are understood through *thoughts*; through thoughts they are invested with a rational form, i.e. with universality and determinacy. This form is *law*; and this it is which the feeling that reserves the right to do what it likes, the conscience that places right in subjective conviction, has reason to regard as its chief foe. The form of right as a duty and a law it feels as a dead, cold letter, as a shackle; for it does not recognize itself in the law and so does not recognize itself as free there, because law is the reason of the thing [*Vernunft der Sache*], and reason refuses to allow feeling to bask in its own particularity. Hence law, as I have remarked somewhere[3] in the course of this textbook, is *par excellence* the shibboleth which marks out these false friends and comrades of what they call the 'people'.

At the present time, the sophistry of wilfulness has usurped the name of *philosophy* and succeeded in giving a wide public the opinion that such triflings are philosophy. The result of this is that it has now become almost a disgrace to go on speaking in philosophical terms about the nature of the state, and honest men cannot be blamed if they become impatient as soon as they hear mention of a philosophical science of the state. Still less is it a matter for surprise that governments have at last directed their attention to this kind of

---

[3] See Hegel's note to *PR* § 258 [p. 231 below].

philosophy, since, apart from anything else, philosophy with us is not, as it was with the Greeks for instance, pursued as a private art, but has an existence in the open, in contact with the public, and especially, or even only, in the service of the state.* Governments have proven their trust in those scholars who have devoted themselves to philosophy by leaving entirely to them the development [*Ausbildung*] and contents of philosophy—though here and there, if you like, it may not have been so much trust that has been shown as indifference to science itself, and professorial chairs of philosophy have been retained only as a tradition (in France, for instance, to the best of my knowledge, chairs of metaphysics at least have been allowed to lapse). Their trust, however, has very often been ill repaid, or alternatively, if you preferred to see indifference, you would have to regard the result, the decay of thorough knowledge, as the penalty for this indifference. Prima facie, superficiality seems to be wholly compatible with outward order and peace, because it fails to touch or even to guess at the substance of things; no action, or at least no police action,[4] would thus have been taken against it in the first instance, had it not been that there still existed in the state a need for a deeper education and insight, a need which the state required [philosophical] science to satisfy. But superficial thinking about the ethical order, about right and duty in general, leads automatically to the principles which constitute superficiality in this sphere, i.e. to the principles of the Sophists which are so clearly outlined for us by Plato.* What is right these principles locate in subjective aims and opinions, in subjective feeling and particular conviction, and from them there follows the ruin of inner ethical life and the upright conscience, of love and right between private persons, no less than the ruin of public order and the law of the state. The significance which such phenomena must acquire for governments is not likely to be diminished by those who feel entitled—by the trust granted to them and by the authority of an official position—to demand that the state should uphold and give scope to what corrupts the substantial source of deeds, namely universal principles, and so even give scope to defiance of the state as if such defiance were quite proper. 'If God gives someone an office, he also gives him sense [*Verstand*]' is an old joke which in these days surely no one will take wholly in earnest.

---

[4] For the wide meaning which Hegel gives to 'police' [*Polizei*], see *PR* §§ 231–49.

In the fresh importance which circumstances have led governments to attach to the character of philosophical work, there is one
element which we cannot fail to notice; this is the protection and support which the study of philosophy now seems to have come to need
in several other directions. Think of the numerous publications in the
field of the positive sciences,* as well as edifying religious works and
vague literature of other kinds, which reveal to their readers the contempt for philosophy I have already mentioned, in that, although the
thought in them is immature to the last degree and philosophy is
entirely alien to them, they treat the latter as something that can be
dismissed. More than this, they expressly rail against it and pronounce its content, namely the conceptual [*begreifend*] knowledge of
God and of physical and spiritual nature, the knowledge of truth, to
be a foolish and even sinful presumptuousness, while *reason*, and
again reason, and reason repeated *ad infinitum*, is arraigned, dispar-
aged, and condemned. At the very least such writings reveal to us
that, to a majority of those engaged in activities supposedly scientific,
the claims of the concept are an embarrassment which nonetheless
they cannot escape. I venture to say that anyone with such phenomena before him may very well begin to think that, *in this respect*, tradition is no longer worthy of respect, nor sufficient to secure for the
study of philosophy either tolerance or a public existence.[5]

The arrogant declamations current in our time against philosophy
present the strange spectacle, on the one hand, of being in the right
by virtue of the superficiality to which that science has been
degraded, and, on the other, of being themselves rooted in this element against which they turn so ungratefully. For by pronouncing
cognition of the truth to be a foolish endeavour, this self-styled philosophizing has reduced all thoughts and all topics to the same level,
just as the despotism of the Roman Empire abolished the distinction
between nobles [*Adel*] and slaves, virtue and vice, honour and dishonour,

---

[5] *Hegel's note*: Similar views occurred to me on reading a letter of Johannes von
Müller* (*Werke* [Tübingen 1810–19], Part VIII, p. 56). In talking of the condition of Rome
in 1803 when the city was under French control, he says: 'Asked how the public educational
institutions were faring, a professor replied: "They are tolerated, like brothels".'*—One
can still even hear people recommending the so-called 'Doctrine of Reason', namely
logic, with the apparent conviction that it is such a dry and profitless science that nobody
will busy himself with it, or that if here and there someone does take it up, he will
thereby acquire mere empty formulae, unproductive and innocuous, and that therefore
in either case the recommendation will do no harm, even if it does no good.

learning and ignorance. The result of this levelling process is that the concepts of truth and the laws of ethical life likewise become nothing more than opinions and subjective convictions. The maxims of the worst of criminals, since they too are *convictions*, are put on the same level of value as those laws;[6] and at the same time any object, however bare and particular, any material, however dry, is given the same worth as that which constitutes the interest of all thinking people and the bonds of the ethical world.

It is therefore to be taken as a piece of *luck* for [philosophical] science—though in actual fact, as I have said,* it is the *necessity* of the thing—that this philosophizing, which like scholastic wisdom might have continued to spin its web within itself, has now been put into closer touch and so into open variance with actuality, in which the principles of rights and duties are a serious matter and which lives in the light of its consciousness of these.

It is just this relation of philosophy to actuality which meets with misunderstandings, and so I revert to what I have said before,* namely that, since philosophy is the *exploration of the rational*, it is for that very reason the *comprehension of the present and the actual*, not the setting up of a beyond, supposed to exist, God knows where—or rather a beyond, of which we can indeed say where it exists, namely in the error of a one-sided, empty ratiocination. In the course of this book,[7] I have remarked that even Plato's *Republic*, which passes proverbially as an empty ideal, is in essence nothing but the grasping of the nature of Greek ethical life. Plato was conscious that there was breaking into that life a deeper principle which could appear in it immediately only as a still unsatisfied longing, and so only as a source of corruption. To combat it, he had to seek aid from that very longing itself. But this aid had to come from on high and all that Plato could do was to seek it initially in a particular *external* form of that same Greek ethical life. By that means he thought to overcome this corruption, and thereby he did the most profound injury to the deeper impulse which underlay it, namely free infinite personality. Still, his greatness of spirit is proved by the fact that the principle on which the distinctive character of his Idea [of the state] turns is precisely the pivot on which the impending world revolution turned.*

---

[6] See the editor's Introduction above, pp. xiii, xxv–xxvi [S.H.]

[7] See the Remark to *PR* § 185.

*What is rational is actual and what is actual is rational.** This conviction is shared by every naive consciousness as well as by philosophy, and from it philosophy starts in its study of the *spiritual* and the *natural* universe. If reflection, feeling, or whatever form subjective consciousness may take, looks upon the *present* as something vacuous and looks beyond it with the eyes of superior wisdom, it finds itself in a vacuum, and because it has actuality in the present alone, it is itself mere vacuity [*Eitelkeit*]. If, on the other hand, the Idea is regarded as 'only an Idea', as something represented [*eine Vorstellung*] in an opinion, philosophy's insight, by contrast, is that nothing is actual except the Idea. The important thing, then, is to recognize in the semblance of the temporal and transient the substance which is immanent and the eternal which is present. For since rationality (which is synonymous with the Idea) enters into external existence [*Existenz*] simultaneously with its actualization,* it emerges with an infinite wealth of forms, shapes, and appearances. Around its core it throws a motley covering in which consciousness is initially at home, a covering which the concept has first to penetrate before it can find the inward pulse and feel it still beating in the external shapes. Yet the infinitely manifold relations which develop in this externality by virtue of the appearance of the essence [*das Scheinen des Wesens*] in it—this endless material and its organization— are not the subject-matter of philosophy. To touch this at all would be to meddle with things which do not concern philosophy, and it may save itself the trouble of giving good advice on such topics. Plato might have omitted his recommendation* to nurses to keep on the move with infants and to rock them continually in their arms. And Fichte too* need not have carried what has been called the 'construction' of his passport regulations to such a pitch of perfection as to require suspects not merely to sign their passports but to have their likenesses painted on them. In such specifications all trace of philosophy is lost, and it can abstain from such ultra-wisdom [*Ultraweisheit*] all the more readily, since its attitude to precisely this infinite multitude of topics should be the most liberal [*am liberalsten*]. In adopting this attitude, [philosophical] science shows itself to be poles apart from the hatred with which the vanity of superior wisdom regards a vast number of affairs and institutions, a hatred in which pettiness takes the greatest delight because only by venting it does it attain a feeling of its self-hood.

This book, then, containing as it does the science of the state, is to be nothing other than the endeavour to *apprehend and present the state*

as something inherently rational. As a work of philosophy, it must be
removed as far as possible from any attempt to construct a *state as it
ought to be.* The instruction which it may contain cannot consist in
teaching the state what it ought to be; it can only show how the state,
the ethical universe, should be understood.[8]

’Ιδού ‘Ρόδος, ἰδού καὶ τὸ πήδημα.
Hic Rhodus, *hic* saltus.*

To comprehend *what is*, this is the task of philosophy, because *what
is*, is reason. Whatever happens, every individual is a *child of his time*;
so philosophy too is *its own time apprehended in thoughts.* It is just as
absurd to fancy that a philosophy can transcend its contemporary
world as it is to fancy that an individual can overleap his own age,
jump over Rhodes. If his theory really goes beyond the world as it is
and builds a world *as it ought to be*, that world exists indeed, but only
in his opinions, a supple element in which anything you please may
be constructed by the imagination.

With hardly an alteration, the proverb just quoted would run:

Here is the rose, dance *here.**

What lies between reason as self-conscious spirit and reason as present actuality, what separates the former from the latter and prevents
it from finding satisfaction in the latter, is the fetter of some abstraction or other which has not been liberated [and so transformed] into
the concept. To recognize reason as the rose in the cross of the
present* and thereby to enjoy the present, this is the rational insight
which *reconciles* us to actuality—the reconciliation which philosophy
affords to those in whom there has once arisen an inner voice bidding
them to *comprehend*, and not only to preserve their subjective freedom in what is substantial, but also to stand with their subjective
freedom in that which is in and for itself rather than in something
particular and contingent.

It is this too which constitutes the more concrete meaning of
what was described above [p. 4] rather abstractly as the *unity of form and
content*; for form in its most concrete signification is reason as
conceptual [*begreifend*] knowing, and content is reason as the substantial essence of actuality, whether ethical or natural. The conscious identity of these two is the philosophical Idea.—It is a great obstinacy, the

[8] See the editor's Introduction above, p. xviii [S.H.]

obstinacy which does honour to humanity, to refuse to recognize in one's disposition anything not justified by thought. This obstinacy is the characteristic of modern times, besides being the distinctive principle of Protestantism. What began with Luther* as faith in [the form of] feeling and the witness of the spirit, is precisely what spirit, since become more mature, has striven to apprehend in the *concept* in order to free itself, and so to find itself, in the present. The saying has become famous* that 'a half-philosophy leads away from God'—and it is the same half-philosophy that locates knowledge in an *approximation* to truth—'while true philosophy leads to God'; and the same is true of philosophy and the state. Reason is not content with an approximation which, as something 'neither cold nor hot', it will 'spew out of its mouth';[9] and it is as little content with the cold despair which concedes that in this earthly life things are truly bad or at best indifferent, but since nothing better can be found here we should live at peace with the world. It is a warmer peace with the world which knowledge supplies.

One word more about giving instruction as to what the world ought to be. Philosophy in any case always comes on the scene too late to give it. As the *thought* of the world, it appears only when actuality has completed its process of formation and attained its finished state. The teaching of the concept, which is also history's inescapable lesson, is that it is only when actuality is mature that the ideal [*das Ideale*]* first appears over against the real and that the ideal grasps this same real world in its substance and builds it up for itself into the shape of an intellectual realm. When philosophy paints its grey in grey,* then has a shape of life grown old. By philosophy's grey in grey it cannot be rejuvenated but only understood. The owl of Minerva begins its flight only with the falling of dusk.*

But it is time to close this preface. After all, as a preface, its only business has been to make some external and subjective remarks about the standpoint of the book it introduces. If a topic is to be discussed philosophically, it spurns any but a scientific and objective treatment, and so too if criticisms of the author take any form other than a scientific discussion of the thing itself, they can count only as a subjective postscript and as capricious assertion, and he must treat them with indifference.

BERLIN, *June 25th*, 1820.

[9] See Revelation 3: 16.

INTRODUCTION

1. The subject-matter of the philosophical science of right is the *Idea* [*Idee*] *of right*, i.e. the concept of right together with the actual-ization of that concept.

Philosophy has to do with Ideas, and therefore not with what are commonly dubbed 'mere concepts'. On the contrary, it exposes such concepts as one-sided and without truth, while showing at the same time that it is the *concept* [*Begriff*] alone (not the mere abstract category of the understanding [*Verstand*] which we often hear called by that name) which has actuality, and further that it gives this actuality to itself. All else, apart from this actuality established through the working of the concept itself, is ephemeral existence, external contingency, opinion, unsubstantial appear-ance, untruth, illusion, and so forth. The shapes which the con-cept assumes in the course of its actualization are indispensable for the knowledge of the concept itself. They are the second essential moment of the Idea, in distinction from the first, i.e. from its form, from its mode of being as concept alone.[10]

Addition: The concept and its existence are two sides of the same thing, distinct and united, like soul and body. The body is the same life as the soul and yet both may be spoken of as lying outside one another. A soul without a body would not be a living thing, nor would a body without a soul. Hence the determinate existence [*Dasein*] of the concept is its body, while its body obeys the soul which brought it into being. The buds have the tree implicit within them and contain the tree's whole strength, although they are not yet the tree itself. The tree corresponds in detail to the simple image of the bud. If the body does not match the soul, it is a poor sort of thing. The unity of determinate existence and the concept, of body and soul, is the Idea. The unity is not a mere harmony, but rather a complete interpenetration. Nothing is alive which is not in some way or other Idea. The Idea of right is freedom, and if it is to be truly understood, it must be known both in its concept and in the determinate existence of that concept.

[10] For more on the 'concept' and 'Idea', see the editor's Introduction and the excerpts from T. M. Knox's Foreword, pp. xvi, xix, xxxiv–xxxv above. [S.H.]

2. The science of right is a section of *philosophy*. Consequently, its task is to develop the Idea—the Idea being the rational factor in any object of study—out of the concept, or, what is the same thing, to look on at the proper immanent development of the thing itself. As a section, it has a definite starting-point, i.e. the result and the truth of what has preceded, and it is what has preceded that constitutes the so-called 'proof' of the starting-point. Hence the concept of right, so far as its coming to be is concerned, falls outside the science of right; it is to be taken up here as given and its deduction is presupposed.*

Addition: Philosophy forms a circle. It has a beginning, a moment of immediacy (for it must begin somewhere), something unproved which is not a result. But the point from which philosophy begins is [also] immediately relative, since it must appear at another end-point as a result. Philosophy is a sequence which does not hang in the air; it is not something that begins immediately; on the contrary, it circles back into itself.

According to the abstract, non-philosophical, method of the sciences, the first thing sought and demanded is a *definition*, or at any rate this demand is made for the sake of preserving the external form of scientific procedure. (The positive science of *right*, however, cannot be very intimately concerned with definitions since it aims primarily to state what is right and legal [*Rechtens*], i.e. what the *particular* legal provisions are, and for this reason the warning has been given: 'in civil law, all definition is hazardous.'* Indeed, the more disconnected and inherently contradictory are the provisions giving determinate character to a right, the less are any definitions in its field possible, for definitions should be stated in universal terms, but these would immediately expose in all its nakedness what is contradictory—that is, in this instance, what is unjust. Thus in Roman law, for example, there could be no definition of 'human being', since 'slave' could not be brought under it—the very status of slave indeed violates the concept of the human being; it would appear just as hazardous to attempt a definition of 'property' and 'proprietor' in many cases.) The deduction of the definition [in the non-philosophical sciences], however, may take its lead from etymology, or proceed above all by abstracting from particular cases, so that it is based on human feelings and ideas [*Vorstellung*]. The correctness of the definition is then made to lie in its correspondence with current ideas. This method neglects what is all-essential for science—i.e. in respect of content, the *necessity* of the thing in and for itself (right, in this instance), and, in respect of form, the nature of the concept.

The truth is that in philosophical knowledge the *necessity* of a concept is the principal thing; and the process of its production as a result is its proof and deduction. Then, once its content has been shown in this way to be necessary on its own account, the second step is to look round for what corresponds to it in our ideas and language. But this concept as it is for itself in its truth not only may be different from our common idea of it, but in fact must be different from it in form and outline. If, however, the common idea of it is not false in content also, the concept may be exhibited as contained in it and as essentially present in it. In other words, the common idea may be raised to the form of the concept. But the common idea is so far from being the standard or criterion of the concept (which is necessary and true on its own account) that it must rather derive its truth from the latter, adjust itself to it, and recognize its own nature by its aid.

But while the above-mentioned abstract way of knowing with its formal definitions, syllogisms, proofs, and the like, is more or less a thing of the past, still it is a poor substitute which a different artifice has provided, namely to adopt and uphold Ideas in general (and in particular the Idea of right and its further specifications) as immediate 'facts of consciousness'* and to make into the source of right our natural or our worked up feelings and the inspirations of our own hearts. This method may be the handiest of all, but it is also the most unphilosophical—not to mention here other aspects of such a view, which has a direct bearing on action and not simply on knowledge.* While the old method, abstract as it is, does at least insist on the *form* of the concept in its definition and the *form* of necessary knowledge in its demonstration, the artifice of feeling and immediate awareness elevates into a guiding principle the subjectivity, contingency, and arbitrariness of knowing. What constitutes scientific procedure in philosophy is expounded in philosophical logic and is here presupposed.[11]

3. Right is *positive* in general (*a*) when it has the *form* of being valid in a particular state, and this legal authority is the guiding principle for the knowledge of right in this positive form, i.e. for the

[11] See *PR* Preface, pp. 3–4 above.

positive science of right. (*b*) Right in this positive form acquires a positive element in its *content*

(α) through the particular national character of a people, its stage of historical development, and the whole complex of relations connected with the necessities of nature;*

(β) because a system of legal right must necessarily involve the application of the universal concept to particular, externally given, characteristics of objects and cases. This application lies outside speculative thought and the development of the concept, and is the subsumption by the understanding [of the particular under the universal];

(γ) through the final determinations requisite for actually making *decisions* [in court].

If inclination, caprice, and the sentiments of the heart are set up in opposition to positive right and the laws, philosophy at least cannot recognize authorities of that sort.—That force and tyranny may be an element in positive right is accidental to the latter and has nothing to do with its nature. Later on in this book, in §§ 211–14, it will be shown at what point right must become positive. The details to be expounded there are being mentioned here only to indicate the limits of the philosophical study of right and to obviate at once any possible supposition, let alone demand, that the outcome of its systematic development should be a code of positive law, i.e. a code such as the one an actual state requires.

Natural law, or right from the philosophical point of view, is distinct from *positive* right; but to pervert their difference into an opposition and a contradiction would be a gross misunderstanding. The relation between them is much more like that between Institutes and Pandects.*

As for the historical element in positive right, mentioned above in § 3, Montesquieu proclaimed the true historical view,* the genuinely philosophical position, namely that legislation both in general and in its particular provisions is to be treated not as something isolated and abstract but rather as a dependent moment of a whole, interconnected with all the other features which make up the character of a nation and an epoch. It is in being so connected that the various laws acquire their true meaning and therewith their justification.—To consider particular determinations of right as they appear and develop in time is a *purely historical* task. Like acquaintance with what can be logically deduced from a comparison of these determinations with previously existing principles of right, this task is appreciated and rewarded in its own sphere and has no relation whatever to the philosophical study of the subject—unless of course the derivation of particular aspects of right from historical events is confused with their derivation from the concept, and the historical explanation and justification is stretched to become a justification that is *valid in and for itself* [*an und für sich*]. This difference, which is very important and should be firmly adhered to, is also very obvious. A particular determination of right may be shown to be wholly grounded in and consistent with the circumstances and with existing institutions of right, and yet it may be wrong and irrational in and for itself, like a number of provisions in Roman private law which followed quite logically from such institutions as Roman matrimony and Roman paternal power.[12] But even if particular determinations of right *are* both right and reasonable, still it is one thing to *prove* that they have that character—which cannot be truly done except by means of the concept—and quite another to describe their appearance in history or the circumstances, contingencies, needs, and events which brought about their enactment. That kind of exposition and (pragmatic) knowledge, based on proximate or remote historical causes, is frequently called 'explanation' [*Erklären*] or preferably 'comprehension' [*Begreifen*], by those who think that to expound history in this way is the only thing, or rather the essential thing, the only important thing, to be done in order to comprehend law or an institution of right;* whereas what is really essential, the concept of the thing, they have not discussed at all. From the same point of view, reference is commonly made also to the Roman or the German 'concepts' of right, i.e. concepts of right as they might be defined in this or that legal code, whereas what is meant are not concepts but only general determinations of right, propositions of the understanding, maxims, positive laws, and the like.

By obscuring the difference between the historical and the philosophical study of right, it becomes possible to shift the point of view and slip over from the problem of the true justification of

---

[12] See Remark and Addition to *PR* § 180.

a thing to a justification by appeal to circumstances, to deductions from presupposed conditions which in themselves may have no higher validity, and so forth. To generalize, by this means the relative is put in place of the absolute and the external appearance in place of the true nature of the thing. When those who try to justify things on historical grounds confound an origin in external circumstances with one in the concept, they unconsciously achieve the very opposite of what they intend. Once the origination of an institution has been shown to be wholly to the purpose and necessary in the circumstances of the time, the demands of the historical point of view have been fulfilled. But if this is supposed to pass for a general justification of the thing itself, it turns out to be the opposite, because, since those circumstances are no longer present, the institution—far from being justified—has by their disappearance lost its meaning and its right. Suppose, for example, that we accept as a vindication of the monasteries their service in cultivating wildernesses and populating them, in keeping learning alive by transcribing manuscripts and giving instruction, and so on, and suppose further that this service has been deemed to be the ground and the purpose of their continued existence, then what really follows from considering this past service is that, since circumstances have now entirely altered, the monasteries are at least in this respect superfluous and inappropriate.

Since the historical meaning of coming to be [*Entstehen*]—the historical method of portraying it and making it comprehensible— is at home in a different sphere from the philosophical survey of the concept of the thing and of a thing's coming to be, philosophy and history are able to that extent to preserve an attitude of mutual indifference. But they are not always at peace in this way, even in scientific circles, and so I quote something, relevant to their contact, which appears in Herr Hugo's *Textbook of the History of Roman Law*,* and which will at the same time lead to further elucidation of the manner in which they can be opposed. Herr Hugo says (fifth edition, § 53) that 'Cicero praises the Twelve Tables* while *looking askance* at the philosophers . . . whereas the philosopher Favorinus treats them exactly as many a great philosopher since his day has treated positive right'. In the same context Herr Hugo provides his final retort to a treatment of the subject such as Favorinus' when he explains that 'Favorinus *understood* the

Twelve Tables *just as little* as these philosophers have understood positive right'.

As far as the correction of the philosopher Favorinus by the jurist *Sextus Caecilius* in [Aulus] Gellius is concerned,*[13] this is in the first place an expression of the enduring and true principle for justifying what is merely positive. 'You must be aware',* Caecilius happily retorts to Favorinus, 'that the advantages and remedies offered by the laws vary and fluctuate in accordance with contemporary customs, types of constitution, considerations of immediate advantage, and the violence of the ills to be remedied. Laws do not persist unchanged in character; on the contrary, the storms of circumstance and chance alter them as storms change the face of the sea and the sky. Has anything ever seemed more salutary than Stolo's proposal . . . more advantageous than the decree . . . carried by Voconius as tribune? What has been taken to be so necessary . . . as the Licinian law? Yet, now that the state has grown wealthy, all these regulations have been blotted out and buried.' These laws are positive insofar as they have their meaning and appropriateness in the *circumstances*, and their value is therefore simply historical; they are for that reason of a transitory nature. The *wisdom* of what legislators and governments did for the circumstances of their day or settled to meet the needs of the hour is a separate matter. It is one properly to be assessed by history, whose recognition of it will be all the deeper the more its assessment is supported by philosophical points of view.

Of Caecilius' further arguments in justification of the Twelve Tables against Favorinus, however, I will give an example, because he introduces in them the eternally deceptive method and argumentation of the understanding, namely the production of a *good reason* for a bad thing and the supposition that the bad thing has thereby been justified. Caecilius is discussing the horrible law that gave a creditor the right after a fixed period of time to kill his debtor or sell him into slavery, or, if there were several creditors, to cut pieces off their debtor and divide him up amongst themselves; there was even a further proviso that if one of them cut off too much or too little, no action was for that reason to be taken against him—a clause which would have benefited Shakespeare's

---

[13] *Hegel's reference*: Aulus Gellius, *Attic Nights* [*Noctes Atticae*], 20. 1.

Shylock in the *Merchant of Venice** and of which he would most
gratefully have availed himself. For this law Caecilius adduces the
good reason that it rendered trust and credit all the more secure and
that because of its horrible character there was never to have been
any question of its application. In his thoughtlessness not only
does the reflection escape him that if the law could never have
been applied, then the aim of securing trust and credit by it was
frustrated, but he even goes on directly afterwards to give an
example of how the law concerning false witness was made
ineffective owing to its immoderate penalties.

It is not clear, however, what Herr Hugo means when he says
that Favorinus did not *understand* the law. Any schoolboy is perfectly capable of understanding it, and Shylock would have understood better than anyone else the clause, cited above, which would
have been so advantageous to him. By 'understand' Herr Hugo
must have meant only that level of understanding which in the
case of such a law is content if it can find a *good reason* for it.

By the way, another misunderstanding of which Favorinus was
convicted by Caecilius in the same context is one to which a philosopher may surely confess without exactly blushing. I mean the failure to understand that *jumentum* (which 'as distinct from *arcera*' is,
according to the law, the only conveyance to be provided for a sick
person who has to appear as a witness in court) is to be interpreted
to mean not only a horse but also a carriage or wagon.* From this
legal proviso Caecilius was able to derive a further proof of the
excellence and precision of the old laws by pointing out that, in
fixing the terms of a summons to a sick witness to appear in court,
they carried precision so far as to distinguish not only between
a horse and a wagon, but even between one wagon and another,
between one covered and 'upholstered', as Caecilius explains, and
one not so comfortable. Here, then, we would have the choice
between the severity of the law and the triviality of such distinctions; but to describe such things, and still more their learned
interpretation, as 'trivial' would be one of the worst of insults to
erudition of this kind and others!

But in the textbook mentioned above Herr Hugo also comes to
speak of *rationality* in connection with Roman law, and what has
struck me in his remarks is the following. In his treatment of the
'period from the origin of the state to the Twelve Tables' (§§ 38–9)

he says that (in Rome) 'people had many wants and were compelled
to work and hence needed the assistance of draught and pack animals, such as we are familiar with ourselves; that in Roman territory hills and valleys alternated and that the city was built on a hill'
and so forth—remarks which were perhaps intended to fulfil
Montesquieu's aims, but in which one will hardly find that his
spirit has been caught. He goes on to say (§ 40) that in this period
'the legal position was still very far from satisfying the *highest*
demands of reason'. (This is quite right: Roman law in respect of
the family, slavery, and so on, fails even to satisfy reason's most
modest demands.) Yet in dealing with later periods of Roman history, Herr Hugo forgets to tell us whether in any of them, and if so
in which, Roman law did 'satisfy the highest demands of reason'.
Concerning the classical jurists in the period of the 'highest matur-
ity of Roman law as a science', however, Herr Hugo writes (§ 289)
that 'it has long since been observed that the classical jurists were
educated through philosophy', yet 'few know' (though more know
now, thanks to the numerous editions of Herr Hugo's textbook)
'that no class of writers is so well entitled as these same Roman
jurists to be compared with mathematicians in respect of the rig-
orous logic of their deductive reasoning or with the new founder
of metaphysics in respect of their quite strikingly distinctive method
of developing their concepts—a contention supported by the curious fact that nowhere are there to be found so many trichotomies
as there are in the classical jurists and in Kant'.—Now logical
deduction, a method commended by Leibniz,* is certainly an
essential characteristic of the science of right, as of mathematics
and any other science of the understanding, but this deductive
method of the understanding has nothing whatever to do with the
satisfaction of the demands of reason or with philosophical science.
Apart from that, however, it is the *illogicality* of the Roman jurists
and praetors that must be regarded as one of their chief virtues,
for by being illogical they evaded unjust and detestable laws and
institutions—though in the process they found themselves
compelled to devise empty verbal distinctions on the sly [*callide*]
(e.g. to call *bonorum possessio* what was nevertheless an inheritance)* and downright foolish subterfuges (and folly also is
illogicality) in order to preserve the letter of the Twelve Tables
(e.g. by the fiction or pretence that a daughter [*filia*] was a son

[*filius*]).*[14]—It is ludicrous though to see the classical jurists compared with Kant because of a few trichotomous divisions, especially those cited as examples in Note 5 to Herr Hugo's remarks, and to see that kind of thing called the 'development of concepts'.

4. The basis of right is, in general, the realm of spirit [*das Geistige*]; its precise place and point of origin is the *will*. The will is *free*, so that freedom is both its substance and its goal, while the system of right is the realm of freedom made actual, the world of spirit [*Geist*] brought forth out of itself as a second nature.

Addition: The freedom of the will is best explained by a reference to physical nature. For freedom is just as fundamental a character of the will as weight is of bodies. If we say: matter is 'heavy', we might mean that this predicate is only contingent; but it is nothing of the kind, for nothing in matter is without weight. Matter is rather weight itself. Heaviness constitutes the body and is the body. The same is the case with freedom and the will, since that which is free is the will. Will without freedom is an empty word, while freedom is actual only as will, as subject.

The following points should be noted about the connection between the will and thought. Spirit is thinking in general, and the human being is distinguished from the animal in virtue of thinking. But one must not imagine that the human being is, on the one hand, thought and, on the other, will, and that he keeps thought in one pocket and will in another, for this would be a foolish idea. The distinction between thought and will is only that between the theoretical attitude and the practical. These, however, are surely not two faculties; the will is rather a particular way of thinking, thinking translating itself into existence, thinking as the urge to give itself existence.

This distinction between thought and will may be described as follows. In thinking an object, I make it into thought and deprive it of its sensuous aspect; I make it into something which is immediately and essentially mine. Since it is only in thought that I am with myself [*bei mir*], I do not penetrate an object until I understand it; it then ceases to stand over against me and I have taken from it the character of its own which it had in opposition to me. Just as Adam said to Eve: 'Thou art flesh of my flesh and bone of my bone,'[15] so spirit says: 'This is spirit of my spirit and its foreign character has disappeared.' An idea is always a generalization, and

---

[14] *Hegel's reference*: J. G. Heineccius, *Illustrated Treatise on Ancient Roman Jurisprudence* [*Antiquitatum Romanarum jurisprudentiam illustrantium Syntagma*] lib. I [Frankfurt, 1771], tit. II, § 24.
[15] See Genesis 2: 23.

generalization is a property of thinking. To generalize means to think. The I is thought and so the universal. When I say 'I', I *eo ipso* abandon all my particular characteristics, my disposition, natural endowment, knowledge, and age. The I is quite empty, a mere point, simple, yet active in this simplicity. The variegated canvas of the world is before me; I stand over against it; by my theoretical attitude to it I overcome its opposition to me and make its content my own. I am at home in the world when I know it, still more so when I have understood it. So much for the theoretical attitude.

The practical attitude, on the other hand, begins in thinking, in the I itself, and it appears first as though opposed to thinking because it immediately sets up a division. Insofar as I am practical or active, i.e. insofar as I act, I determine myself, and to determine myself simply means to posit a difference. But these differences which I posit are still mine all the same; the determinations are mine and the aims to which I am driven belong to me. If I now let these determinations and differences out, i.e. if I posit them in the so-called external world, they nonetheless still remain mine. They are what I have done, what I have made; they bear the trace of my spirit.

Such is the distinction between the theoretical attitude and the practical, but now the relation between them must be described. The theoretical is essentially contained in the practical; we must decide against the idea that the two are separate, because we cannot have a will without intelligence. On the contrary, the will contains the theoretical in itself. The will determines itself and this determination is in the first place something inward, because what I will I hold before my mind as an idea; it is the object of my thought. An animal acts on instinct, is driven by an inner impulse and so it too is practical, but it has no will, since it does not bring before its mind the object of its desire. A human being, however, can just as little be theoretical or think without a will, because in thinking he is of necessity being active. The content of something thought has the form of being; but this being is something mediated, something established through our activity. Thus these distinct attitudes cannot be divorced; they are one and the same; and in any activity, whether of thinking or willing, both moments are present.

In considering the freedom of the will, we may recall the old method of cognition. The procedure was to presuppose the idea [*Vorstellung*] of the will and to attempt to establish a definition of the will by deriving it from that idea; then the so-called 'proof' of the will's freedom was extracted, in the manner of the old empirical psychology, from the various feelings and phenomena of ordinary consciousness, such as remorse, guilt, and the like, by maintaining that they were to be explained only in the light of a will that was free.

But it is more convenient of course to arrive at the same point by taking the short cut of supposing that freedom is given as a 'fact of consciousness' and that we must simply *believe* in it!

That the will is free and *what* the will and freedom are, can be deduced (as has already been pointed out in § 2) only in the context of the whole [of philosophy]. The fundamental premisses of this deduction are that spirit to start with is *intelligence*, that the phases through which it passes in its development from feeling, through representational thinking [*Vorstellen*], to thinking proper are the road along which it produces itself as will, and that will, as practical spirit in general, is the truth of intelligence, the stage next above it. These premisses I have expounded in my *Encyclopaedia of the Philosophical Sciences* (Heidelberg, 1817), §§ 363–99, and I hope by and by to be able to elaborate them still further.* There is all the more need for me by so doing to make my contribution to what I hope is the deeper knowledge of the nature of spirit in that, as I have said in the *Encyclopaedia* (Remark to § 367 [3rd edition § 444]), scarcely any philosophical science is so neglected and in so bad a condition as the theory of spirit [or mind] which is usually called 'psychology'. The moments in the concept of the will which are dealt with in this and the following paragraphs of this Introduction result from the premisses to which I have just referred, but in addition anyone may find help towards forming an idea of them by calling on his own self-consciousness. In the first place, anyone can discover in himself the ability to abstract from everything whatever, and in the same way to determine himself, to posit any content in himself by his own effort; and similarly the other specific characteristics of the will are exemplified for him in his own consciousness.

5. The will contains (α) the element of *pure indeterminacy* or that pure reflection of the I into itself which involves the dissolution of every restriction and every content either immediately presented by nature, by needs, desires, and impulses, or given and determined by any means whatever. This is the unrestricted infinity of *absolute abstraction* or *universality*, the pure *thought* of oneself.

Those who regard thinking as one particular, distinctive faculty, separate from the will as another distinctive faculty, and who even proceed to contend that thinking is prejudicial to the will, especially the good will, reveal at the very outset their complete ignorance of the nature of the will—a remark we shall have to make rather often when dealing with this same subject.

In § 5, it is only one side of the will which is described, namely this absolute possibility of *abstraction* from every determination in which I may find myself or which I may have set up in myself, my flight from every content as from a restriction. When the will's self-determination consists in this alone, or when representational thinking regards this side by itself as freedom and clings fast to it, then we have *negative* freedom, or freedom as the understanding conceives it.—This is the freedom of the void which rises to a passion and takes shape in the world; while still remaining theoretical, it takes shape in religion as the Hindu fanaticism of pure contemplation, but when it turns to actual practice, it takes shape in religion and politics alike as the fanaticism of destruction (of the whole subsisting social order), as the elimination of individuals who are objects of suspicion to a given social order, and as the annihilation of any organization which tries to rise anew from the ruins.* Only in destroying something does this negative will possess the feeling of itself as existent. Of course it imagines that it is willing some positive state of affairs, such as universal equality or universal religious life, but in fact it does not will that this shall be positively actualized, and for this reason: such actuality leads at once to some sort of order, to a particularization of organizations and individuals alike, while it is precisely out of the annihilation of particularity and objective determination that the self-consciousness of this negative freedom proceeds. Consequently, whatever negative freedom means to will can never be anything in itself but an abstract idea, and giving effect to this idea can only be the fury of destruction.

Addition: In this element of the will is rooted my ability to free myself from everything, abandon every aim, abstract from everything. The human being alone can sacrifice everything, his life included; he can commit suicide. An animal cannot; it always remains merely negative, in an alien determination to which it merely accustoms itself. The human being is the pure thought of himself, and only in thinking is he this power to give himself universality, i.e. to extinguish all particularity, all determinacy. This negative freedom, or freedom as the understanding conceives it, is one-sided; but what is one-sided always contains an essential determination and therefore is not to be discarded. But the understanding is defective in exalting a one-sided determination to be the sole and the supreme one.

In history this form of freedom is a frequent phenomenon. Amongst the Hindus, for instance, the highest life is held to entail persisting in the bare knowledge of one's simple identity with oneself, remaining in this empty space of one's inner life, as light remains colourless in pure vision, and sacrificing every activity in life, every aim, and every idea. In this way the human being becomes Brahman; there is no longer any distinction between the finite human being and Brahman. In fact in this universality every difference has disappeared.

This form of freedom appears more concretely in the active fanaticism of both political and religious life. For instance, during the Terror in the French Revolution all differences of talent and authority were supposed to have been superseded. This period was an upheaval, an agitation, an intolerance of everything particular. Since fanaticism wills an abstraction only, nothing articulated, it follows that, when distinctions appear, it finds them antagonistic to its own indeterminacy and annuls them. For this reason, the people during the French Revolution destroyed once more the institutions which they had made themselves, since any institution whatever is antagonistic to the abstract self-consciousness of equality.

6. (β) At the same time, the I is also the transition from undifferentiated indeterminacy to the *differentiation*, *determination*, and *positing* of a determinacy as a content and object. Now further, this content may either be given by nature or engendered by the concept of spirit. Through this positing of itself as something determinate, the I steps into *determinate existence* [*Dasein*] in general. This is the absolute moment of the *finitude* or *particularization* of the I.

This second moment—determination—is negativity and cancellation [*Aufheben*] like the first, i.e. it cancels the abstract negativity of the first. Since in general the particular is contained in the universal, it follows that this second moment is already contained in the first and is simply an explicit positing of what the first already is in itself [*an sich*]. The first moment—namely as it is for itself— is not true infinity or concrete universality, not the concept, but only something determinate, one-sided; i.e., being abstraction from all determinacy, it is itself not without determinacy; and to be something abstract and one-sided constitutes its determinacy, its defectiveness, and its finitude.

The determination and differentiation of the two moments which have been mentioned is to be found in the philosophies of

Fichte, Kant, and others; only, in Fichte—to confine ourselves to his exposition—the I, as that which is without limitation, is taken (in the first proposition of his *Science of Knowledge*) purely and simply as something *positive* and so as the universality and identity of the understanding. The result is that this abstract I by itself is supposed to be the truth, and therefore the restriction—the *negative* in general, whether as a given external limitation or as an activity of the I itself—appears (in the second proposition) merely as an addition.*

To apprehend the negativity immanent in the universal or self-identical, as in the I, was the next step which speculative philosophy had to take—a step of whose necessity they have no inkling who hold to the dualism of infinite and finite and do not even grasp it in that immanence and abstraction in which Fichte did.

Addition: This second moment appears as the moment opposed to the first; it is to be grasped in its general character; it belongs to freedom, although it does not constitute the whole of freedom. Here the I leaves undifferentiated indeterminacy and proceeds to differentiate itself, to posit a content or object and so to give itself determinacy. My willing is not pure willing but the willing of *something*. A will which, like that expounded in § 5, wills only the abstract universal, wills nothing and is therefore no will at all. The particular volition is a restriction, since the will, in order to be a will, must restrict itself in some way or other. The fact that the will wills *something* is restriction, negation. Thus particularization is what as a rule is called finitude. Reflective thinking [*Reflexion*] usually takes the first moment, i.e. indeterminacy, as the higher and absolute moment, while it regards restriction as a mere negation of this indeterminacy. But this indeterminacy is itself only a negation in contrast with the determinate, with finitude; the I is this solitude and absolute negation.* The indeterminate will is to this extent just as one-sided as the will rooted in sheer determinacy.

7. (γ) The will is the unity of both these moments. It is particularity reflected into itself and so brought back to universality, i.e. it is *individuality*. It is the *self*-determination of the I, which means that at one and the same time the I posits itself as its own negative, i.e. as restricted and determinate, and yet remains with itself, i.e. in its self-identity and universality. It determines itself and yet at the same time binds itself together with itself.—The I determines itself in so far as it is the relating of negativity to itself. As this self-relation, it is equally indifferent to this determinacy; it knows it as something which is its own, something which is only ideal [*ideell*],* a mere *possibility* by

which it is not constrained and in which it is confined only because it has put itself in it.—This is the freedom of the will and it constitutes the concept or substantiality of the will, its weight, so to speak, just as weight constitutes the substantiality of a body.

Every self-consciousness knows itself (i) as universal, as the possibility of abstracting from everything determinate, and (ii) as particular, with a determinate object, content, and aim. Still, both these moments are only abstractions; what is concrete and true (and everything true is concrete) is the universality which has the particular as its opposite, but the particular which by its reflection into itself has been equalized with the universal. This unity is *individuality*, not individuality in its immediacy as a unit, our first idea of individuality, but individuality in accordance with its concept;[16] indeed, individuality in this sense is precisely the concept itself. The first two moments—(i) that the will can abstract from everything, and (ii) that it is also determined in some specific way either by itself or by something else—are readily admitted and grasped because, taken independently, they lack truth and are moments of the understanding. But the third moment, which is true and speculative (and everything true must be thought speculatively if it is to be comprehended) is the one into which the understanding declines to advance, for it is precisely the concept which it persists in calling the inconceivable. It is the task of logic as purely speculative philosophy to prove and explain further this innermost secret of speculation, of infinity as negativity relating itself to itself, this ultimate spring of all activity, life, and consciousness.— Here attention can only be drawn to the fact that when people say '*the will* is universal, *the will* determines itself', the words they use to describe the will presuppose it to be a subject or substratum from the start. But the will is not something complete and universal prior to its determining itself and prior to its superseding and idealizing this determination. The will is not a will until it is this self-mediating activity, this return into itself.

Addition: What is properly called the will includes in itself both the preceding moments. The I as such is in the first place pure activity, the universal which is with itself [*bei sich*]. But this universal determines itself and to that extent is no longer with itself but posits itself as an other and ceases

[16] *Hegel's reference*: *Encyclopaedia*, §§ 112–14 [3rd edn. §§ 163–5].

to be the universal. Now the third moment is that, in its restriction, in this other, the will is with itself; in determining itself it still remains with itself and does not cease to keep hold of the universal. This moment, then, is the concrete concept of freedom, while the two previous moments have been found to be through and through abstract and one-sided.

Freedom in this sense, however, we already possess in the form of feeling—in friendship and love, for instance. Here we are not inherently one-sided; we restrict ourselves gladly in relating ourselves to another, but in this restriction know ourselves as ourselves. In this determinacy a human being should not feel determined; on the contrary, by treating the other as other he first arrives at the feeling of his own selfhood. Thus freedom lies neither in indeterminacy nor in determinacy; it is both of these at once. The will which restricts itself simply to a *this* is the will of the stubborn individual who supposes that he is not free unless he has *this will*. But the will is not tied to something restricted; it must go beyond the restriction, since the nature of the will is other than this one-sidedness and constraint. Freedom is to will something determinate, yet in this determinacy to be with oneself and to revert once more to the universal.

8. The more detailed process of particularization (see § 6) constitutes the difference between the forms of the will: (*a*) If the will's determinate character lies in the formal opposition of its subjectivity to the objectivity of external immediate existence, then this is the *formal* will as self-consciousness which *finds* an external world *confronting* it. As individuality returning in its determinacy into itself, this will is the process of *translating the subjective purpose* into *objectivity* through the mediation of its own activity and some external means. In spirit as it is in and for itself [*wie er an und für sich ist*], in which its determinacy is true and simply its *own*,[17] the relation of consciousness constitutes only the *appearance* of the will, which is not considered *separately* [*für sich*] any further here.*

Addition: The consideration of the will's determinacy properly belongs to the understanding and is in the first instance not speculative. The will is determined in two senses, i.e. in both content and form. Its determinacy in form is its purpose and the fulfilment of its purpose. My purpose is at first only something inward, something subjective, but it should also become objective and cast aside the defect of mere subjectivity. At this point you may ask why it has this defect. If what has a defect does not at the same time stand above its defect, the defect is not for it a defect. An animal is deficient from our point of view, not from its own. My purpose,

---

[17] *Hegel's reference*: *Encyclopaedia*, § 363 [3rd edn. § 440].

so far as it is still only mine, is felt by me as a defect since freedom and will are for me the unity of the subjective and objective. Hence the purpose must be established objectively and thereby it attains not a new one-sided determination but only its realization.

9. (b) In so far as the determinations of the will are its *own* or, in general, its particularization reflected into itself, they are its *content*. This content, as content of the will, is, in accordance with the form described in (a), its *purpose*,* either its inward or subjective purpose when the will merely represents its object, or else its purpose actualized and achieved by means of its activity of translating its subjective purpose into objectivity.

10. This content, or the will's distinct determination, is in the first place *immediate*. Consequently the will is free only *in itself* or *for us*, or, to speak generally, it is the will in its concept. It is not until it has itself as its object* that the will is *for itself* what it is in itself.*

Finitude consists therefore in this, that what something is in itself or in accordance with its concept is one phenomenon or exists in one way, while what it is for itself is a different phenomenon or exists in another way; so, for example, in itself the abstract externality of nature is space, but *for itself* it is time.* In this connection, two things are to be noticed: (i) The true is the Idea and the Idea alone, and hence if you take an object or a category only as it is in itself or in its concept, you have not yet grasped it in its truth. (ii) A thing which is in itself or as concept is also existent in some way and its existence in such a way is a shape proper to the thing itself (as space is in the example just given). The gulf present in the sphere of the finite between 'being-in-itself' [*Ansichsein*] and 'being-for-itself' [*Fürsichsein*] constitutes at the same time that sphere's mere existence or *appearance*. (Examples of this—in the natural will and then in formal right, and so on—will be forthcoming directly.)

The understanding goes no further than mere being-in-itself and consequently calls the freedom which accords with this being-in-itself a 'capacity' [*Vermögen*], because such freedom is indeed mere *possibility*. But the understanding regards this determination as absolute and perennial; and it takes the relation of freedom to what it wills, or in general to the object in which it is realized, as merely a matter of its *application* to a given material, not belonging to the essence of freedom itself. Thus it has to do with the abstract only, not with its Idea and its truth.

Addition: The will which is a will only in accordance with its concept is free in itself but at the same time it is also unfree, for it would become truly free only as truly determinate content. At that point it is free for itself, has freedom as its object, and *is* freedom. What is still only in accordance with its concept, what is merely in itself [*an sich*], is only immediate, only natural. In our ordinary ways of thinking we are familiar with this. The child is *in itself* a human being. At first it possesses reason only *in itself* [or implicitly]; it begins by being the possibility of reason and freedom, and so is free only in accordance with its concept. Now what exists only in itself in this way does not yet exist in its actuality. The human being is *in himself* [or implicitly] rational, but he must also become so *for himself* [or explicitly] by working to create himself, not only by going outside himself but also by developing himself internally.

11. The will which is free only in itself [*an sich*] is the *immediate* or *natural* will.* The determinations of difference which the self-determining concept posits within the will appear in the natural will as an immediately existing content, i.e. as the impulses, desires, inclinations, whereby the will finds itself determined in the course of nature. This content, together with the determinations developed within it, arises from the rationality of the will and so is in itself rational; but, poured out in this way into the mould of immediacy, it still lacks the form of rationality. It is true that this content has *for me* the general character of being *mine*; but this form is still different from the content, and hence the will is still a will finite in character.

Empirical psychology details and describes these impulses and inclinations, and the needs arising from them, as it finds them, or presumes it finds them, in experience, and it proceeds in the usual way to classify this given material. Consideration is given below[18] to the objective element in these impulses, both to its true character stripped of the form of irrationality which it possesses as impulse and also to the manner in which at the same time it is shaped externally.

Addition: An animal too has impulses, desires, inclinations, but it has no will and must obey its impulse if nothing external deters it. The human being, however, the wholly undetermined, stands above his impulses and

---

[18] See *PR* §§ 19 and 150 with the Remarks thereto.

may make them his own, posit them in himself as his own. An impulse is something natural, but to posit it in the I depends on my will which thus cannot fall back on the plea that the impulse has its basis in nature.

12. The system of this content, as we *find* it in its immediacy in the will, is there only as a medley and multiplicity of impulses, each of which as such is 'mine' but exists alongside others which are likewise all 'mine', and each of which is at the same time something universal and indeterminate, aimed at all kinds of objects and satiable in all kinds of ways. When, in this twofold indeterminacy,* the will gives itself the form of *individuality* (see § 7), this constitutes the resolution of the will, and it is only in so far as it resolves that the will is an actual will at all.

To *resolve* on something is to cancel the state of indeterminacy in which one content is prima facie just as much of a possibility as any other. As an alternative to *etwas beschliessen* [to resolve on something] the German language also contains the expression *sich entschliessen.** This expresses the fact that the indeterminate character of the will itself, as itself neutral yet infinitely prolific, the original seed of all determinate existence, contains its determinations and aims within itself and simply brings them forth out of itself.

13. By resolving, the will posits itself as the will of a specific individual and as a will separating itself off against another individual. But apart from this *finitude* as consciousness (see § 8), the immediate will is *formal* on account of the difference between its form and its content (see § 11). It is capable only of *abstract* resolution [or decision] and its content is not yet the content and product of its *freedom*.

In so far as intelligence thinks, its object and content remain something universal, while its own behaviour consists of a universal activity. In the will, 'the universal' also means in essence 'mine', 'individuality'; and in the immediate will—the will which is only a formal will—it means abstract individuality, individuality not yet filled with its free universality. Hence it is in the will that the *intrinsic finitude* of intelligence has its beginning; and it is only by raising itself to become thought again, and endowing its aims with immanent universality, that the will cancels the difference of form and content and makes itself the objective, infinite, will. Thus they understand little of the nature of thinking* and willing who suppose that while, in willing as such, the human being is infinite, in thinking, he, or even reason itself, is restricted. In so far as thinking and willing are still distinguished, the opposite is rather the truth, and will is thinking reason resolving itself to finitude.

Addition: A will which resolves on nothing is no actual will; a characterless human being never reaches a decision. The reason for indecision may also lie in a tenderness of feeling which knows that, in willing something determinate, it is engaging with finitude, imposing a restriction on itself and sacrificing the infinite; yet it will not renounce the totality after which it hankers. However 'beautiful' such a disposition may be,* it is nevertheless dead. As Goethe says: 'Whoever wills something great must be able to restrict himself.'* Only by resolving can a human being step into actuality, however bitter this may be to him. Inertia lacks the will to abandon the inward brooding which allows it to retain everything as a possibility. But possibility is not yet actuality. The will which is sure of itself does not *eo ipso* lose itself in its determinate volition.

14. The finite will as, in respect of its form, though only its form, the self-reflecting, independent, and infinite I (see § 5), *stands over* its content, i.e. its various impulses, and also over the further separate ways in which these are actualized and satisfied. At the same time, since it is infinite in form only, it is *tied* to this content (see §§ 6 and 11) as to the specific determinations of its nature and its external actuality; though since it is indeterminate, it is not tied to *this* or *that* specific content. From the point of view of the I reflected into itself, this content is only a possible one, i.e. it may be mine or it may not; and the I similarly is the *possibility* of determining myself to this or to something else, of *choosing* between these specific determinations, which at this point I regard as external to me.

15. According to this determination, the freedom of the will is *arbitrariness* [*Willkür*] and this involves two factors: (*a*) free reflection, abstracting from everything, and (*b*) dependence on a content and material given either from within or from without. Because this content, necessary in itself as purpose, is at the same time qualified in the face of free reflection as possible, it follows that arbitrariness is *contingency* manifesting itself as will.

The idea which people most commonly have of freedom is that it is arbitrariness—the middle position of reflection between the will wholly determined by natural impulses and the will that is free in and for itself [*an und für sich*]. If we hear it said that the definition of freedom is the ability to do what we please, such an idea can only be taken to reveal an utter immaturity of thought, for it contains not even an inkling of the free will in and for itself, of right, ethical life, and so forth. Reflection, the formal universality and unity of self-consciousness, is the will's abstract certainty of its freedom, but it is not yet the truth of freedom, because it has not yet got *itself* as its content and aim, and consequently the subjective side is still other than the objective; the content of this self-determination, therefore, also remains purely and simply finite. Instead of being the will in its truth, arbitrariness is rather the will as contradiction.

In the controversy carried on especially at the time of Wolff's metaphysics* as to whether the will is really free or whether the conviction of its freedom is only a delusion, it was arbitrariness which was in view. In opposition to the certitude of this abstract self-determination, determinism has rightly pointed to the content which, as something *encountered*, is not contained in that certitude and so comes to it from outside, although 'outside' in this case means impulses, ideas, or, in general, consciousness so filled in one way or another that its content is not intrinsic to its self-determining activity as such. Since, then, arbitrariness has immanent in it only the formal element in willing, i.e. free self-determination, while the other element is something *given* to it, we may readily allow that, if arbitrariness is supposed to be freedom, it may indeed be called an illusion. In every philosophy of reflection, like Kant's, and Kant's deprived of all its depth by Fries, freedom is nothing else but this formal self-activity.

Addition: Since it is possible for me to determine myself in this way or that, or in other words since I can choose, I possess the arbitrary will, and to possess this is what is usually called freedom. The choice which I have is grounded in the universality of the will, in the fact that I can make this or that mine. This thing that is mine is particular in content and therefore not adequate to me and so is separate from me; it is only possibly mine, while I am the possibility of linking myself to it. Choice, therefore, is grounded in the indeterminacy of the I and the determinacy of a content. Thus the will, on account of this content, is not free, although it has an infinite aspect in virtue of its form. No single content is adequate to it and in no single content is it truly itself. Arbitrariness implies that the content is made mine not by the nature of my will but by *contingency*. Thus I am dependent on this content, and this is the contradiction lying in arbitrariness. The ordinary person thinks he is free if it is open to him to act as he pleases but his very arbitrariness implies that he is not free. When I will what is rational, then I am acting not as a particular individual but in accordance with the concepts of ethical life in general. In an ethical action, what I vindicate is not myself but the thing. But in doing a perverse action, it is my particularity that I bring on to the centre of the stage. The rational is the high road where everyone travels, where no one is conspicuous. When great artists complete a work, we can say: *that* is how it must be; that is, the artist's particularity has completely disappeared and no mannerism is detectable in it. Pheidias has no mannerisms;* the shape itself lives and stands forth. But the worse the artist is, the more we see in his work the artist, his particularity, his arbitrariness. If you stop at the consideration that, having an arbitrary will, a human being can will this or that, then of course his freedom consists in that ability. But if you keep firmly in view that the content of his willing is a given one, then he is determined thereby and in that respect at all events is free no longer.

16. What the will has decided to choose (see § 14) it can equally easily renounce (see § 5). But its ability to go beyond any other choice which it may substitute, and so on *ad infinitum*, never enables it to get beyond its own finitude, because the content of every such choice is something other than the form of the will and therefore something finite, while the opposite of determinacy, namely indeterminacy, i.e. indecision or abstraction from any content, is only the other, equally one-sided, moment of the will.

17. The contradiction, which the arbitrary will is (see § 15), comes into appearance as a *dialectic* of impulses and inclinations; each of them is in the way of every other—the satisfaction of one is unavoidably subordinated or sacrificed to the satisfaction of another, and so on. An impulse is simply a unidirectional urge and thus has no measuring-rod in itself, and so this determination of its subordination or sacrifice is the contingent decision of the arbitrary will which, in deciding, may proceed either by using understanding to calculate which impulse will give most satisfaction, or else in accordance with any other optional consideration.

Addition: Impulses and inclinations are in the first instance a content of the will, and reflection alone stands above them. But these impulses themselves begin to impel, they drive one another, stir each other, and all of them demand satisfaction. Now if I neglect all the others and put myself in one of them by itself, I find myself under a restriction which destroys me, since just by so doing I have surrendered my universality, which is a system of all impulses. But it is just as little help to make a mere hierarchy of impulses—a device to which the understanding usually resorts—since no criterion for so ordering them is available here, and therefore the demand for such a hierarchy runs out in the tedium of generalities.

18. In connection with the *judging* of impulses, this dialectic appears in the following form: (*a*) As *immanent* and so positive, the determinations of the immediate will are *good*; thus human beings are said to be by nature good. (*b*) But, insofar as these determinations are *natural* and thus are in general opposed to freedom and the concept of spirit, and hence negative, they must be uprooted, and so human beings are said to be by nature *evil*.—At this point a decision in favour of either thesis depends equally on subjective arbitrariness.

Addition: The Christian doctrine that human beings are by nature evil is superior to the other which takes them to be by nature good. This doctrine is to be understood as follows in accordance with the philosophical exegesis of it: As spirit, the human being is a free being who is in the position of not allowing himself to be determined by natural impulses; when his condition is immediate and undeveloped, the human being is in a situation in which he ought not to be and from which he must free himself. This is the meaning of the doctrine of original sin without which Christianity would not be the religion of freedom.

19. In the demand for the *purification* of impulses there lies the general notion that they should be freed both from their form as immediate and natural determinations, and also from the subjectivity and contingency of their content, and so brought back to their substantial essence. The truth behind this vague demand is that the impulses should become the rational system of the will's volitions. To grasp them like that, proceeding out of the concept of the will, is the content of the philosophical science of right.

The content of this science through every single one of its moments, e.g. right, property, morality, family, state, and so forth, may be expounded in the form: human beings have by nature the *impulse* towards right, also the impulse to property and morality, also the impulse of love between the sexes, the impulse to sociability, and so on. This form is to be found in empirical psychology. But if in its stead the greater dignity of a philosophical dress is desired, then according to what, as was remarked before,[19] has passed in

[19] See Remarks to *PR* §§ 2 and 4.

recent times, and still passes, for philosophy, this dress may be
had cheap by the simple device of saying that the human being
discovers within himself as a 'fact of his consciousness' that right,
property, the state, and so on, are objects of his volition. Later in
the book,[20] this same subject-matter, which appears here in the
shape of impulses, will come on the scene in another form, i.e. in
the shape of *duties*.

20. When reflection is brought to bear on impulses, they are
imaged, estimated, compared with one another, with their means of
satisfaction and their consequences, and so on, and with a sum of satisfaction (i.e. with *happiness*). In this way reflection invests this material with formal universality and in this external manner purifies it
of its crudity and barbarity. This growth of the universality of
thought is the absolute value in *education* [*Bildung*] (compare § 187).

Addition: In happiness thought has already a mastery over the natural force
of impulses, since the thinker is not content with the momentary but
demands a whole happiness. This requirement is connected with education in that it is education which vindicates a universal. In the ideal of happiness, however, there are two moments: (i) a universal which is superior
to all particularity; but (ii) since the content of this universal is still only
universal *pleasure*, there appears here once again the singular, the particular, i.e. something finite, and a return must therefore be made to impulse.
Since the content of happiness lies in everyone's subjectivity and feeling,
this universal end is for its part particular, and consequently there is still
not present in it any genuine unity of form and content.

21. The truth, however, of this formal universality, which is indeterminate for itself and finds its determinacy in the material mentioned in § 20, is *self-determining universality*, the will, freedom. In
having universality, or itself *qua* infinite form,* for its object, content, and aim, the will is free not only *in* itself but *for* itself also; it is
the Idea in its truth.

(i) When the will's self-consciousness takes the form of desire and
impulse, this self-consciousness is *sensuous*, just as sensation in
general denotes externality and therefore the condition in which
self-consciousness is external to itself. (ii) When the will is *reflective*,
it contains two elements—this sensuous moment and the universality of thought. (iii) When the will is will *in and for itself*, then it

---

[20] See *PR* § 148 and esp. Remark to *PR* § 150.

has for its object the will itself as such, and so the will in its sheer universality—a universality which is what it is simply because it has superseded [*aufgehoben*] in itself the immediacy of natural desire and the particularity which is produced by reflection and with which such desire *eo ipso* becomes imbued. But this process of supersession or elevation to universality is what is called the activity of *thought*. The self-consciousness which purifies its object, content, and aim, and raises them to this universality effects this as thinking *asserting* itself in the will. Here is the point at which it becomes clear that it is only as thinking intelligence that the will is genuinely a will and free. The slave does not know his essence, his infinity, his freedom; he does not know himself to be an essence; and he lacks this knowledge of himself because he does not *think* himself. This self-consciousness which apprehends itself through thinking as an essence, and thereby frees itself from the contingent and the untrue, is the principle of right, morality, and all ethical life. Philosophical utterances about right, morality, and ethical life from those who would banish thought and have recourse instead to feeling, enthusiasm, the heart and the breast, are expressive of the utterly contemptible position into which thought and philosophical science have fallen, because what this amounts to is that even philosophical science itself, plunged in self-despair and extreme exhaustion, is taking as its principle barbarity and absence of thought, and would do its best to rob humanity of all truth, worth, and dignity.

Addition: Truth in philosophy means that concept and reality correspond. For example, the body is the reality, while the soul is the concept; but soul and body ought to be adequate to one another. Therefore a corpse is still an existent, but its existence is no true existence; the concept has left it; and for this reason a dead body putrefies. So a will is truly a will only when what it wills, its content, is identical with itself, when, that is to say, freedom wills freedom.

22. It is the will in and for itself which is *truly infinite*, because its object is itself and so is not for it an 'other' or a limitation; on the contrary, in its object this will has simply turned back into itself. Further this will is not mere possibility, predisposition, capacity (*potentia*), but the *infinite in actuality* (*infinitum actu*), since the concept's existence or its objective externality is inwardness itself.

Thus, if anyone speaks simply of the 'free will' as such, without specifically referring to the will which is free in and for itself, he is speaking only of the *predisposition* towards freedom, or of the natural and finite will (see § 11), and not by any means therefore of the free will, despite his intention and the words he uses.

Since the understanding takes the infinite only as something negative and so as something 'beyond', it supposes that it is doing all the more honour to the infinite, the more it pushes it into the distance away from itself and removes it from itself as something alien. In the free will, the truly infinite becomes actual and present; the free will itself is this Idea whose nature it is to be present here and now.

Addition: Infinity has rightly been represented figuratively as a circle, because a straight line goes on and on for ever and denotes the purely negative, bad infinite which, unlike the true infinite, has no return into itself. The free will is truly infinite, since it is not just a possibility and a predisposition. On the contrary, its external existence is its own inwardness, is itself.

23. Only in freedom of this kind is the will with itself without qualification, because then it is related to nothing except itself and so is released from every relation of dependence on anything else. The will is then true, or rather truth itself, because its self-determination consists in a correspondence between what it is in its existence (i.e. what it is as objective to itself) and its concept; or in other words, the pure concept of the will has the intuition of itself for its goal and its reality.

24. The will is then universal, because all restriction and all particular individuality have been superseded within it. These lie only in the difference between the concept and its content or object, or, to put it otherwise, in the difference between its being-in-itself [*Ansichsein*] and its subjective being-for-itself [*Fürsichsein*], or between its universality and its exclusive individuality, the individuality which resolves.

The various determinations of universality are developed in logic.[21] In connection with this word 'universality', what strikes representational thinking [*Vorstellen*] first is the idea of abstract and external universality; but in connection with universality in and for itself—and the universality here in question is of this character— we have to think neither of the universality of reflection, i.e. 'all-ness'

[21] *Hegel's reference*: See *Encyclopaedia*, §§ 118–26 [3rd edn. §§ 169–78].

or the universal as a common characteristic, nor of the abstract universality which stands outside and over against the individual, the abstract identity of the understanding (see Remark to § 6). It is the universality concrete in character and so universal for itself which is the substance of self-consciousness, its immanent generic essence, or its immanent Idea. This—the concept of the free will— is the universal which embraces its object, thoroughly permeates its determination and therein remains identical with itself. The universal in and for itself is definable as what is called the '*rational*', and it can be apprehended only in this speculative way.

25. The *subjective*, in relation to the will in general, means the will's self-conscious side, its individuality (see § 7) in distinction from its concept in itself. The subjectivity of the will means therefore

(α) the *pure form* of the will, the absolute unity of self-consciousness with itself (a unity in which self-consciousness, as I = I, is purely and simply inward and abstractly self-dependent), the pure certainty of itself, as distinguished from the truth;

(β) the *particularity* of the will as the arbitrary will and the contingent content of optional aims;

(γ) in general, the one-sided form of the will (see § 8) in which the thing willed, whatever its content, is but a content belonging to self-consciousness and an aim unfulfilled.

26. (α) The will is purely and simply *objective* insofar as it has itself for its determination and so is in correspondence with its concept and genuinely a will;

(β) but the objective will, *without the infinite form* of self-consciousness, is the will absorbed in its object or condition, whatever the content of these may be; it is the will of the child, the ethical will,* also the will of the slave, the superstitious person, and so on;

(γ) objectivity, finally, is the one-sided form opposed to the subjective volition, and hence it is the immediacy of existence as external reality; the will first becomes objective to itself in this sense through the fulfilment of its aims.

These logical categories—subjectivity and objectivity—have been set forth in detail here primarily with a view to pointing out expressly in relation to them, since they are often used in the sequel, that they, like other distinctions and opposed determinations of reflection, pass over into their opposites as a result of their finitude and their dialectical character. Other such opposed determinations, however, retain a hard and fast meaning for representational thinking and the understanding, because their identity is still only something *inward*. In the will, on the other hand, the opposed aspects are supposed to be at one and the same time abstractions *and* determinations *of the will*, which can be known only as something concrete, and so they lead by themselves to their identity and to the confusion of their meanings—a confusion into which the understanding slips quite unconsciously. Thus, for example, the will as inward freedom is subjectivity itself; subjectivity therefore is the concept of the will and so its objectivity. But its subjectivity contrasted with objectivity is finitude, and yet, because of this very contrast, the will is not with itself but is entangled with its object, and so its finitude consists quite as much in the fact that it is not subjective—and so on. Hence the meaning to be attributed in what follows to 'subjective' or 'objective' in respect of the will must each time appear from the context, which defines their position in relation to the will as a whole.

Addition: It is usually supposed that subjective and objective stand rigidly in opposition to one another. But this is not the case; it would be truer to say that they pass over into each other, since they are not abstract categories like positive and negative but already have a more concrete significance.

Consider first the word 'subjective'. We may call 'subjective' an end which is only the end of one specific subject. In this sense a very bad work of art, one which is not quite the thing, is purely 'subjective'. The word may also be applied, however, to the content of the will, and it is then almost synonymous with 'arbitrary'; a 'subjective' content is that which belongs to the subject alone. Hence bad actions, for example, are purely 'subjective'. But, further, it is just that pure empty I which may be called 'subjective', the I which has itself alone for its object and possesses the power to abstract from any other content. Thus subjectivity sometimes means something wholly particular, and at other times something with the highest justification, since everything which I am to recognize has also the task of becoming mine and attaining its validity in me. Subjectivity is insatiably greedy to concentrate and drown everything in this simple spring of the pure I.

No less varied are the ways in which we may take 'objective'. We may understand by it everything which we make an object to ourselves, whether actual existences or mere thoughts which we bring before our minds. We also include under this category the immediacy of existence in which the end is to be realized; even if the end is itself wholly particular and subjective, we nonetheless call it 'objective' on its appearance. But the 'objective' will is also that in which truth lies, and thus God's will, the ethical will, is an 'objective' one. Finally, we may also call 'objective' the will which is entirely absorbed in its object, as for example the will of the child, which is rooted in trust without subjective freedom, and the will of the slave, which does not yet know itself as free and on that account is a will-less will. In this sense any will is 'objective' which acts under the guidance of an alien authority and has not yet completed its infinite return into itself.

27. The absolute determination, or, if you like, the absolute impulse, of the free spirit (see § 21) is to make its freedom its object, i.e. to make freedom objective, both in the sense that freedom is to be the rational system of spirit and in the sense that this system is to be the world of immediate actuality (see § 26). In making freedom its object, spirit's purpose is to be for itself, as Idea, what the will is in itself. The abstract concept of the Idea of the will is in general *the free will which wills the free will*.

28. The will's activity consists in annulling [*aufzuheben*] the contradiction between subjectivity and objectivity and giving its aims an objective instead of a subjective character, while at the same time remaining with itself even in objectivity. Aside from the formal mode of consciousness (see § 8), where objectivity is present only as immediate actuality, this activity is in essence the development of the substantial content of the Idea (see § 21)—a development through which the concept determines the *Idea*, *itself* at first *abstract*, until it becomes a systematized whole. This whole, as what is substantial, is independent of the opposition between a merely subjective aim and its realization and is the same in both despite their difference in form.

29. Right [*Recht*] is any existence at all which is the *existence* [*Dasein*] *of the free will*. Right therefore is by definition freedom as Idea.

The crucial point in both the Kantian and the generally accepted definition of right (see the Introduction to Kant's *Doctrine of Right*)* is the '*restriction* which makes it possible for my freedom or self-will to coexist with the self-will of each and all according to a universal law'. On the one hand, this definition contains only a negative determination, that of restriction, while on the other hand the positive factor—the universal law or the so-called 'law of reason', the correspondence of the arbitrary self-will [*Willkür*] of one individual with that of another—is tantamount to the principle of contradiction and the familiar notion of formal identity. The definition of right which I have quoted involves that way of looking at the matter, especially popular since Rousseau,* according to which what is fundamental, substantial, and primary is supposed to be the will of an individual in his own arbitrary self-will, not the rational will in and for itself, and spirit as a particular individual, not spirit as it is in its truth. Once this principle is adopted, of course the rational can come on the scene only as a restriction on the type of freedom which this principle involves, and so also not as something immanently rational but only as an external, formal universal. This view is devoid of any speculative thinking and is repudiated by the philosophical concept. And the phenomena which it has produced both in people's heads and in the world are of a frightfulness parallel only to the superficiality of the thoughts on which they are based.*

30. It is precisely because right is the existence of the absolute concept or of self-conscious freedom that it is something *sacrosanct* [*heilig*].—The *formalism* of right (and of duty also, as we shall see [§§ 133–5]) arises, however, out of differences in the development of the concept of freedom. By contrast with the right which is more formal (i.e. more abstract) and so more restricted, a higher right belongs to the sphere and stage of spirit in which spirit has determined and actualized within itself the further moments contained in its Idea; and it belongs to this sphere as the sphere which is more concrete, intrinsically richer, and more genuinely universal.

Every stage in the development of the Idea of freedom has its own special right, since it is the existence of freedom in one of its own determinations. When there is said to be a clash between the moral or the ethical and right, the right in question is only the initial, formal, right of abstract personality. Morality, ethical life, the interest of the state, each of these is a distinctive right because each of them is a specific determination and existence of freedom. They can come into collision with each other only insofar as they are all equally rights. If spirit's moral standpoint were not also a right, or freedom in one of its forms, it could not possibly come into collision with the right of personality or with any other right, because any right whatever has inherent in it the concept of freedom, i.e. the highest category of spirit, in contrast with which anything else is without substance. Yet at the same time collision involves another moment, namely the fact that it is restrictive, and so if two rights collide one is subordinated to the other. It is only the right of the world-spirit [*Weltgeist*] which is absolute without qualification.

31. The method whereby, in philosophical science, the concept develops itself out of itself is expounded in logic and is here likewise presupposed.[22] Its development is a purely *immanent* progress and engendering of its determinations. Its advance is not effected by the assertion that various things 'exist' and then by the 'application' of the universal to extraneous material of that sort culled from elsewhere.

The concept's moving principle, which alike engenders and dissolves the particularizations of the universal, I call '*dialectic*', though I do not mean that dialectic which takes an object, proposition, and so on, given to feeling or, in general, to immediate consciousness, and explains it away, confuses it, pursues it this way and that, and has as its sole task the deduction of the contrary of that with which it starts—a negative type of dialectic commonly appearing even in Plato.* Dialectic of this kind may regard as its final result either the contrary of the idea with which it begins, or, if it is as incisive as the scepticism of the ancients, the contradictory of this idea, or again, it may be feeble enough to be content with an 'approximation' to the truth, a modern half-measure.[23] The higher dialectic of the concept consists not simply in producing the determination as a contrary and a restriction, but in producing and seizing upon the *positive* content and outcome of the determination, because it is this which makes it solely a *development* and an immanent progress. Moreover, this dialectic is not an activity of subjective thinking applied to some matter externally, but is rather the matter's *very soul* putting forth its branches and fruit organically. This development of the Idea is the proper activity of its rationality, and thinking, as something subjective, merely looks on at it without for its part adding to it any ingredient of its own. To consider a thing rationally means not to bring reason to bear on the object from the outside and so to work on it, but to find that the object is rational on its own account [*für sich*]; here it is spirit in its freedom, the culmination of self-conscious reason,

---

[22] See *PR* Preface, pp. 3–4 above. [S.H.]
[23] See *PR* Preface, p. 16 above. [S.H.]

which gives itself actuality and engenders itself as an existing world. The sole task of philosophical science is to bring into consciousness this proper work of the reason of the thing itself.

32. The determinations of the concept in the course of its development are from one point of view themselves concepts, but from another they take the form of existents, since the concept is in essence Idea. The series of concepts which this development yields is therefore at the same time a series of shapes [*Gestaltungen*], and philosophical science must treat them accordingly.

In a more speculative sense, a concept's determinacy [*Bestimmtheit*] and its mode of existence [*Dasein*] are one and the same thing. Yet it is to be noticed that the moments, whose result is a further determined form of the concept, precede it in the philosophical development of the Idea as determinations of the concept, but they do not come before it in its temporal development as shapes. Thus, for instance, the Idea determined as the family, presupposes the determinations of the concept from which the family will later on in this work be shown to result. But the explicit existence of these inner presuppositions as shapes also, e.g. as the right of property, contract, morality, and so forth, is the other aspect of the development, and it is only in a higher and more complete civilization that the development has gone so far as to endow its moments with this distinctively shaped existence.*

Addition: The Idea must further determine itself within itself continually, since in the beginning it is no more than an abstract concept. But this original abstract concept is never abandoned. It merely becomes continually richer in itself and the final determination is therefore the richest. In this process its earlier determinations, which exist only in themselves [*an sich*], attain their free self-subsistence but in such a way that the concept remains the soul which holds everything together and attains its own proper differentiation only through an immanent process. It therefore cannot be said that the concept reaches anything new; on the contrary, its final determination coincides with its first. Even if the concept seems in its existence to have fallen apart, this is nothing but a semblance [*Schein*] revealing itself in due course as a semblance, because all details revert at last to the concept of the universal. In the empirical sciences one usually analyses what is found in representation [*Vorstellung*], and when the single instance has been brought back to the common character, the latter is then called the concept. This is not our procedure; we only wish to look on at the way in which the concept determines itself and to restrain ourselves from adding thereto anything of our thoughts and opinions. What we acquire in this way, however, is a series of thoughts and another series of existent shapes; to which I may add that the time order in which the latter actually appear is other than the logical order. Thus, for example, we cannot say that property *existed* before the family, yet, in spite of that, property must be dealt with first.

Consequently you might raise here the question why we do not begin at the highest point, i.e. with the concretely true. The answer is that it is precisely the truth in the form of a result that we are looking for, and for this purpose it is essential to start by grasping the abstract concept itself. What is actual, the shape in which the concept is embodied, is for us therefore the further thing and the sequel, even if it were itself first in the actual world. The development we are studying is that whereby the abstract forms reveal themselves not as existing for themselves but as untrue.

Division of the Subject

33. According to the stages in the development of the Idea of the absolutely free will, the will is:

A. immediate; its concept therefore is abstract, namely personality, and its existence [*Dasein*] is an immediate external thing—the sphere of *abstract* or *formal right*;

B. reflected from its external existence into itself—it is then characterized as subjective individuality in opposition to the universal. The universal here is characterized as something inward, the good, and also as something outward, a world presented to the will; both these sides of the Idea are here mediated only by each other. This is the Idea in its division or in its existence [*Existenz*] as particular; and here we have the right of the subjective will in relation to the right of the world and the right of the Idea, though only the Idea *in itself*— the sphere of *morality* [*Moralität*];

C. the unity and truth of both these abstract moments—the Idea of the good not only apprehended in thought but so realized both in the will reflected into itself and in the external world that freedom exists as *substance*, as actuality and necessity, no less than as *subjective* will; this is the Idea in its universal existence in and for itself— *ethical life* [*Sittlichkeit*].

But the ethical substance is likewise

(a) natural spirit, the *family*;

(b) in its division and appearance, *civil society*;

(c) the *state* as freedom, freedom universal and objective even in the free self-subsistence of the particular will. This actual and organic spirit (α) of a people [*Volk*] (β) reveals and actualizes itself through the interrelation of the particular national spirits until (γ) in the process of world-history it reveals and actualizes itself as the universal world-spirit whose right is supreme.

The fact that when a thing or a content is posited first of all in accordance with its *concept* or as it is *in itself*, it then has the form of *immediacy* or *pure being*, is the doctrine of speculative logic, here presupposed;[24] the concept which is for itself in the *form of the concept* is a different thing and no longer something immediate.

The principle which determines the division of the subject is likewise here presupposed.[25] The division may also be looked upon as a predeclaration in historical form of the parts of the book, since the various stages must engender themselves out of the subject-matter itself as moments in the development of the Idea. A philosophical division is far from being an external one, i.e. it is not an external classification of a given material in accordance with one or more borrowed bases of division, but, on the contrary, is the immanent self-differentiation of the concept.

'Morality' [*Moralität*] and 'ethical life' [*Sittlichkeit*],* which are perhaps usually regarded as synonyms, are taken here in essentially different senses. Yet even commonplace thinking seems now to be distinguishing them; Kant generally prefers to use the word 'morality' and, since the principles of action in his philosophy are always limited to this conception, they make the standpoint of ethical life completely impossible, in fact they explicitly nullify and spurn it. But even if 'moral' and 'ethical' meant the same thing etymologically, that would in no way hinder them, once they had become different words, from being used for different conceptions.

Addition: In speaking of right [*Recht*] here, we mean not merely what is generally understood by the word, namely civil right, but also morality, ethical life, and world-history; these belong just as much to our topic, because the concept brings thoughts together into a true system. If the free will is not to remain abstract, it must in the first place give itself an existence, and the first sensuous material available for such existence are things,

---

[24] See *Encyclopaedia* (1830), §§ 84 ff. [S.H.]
[25] See *Encyclopaedia* (1830), §§ 237–43.

i.e. objects outside us. This primary mode of freedom is the one which we are to become acquainted with as *property*, the sphere of formal and abstract right. To this sphere there also belong property in its mediated form as *contract*, and right in its infringement as *crime* and *punishment*. The freedom which we have here is what is called a person, i.e. the subject who is free, free indeed for himself, and who gives himself an existence in things.

The sheer immediacy of existence, however, is not adequate to freedom, and the negation of this determination is the sphere of *morality*. I am now free, not merely in this immediate thing, but also after the immediacy has been superseded, i.e. I am free in myself, in my subjectivity. In this sphere the main thing is my insight, my intention, my purpose, because externality has now been posited as indifferent. Good, however, which here is the universal end, should not simply remain in my inner life; it should realize itself. That is to say, the subjective will demands that what is internal to it, i.e. its end, shall acquire an external existence, that the good shall in this way be consummated in the external world.

Morality and formal right are two abstract moments whose truth is *ethical life* alone. Hence ethical life is the unity of the will in its concept with the will of the individual, i.e. of the subject. Its first existence is again something natural, whose form is love and feeling—the *family*. Here the individual has transcended his self-enclosed personality and finds himself and his consciousness of himself in a whole. At the next stage, however, we see substantial unity disappearing along with ethical life proper; the family falls asunder and its members relate themselves to each other as self-subsistent, since their only bond of connection is reciprocal need. This stage—*civil society*—has often been looked upon as the state, but the *state* is first present at the third stage, the stage of ethical life and of spirit in which the prodigious unification of self-subsistent individuality with universal substantiality has been achieved. The right of the state therefore stands above the preceding stages; it is freedom in its most concrete shape and as such is subordinate to one thing alone—the supreme absolute truth of the world-spirit.

ABSTRACT RIGHT

34. The will that is free in and for itself, at the stage when its concept is *abstract*, has the determinate character of *immediacy*. Accordingly this stage is its abstractly self-related actuality, which is negative in contrast with reality—the inherently *individual* will of a subject. According to the moment of the particularity of the will it has in addition a content consisting of determinate aims, and, as *exclusive individuality*, it has this content at the same time as an external world directly confronting it.

Addition: When I say that 'the will that is free in and for itself, at the stage when its concept is abstract, has the determinate character of immediacy', what I mean is this: when the concept has fully realized itself and when the existence of the concept has become nothing but the unfolding of its own self, then that state of affairs is the fully developed Idea of the will. But at the start the concept is abstract, which means that all its determinations are contained within it, but still only contained within it; they are only implicit [*an sich*] and not yet developed to be a totality in themselves. If I say 'I am free', the I is still this inwardness [*Insichsein*] without opposition. In morality, on the other hand, there is opposition from the start, since I stand in the moral sphere as an *individual will* while the good is the *universal* even though it is within myself. Thus at that level, the will has in itself the different moments of individuality and universality, and this gives it its determinate character. But, to begin with, no such difference is present, since at the first stage, that of abstract unity, there is no advance and no mediation and so the will has the form of immediacy, of mere being. The essential point of view to be taken here then is that this original indeterminacy is itself a determinacy. The indeterminacy lies in the fact that there is as yet no difference between the will and its content; but indeterminacy, opposed to the determinate, acquires the character of being something determinate. It is abstract identity which here constitutes determinacy; the will therefore becomes an individual will, a *person*.

35. The *universality* of this will that is free for itself is formal universality, the self-conscious but otherwise contentless and *simple* relation of itself to itself in its individuality, and from this point of view the subject is a person [*Person*]. Personality implies that as *this* person: (i) I am completely determined on every side (in my inner caprice, impulse, and desire, as well as by immediate external existence) and so finite, yet (ii) nonetheless I am simply and solely self-relation, and therefore in finitude I know myself as something *infinite, universal*, and *free*.

Personality begins not with the subject's mere general consciousness of himself as an I concretely determined in some way or other, but rather with his consciousness of himself as a completely abstract I in which every concrete restriction and value is negated and without validity. In personality, therefore, knowledge is knowledge of oneself as an object, but an object raised by thinking to the level of simple infinity and so an object that is purely self-identical. Individuals and peoples have no personality until they have achieved this pure thought and knowledge of themselves. Spirit that is in and for itself differs from spirit in its appearance in this, that in the same respect in which the latter is only *self-consciousness*—a consciousness of self but only in accordance with the natural will and its still external oppositions[26]—the former has itself, as the abstract and free I, for its object and aim, and so is a *person*.

Addition: The will that is abstract or for itself is the person. The highest thing for a human being is to be a person, and yet in spite of that the bare abstraction, 'person', is somewhat contemptuous in its very expression. 'Person' is essentially different from 'subject', since 'subject' is only the possibility of personality; every living thing of any sort is a subject. A person, then, is a subject aware of this subjectivity, since in personality I am for myself as such. The person is the individuality of freedom in its pure being-for-self. As *this* person, I know myself to be free in myself. I can abstract from everything, since nothing confronts me save pure personality, and yet as *this* person I am something wholly determinate, e.g. I am of a certain age, a certain stature, I occupy this space, and so on through whatever other details you like. Thus personality is at once the sublime and the trivial. It implies this unity of the infinite with the purely finite, of the wholly limitless with determinate limitation. It is the sublimity of personality that is able to sustain this contradiction, a contradiction which nothing merely natural contains or could endure.

---

[26] *Hegel's reference*: See *Phenomenology of Spirit* (Bamberg and Würzburg, 1807), 101 ff. [Miller trans., 104–5], and *Encyclopaedia*, § 344 [3rd edn. § 424]).

36. (1) Personality essentially involves the capacity for rights and constitutes the concept and the basis (itself abstract) of the system of abstract and therefore formal right. Hence the imperative of right is: 'Be a person and respect others as persons.'

37. (2) The *particularity* of the will is a moment in the consciousness of the will as a whole (see § 34), but it is not yet contained in abstract personality as such. Therefore, it is present at this point, but as still sundered from personality, from the character of freedom, present as desire, need, impulse, casual whim, and so forth. In formal right, therefore, it is not a matter of particular interests, of my advantage or my welfare, any more than of the particular motive behind my volition, of insight and intention.

Addition: Since, in personality, particularity is not present as freedom, everything which depends on particularity is here a matter of indifference. To have no interest except in one's formal right may be pure obstinacy, often a fitting accompaniment of a cold heart and restricted sympathies: for it is uncultured people who insist most on their rights, while noble minds look on other aspects of the thing. Thus abstract right is nothing but a bare possibility and in that respect something formal as compared with the whole range of the situation. On that account, to have a right gives one a warrant, but it is not absolutely necessary that one should insist on one's rights, because that is only one aspect of the whole situation. That is to say, possibility is being which has the significance of also not being.

38. In relation to action in the concrete and to moral and ethical relations, abstract right is, in contrast with the further content which these involve, only a *possibility*, and to have a right is therefore to have only a *permission* or a *warrant*. The unconditional commands of abstract right are restricted, once again because of its abstractness, to the negative: 'Do not infringe personality and what personality entails.' The result is that there are only *prohibitions* in the sphere of right, and the positive form of any command in this sphere is based in the last resort, if we examine its ultimate content, on prohibition.

39. (3) As *immediate* individuality, a person in making decisions is related to a world of nature directly confronting him, and thus the personality of the will stands over against this world as something subjective. For personality, however, as inherently infinite and universal, the restriction of being only subjective is a contradiction and a nullity. Personality is that which acts to overcome [*aufzuheben*] this restriction and to give itself reality, or in other words to claim that external world as its own.

40. Right is in the first place the immediate existence which freedom gives itself in an immediate way, i.e. (*a*) possession, which is *property*-ownership. Freedom is here the freedom of the abstract will in general or, *eo ipso*, the freedom of an individual person related only to himself. (*b*) A person by distinguishing himself from himself relates himself to another person, and it is only as owners that these two persons really exist for each other. Their implicit [*an sich seiend*] identity is realized through the transference of property from one to the other in conformity with a common will and without detriment to the rights of either. This is *contract*. (*c*) The will which is differentiated not in the sense of (*b*) as being contrasted with another person, but in the sense of (*a*) as related to itself, is as a *particular* will at variance with and opposed to itself as a will *that is in and for itself*. This opposition is wrongdoing and *crime*.

The classification of the system of rights* into the right of *persons* and the right to *things*, on the one hand, and the right of action, on the other, like the many other similar classifications, has as its primary aim the imposition of an external order on the mass of unorganized material confronting the classifier. The striking thing about this classification is the confusion in it due to the disorderly intermixture of rights which presuppose substantial relations, e.g. those of family and state, and rights which only concern abstract personality as such. This confusion is exemplified in the classification of rights (adopted by Kant and since favoured by others)[27] into rights to *things*, rights of *persons*, and *personal* rights of a *real* [*dinglich*] kind.

To develop the perversity and lack of conceptual thought in the classification of rights into rights of *persons* and rights to *things*, which lies at the root of Roman law (rights of action concern the administration of justice and are of a different order altogether), would take us too far afield. Here this much at least is clear: it is *personality* alone which can confer a right to things and therefore the right of persons in its essence is a right to things, 'thing' [*Sache*] being taken here in its general sense as anything external to my freedom, including even my body and my life. In this sense,

[27] For the relevant passage in Kant's *Doctrine of Right*, see § 10 [Gregor trans., 81]. For full bibliographical details see explanatory note to p. 46 [p. 334 below].

the right to things is the right of *personality as such*. From the point of view of what is called the right of persons in Roman law, however, someone is reckoned a person only when he is treated as possessing a certain *status*.[28] Hence in Roman law, even personality itself is only a certain standing [*Stand*] or condition [*Zustand*] contrasted with slavery. Apart from the right over slaves (and children, who also count roughly as 'slaves'), as well as the status (called *capitis diminutio*)* of having lost one's rights, the so-called Roman law of 'personal' rights is concerned with *family relationships*. (In Kant, by the way, family relationships fall under *personal* rights of a *real* kind.)[29] The Roman right of persons is therefore not the right of the person as person but at most the right of a person in his *particular* capacity. (Later on in this book [§§ 163, 167–8], it will be shown that the substantial basis of family relationships is rather the sacrifice of personality.) It must now be obvious that it is perverse to treat the right of a specific person in his *particular* capacity before the universal right of personality as such.

Kant's *personal rights* are the rights issuing from a contract whereby I undertake to give something or to perform something[30]—the *jus ad rem* [right to a thing] conferred by an *obligatio* in Roman law. To be sure, it is only a person who is required to execute the covenants of a contract, just as it is also only a person who acquires the right to their execution. But a right of this sort cannot for this reason be called a 'personal' right; rights of *every* sort belong to a person alone. Objectively considered, a right arising from a contract is never a right over a person, but only a right over something external to a person or something which he can alienate, always a right over a thing.

SUB-SECTION I

PROPERTY

41. A person must translate his freedom into an external sphere in order to exist as Idea. Personality is the first, still wholly abstract,

---

[28] *Hegel's reference*: J. G. Heineccius, *Elements of Civil Law* [*Elementa Juris Civilis*] (1728), § 75.

[29] See Kant, *Doctrine of Right*, § 22 [Gregor trans., 95].

[30] These personal rights are treated by Kant under the heading of 'contract right'; see Kant, *Doctrine of Right*, §§ 18–21 [Gregor trans., 90–5].

determination of the infinite will in and for itself, and therefore this sphere distinct from the person, the sphere capable of embodying his freedom, is likewise determined as what is *immediately* different and separable from him.

Addition: The rationale of property is to be found not in the satisfaction of needs but in the supersession of the pure subjectivity of personality. In his property a person exists for the first time as reason. Even if my freedom is here realized first of all in an external thing, and so poorly realized, nevertheless abstract personality in its immediacy can have no other existence save one characterized by immediacy.

42. What is immediately different from free spirit is that which, both for spirit and in itself, is the external pure and simple, a thing, something not free, not personal, without rights.

'Thing' [*Sache*], like 'the objective', has two opposed meanings. If we say 'that's the thing' or 'the thing is what matters, not the person', 'thing' means what is substantial. On the other hand, when 'thing' is contrasted with 'person' as such, not with the particular subject, it means the opposite of what is substantial, i.e. that whose determinate character lies in its pure externality. From the point of view of free spirit, which must, of course, be distinguished from mere consciousness, the external is external in and for itself [*an und für sich*], and it is for this reason that the determinate character assigned to *nature* by the concept is inherent *externality*.

Addition: Since a thing lacks subjectivity, it is external not merely to the subject but to itself. Space and time are external in this way. As sentient, I am myself external, spatial, and temporal. In so far as I have sensuous intuitions, I have them from something which is external to itself. An animal can intuit, but the soul of an animal has for its object not its soul, itself, but something external.

43. As the concept in its *immediacy,* and so as in essence an individual, a person has a natural existence partly within himself and partly of such a kind that he is related to it as to an external world.— It is only these things* in their immediacy as things, not determinations that become such through the mediation of the will, which are in question here where the topic under discussion is personality, itself at this point still in its initial immediacy.

Mental [*geistig*] aptitudes, erudition, artistic skill, even things ecclesiastical (like sermons, masses, prayers, consecration of votive objects), inventions, and so forth, become subjects of a contract, brought to parity, through being bought and sold, with things recognized as things. It may be asked whether the artist, scholar, etc., is from the legal point of view in possession of his art, erudition, ability to preach a sermon, sing a mass, etc., that is, whether such attainments are 'things'. We may hesitate to call such abilities, attainments, aptitudes, etc., 'things', for while possession of these may be the subject of business dealings and contracts, as if they were things, there is also something inward and mental about it, and for this reason the understanding may be in perplexity about how to describe such possession in legal terms, because its field of vision is as limited to the dilemma that this is 'either a thing or not a thing' as to the dilemma 'either finite or infinite'. Attainments, erudition, talents, and so forth, belong, of course, to free spirit and are something internal and not external to it, but even so, by expressing them it may embody them in something external and alienate [*veräußern*] them (see below [§§ 65 ff.]), and in this way they are put into the category of 'things'. Therefore they are not immediate at the start but only acquire this character through the mediation of spirit which reduces its inner possessions to immediacy and externality. It was an unjustifiable and unethical proviso of Roman law that children were from their father's point of view 'things'. Hence he was legally the owner of his children, although, of course, he still also stood to them in the ethical relation of love (though this relation must have been much weakened by the injustice of his legal position). Here, then, the two qualities 'being a thing' and 'not being a thing' were united, though quite wrongly.

In the sphere of abstract right, we are concerned only with the person as person, and therefore with the particular (which is indispensable if the person's freedom is to have scope and reality) only insofar as it is something separable from the person and immediately different from him, no matter whether this separability constitutes the essential nature of the particular, or whether the particular receives it only through the mediation of the subjective will. Hence in this sphere we are concerned with mental aptitudes, erudition, etc., only insofar as they are possessions in a legal sense; we have not to treat here the possession of our body and spirit which we can achieve through education, study, habit, etc., and which exists as an *inward* property of spirit. But it is not until we come to deal with alienation that we need begin to speak of the *transition* of such spiritual property into the external world where it falls under the category of property in the legal sense.

44. A person has as his substantial end the right of putting his will into any and every thing and thereby making it his, because it has no such end in itself and derives its determination and soul from his will. This is the absolute *right of appropriation* which human beings have over all 'things'.

The so-called 'philosophy' which attributes reality in the sense of self-subsistence and genuine being-for-and-within-itself [*Für- und Insichsein*] to unmediated single things, to the non-personal, is directly contradicted by the free will's attitude to these things. The same is true of the other philosophy which assures us that the mind cannot apprehend the truth or know the nature of the thing-in-itself.* While so-called 'external' things have a semblance [*Schein*] of self-subsistence for consciousness, intuition, and representational thinking, the free will idealizes such actuality and so is its truth.*

Addition: All things may become the property of a human being, because the latter is free will and consequently is in and for itself, while what stands over against him lacks this quality. Thus everyone has the right to make his will the thing or to make the thing his will, or in other words to supersede [*aufzuheben*] the thing and transform it into his own; for the thing, as externality, has no end in itself; it is not infinite self-relation but something external to itself. A living thing (an animal) is also external to itself in this way and is so far itself a thing. Only the will is the infinite, absolute in contrast with everything other than itself, while that other is on its side only relative. Thus 'to appropriate' means at bottom only to manifest the pre-eminence of my will over the thing and to prove that the latter is not absolute [*an und für sich*], is not an end in itself. This is made manifest when I endow the thing with some purpose not directly its own. When the living thing becomes my property, I give to it a soul other than the one it had before, I give to it my soul. The free will, therefore, is the idealism which does not take things as they are to be in and for themselves, while realism pronounces them to be absolute, even if they only exist in the form of finitude. Even an animal has gone beyond this realist philosophy since it devours things and so proves that they are not absolutely self-subsistent.

45. To have power over a thing *ab extra* constitutes *possession*. The particular aspect of the matter, the fact that I make something my own as a result of my natural need, impulse, and caprice, is the particular interest satisfied by possession. But I as free will am an object to myself in what I possess and thereby also for the first time am an actual will, and this is the aspect which constitutes the determination of *property*, the true and rightful factor in possession.

If emphasis is placed on my needs, then the possession of property appears as a means to their satisfaction, but the true position is that, from the standpoint of freedom, property is the first existence [*Dasein*] of freedom and so is in itself a substantial end.

46. Since my will, as the will of a person, and so as an individual will, becomes objective to me in property, property acquires the character of *private property*; and common property of such a nature that it may be owned by separate persons acquires the character of an inherently dissoluble partnership in which the retention of my share is explicitly a matter of my arbitrary preference.

The nature of the elements* makes it impossible for the use of them to become so particularized as to be the private possession of anyone.

In the Roman *agrarian laws** there was a clash between public and private ownership of land. The latter is the more rational and therefore had to be given preference even at the expense of other rights.

One factor in *family testamentary trusts** contravenes the right of personality and so the right of private property. But the specific characteristics pertaining to private property may have to be subordinated to a higher sphere of right (e.g. to a society or the state), as happens, for instance, when private property is put into the hands of a so-called 'artificial' person [*moralische Person*] and into mortmain.* Still, such exceptions to private property cannot be grounded in chance, in private caprice, or private advantage, but only in the rational organism of the state.

The general principle that underlies Plato's ideal state violates the right of personality by forbidding the holding of private property.* The idea of a pious or friendly and even a compulsory brotherhood of men holding their goods in common and rejecting the principle of private property may readily present itself to the disposition which mistakes the true nature of the freedom of spirit and right and fails to apprehend it in its determinate moments. As for the moral or religious view behind this idea, when Epicurus' friends proposed to form such an association holding goods in common, he forbade them, precisely on the ground that their proposal betrayed distrust and that those who distrusted each other were not friends.[31]

Addition: In property my will is the will of a person; but a person is *this* person and so property becomes the personal aspect of this specific will. Since property is the means whereby I give my will existence, property must also have the character of being 'this' or 'mine'. This is the important doctrine of the necessity of private property. While the state may cancel private ownership in exceptional cases, it is nevertheless only the state that can do this; but frequently, especially in our day, private property has been reintroduced by the state. For example, many states have dissolved the monasteries, and rightly, for in the last resort no community has so good a right to property as a person has.

47. As a person, I am myself an *immediate* individual; if we give further precision to this expression, it means in the first instance that I am alive in this *organic body* which is my external existence, universal in content and undivided,* the real possibility of all further-determined existence. But, all the same, as person, I possess my life and my body, like other things, only insofar as my will is in them.

The fact that, considered as existing not as the concept that is for itself but only as the concept in its immediacy, I am alive and have an organic body, depends on the concept of life and on the concept of the spirit as soul—on moments which are taken over here from the philosophy of nature[32] and from [philosophical] anthropology.[33]

I possess the members of my body, my life, only so long as I will to possess them. An animal cannot maim or destroy itself, but a human being can.

Addition: Animals are in possession of themselves; their soul is in possession of their body. But they have no right to their life, because they do not will it.

48. Insofar as the body is an immediate existent, it is not in conformity with spirit. If it is to be the willing organ and soul-endowed

---

[31] *Hegel's reference*: Diogenes Laertius,* 10. 6.
[32] *Hegel's reference*: *Encyclopaedia*, §§ 259 ff.; cf. §§ 161, 164, 298 [3rd edn. §§ 336 ff.; cf. §§ 213, 216, 376].
[33] *Hegel's reference*: *Encyclopaedia*, § 318 [3rd edn. §§ 388 ff.].

instrument of spirit, it must first be *taken into possession* by spirit (see § 57). But from the point of view of *others*, I am in essence a free entity in my body while my possession of it is still immediate.

It is only because I am alive as a free entity in my body that this living existent ought not to be misused by being made a beast of burden. While I am alive, my soul (the concept and, to use a higher term, the free entity) and my body are not separated; my body is the existence of my freedom and it is with my body that I feel. It is therefore only sophistical understanding, devoid of the Idea [*ideelos*], which can so distinguish body and soul as to hold that the 'thing-in-itself', the soul, is not touched or attacked if the body is maltreated and the existent embodiment [*Existenz*] of personality is subjected to the power of another. I can withdraw into myself out of my bodily existence and make my body something external to myself; particular feelings I can regard as something outside me, and in chains I can still be free. But this is *my* will; so far as *others* are concerned, I am in my body. To be free from the point of view of *others* is identical with being free in my *determinate existence* [*Dasein*].[34] If another does violence to *my body*, he does violence to *me*.

If my body is touched or suffers violence, then, because I feel, I am touched myself actually, here and now. This creates the distinction between personal injury and damage to my external property, for in such property my will is not actually present in this direct fashion.

49. In relation to external things, the *rational* aspect is that I possess property, but the *particular* aspect comprises subjective aims, needs, arbitrariness, abilities, external circumstances, and so forth (see § 45). On these mere possession as such depends, but this particular aspect has in this sphere of abstract personality not yet been posited as identical with freedom. What and how much I possess, therefore, is a matter of indifference so far as rights are concerned.

If at this stage we may speak of more persons than one, although no such distinction has yet been made, then we may say that in

---

[34] *Hegel's reference*: See my *Science of Logic* (1st edn. 1812), i. 49 ff. [Miller trans., 116 ff.]. [The Miller translation is a translation of the second edn. (1832), in which the passage in question was revised. S.H.]

respect of their personality persons are equal. But this is an empty tautology, for the person, as something abstract, has not yet been particularized or posited as distinct in some specific way.

'Equality' is the abstract identity of the understanding; reflective thought and all kinds of intellectual mediocrity stumble on it at once when they are confronted by the relation of unity to a difference. At this point, equality could only be the equality of abstract persons as such, and therefore the whole field of possession, this terrain of inequality, falls outside it.

The demand sometimes made for an equal division of land, and other available resources too, is an intellectualism all the more empty and superficial in that at the heart of particular differences there lies not only the external contingency of nature but also the whole compass of spirit, endlessly particularized and differentiated, and its rationality developed into an organism.*

We may not speak of the injustice of nature in the unequal distribution of possessions and resources, since nature is not free and therefore is neither just nor unjust. That everyone ought to have subsistence enough for his needs is a moral wish and thus vaguely expressed is well enough meant, but like anything that is only well meant it lacks objectivity. On the other hand, subsistence is not the same as possession and belongs to another sphere, i.e. to civil society.[35]

Addition: The equality which might be set up, e.g. in connection with the distribution of goods, would soon be destroyed again anyway, because wealth depends on diligence. But if a project cannot be executed, it ought not to be executed. Of course people are equal, but only *qua* persons, that is, with respect only to the source from which possession springs; the inference from this is that everyone must have property. Hence, if you wish to talk of equality, it is this equality which you must have in view. But this equality is something apart from the fixing of particular amounts, from the question of how much I own. From this point of view it is false to maintain that justice requires everyone's property to be equal, since it requires only that everyone shall own property. The truth is that particularity is just the sphere where there is room for inequality and where equality would be wrong. True enough, people often covet the goods of others, but that is just doing wrong, since right is that which remains indifferent to particularity.

[35] See *PR* §§ 199 ff., 230, 237 ff.

50. The principle that a thing belongs to the person who happens to be the first in time to take it into his possession is immediately self-explanatory and superfluous, because a second person cannot take into his possession what is already the property of another.

Addition: The points made so far have been mainly concerned with the proposition that personality must have existence in property. Now the fact that the first person to take possession of a thing should also be its owner is an inference from what has been said. The first is the rightful owner, however, not because he is the first but because he is a free will, for it is only by another's succeeding him that he becomes the first.

51. Since property is the *existence* of personality, my inward idea and will that something is to be mine are not enough to make it my property; to secure this end I must *take possession* of it. The existence which my willing thereby attains entails its capacity to be recognized by others.—The fact that a thing of which I can take possession should be without an owner [*herrenlos*] is (see § 50) a self-explanatory negative condition of taking possession, or rather it bears on the anticipated relation to others.*

Addition: That a person puts his will into a thing is just the concept of property, and the next step is the *realization* of this concept. The inner act of will which consists in saying that something is mine must also become recognizable by others. If I make a thing mine, I give to it a predicate, 'mine', which must appear in it in an external form and must not simply remain in my inner will. It often happens that children lay stress on their prior willing in preference to the seizure of a thing by others. But for adults this willing is not sufficient, since the form of subjectivity must be removed and must work its way beyond the subjective to objectivity.

52. Taking possession makes the *matter* of the thing my property, since matter in itself [*für sich*] does not belong to itself.

Matter offers resistance to me—and matter is nothing except the resistance it offers to me—that is, it presents itself to me as something abstractly independent, only when my spirit is taken abstractly as sensation. (Sense-perception perversely takes spirit's sensuous being to be concrete and reason to be abstract.) In relation to the will and property, however, this independence [*Fürsichsein*] of matter has no truth. Taking possession, as an *external activity* whereby we actualize our universal right of appropriating natural objects, comes to be conditioned by physical strength, cunning, dexterity, the means of one kind or another whereby we take physical possession of things. Owing to the qualitative differences between natural objects, mastery and occupancy of these has an infinite variety of meanings and involves a restriction and contingency that is just as infinite. Apart from that, a 'kind' of thing, or an element as such, is not the correlative *object of an individual person*. Before it can become such and be appropriated, it must first be individualized into a breath of air or a drink of water. In the fact that it is impossible to take possession of an external 'kind' of thing as such, or of an element, it is not the external physical impossibility which must be looked on as ultimate, but the fact that a person, as will, is characterized as individual, while as person he is at the same time *immediate* individuality; hence as person he is related to the external world as to individual things (see Remark to § 13 and § 43).

Thus the mastery and external possession of things becomes, in ways that again are infinite, more or less indeterminate and incomplete. Yet matter is never without an essential form of its own and only because it has one is it anything. The more I appropriate this form, the more do I enter into actual possession of the thing. The consumption of food is an out and out alteration of its qualitative character, the character on the strength of which it was what it was before it was eaten. The training of my body in dexterity, like the education of my spirit, is likewise a more or less complete occupancy and penetration of it. It is my spirit which of all things I can make most completely my own. Yet actually taking possession is different from property as such because property is completed by the free will. In face of the free will, the thing retains nothing proper to itself even though in possession, as an external relation to an object, there still remains something external. The empty abstraction of a matter without properties which, when a thing is my property, is supposed to remain outside me and the property of the thing, is something which thought must overcome.

Addition: Fichte has raised the question whether the matter too belongs to me if I impose a form on it.* On his argument, after I had made a golden cup, it would have to be open to someone else to take the gold provided that in so doing he did no damage to my work. However separable the matter may be in thought [*Vorstellung*], still in reality this distinction is an empty subtlety, because, if I take possession of a field and plough it, it is not only the furrow that is my property, but the rest as well, the furrowed earth. That is to say, I will to take this matter, the whole thing, into my possession; the matter therefore does not remain without an owner nor does it remain its own property. Further, even if the matter remains external to the form which I have given to the object, the form is precisely a sign that I claim the thing as mine. The thing therefore does not remain external to my will or outside what I have willed. Hence there is nothing left to be taken into possession by someone else.

53. The more precise determinations of property are to be found in the will's relation to the thing. This relation is

(A) *taking possession* of the thing directly (here it is in the thing *qua* something positive that the will has its existence);

(B) *use* (the thing is negative in contrast with the will and so it is in the thing as something to be negated that the will has its existence);

(C) *alienation* [*Veräußerung*], the reflection of the will out of the thing back into itself.

These three are respectively the positive, negative, and infinite judgements* of the will on the thing.

A. *Taking Possession*

54. We take possession of a thing (α) by directly grasping it physically, (β) by forming it, and (γ) by merely marking it as ours.

Addition: These modes of taking possession involve the advance from the category of individuality to that of universality. It is only of an individual thing that we can take possession physically, while marking a thing as mine is taking possession of it in idea [*Vorstellung*]. In the latter case I have an idea of the thing and mean that the thing as a whole is mine, not simply the part which I can take into my possession physically.

55. (α) From the point of view of sensation, to grasp a thing physically is the most complete of these modes, because then I am directly present in this possession, and therefore my will is recognizable in it. But at bottom this mode is only subjective, temporary, and seriously restricted in scope, as well as by the qualitative nature of the things grasped.—As a result of the connection which I may effect between something and things which have already become my property in other ways, or into which something may otherwise be accidentally

brought, the scope of this method is somewhat enlarged, and the same result is produced by other means also.

Mechanical forces, weapons, tools, extend the range of my power. Connections between my property and something else may be regarded as making it more easily possible for me than for another owner, or sometimes possible for me alone, to take possession of something or to make use of it. Instances of such connections are that my land may be on the seashore, or on a river bank; or my estate may border on hunting country or pasture or land useful for some other purpose; stone or other mineral deposits may be under my fields; there may be treasure in or under my ground, and so on. The same is true of connections arising only in the course of time and by chance, like some of what are called 'natural accessions' such as alluvial deposits, etc., and jetsam. (Young born to animals in my possession [*foetura*] constitute an accession to my wealth too, but the connection here is an organic one, it is not a case of a thing being added *ab extra* to another thing already in my possession; and therefore *foetura* is of a type quite different from the other accessions.) Alternatively, the addition to my property may be looked upon as a non-self-subsistent accident of the thing to which it has been added. In every case, however, these are *external* conjunctions whose bond of connection is neither life nor the concept. It devolves, therefore, on the understanding to adduce and weigh their pros and cons, and on positive legislation to make decisions about them in accordance with the extent to which the relation between the things conjoined has or has not any essentiality.

Addition: Taking possession is always piecemeal in type; I take into possession no more than what I touch with my body. But here comes the second point: external objects extend further than I can grasp. Therefore, whatever I have in my grasp is linked with something else. It is with my hand that I manage to take possession of a thing, but its reach can be extended. What I hold in my hand—that magnificent tool which no animal possesses—can itself be a means to gripping something else. If I am in possession of something, understanding immediately draws the inference that it is not only the immediate object in my grasp which is mine but also what is connected with it. At this point positive right must enact its statutes since nothing further on this topic can be deduced from the concept.*

56. (β) When I impose a form on something, the thing's determinate character *as* mine acquires an independent [*für sich bestehend*]

externality and ceases to be restricted to my presence here and now and to the presence of my knowledge and will.

To impose a form on a thing is the mode of taking possession most in conformity with the Idea [*Idee*] to this extent, that it implies a union of subject and object, although it varies endlessly with the qualitative character of the objects and the variety of subjective aims. Under this head there also falls the formation of the organic. What I do to the organic does not remain external to it but is assimilated by it. Examples are the tilling of the soil, the cultivation of plants, the taming and feeding of animals, the preservation of game, as well as contrivances for utilizing raw materials or the forces of nature and processes for making one material produce effects on another, and so forth.

Addition: Empirically, this forming of an object may assume the most various guises. In farming land I impose a form on it. Where inorganic objects are concerned, the imposition of a form is not always direct. For example, if I build a windmill, I have not imposed a form on the air, but I have formed something for utilizing the air, which latter cannot be taken away from me just because I have not formed it myself. Further, the preserving of game may be regarded as a way of forming game, for it is a mode of behaviour directed towards maintaining the object in question. [The same is true of] the training of animals, only of course that is a more direct way of forming them and it depends on me to a greater extent.

57. The human being, in his *immediate* existence in himself, is something natural, external to his concept. It is only through the development of his own body and spirit, essentially through his *self-consciousness's apprehension of itself as free*, that he takes possession of himself and becomes his own property and no one else's. This taking possession of oneself, looked at from the opposite point of view, is the translation into *actuality* of what one is according to one's concept, i.e. a possibility, capacity, predisposition. In that translation one's self-consciousness is posited for the first time as one's own, as one's object also and distinct from self-consciousness pure and simple, and thereby capable of taking the form of a 'thing' (compare Remark to § 43).

The alleged justification of slavery (with all its more specific explanations through physical force, capture in war, the saving and preservation of life, sustenance, education, philanthropy, the slave's

own acquiescence, and so forth), as well as the justification of
slave-ownership as simple lordship in general, and all historical
views of the justice of slavery and lordship, depend on regarding
the human being as a *natural entity* pure and simple, as an existent
not in conformity with its concept (an existent also to which arbitrariness is appropriate). The argument for the absolute injustice
of slavery, on the other hand, adheres to the concept of the human
being as spirit, as something inherently [*an sich*] free. This view is
one-sided in so far as it regards the human being as free *by nature*,
or, in other words, takes the concept as such in its immediacy, not
the Idea, as the truth. This *antinomy* rests, like all others, on the
formal thinking which asserts both the moments of an Idea in
separation from one another and clings to each of them in its independence and so in its inadequacy to the Idea and in its untruth.
Free spirit consists precisely (see § 21) in its being no longer
implicit [*an sich*] or concept alone, but in its superseding this
formal stage of its being and *eo ipso* its immediate natural existence, until the existence which it gives to itself is one which is
solely its own and free. The side of the antinomy which asserts
the concept of freedom therefore has the merit of containing the
absolute starting-point, though only the starting-point, for the
discovery of truth, while the other side goes no further than existence without the concept and therefore excludes the outlook of
rationality and right altogether. The position of the free will, with
which right and the science of right begin, is already beyond the
untrue point of view, which sees the human being, as a natural
entity and only the implicit [*an sich seiend*] concept, as capable of
being enslaved. This earlier, untrue phenomenon of slavery is one
which befalls spirit when spirit is only at the level of consciousness. The dialectic of the concept and of the purely immediate
consciousness of freedom brings about at that point the *struggle for
recognition* and the relationship of *master* and *slave*.[36]

Objective spirit, the content of right, should not itself be apprehended in its subjective concept alone, and the fact that the human
being in and for himself is not destined to be a slave should not
itself be understood as a mere 'ought'. These demands are fulfilled,

---

[36] *Hegel's reference*: See *Phenomenology*, 115 ff. [Miller trans., 111 ff.], and
Encyclopaedia, §§ 352 ff. [3rd edn. §§ 430 ff.].

however, only when we recognize that the Idea of freedom is actual only as the *state*.

Addition: To hold fast to the idea that the human being is free in and for himself is *eo ipso* to condemn slavery. Yet if someone is a slave, his own will is responsible for his slavery, just as it is its will which is responsible if a people is subjugated. Hence the wrong of slavery lies at the door not simply of enslavers or conquerors but of the slaves and the conquered themselves. Slavery occurs in humanity's transition from the state of nature to genuinely ethical conditions; it occurs in a world where a wrong is still right. At that stage wrong has validity and so is necessarily in place.

58. (γ) The mode of taking possession which in itself [*für sich*] is not actual but is only *representative* of my will is to mark the thing with a *sign*, whose meaning is supposed to be that I have put my will into the thing. In its objective scope and its meaning, this mode of taking possession is very indeterminate.

Addition: To take possession by marking a thing with a sign is of all the ways of taking possession the most complete, since the sign is implicitly at work to some extent in the other ways too. When I grasp a thing or form it, this is also in the last resort a sign, a sign given to others in order to exclude them and show that I have put my will into the thing. The concept of the sign, that is to say, is that the thing does not count as the thing which it is but as what it is supposed to signify. A cockade, for instance, signifies citizenship of a state, though the colour has no connection with the nation and represents not itself but the nation. Precisely by being able to mark things with a sign and thereby to acquire them, the human being shows his mastery over things.

B. *Use of the Thing*

59. By being taken into possession, the thing acquires the predicate 'mine' and my will is related to it positively. Within this identity, the thing is equally posited as something *negative*, and my will in this situation is a *particular* will, i.e. need, inclination, and so forth. Yet my need, as the particular aspect of one will, is the positive element which finds satisfaction, and the thing, as something negative in itself, exists only for my need and is at its service.—The use of the thing is my need being externally realized through the change, destruction, and consumption of the thing. The thing thereby stands revealed as naturally selfless and so fulfils its destiny [*Bestimmung*].

The fact that property is realized and actualized only in use floats before the minds of those who look upon property as derelict and ownerless if it is not being put to any use, and who excuse its unlawful occupancy on the ground that it has not been used by its owner. But the owner's will, in accordance with which a thing is his, is the primary substantial basis of property; use is a further modification of property, secondary to that universal basis, and is only its manifestation and particular mode.

Addition: While in marking a thing with a sign I am taking possession in a universal way of the thing as such, the use of it implies a still more universal relation to the thing, because, when it is used, the thing in its particularity is not recognized but is negated by the user.* The thing is reduced to a means to the satisfaction of my need. When I and the thing meet, an identity is established and therefore one or other must lose its qualitative character. But I am alive, a being who wills and is truly affirmative; the thing on the other hand is something natural. Therefore the thing must be destroyed while I preserve myself. This, in general terms, is the prerogative and the rationality [*Vernunft*] of the organic.

60. The use of a thing by grasping it directly is in itself [*für sich*] an *individual* act of taking possession. But if my use of it is grounded on a persistent need, and if I make repeated use of a product which continually renews itself, restricting my use if necessary to safeguard that renewal, then these and other circumstances transform the immediate individual seizure of the thing into a sign, intended to indicate that I am taking it into my possession in a universal way, and thereby taking possession of the elemental or organic basis of such products, or of anything else that conditions them.

61. Since the substance of the thing which is my property is, if we take the thing by itself, its externality, i.e. its non-substantiality—in contrast with me it is not an end in itself (see § 42)—and since in my use or employment of it this externality is realized, it follows that my full use or employment of a thing is the thing in its entirety, so that if I have the full use of the thing I am its owner. Over and above the entirety of its use, there is nothing left of the thing which could be the property of another.

Addition: The relation of property to use is the same as that of substance to accident, inner to outer, force to its manifestation. Just as force exists only in manifesting itself, so arable land is arable land only in bearing crops.

Thus he who has the use of arable land* is the owner of the whole, and it is an empty abstraction to recognize still another property in the object itself.

62. My merely partial or temporary use of a thing, like my partial or temporary possession of it (a possession which itself is simply the partial or temporary possibility of using it) is therefore to be distinguished from ownership of the thing itself. If the whole and entire use of a thing were mine, while the abstract ownership was supposed to be someone else's, then the thing as mine would be penetrated through and through by my will (see §§ 52 and 61), and at the same time there would remain in the thing something impenetrable by me, namely the will, the empty will, of another. As a positive will, I would be at one and the same time objective and not objective to myself in the thing—an absolute contradiction. Ownership therefore is in essence *free and complete*.

To distinguish between the right to the entire use of a thing and ownership in the abstract is the work of the empty understanding for which the Idea—i.e. in this instance, the unity of (*a*) ownership (or even the person's will as such) and (*b*) its realization—is not the truth, but for which these two moments in their separation from one another pass as something which is true. This distinction, then, as an actual relation, is that of an empty mastery, and this might be called an 'insanity of personality' (if we may mean by 'insanity' not merely the immediate contradiction between a person's purely subjective ideas and his actuality), because 'mine' as applied to *one* object would have to mean the direct presence in it of both my individual exclusive will and the individual exclusive will of someone else.

In the *Institutes* [of Justinian], Book 2, chapter 4, we read: 'usufruct is the right of using *another's* property, of enjoying its fruits while preserving its *substance*. . . . Nevertheless, in order that properties should not become *useless* through the *permanent* cessation of usufruct, the law has *resolved* [*placuit*] that in certain circumstances the right of usufruct shall be annulled and that the land shall revert to the proper owner.'* '*Has resolved*'—as if it were in the first instance a whim or a fiat to make this proviso and thereby give some sense to that empty distinction! A property which suffered 'the *permanent* cessation of usufruct' [*proprietas semper abscendente usufructu*] would not merely be 'useless' [*inutilis*], it would no longer be a 'property' [*proprietas*] at all.

To examine other distinctions in property itself, e.g. between *res mancipi* and *nec mancipi, dominium quiritarium* and *bonitarium*,* etc., is inappropriate here since they have no bearing on any of the modifications of property determined by the concept and are merely titbits culled from the history of the right of property. The empty distinction discussed above, however, is in a way contained in the relations of *dominium directum* and *dominium utile*, in the *emphyteutic* contract,* and in the further relations involved in estates held in fief with their hereditary rents and other taxes, dues, feudal tributes, etc. in their sundry modifications, in cases where such burdens are irredeemable. But from another point of view, these relations preclude that distinction. They preclude it insofar as *dominium utile* is associated with burdens, with the result that *dominium directum* becomes at the same time a *dominium utile*.* Were there nothing in these relations except that distinction in its rigid abstraction, then in them we would not have two overlords (*domini*) in the strict sense, but an owner on the one hand and an overlord who was the overlord of nothing on the other. But on account of the burdens imposed there are two owners standing in relation to each other. Although their relation is not that of being common owners of a property, still the transition from it to common ownership is very easy—a transition which has already begun when, under *dominium directum*, the yield of the property is calculated and looked upon as the essential thing, so that the incalculable factor in the overlordship of a property, which has perhaps been regarded as the *noble* thing about property, is subordinated to the *utile* [the usefulness of property] which here is the rational factor.*

It is about a millennium-and-a-half since the freedom of personality began through the spread of Christianity to blossom and gain recognition as a universal principle from a part, though still a small part, of the human race. But it was only yesterday, we might say, that the principle of the freedom of property became recognized in some places. This example from history may serve to rebuke the impatience of opinion and to show the length of time that spirit requires for progress in its self-consciousness.

63. A thing in use is an individual thing determined quantitatively and qualitatively and related to a specific need. But its specific utility, being quantitatively determinate, is at the same time comparable

with [the specific utility of] other things of like utility. Similarly, the specific need which it satisfies is at the same time need in general and thus is comparable on its particular side with other needs, while the thing in virtue of the same considerations is comparable with things meeting other needs. This, the thing's *universality*, whose simple determinate character arises from the particularity of the thing, in such a way that it is at the same time abstracted from the thing's specific quality, is the thing's *value,* wherein its genuine substantiality becomes determinate and an object of consciousness. As full owner of the thing, I am *eo ipso* owner of its value as well as of its use.

The distinctive character of the property of a feudal tenant is that he is supposed to be the owner of the use only, not of the *value* of the thing.

Addition: The qualitative disappears here in the form of the quantitative; that is to say, when I speak of 'need', I use a term under which the most various things may be brought; they share it in common and so become commensurable. The advance of thought here therefore is from a thing's specific quality to a character which is indifferent to quality, i.e. quantity. A similar thing occurs in mathematics. The definition of a circle, an ellipse, and a parabola reveals their specific difference. But, in spite of this, the distinction between these different curves is determined purely quantitatively, i.e. in such a way that the only important thing is a purely quantitative difference which rests on their coefficients alone, on purely empirical magnitudes. In property, the quantitative character which emerges from the qualitative is *value.* Here the qualitative provides the quantity with its quantum and in consequence is as much preserved in the quantity as superseded by it. If we consider the concept of value, we must look on the thing itself only as a sign; it counts not as itself but as what it is worth. A bill of exchange, for instance, does not represent what it really is—paper; it is only a sign of another universal—value. The value of a thing may be very heterogeneous; it depends on need. But if you want to express the value of a thing not in its specificity but in the abstract, then it is money which expresses this. Money represents any and every thing, though since it does not portray the need itself but is only a sign of it, it is itself controlled by the specific value [of the commodity]. Money, as something abstract, merely expresses this value. It is possible in principle to be the owner of a thing without at the same time being the owner of its value. If a family can neither sell nor pawn its goods, it is not the owner of their value. But since this form of property is not in accordance with the concept of property, such restrictions on ownership (feudal tenure, testamentary trusts) are mostly in course of disappearing.

64. The form given to a possession and the sign it presents are themselves externalities but for the subjective presence of the will which alone constitutes their meaning and value. This presence, however, which is use, employment, or some other mode in which the will expresses itself, falls within time, and what is objective in time is the continuance of this expression of the will. Without this the thing becomes ownerless, because it has been deprived of the actuality of the will and possession. Therefore I gain or lose possession of property through *prescription* [*Verjährung*].*

Prescription, therefore, has not been introduced into right solely from an external consideration running counter to right in the strict sense, i.e. with a view to truncating the disputes and confusions which old claims would introduce into the security of property. On the contrary, prescription rests at bottom on the specific character of property as 'real',* on the fact that the will to possess something must express itself.

Public memorials are national property, or, more precisely, like works of art in general so far as their enjoyment is concerned, they have life and count as ends in themselves so long as they enshrine the spirit of remembrance and honour. If they lose this spirit, they become in this respect ownerless in the eyes of a nation and the private possession of the first comer, like e.g. the Greek and Egyptian works of art in Turkey.

The right of private property which the family of an author has in his publications dies out for a similar reason; such publications become ownerless in the sense that like public memorials, though in an opposite way,* they become public property, and their particular handling of their topic can become the private property of anyone.

Vacant land consecrated for a burial ground, or even to lie unused in perpetuity, embodies an empty absent arbitrary will. If such a will is infringed, nothing actual is infringed, and hence respect for it cannot be guaranteed.

Addition: Prescription rests on the presumption that I have ceased to regard the thing as mine. If a thing is to remain mine, my will must continue in it, and using it or keeping it safe shows this continuance. That public memorials may lose their value was frequently shown during the Reformation in the case of foundations, endowments, etc., for the Mass. The spirit of the old faith, i.e. of these foundations, had fled, and consequently they could be seized as private property.

C. *Alienation of Property*

65. The reason I can alienate my property is that it is mine only insofar as I put my will into it. Hence I may abandon (*derelinquiere*) as ownerless anything that I have or yield it to the will of another and so into his possession, provided always that the thing in question is a thing external by nature.

Addition: While prescription is an alienation with no direct expression of the will to alienate, alienation proper is an expression of my will, of my will no longer to regard the thing as mine. The whole matter may also be so viewed that alienation is seen to be a true mode of taking possession. To take possession of the thing immediately is the first moment in property. Use is likewise a way of acquiring property. The third moment then is the unity of these two, taking possession of the thing through alienation.

66. Therefore those goods, or rather substantial characteristics, which constitute my very own person and the universal essence of my self-consciousness are inalienable and my right to them is imprescriptible. Such characteristics are my personality as such, my universal freedom of will, my ethical life, my religion.

The fact that what spirit is in accordance with its concept or implicitly [*an sich*] it also should be explicitly [*für sich*] and in existence (the fact that thus spirit should be a person, be capable of holding property, should have an ethical life, a religion) is the Idea which is itself the concept of spirit. As *causa sui*, i.e. as free causality, spirit is that 'whose nature cannot be conceived except as existing'.*[37]

It is just in this concept of spirit, as that which is what it is only through itself and as infinite return into itself out of the natural immediacy of its existence, that there lies the possibility of a clash: i.e. what it is only in itself [*an sich*] it may not be for itself [*für sich*] (see § 57), and vice versa what it is only for itself may be other than what it is in itself (as with evil in the case of the will). Herein lies the possibility of the alienation of personality and its substantial being, whether this alienation occurs unconsciously or intentionally. Examples of the alienation of personality are slavery, serfdom, disqualification from holding property, encumbrances on property, and so forth. Alienation of intelligence and rationality,

[37] *Hegel's reference*: Spinoza, *Ethics*, Part 1, Definition 1.

of morality, ethical life, and religion, is exemplified in superstition, in ceding to someone else full power and authority to fix and prescribe what actions are to be done (as when an individual binds himself expressly to steal or to murder, etc., or to a course of action that may involve crime), or what duties are binding on one's conscience or what religious truth is, etc.

The right to what is in essence inalienable is imprescriptible, since the act whereby I take possession of my personality, of my substantial essence, and make myself a responsible being, capable of possessing rights and with a moral and religious life, takes away from these characteristics of mine just that externality which alone made them capable of passing into the possession of someone else. When I have thus annulled their externality, I cannot lose them through lapse of time or from any other reason drawn from my prior consent or willingness to alienate them. This return of mine into myself, whereby I make myself existent as Idea, as a person with rights and moral principles, annuls the previous position and the wrong done to my concept and my reason by others and myself when the infinite existence [*Existenz*] of self-consciousness has been treated as something external and has been allowed to be so treated. This return into myself makes clear the contradiction in supposing that I have given into another's possession my capacity for rights, my ethical life and religious feeling; for either I have given up what I myself did not possess, or I am giving up what, so soon as I possess it, exists in essence as mine alone and not as something external.

Addition: It is in the nature of the case that a slave has an absolute right to free himself and that if anyone has prostituted his ethical life by hiring himself to thieve and murder, this is a nullity in and for itself and everyone has a warrant to repudiate this contract. The same is the case if I place my religious feeling at the disposal of a priest who is my confessor, for such an inward matter a person has to settle with himself alone. A religious feeling which is partly under the control of someone else is no proper religious feeling at all. The spirit is only one [*Einer*] and should dwell in me. The unification of being-in-and-for-itself should belong to *me*.

67. Single products of my particular physical and mental [*geistig*] skill and of my power to act I can alienate to someone else and I can give him the use of my abilities for a restricted period, because, on the strength of this restriction, my abilities acquire an external relation to the totality and universality of my being. By alienating the

whole of my time, as crystallized in my work, and everything I produced, I would be making into another's property the substance of my being, my universal activity and actuality, my personality.

The relation here between myself and the exercise of my abilities is the same as that between the substance of a thing and its use (see § 61). It is only when use is restricted that a distinction between use and substance arises. So here, the use of my powers differs from my powers and therefore from myself, only insofar as it is quantitatively restricted. Force is the totality of its manifestations, substance of its accidents, the universal of its particulars.

Addition: The distinction here explained is that between a slave and a modern domestic servant or day-labourer. The Athenian slave perhaps had an easier occupation and more intellectual [*geistigere*] work than is usually the case with our servants, but he was still a slave, because the whole range of his activity had been alienated to his master.

68. What is peculiarly mine in a product of my spirit may, owing to the method whereby it is expressed, turn at once into something external like a 'thing' which *eo ipso* may then be produced by other people. The result is that by taking possession of a thing of this kind, its new owner may make his own the thoughts communicated in it or the technical invention which it contains, and it is the ability to do this which sometimes (i.e. in the case of books) constitutes the value of these things and the only purpose of possessing them. But besides this, the new owner at the same time comes into possession of the *universal methods* of so expressing himself and producing numerous other things of the same sort.

In the case of works of art, the form—the portrayal of thought in an external medium—is, regarded as a thing, so peculiarly the property of the individual who produces it that a copy of a work of art is essentially a product of the copyist's own mental [*geistig*] and technical ability. In the case of a literary work, the form in virtue of which it is an external thing is of a *mechanical* kind, and the same is true of the invention of a technical device; for in the first case the thought is presented not in a concrete image, like a statue, but in a series of distinct abstract signs, while in the second case the thought has a mechanical content throughout. The ways and means of producing things of that mechanical kind as things are commonplace accomplishments.

But between the work of art at one extreme and the routine products of craft at the other there are transitional stages which to a greater or lesser degree partake of the character of one or other of the extremes.

69. Since the owner of such a product, in owning a copy of it, is in possession of the entire use and value of that copy *qua* an individual thing, he has complete and free ownership of that copy *qua* an *individual* thing, even if the author of the book or the inventor of the technical device remains the owner of the *universal* ways and means of reproducing such products and things. *Qua* universal ways and means of expression, he has not immediately alienated them, but may reserve them to himself as means of expression which belong to him.

The substance of an author's or an inventor's right is not to be sought in the first instance in the idea that when he disposes of a single copy of his work, he arbitrarily makes it a *condition* that the power to produce facsimiles as things, a power which thereupon passes into another's possession, should not become the property of the other but should remain his own. The first question is whether such a separation between ownership of the thing and the power to produce facsimiles which is given with the thing is compatible with the concept of property, or whether it does not cancel complete and free ownership (see § 62)—so that it depends on the arbitrariness of the original producer of intellectual [*geistig*] work whether he will reserve to himself the power to reproduce, or part with this power as a thing of value, or attach no value to it at all and surrender it together with the single exemplar of his work. I reply that this power to reproduce has a special character, viz. it is that in virtue of which the thing is not merely a possession but a *resource* [*Vermögen*] (see §§ 170 ff.); the fact that it is such a resource depends on the particular way in which the thing is put to external use, a way distinct and separable from the use to which the thing is immediately destined (the resource here is not what people call a 'natural accession' [*accessio naturalis*] like young born to animals in my possession [*foetura*]). Since, then, this distinction falls into the sphere of that whose nature entails its divisibility, into the sphere of *external* use, to retain part of a thing's use while alienating another part is not to retain proprietorship without use [*utile*].*

The purely negative, though the primary, means of advancing the sciences and arts is to guarantee scientists and artists against theft and to enable them to benefit from the protection of their property, just as it was the primary and most important means of advancing trade and industry to guarantee it against highway robbery.

There is, however, a further point: the purpose of a product of the intellect is that people other than its author should understand it and make it the possession of their ideas, memory, thinking, etc. Their mode of expression, whereby in turn they make what they have *learnt* (for 'learning' means more than 'learning things by heart', 'memorizing them'; the thoughts of others can be apprehended only by thinking, and this rethinking the thoughts of others is learning too) into a 'thing' which they can alienate, very likely has some special form of its own in every case. The result is that they may regard as their own property the resource accruing from their learning and may claim for themselves the right to reproduce their learning in books of their own. Those engaged in the propagation of knowledge of all kinds, in particular those whose appointed task is teaching, have as their specific function and duty (above all in the case of the positive sciences, the doctrine of a church, jurisprudence, etc.) the repetition of well-established thoughts, taken up *ab extra* and all of them given expression already. The same is true of writings devised for teaching purposes and the spread and propagation of the sciences. Now to what extent does the new form which arises when something is expressed again and again transform the available stock of knowledge, and in particular the thoughts of others who still retain *external* property in those intellectual productions of theirs, into a special intellectual property of the individual reproducer and thereby give him or fail to give him the right to make them his *external* property as well? To what extent is such repetition of another's material in one's book a plagiarism? There is no precise principle of determination available to answer these questions, and therefore they cannot be finally settled either in principle or by law. Hence plagiarism would have to be a matter of honour and be held in check by honour.

Thus copyright legislation attains its end of securing the property rights of author and publisher only to a very restricted extent, though it does attain it within limits. The ease with which we may deliberately change something in the form of what we are expounding or invent a trifling modification in a large body of knowledge or a comprehensive theory which is another's work, and even the impossibility of sticking to the author's words in expounding something we have learnt, all lead of themselves (quite apart from the particular purposes for which such repetitions are required) to an endless multiplicity of alterations which more or less superficially stamp someone else's property as one's own. For instance, the hundreds and hundreds of compendia, selections, anthologies, etc., arithmetics, geometries, devotional tracts, etc., show how every new idea in a review or annual or encyclopedia, etc., can be forthwith repeated over and over again under the same or a different title, and yet may be claimed as something peculiarly the writer's own. The result of this may easily be that the profit promised to the author, or the projector of the original undertaking, by his work or his original idea becomes negligible or reduced for both parties or lost to all concerned.

But as for the effectiveness of honour in checking plagiarism, what has happened is that nowadays we scarcely hear the word 'plagiarism', nor are scholars accused of stealing each other's results. It may be that honour has been effective in abolishing plagiarism, or perhaps plagiarism has ceased to be dishonourable and feeling against it is a thing of the past; or possibly a trivial idea, and a change in external form, is rated so highly as originality and a product of independent thinking that the thought of plagiarism never dawns on anyone.

70. The comprehensive totality of external activity, i.e. life, is not external to personality which is itself immediate and a *this*. The disposal [*Entäußerung*] or sacrifice of life is not the existence of *this* personality but the very opposite. I have, therefore, no right whatsoever to dispose of my life. Only an ethical Idea,* in which *this* immediately individual personality is, in itself, immersed and to whose power it is actually subjected, has such a right [to dispose of my life]. Just as life as such is immediate, so death is its immediate negativity and hence must come from without, either by natural causes, or else, in the service of the Idea, by the hand of a foreigner [*von fremder Hand*].

Addition: An individual person is certainly something subordinate, and as such he must dedicate himself to the ethical whole. Hence if the state claims life, the individual must surrender it. But may a human being take his own life? Suicide may at a first glance be regarded as an act of courage, but only the false courage of tailors and servant girls. Or again it may be looked upon as a misfortune, since it is inward distraction which leads to it. But the fundamental question is: Have I a *right* to take my life? The answer will be that I, as this individual, am not master of my life, because life, as the comprehensive totality of my activity, is nothing external to personality, which itself is immediately this personality. Thus when a person is said to have a right over his life, the words are a contradiction, because they mean that a person has a right over himself. But he has no such right, since he does not stand over himself and he cannot pass judgement on himself. When Hercules destroyed himself by fire and when Brutus fell on his sword,* this was the conduct of a hero against his personality. But as for the simple *right* to suicide, this may be denied even to heroes.

Transition from Property to Contract

71. Existence [*Dasein*] as determinate being is in essence being for another (see Remark to § 48). One aspect of property is that it is an existent as an external thing, and in this respect property exists for other external things and is connected with their necessity and contingency. But it is also the existence of the *will*, and from this point of view the 'other' for which it exists can only be the will of another person. This relation of will to will is the true and proper ground in which freedom has existence.—The sphere of *contract* is made up of this mediation whereby I hold property not merely by means of a thing and my subjective will, but by means of another person's will as well and so hold it in virtue of my participation in a common will.

Reason makes it just as necessary for human beings to enter into contractual relationships—gift, exchange, trade, etc.—as to possess property (see Remark to § 45). All they are conscious of is that they are led to make contracts by need in general, by benevolence, advantage, etc.; implicitly [*an sich*], however, they are led to do this by reason, i.e. by the Idea of the real existence of free personality, 'real' [*reell*] here meaning 'present in the will alone'.

Contract presupposes that the parties entering it *recognize* each other as persons and property owners. It is a relationship at the level of objective spirit, and so contains and presupposes from the start the moment of recognition (compare § 35 and Remark to § 57).

Addition: In a contract I hold property on the strength of a common will; that is to say, it is the interest of reason that the subjective will should become universal and raise itself to this degree of actualization. Thus in contract my will still has the character of being *this* will, though it has it in community with another will. The universal will, however, still appears here only in the form and shape of community [*Gemeinsamkeit*].

SUB–SECTION 2

CONTRACT

72. Contract brings into existence the property whose external side, its side as an existent, is no longer a mere 'thing' but contains the moment of a will (and consequently the will of a second person). Contract is the process in which there is revealed and mediated the contradiction that I *am* and *remain* the independent owner of something from which I exclude the will of another only insofar as in identifying my will with the will of another I *cease* to be an owner.

73. I have power to alienate a property as an external thing (see § 65); but more than this, the concept *compels* me to alienate it *qua* property in order that thereby my will may become objective to me as determinately existent [*daseiend*]. In this situation, however, my will as alienated is at the same time *another's* will.* Consequently this situation wherein this necessity of the concept is realized is the unity of different wills and so a unity in which both surrender their difference and their own special character. Yet this identity of their wills implies also (at this stage) that each will still is and remains *not* identical with the other but retains from its own point of view a special character of its own.

74. This contractual relationship, therefore, is the means whereby one identical will persists within the absolute difference between independent property-owners. It implies that each, in accordance with the common will of both, *ceases* to be an owner and yet *remains* and *becomes* one. It is the mediation of the will to give up a property, an individual property, and the will to take up another, i.e. another belonging to someone else; and this mediation takes place when the

two wills are associated in an identity in the sense that one of them comes to its decision only in the presence of the other.

75. The two contracting parties are related to each other as *immediate* self-subsistent persons. Therefore (α) contract arises from the *arbitrary will*. (β) The identical will which is brought into existence by the contract is only one *posited* by the parties, and so is only a will shared in common and not a will that is universal in and for itself. (γ) The object about which a contract is made is an individual external thing, since it is only things of that kind which the parties' purely arbitrary will has it in its power to alienate (see §§ 65 ff.).

To subsume *marriage* under the concept of contract is thus quite impossible; this subsumption—though shameful is the only word for it—is propounded in Kant's *Doctrine of Right*.[38] It is equally far from the truth to ground the nature of the *state* on the contractual relation, whether the state is supposed to be a contract of all with all, or of all with the monarch and the government.

The intrusion of this contractual relation, and relationships concerning private property generally, into the relation between the individual and the state has been productive of the greatest confusion in both constitutional law and actuality. Just as at one time* political rights and duties were considered and maintained to be an immediate private property of particular individuals, something contrasted with the right of the monarch and the state, so also in more recent times the rights of the monarch and the state have been regarded as the subjects of a contract and as grounded in contract, as something embodying merely a common will and resulting from the arbitrariness of parties united into a state. However different these two points of view may be, they have this in common, that they have transferred the characteristics of private property into a sphere of a quite different and higher nature. (See below [esp. §§ 258, 278, 294], ethical life and the state.)

Addition: It has recently become very popular to regard the state as a contract of all with all. Everyone makes a contract with the monarch, so the argument runs, and he again with his subjects. This point of view arises from thinking superficially only of *one* unity of different wills. In contract, however, there are two identical wills who are both persons and wish to remain property-owners. Thus contract springs from a person's arbitrary

---

[38] See Kant, *Doctrine of Right*, §§ 24–7 [Gregor trans., 96–8].

will, an origin which marriage too has in common with contract. But the case is quite different with the state; it does not lie with an individual's arbitrary will to separate himself from the state, because we are already citizens of the state by birth. The rational end of humanity is life in the state, and if there is no state there, reason at once demands that one be founded. Permission to enter a state or leave it must be given by the state; this then is not a matter which depends on an individual's arbitrary will and therefore the state does not rest on contract, for contract presupposes arbitrariness. It is false to maintain that the foundation of the state is dependent on the arbitrary will of all. On the contrary, it is absolutely necessary for every individual to be a citizen of a state. The great advance of the state in modern times is that it remains an end in and for itself; it is no longer open to individuals, as it was in the Middle Ages, to make private stipulations in connection with it.

76. Contract is *formal* when the double consent whereby the common will is brought into existence is apportioned between the two contracting parties so that one of them has the negative moment—the alienation of a thing—and the other the positive moment—the appropriation of the thing. Such a contract is *gift*. But contract may be called *real* [*reell*] when each of the two contracting wills is the totality of these mediating moments and therefore in such a contract becomes a property owner and remains so. This is a contract of *exchange*.

Addition: Contract implies two consenting parties and two things. That is to say, in a contract my purpose is both to acquire property and to surrender it. Contract is real when the action of both parties is complete, i.e. when both surrender and both acquire property, and when both remain property-owners even in the act of surrender. Contract is formal where only one of the parties acquires property or surrenders it.

77. Since in real contract each party retains the same property with which he enters the contract and which at the same time he surrenders, what remains identical throughout as the intrinsic [*an sich seiend*] property in the contract is distinct from the external things whose owners change when the exchange is made. What remains identical is the *value*, in respect of which the objects of the contract are equal to one another whatever the qualitative external differences of the things exchanged. Value is their *universal* aspect (see § 63).

The legal provision that excessive damage (*laesio enormis*)* annuls the obligation arising out of the making of a contract has its source, therefore, in the concept of contract, particularly in this moment of it, that the contracting party by alienating his property still remains a property owner and, more precisely, an owner of the quantitative equivalent of what he alienates. But the damage is not merely excessive (as it is taken to be if it exceeds one-half of the value) but infinite, if someone has entered on a contract or made a stipulation of any sort for the alienation of *inalienable* goods (see § 66).

A *stipulation*, moreover, differs from a contract, first, in its *content*, because it signifies only some single part or moment of the whole contract, and secondly, because it is the *form* in which the contract is settled (a point on which more will be said later [§ 217]). So far as its content is concerned, it comprises only the formal determination of the contract, i.e. the willingness of one party to give something and the willingness of the other to accept it; for this reason, the stipulation has been enumerated amongst so-called 'unilateral' contracts. The distinction between unilateral and bilateral contracts, and distinctions in Roman law between other types of contract,* are sometimes superficial juxtapositions made from an isolated and often external point of view such as that of the different types of contractual form; or sometimes they confuse determinations intrinsic to contract itself with others which only arise later in connection with the administration of justice (*actiones*) and the legal processes giving effect to positive laws, and which are often derived from quite external circumstances and contravene the concept of right.

78. The distinction between property and possession, the substantial and external aspects of ownership (see § 45), appears in the sphere of contract as the distinction between a common will and its actualization, or between a *covenant* and its *performance*. Once made, a covenant taken by itself in distinction from its performance is something held before the mind [*ein Vorgestelltes*], something therefore to which a particular determinate existence must be given in accordance with the distinctive mode of giving determinate existence to ideas through signs.[39] This is done, therefore, by expressing the *stipulation* in formalities such as gestures and other symbolic actions, particularly by declaring it with precision in

---

[39] *Hegel's reference: Encyclopaedia*, §§ 379 ff. [3rd edn. §§ 458 ff.].

language, the most worthy medium for the expression of intellectual representations.

The stipulation accordingly is the form given to the content of a contract, i.e. to what is agreed in it, whereby this content attains its determinate existence as something as yet only *represented*. But this representation is only a form, and does not mean that the content [itself] is still something subjective, a desire or a wish for so and so. On the contrary, the content is what has finally been decided by the will concerning such matters.

Addition: Just as in the theory of property we had the distinction between ownership and possession, between the substance of the matter and its purely external side, so here in contract we have the difference between a common will—covenant—and a particular will—performance. It lies in the nature of contract that it should be an expression of both the common and the particular will of the parties, because in it will is related to will. The covenant, made manifest in a sign, and its performance are quite distinct from each other amongst civilized peoples, though amongst savages they may coincide. In the forests of Ceylon there is a tribe of traders who put down their property and wait quietly until others come to put theirs down opposite. Here there is no difference between the dumb declaration of will and the performance of what is willed.

79. In contract it is the will, and therefore the *substance* of what is right in contract, that the stipulation enshrines. In contrast with this substance, the possession which is still being retained while the contract remains unfulfilled is in itself only something external, dependent for its determination on the will alone. By making the stipulation, I have given up a property and withdrawn my particular arbitrary will from it, and it has *eo ipso* become the property of another. If, therefore, I agree to stipulated terms, I am immediately bound by right to carry them out.

The difference between a mere promise and a contract lies in the fact that a promise is a statement that I will give or do or perform something in the *future*, and a promise still remains a subjective volition which because it is subjective I can still alter. A stipulation in a contract, on the other hand, is itself already the *existence* of the will's decision in the sense that by making the stipulation I have alienated my property, it has *now* ceased to be mine, and I already recognize it as the property of another. The distinction in Roman law between *pactum* and *contractus* is a bad one.*

Fichte at one time[40] maintained that my obligation to keep a contract begins only when the other party starts fulfilling his side of it; his reason was that up to that point I am uncertain whether the other party's declarations are seriously meant. In that case it would follow that the obligation to keep a contract before it was carried out would only be a *moral* one, not an obligation by rights.—But the expression of the stipulation is not simply a declaration of a general character; it embodies a common will which has been brought into existence and which has superseded the arbitrary and alterable dispositions of the parties. The question therefore is not whether the other party could have had different inner intentions when the contract was made or afterwards, but whether he had any right to have them. Even if the other party begins to fulfil his side of the contract, it is equally open to me to do wrong if I like. The nullity of Fichte's view is also shown by the fact that it would base contractual rights on the bad infinite, i.e. on the progress *ad infinitum** involved in the infinite divisibility of time, matter, action, etc. The *existence* of the will in formal gestures or in explicit and precise language is already the complete existence of the will as an intelligent entity, and the performance of the covenant so embodied is only the selfless [*selbstlos*] consequence.

It is true that in positive right there are so-called 'real' contracts [*Real-Kontrakte*] as distinguished from 'consensual' contracts, in the sense that the former are looked upon as fully valid only when the actual performance (*res*, *traditio rei*) of the undertaking supervenes upon the willingness to perform it; but this has nothing to do with the thing at issue. For one thing, these 'real' contracts cover particular cases where it is only this delivery by the other party which puts me in a position to fulfil my side of the bargain, and where my obligation to do my part relates only to the thing after it has come into my hands, as happens for instance in loans, contracts of lease, or deposits. (The same may also be the case in other contracts.) But this is a matter which concerns not the nature of the relation of the stipulation to performance but only the manner of performance.—For another thing, it is always open

[40] See J. G. Fichte, *An Attempt to Correct the Public's Judgements Concerning the French Revolution* [*Beitrag zur Berichtigung der Urteile des Publicums über die französische Revolution*], in *Fichtes Werke*, ed. I. H. Fichte (Berlin, 1845), vi. 111 ff.

to the parties at their discretion to stipulate in any contract that
the obligation of one party to perform his side shall not lie in the
making of the contract itself as such, but shall arise only from the
performance by the other party of his side.

80. The classification of contracts and an intelligent treatment of
their various species once classified is not here to be derived from
external circumstances but from distinctions lying in the very nature
of contract. These distinctions are those between formal and real
[*reell*] contracts,* between ownership and possession and use,
between value and specific thing, and they yield contracts of the following sorts (the classification given here agrees on the whole with
that of Kant's *Metaphysical First Principles of the Doctrine of Right*,
120 ff.,[41] and one would have expected that the usual humdrum
classification of contracts as real [*Real-*] and consensual, nominate
and innominate,* etc., would have been long since abandoned in
favour of this rational classification):

A. *Gift*.

  (1) Gift of a thing—gift properly so called.

  (2) Loan [*Leihen*] of a thing—i.e. the gift of a portion of it or of
restricted use and enjoyment of it; here the lender remains the owner
of the thing (*mutuum* and *commodatum* without payment of interest).*
Here the thing lent is either a specific thing, or, even though it be
something specific, it may still be looked on as universal, or it may be
a thing which counts (like money) as a thing universal in itself.

  (3) Gift of service of any sort, e.g. the mere safe-keeping of a
property (*depositum*). The gift of a thing on the special condition
that its recipient shall not become its owner until the date of the
donor's death, i.e. the date at which he ceases in any case to be an
owner of property, is *testamentary* disposition; this is not contained
in the concept of contract but presupposes civil society and positive
legislation.[42]

B. *Exchange*.

  (1) Exchange as such:

  (α) exchange of a thing pure and simple, i.e. exchange of one
specific thing for another of the same kind;

---

[41] See Kant, *Doctrine of Right*, § 31 [Gregor trans., 102–3].
[42] See *PR* §§ 179 ff.

(β) purchase or sale (*emtio, venditio*); exchange of a specific thing for one characterized as universal, one which counts as value alone and which lacks the other specific determination of utility—i.e. for money.

(2) Letting (*locatio, conductio*); alienation of the temporary use of a property in return for rent:

(α) letting of a specific thing—letting in the proper sense; or

(β) letting of a universal thing, so that the lessor remains only the owner of this universal, or in other words of the value—loan [*Anleihe*] (*mutuum*, or even *commodatum* since rent is charged).*

The additional empirical characteristics of the thing (which may be, e.g., a flat, furniture, a house, *res fungibilis* or *non fungibilis*, etc.) entail (as in A.2 above) other particular though unimportant subdivisions.

(3) Contract for wages (*locatio operae*)—alienation of my productive capacity or my services so far, that is, as these are alienable, the alienation being restricted in time or in some other way (see § 67).

Akin to this are mandates and other contracts whose fulfilment depends on character, good faith, or superior gifts, and where an incommensurability arises between the services rendered and a value in terms of cash. (In such cases the cash payment is called not 'wages' but an 'honorarium'.)

C. *Completion of a contract (cautio) through giving a pledge.*

In the contracts whereby I part with the *use* of a thing, I am no longer in possession of the thing though I am still its owner, as for example when I let a house. Further, in gifts or contracts for exchange or purchase, I may have become the owner of a thing without as yet being in possession of it, and the same cleavage between ownership and possession arises in respect of the implementing of any undertaking which is not completed in one go. Now what the *pledge* effects is that in the one case I remain, and in the other case I am put, in actual possession of the *value* as that which is still or has already become my property, without in either case being in possession of the specific thing which I am handing over or which is to be mine. The pledge is a specific thing but one which is my property only to the extent of the value of the property which I have handed over into another's possession or which is due to me; its specific character as a thing and any excess value it may have still belong to the person who gave the pledge. Giving a pledge, therefore, is not itself a contract but only a stipulation (see [Remark to] § 77), i.e. it is the moment which brings a contract to completion so far as the possession of the property is concerned.* Mortgage and surety are particular forms of pledge.

Addition: In contract we drew the distinction between the covenant or stipulation (which made the property mine though it did not give me possession) and performance (which first gave me possession). Now if I am already the out-and-out owner of the property, the object of the pledge is to put me simultaneously in possession of the value of the property and thereby to guarantee the covenant's performance at the very time the covenant is made. Surety is a particular kind of pledge whereby someone gives his promise or pledges his credit as a guarantee for my performance. Here a person fulfils the function which is fulfilled by a mere thing in the case of a pledge proper.

81. In any relation of *immediate* persons to one another, their wills, while in themselves [*an sich*] identical and in contract posited by them as common, are yet particular. Because they are *immediate* persons, it is a matter of chance whether or not their particular wills actually correspond with the will in itself, although it is only through the former that the latter has its real existence. If the particular will is for itself [*für sich*] at variance with the universal, it assumes a way of looking at things and a volition that are capricious and fortuitous and comes on the scene in opposition to that which is right in itself [*an sich Recht*]. This is *wrong*.

The transition to wrong is made by the logical higher necessity that the moments of the concept—here right in itself or the will as universal, and right in its existence [*Existenz*], which is just the particularity of the will—should be posited as explicitly different. This happens when the concept is *realized abstractly*. But this particularity of the will for itself is arbitrariness and contingency, and in contract I have surrendered these only as arbitrariness in the case of an individual thing and not as the arbitrariness and contingency of the will itself.

Addition: In contract we had the relation of two wills as a common will. But this identical will is only relatively universal, posited as universal, and so is still opposed to the particular will. In contract, to be sure, making a covenant entails the right to require its performance. But this performance is dependent again on the particular will which *qua* particular may act in contravention of right in itself. At this point then the negation, which was already present at the start in the will in itself, comes into view, and this negation is just what wrong is. The overall progression entails purifying the will of its immediacy and thereby summoning from the common will particularity which then comes on the scene as opposed to the common will. In contract the parties still retain their particular wills; contract therefore is not yet beyond the stage of arbitrariness, with the result that it remains at the mercy of wrong.

SUB-SECTION 3
WRONG

82. In contract right in itself is present as something *posited*, while its inner universality is there as something common in the arbitrariness and particular will of the parties. This *appearance* [*Erscheinung*] of right, in which right and its essential existence, the particular will, correspond immediately, i.e. fortuitously, proceeds in wrong to become a *semblance* [*Schein*],* an opposition between right in itself and the particular will as that in which right becomes a particular right. But the truth of this semblance is its nullity and the fact that right reasserts itself by negating this negation of itself. In this process right is mediated by returning into itself out of the negation of itself; it thereby makes itself *actual* and *valid*, while at the start it was only in itself [*an sich*] and something immediate.

Addition: Right in itself, the universal will, is essentially determined through the particular will, and so is in relation with something which is inessential. This is the relation of essence to its appearance. Even if the appearance corresponds with the essence, still, looked at from another point of view, it fails to correspond with it, since appearance is the stage of contingency, essence related to the inessential. In wrong, however, appearance proceeds to become a semblance. A semblance is a determinate existence inadequate to the essence, the empty detachment and positedness [*Gesetztsein*] of the essence, so that in both essence and semblance the distinction of the one from the other is present as sheer difference.

The semblance, therefore, is the untrue which disappears in claiming to be for itself; and in the course of the semblance's disappearance the essence reveals itself as essence, i.e. as the power over semblance. The essence has negated its own negation and so is corroborated. Wrong is a semblance of this kind, and, when it disappears, right acquires the character of something fixed and valid. What is here called the essence is just right in itself, and in contrast with it the particular will annuls itself as untrue. Hitherto the being of right has been immediate only, but now it becomes *actual* because it returns out of its negation. The actual is what is effective; in its otherness it still preserves itself, while anything immediate remains susceptible of negation.

83. When right is something *particular* and therefore manifold in contrast with its intrinsic [*an sich seiend*] universality and simplicity, it acquires the form of a *semblance*. (*a*) This semblance of right is in itself or immediate—non-malicious wrong or a civil offence; (*b*) right is posited as a semblance by the subject—fraud; (*c*) it is posited by the subject as altogether null and void—crime.

Addition: Wrong is thus the semblance of the essence that posits itself as self-subsistent. If the semblance is only in itself or implicit [*an sich*] and not also for itself or explicit [*für sich*], i.e. if the wrong passes in my eyes as right, the wrong is non-malicious. The semblance here is a semblance from the point of view of right but not from my point of view.

The second type of wrong is fraud. Here the wrong is not a semblance from the point of view of right in itself. The position is that I create a semblance to deceive the other party. In fraud right is in my eyes only a semblance. In the first case, the wrong was a semblance from the point of view of right. In the second case, from my own point of view, from the point of view of wrong, right is only a semblance.

Finally, the third type of wrong is crime. This is wrong both in itself and for me. But here I will the wrong and make no use of even the semblance of right. I do not intend the other against whom the crime is committed to regard as right what is wrong in and for itself. The distinction between crime and fraud is that in the latter the form of acting still implies a recognition of right, and this is just what is lacking in crime.

A. *Non-malicious Wrong*

84. Taking possession (see § 54) and contract—both for themselves and in their particular species—are in the first instance different expressions and consequences of my willing pure and

simple; but since the will is the inherently universal, they are, through their recognition by others, grounds of title [*Rechtsgründe*]. Such grounds are external to one another and multiple, and this implies that different persons may have them in relation to one and the same thing. Each person may look upon the thing as his property on the strength of the particular ground on which he bases his title. It is in this way that one person's right may clash with another's.

85. This clash which arises when a thing has been claimed on some ground, and which comprises the sphere of civil suits, entails the *recognition* of right as the universal and decisive factor, so that it is common ground that the thing in dispute should belong to the party who has the right to it. The suit is concerned only with the subsumption of the thing under the property of one or other of the parties—a straightforward negative judgement, where, in the predicate 'mine', only the particular is negated.*

86. The recognition of right by the parties is bound up with their opposed particular interests and points of view. In opposition to this semblance of right, yet within this semblance itself (see the preceding Paragraph), right in itself arises as something kept in view [*vorgestellt*] and demanded by the parties. But at first it arises only as an 'ought-to-be' because the will is not yet present here as a will so freed from the immediacy of interest as, despite its particularity, to have the universal will for its aim; nor is it yet at this point determined as a recognized actuality of such a sort that in face of it the parties would have to renounce their particular interest and point of view.

Addition: There is a determinate ground for what is right in itself, and the wrong which I hold to be right I also defend on some ground or other. The nature of the finite and particular is to allow room for contingencies. Thus here collisions must occur, because here we are on the level of the finite. This first type of wrongdoing negates the particular will only, while universal right is respected. Consequently this is the most venial of the types of wrongdoing. If I say 'a rose is not red', I still recognize that it has a colour. Hence I do not deny the genus; all that I negate is the particular colour, red. Similarly, right is recognized here. Each of the parties wills what is right, and each is supposed to receive only what is right. The wrong of each consists simply in his holding that what he wants is right.

B. *Fraud*

87. Right in itself, as distinct from right as particular and as determinately existent, is determined as what is *demanded*, as the essential
thing; but as such, it is still *only* something demanded and from that
point of view something merely subjective, and so inessential—a mere
semblance. When the universal is *reduced* to a mere semblance by the
particular will, as happens initially when the universal is reduced, in
contract, to a merely external community of wills, we have *fraud*.

Addition: At this second level of wrongdoing, the particular will is
respected, but universal right is not. In fraud, the particular will is not
infringed, because the party defrauded is given to believe that he is receiving his right. Thus the right which he demands is posited as something
subjective, as a mere semblance, and it is this which constitutes fraud.

88. In contract I acquire a property for the sake of its particular
characteristics and at the same time in light of the inner universality
which it possesses partly through its *value* and partly through having
been the *property* of another. If the other so wills, a false semblance
may be given to the thing I acquire, so that the contract is right
enough so far as it is an exchange, voluntary on both sides, of *this*
thing in its immediacy and uniqueness, but still the aspect of intrinsic [*an sich seiend*] universality is lacking. (Here we have an infinite
judgement expressed positively or as a tautology.)* [43]

89. Here again all there is, is the *demand** that the objective or universal element—as opposed to the acceptance of the thing simply as
this thing and to the mere opinions and arbitrariness of the will—be
recognizable as *value* and have validity as right, and that the subjective
arbitrary will, opposing itself to right, be superseded [*aufgehoben*].

Addition: In the case of civil and non-malicious wrong no punishment is
imposed, because in such cases the wrongdoer has willed nothing in opposition to right. In the case of fraud, on the other hand, punishments come
in, because here it is a matter of the infringement of right.

C. *Coercion and Crime*

90. In owning property I place my will in an external thing, and
this implies that my will, just by being thus reflected in the object,

---

[43] *Hegel's reference*: Encyclopaedia, § 121 [3rd edn. § 173].

may be seized in it and brought under compulsion. It may simply be subjected in the thing to force as such, or it may be constrained to sacrifice something or to do some action as a condition of retaining one or other of its possessions or embodiments—it may be *coerced*.

Addition: Wrong in the full sense of the word is crime, where there is no respect either for right in itself or for what seems right to me, where, then, both sides, the objective and the subjective, are infringed.

91. As a living thing a human being may be coerced, i.e. his body or anything else external about him may be brought under the power of others; but the free will cannot be coerced at all (see § 5), except in so far as *it fails to withdraw itself out of the external object* in which it is held fast, or rather out of its idea of that object (see § 7). Only the will which *allows* itself to be *coerced* can in any way be coerced.

92. Since it is only insofar as the will has an existence in something determinate that it is Idea or actually free, and since the existent in which it has laid itself is freedom in being [*Sein der Freiheit*], it follows that force or coercion is in its concept immediately self-destructive because it is an expression of a will which annuls the expression or determinate existence of a will. Hence force or coercion, taken abstractly, is wrong.

93. That coercion is in its concept self-destructive is exhibited in reality by the fact that *coercion is annulled by coercion*; coercion is thus shown to be not only right under certain conditions but necessary, i.e. as a *second* act of coercion which is the annulment of one that has preceded.

Breaking a contract by failing to carry out its stipulated terms, or neglect of duty rightly owed to family or state, or action in defiance of that duty, is the first act of coercion or at least force, in that it involves depriving another of his property or evading a service due to him.

Coercion by a schoolmaster, or coercion directed against savagery and brutishness, seems at first sight to be an initial act of coercion, not a second following on one that has preceded. But the merely natural will is *in itself* a force against the intrinsic [*an sich seiend*] Idea of freedom which must be protected against such an uncivilized will and be made to prevail in it. Either an ethical institution has already been established in family or government, and the natural will is a mere display of force against it; or else there is only a state of nature, a state of affairs where mere force prevails and against which the Idea establishes a *right of heroes*.

Addition: Once the state has been founded, there can no longer be any heroes. They come on the scene only in uncivilized conditions. Their aim is right, necessary, and political, and this they pursue as their own affair. The heroes who founded states, introduced marriage and agriculture, did not do this as their recognized right, and their conduct still has the appearance of being their particular will. But as the higher right of the Idea against nature, this heroic coercion is a rightful coercion. Mere goodness can achieve little against the power of nature.

94. Abstract right is a *right to coerce*, because the wrong which transgresses it is an exercise of force against the existence of my freedom in an external thing. The maintenance of this existence against the exercise of force therefore itself takes the form of an external act and an exercise of force annulling the force originally brought against it.

To define abstract right, or right in the strict sense, at the very outset as a right in the name of which coercion may be used, is to interpret it in light of a consequence that arises only through the indirect route of wrong.

Addition: Special attention must be paid at this point to the difference between the right and the moral. In morality, i.e. when I am reflected into myself, there is also a duality, because the good is my aim and I ought to determine myself by reference to that Idea. The good is given existence in my decision and I actualize the good in myself. But this existence is purely inward and therefore cannot be coerced. The laws of the state therefore cannot possibly seek to reach as far as a person's disposition, because, in the moral sphere, I exist for myself alone, and force in that context is meaningless.

95. The initial act of coercion as an exercise of force by the free agent, an exercise of force which infringes the existence of freedom in its concrete sense, infringes right as right, is *crime*—a negatively infinite judgement in its full sense,*[44] whereby not only the particular (i.e. the subsumption of a thing under my will—see § 85) is negated, but also the universality and infinity in the predicate 'mine' (i.e. my capacity for rights). Here the negation does not come about through

---

[44] *Hegel's reference*: See my *Science of Logic*, ii. 99 [Miller trans., 641–3].

the mediation of my opinion (as it does in fraud—see § 88) but in defiance of it. This is the sphere of criminal law [*peinliches Recht*].

Right, the infringement of which is crime, has so far only those formations which we have seen in the preceding Paragraphs; hence crime also, to begin with, has its more precise significance in relation to these specific rights. But the substance of these forms is the universal which remains the same throughout its further development and formation, and consequently its infringement, crime, also remains the same and accords with its concept. Thus the specific characteristic of crime [in general] to be noticed in the next Paragraph is characteristic also of the particular, more determinate, content in e.g. perjury, treason, counterfeiting, forgery, etc.

96. It is only the existent [*daseiend*] will that can suffer injury. In becoming existent in something, however, the will enters the sphere of quantitative extension and qualitative determinations, and hence varies accordingly. For this reason, it makes a difference to the objective aspect of crime whether the will so objectified and its specific quality is injured throughout its entire extent, and so in the infinity which is equivalent to its concept (as in murder, slavery, enforced religious observance, etc.), or whether it is injured only in a single part or in one of its qualitative determinations, and if so, in which of these.

The Stoic view* that there is only one virtue and one vice, the laws of Draco* which prescribe death as a punishment for every offence, the crude formal code of honour which takes any insult as an offence against the infinity of personality, all have this in common, that they go no further than the abstract thought of the free will and personality and fail to apprehend it in the concrete and determinate existence which it must possess as Idea.

The distinction between robbery and theft is qualitative; when I am robbed, personal violence is done to me and I am injured in my character as consciousness existing here and now and so as this subjective infinity.

Many qualitative characteristics of crime, e.g. its danger to public safety,[45] have their basis in more concrete circumstances, but they are often apprehended only indirectly through their consequences

---

[45] See *PR* § 218 and Remark to *PR* § 319.

rather than through the concept of the thing. Thus the crime which taken by itself is the more dangerous in its immediate character is an injury of a more serious type in its range or its quality.

The subjective, *moral* quality of crime rests on the higher distinction implied in the question how far an event or deed is at all an action, and concerns the subjective character of the action itself, on which see below [§§ 113 ff.].

Addition: How any given crime is to be punished cannot be settled by mere thinking; positive determinations are necessary. But with the advance of education, opinions about crime become less harsh, and today a criminal is not so severely punished as he was a hundred years ago. It is not exactly crimes or punishments which change but the relation between them.

97. The infringement of right as right is something that happens and has positive existence in the external world, though inherently it is null and void. The *manifestation* of its nullity is that the annihilation of the infringement also comes into existence. This is right actualized, the necessity of right mediating itself with itself by annulling what has infringed it.

Addition: A crime alters something in some way, and the thing has its existence in this alteration. Yet this existence is a self-contradiction and to that extent is inherently a nullity. The nullity is that the crime has cancelled [*aufgehoben*] right as such. For right, as something absolute, cannot be cancelled, and so committing a crime is in itself a nullity and this nullity is the essence of what a crime effects. A nullity, however, must reveal itself to be such, i.e. manifest itself as vulnerable. A crime, as an act, is not something positive, not a first thing, on which punishment would supervene as a negation. It is something negative, so that its punishment is only a negation of the negation. Right in its actuality, then, annuls what infringes it and therein displays its validity and proves itself to be a necessary, mediated, existence.

98. Insofar as the infringement of right is only an injury to a possession or to something which exists externally, it is something bad, or damage, done to some kind of property or resource. The annulling of the infringement, so far as the infringement is productive of damage, is the satisfaction given in a civil suit, i.e. *compensation* for the wrong done, so far as any such compensation can be found.

Concerning such satisfaction, the universal character of the damage, i.e. its *value*, must here again take the place of its specific qualitative character in cases where the damage done amounts to destruction and is quite irreparable.

99. But the injury which has befallen the will *in itself* (and this means the will of the *injuring* party as well as that of the injured and everyone else) has as little positive existence in this will as such as it has in the mere state of affairs which it produces. For itself this will in itself (i.e. right or law in itself) is rather that which has no external existence and which for that reason cannot be injured. Equally, the injury from the point of view of the particular will of the injured party and of onlookers is only something negative. The *positive* existence of the injury consists solely in the *particular will of the criminal.** Hence to injure this particular will as a determinately existent will is to annul the crime, *which otherwise would be held valid*, and to restore right.

The theory of punishment is one of the topics which have come off worst in the recent study of the positive science of right, because in this theory the understanding is insufficient; the essence of the matter depends on the concept.

If crime and its annulment [*Aufhebung*] (which will be further determined as punishment [see § 220]) are treated as if they were unqualified evils [*Übel*], it must, of course, seem quite unreasonable to will an evil *merely because another evil is there already*.[46] To give punishment this superficial character of an evil is, amongst the various theories of punishment, the fundamental presupposition of those which regard it as a preventive measure, a deterrent, a threat, as reformative, etc., and what on these theories is supposed to result from punishment is characterized equally superficially as a good. But it is not merely a question of an evil or of this, that, or the other good; the precise point at issue is *wrong* and the righting of it, that is, *justice* [*Gerechtigkeit*]. If you adopt that superficial attitude to punishment, you brush aside the objective consideration of justice, which is the primary and fundamental point of view in relation to crime; and the natural consequence is that you take as essential the moral point of view, i.e. the subjective aspect of crime, intermingled with trivial psychological ideas

---

[46] *Hegel's reference*: [E. F.] Klein, *Principles of Common German and Prussian Penal Law** [*Grundsätze des gemeinen deutschen und preußischen peinlichen Rechts*] (Halle, 1796), §§ 9 ff.

of stimuli, impulses too strong for reason, and psychological factors coercing and working on our ideas (as if freedom were not equally capable of thrusting an idea aside and reducing it to something contingent). The various considerations which are relevant to punishment as a phenomenon and to the bearing it has on the particular consciousness, and which concern its effects (deterrent, reformative, etc.) on the imagination, are an essential topic for examination in their place, especially in connection with the modality of punishment, but all these considerations presuppose as their foundation the fact that punishment is in and for itself *just*. In discussing this matter the only important things are, first, that crime is to be annulled, not because it is the producing of an evil, but because it is an infringement of right as right, and secondly, the question of what that positive existence is which crime possesses and which must be annulled; it is this existence which is the real evil to be removed, and the essential point is the question of where it lies. So long as the concepts here at issue are not clearly apprehended, confusion must continue to reign in the theory of punishment.

Addition: Feuerbach bases his theory of punishment on threat* and thinks that if anyone commits a crime despite the threat, punishment must follow because the criminal was aware of it beforehand. But what about the justification of the threat? A threat presupposes that a person is not free, and its aim is to coerce him by the idea of an evil. But right and justice must have their seat in freedom and the will, not in the lack of freedom on which a threat turns. To base a justification of punishment on threat is to liken it to the act of someone who lifts a stick to a dog. It is to treat a human being like a dog instead of with the freedom and respect due to him as a human being. But a threat, which may ultimately rouse a person to demonstrate his freedom in spite of it, discards justice altogether.—Coercion by psychological factors can concern only differences of quantity and quality in crime, not the nature of crime itself, and therefore any legal codes that may be products of this doctrine lack their proper foundation.

100. The injury which falls on the criminal is not merely just *in itself*—as just, it is *eo ipso* his will as it is in itself, an existence of his freedom, *his* right—but it is also a right *posited in the criminal himself*, i.e. in his objectively existent will, in his action. For his action is the action of a rational being and this implies that it is something universal and that by doing it the criminal has set up a law which he has explicitly recognized in his action and under which in consequence he should be subsumed as under his right.

As is well known, Beccaria* denied to the state the right of inflicting capital punishment. His reason was that it could not be presumed that the readiness of individuals to allow themselves to be executed was included in the social contract, and that in fact the contrary would have to be assumed. But the state is not a contract at all (see [Remark to] § 75) nor is its fundamental essence the unconditional protection and guarantee of the life and property of individuals as such. On the contrary, it is that higher entity which even lays claim to this very life and property and demands its sacrifice. Further, what is involved in the action of the criminal is not only the *concept* of crime—the rational aspect present in crime as such whether the individual wills it or not, the aspect which the state has to vindicate—but also the formal rationality of the individual's *volition*. Since that is so, punishment is regarded as containing the criminal's right, and hence by being punished he is honoured as a rational being. He does not receive this due of honour unless the concept and measure of his punishment are derived from his own act. Still less does he receive it if he is treated either as a harmful animal who has to be made harmless, or with a view to deterring and reforming him.

Furthermore, apart from these considerations, the form in which justice exists in the state, namely *punishment*, is not its only form, nor is the state the pre-condition of justice in itself.

Addition: Beccaria's requirement that people should give their consent to being punished is right enough, but the criminal gives his consent already by his very act. The nature of the crime, no less than the criminal's own will, requires that the injury initiated by the criminal should be annulled. However that may be, Beccaria's endeavour to have capital punishment abolished has had beneficial effects. Even if neither Joseph II* nor the French ever succeeded in entirely abolishing it, still we have begun to see which crimes deserve the death penalty and which do not. Capital punishment has in consequence become rarer, as in fact should be the case with this most extreme punishment.

101. The annulment [*Aufheben*] of the crime is *retribution* insofar as (*a*) retribution according to its concept is the 'injury of an injury' and (*b*), since as existent a crime is something determinate in its scope both qualitatively and quantitatively, its negation as existent is similarly determinate. This identity rests on the concept, but it is not an equality between the specific character of the crime and that of its negation; on the contrary, the two injuries are equal only in respect of their intrinsic [*an sich seiend*] character, i.e. in respect of their *value*.

Empirical science requires that the definition of a concept (punishment in this case) shall be drawn from ideas universally present to conscious psychological experience. This method would prove that the universal feeling of peoples and individuals about crime is and has been that it deserves punishment, that as the criminal has done, so should it be done to him. (It is not clear how these sciences, which find the source of their concepts in ideas universally shared, come on other occasions to take for granted propositions contradictory of such universal 'facts of consciousness'.)

But a point of great difficulty has been introduced into the idea of retribution by the category of *equality*, though it is still true that the justice of specific types or amounts of punishment is a further matter, subsequent to the substance of the thing itself. Even if to determine the later question of specific punishments we had to look round for principles other than those determining the universal character of punishment, still the latter remains what it is. Yet the concept itself must in general contain the *fundamental* principle for determining the particular too. But the determinate character given by the concept to punishment is just that necessary connection between crime and punishment already mentioned: crime, as the will which is null in itself, *eo ipso* contains its negation in itself and this negation is manifested as punishment. It is this inner identity whose reflection in external existence appears to the understanding as 'equality'. Now the qualitative and quantitative characteristics of crime and its annulment fall into the sphere of externality, and in this sphere no absolute determinacy is in any case possible (compare § 49). In the field of the finite, absolute determinacy [thus] remains only a demand, a demand which the understanding has increasingly to delimit—a fact of the greatest importance—but which continues *ad infinitum* and which allows only of perennially approximate satisfaction.

If we overlook this nature of the finite and then into the bargain refuse to go beyond abstract and *specific equality*, we are faced with the insuperable difficulty of fixing punishments (especially if psychology adduces in addition the strength of sensual impulses and consequentially either the greater strength of the evil will or the greater weakness, or the restricted freedom, of the will as such—we may choose which we please). Furthermore, it is easy enough from this point of view to exhibit the retributive character of punishment as an absurdity (theft for theft, robbery for robbery, an eye for an eye, a tooth for a tooth[47]—and then you can go on to suppose that the criminal has only one eye or no teeth). But the concept has nothing to do with this absurdity, for which indeed the introduction of this *specific equality* is solely to blame. *Value*, as the inner equality of things which in their outward existence are specifically different from one another in every way, is a category which has appeared already in connection with contracts (see § 77), and also in connection with injuries that are the subject of civil suits (see Remark to § 98);[48] and by means of it our idea of a thing is raised above its immediate character to its universality. In crime, whose basic determination is the infinite aspect* of the deed, the purely external specific character disappears all the more obviously, and equality remains the basic rule determining what the criminal essentially deserves, though not the specific external form that it should take. It is only in respect of that form that there is a plain inequality between theft and robbery on the one hand, and fines, imprisonment, etc., on the other. In respect of their value, however, i.e. in respect of their universal property of being injuries, they are comparable. Thus, as was said above, it is a matter for the understanding to look for something approximately equal to their value in this sense. If the intrinsic interconnection of crime and its negation, and if also the thought of *value* and the comparability of crime and punishment in respect of their value are not apprehended, then it may become possible to see in a punishment proper only an *arbitrary* connection of an evil with an unlawful action.[49]

Addition: Retribution is the inner connection and the identity of two determinations which are different in appearance and which also have a different external existence in relation to one another. Retribution is

---

[47] See Exodus 21: 24. [S.H.]

[48] All editions have '§ 95'. For '§ 77' just preceding, all editions have simply 'see above'.

[49] *Hegel's reference*: Klein, *Principles of Common German and Prussian Penal Law*, § 9.

inflicted on the criminal and so it has the look of an alien destiny [*Bestimmung*], not intrinsically his own. Nevertheless punishment, as we have seen, is only crime made manifest, i.e. is the second half which necessarily presupposes the first. Prima facie, the objection to retribution is that it looks like something immoral, i.e. like revenge, and that thus it may pass for something personal. Yet it is not something personal, but the concept itself, which carries out retribution. 'Vengeance is mine, saith the Lord', as the Bible says.[50] And if something in the word 'retribution' [*Wiedervergeltung*] calls up the idea of a particular caprice of the subjective will, it must be pointed out that what is meant is only that the form which crime takes is turned round against itself. The Eumenides sleep,* but crime awakens them, and hence it is one's own deed that asserts itself. Now although requital cannot simply be made specifically equal to the crime, the case is otherwise with murder, which is of necessity liable to the death penalty; the reason is that since life is the full compass of [a human being's] existence, the punishment here cannot simply consist in a *value*, for none is great enough, but can consist only in taking away a second life.

102. The annulling of crime in this sphere where right is immediate is initially *revenge*, which is just in its *content* insofar as it is retributive. But in its *form* it is an act of a subjective will which can place its infinity in every act of transgression and whose justice, therefore, is in all cases contingent, while to the other party too it appears as only particular. Hence revenge, because it is a positive action of a particular will, becomes a new transgression; as thus contradictory in character, it falls into an infinite progression and descends from one generation to another *ad infinitum*.

In cases where crimes are prosecuted and punished not as public crimes [*crimina publica*] but as private crimes* [*crimina privata*] (e.g. in Jewish law and Roman law, theft and robbery; in English law to this day, certain crimes, etc.) punishment is still, at least to some extent, revenge. There is a difference between private revenge and the revenge of heroes, knights-errant, etc., which is part of the founding of states.

Addition: In that condition of society when there are neither magistrates nor laws, punishment always takes the form of revenge; revenge remains defective inasmuch as it is the act of a subjective will and therefore does not correspond with the content. Members of a court of law are, indeed, also persons, but their will is the universal will of the law and they aim to import into the punishment nothing except what is implied in the nature of the thing. The person wronged, however, views the wrong not as something qualitatively and quantitatively limited but only as wrong pure and simple, and in requiting the injury he may go too far, and this would lead to a new wrong. Amongst uncivilized peoples, revenge is undying; amongst the Arabs, for instance, it can be checked only by superior force or by the impossibility of its satisfaction. A residue of revenge still lingers in comparatively modern legislation in those cases where it is left to the option of individuals whether to prosecute or not.

103. The demand that this contradiction, which is present here in the manner in which wrong is annulled, be resolved like contradictions in the case of other types of wrong (see §§ 86, 89), is the demand for a justice freed from subjective interest and a subjective form and no longer contingent on power, i.e. it is the demand for justice not as revenge but as *punishment*. Therein lies, initially, the demand for a will which, though particular and *subjective*, yet wills the universal as such. But this concept of *morality* is not simply something demanded; it has emerged in the course of this movement itself.

Transition from Right to Morality

104. That is to say, crime, and justice in the form of revenge, display (i) the shape which the will's development takes when it has passed over into the distinction between the universal will in itself [*an sich*] and the individual will that is for itself [*für sich*] in opposition to the universal; and (ii) the fact that the will that is in itself, returning into itself through superseding this opposition, has now itself come to be *for itself* and *actual*. In this way, right, upheld in face of the individual will that is merely for itself, *is* and *is recognized* as actual by virtue of its necessity.—At the same time, however, the shape that the will has here is *eo ipso* a step forward in the inner determination of the will by the concept. The will's immanent actualization in accordance with its concept is the process whereby it supersedes its being-in-itself [*Ansichsein*] and the form of immediacy in which it begins and which is the shape it assumes in abstract right (see [Remark to] § 21). This means that it first posits itself in the opposition between the universal will in itself and the individual will that is for itself; and then, through the supersession of this opposition (through the negation of the negation), it determines itself as will in its *existence* [*Dasein*], so that it is a free will not only in itself

but *for itself* also, i.e. it determines itself as self-related negativity. It now has its personality—in abstract right the will is personality and no more—for its *object*; the infinite subjectivity of freedom, a subjectivity that has come to be *for itself* in this way, is the principle of the *moral* [*moralisch*] standpoint.

Let us look back more closely over the moments through which the concept of freedom develops itself from the will's determinate character as originally abstract to its character as self-related, and so to its *self-determination as subjectivity*. In property this determinate character is the abstract one, 'mine', and is therefore found in an external thing. In contract, 'mine' is mediated by the wills of the parties and means only something common. In wrong the will of the sphere of right has its abstract being-in-itself or immediacy posited as contingency by the individual will that is itself contingent. At the moral standpoint, the abstract determinacy of the will in the sphere of right has been so far overcome that this contingency itself is, as reflected into itself and self-identical, the infinite inward contingency of the will, i.e. its *subjectivity*.

Addition: Truth entails that the concept shall be, and that this existence shall correspond with the concept. In the sphere of right, the will is existent in something external, but the next requirement is that the will should be existent in something inward, in itself. It must be for itself, be subjectivity, and have itself over against itself. This relation to itself is the moment of *affirmation*, but it can attain it only by superseding its immediacy. The immediacy superseded in crime leads, then, through punishment, i.e. through the nullity of this nullity, to affirmation, i.e. to *morality*.

SECOND PART
MORALITY

105. The standpoint of morality is the standpoint of the will which is infinite not merely in itself but *for itself* (see § 104). This reflection of the will into itself and its identity for itself, in contrast to its being-in-itself and immediacy and the determinate characteristics developed therein, makes the person into the *subject*.

106. Since subjectivity now constitutes the determinacy of the concept and is distinct from the concept as such, i.e. from the will in itself, and, indeed, since the will of the subject—as that of the individual that is for itself—at the same time *is* [*ist*] (i.e. still has immediacy in it), subjectivity constitutes the *existence* [*Dasein*] of the concept. In this way a higher ground has been determined for freedom; the Idea's aspect of existence [*Existenz*], or its moment of reality, is now the *subjectivity* of the will. Only in the will as subjective can freedom or the will in itself be actual.

The second sphere, morality, therefore throughout portrays the real aspect of the concept of freedom, and the movement of this sphere is as follows: the will, which initially is only for itself and is immediately identical only *in itself* with the universal will or the will that is in itself, is superseded and raised above its difference from the universal will, above this situation in which it sinks deeper and deeper into itself, and so is posited as identical *for itself* with the will that is in itself.* This process is accordingly the cultivation of the ground in which freedom is now set, i.e. subjectivity. What happens is that subjectivity, which is abstract at the start, i.e. distinct from the concept, is equated with it, and the Idea thereby acquires its genuine realization. The result is that the subjective will determines itself as objective too and so as truly concrete.

Addition: So far as right in the strict sense was concerned, it was of no importance what my intention or my principle was. This question about the self-determination and motive of the will, like the question about its purpose, now enters at this point in connection with morality. Since the human being wishes to be judged in accordance with his own self-determination, he is free in this relation to himself whatever the external situation may impose upon him. No one can break in upon this inner conviction of humanity, no violence can be done to it, and the moral will, therefore, is inaccessible. The worth of a human being is estimated by reference to his inward action and hence the standpoint of morality is that of freedom that is for itself.

107. The *self-determination* of the will is at the same time a moment in the concept of the will, and subjectivity is not merely its existential aspect but its own determination (see § 104). The will that is free for itself and determined as subjective is at the start concept alone, but itself has *determinate existence* [*Dasein*] in order to exist as *Idea*. The moral standpoint therefore takes shape as the *right of the subjective will*.* In accordance with this right, the will *recognizes* something and *is* something, only insofar as that thing is its *own* and as the will is present to itself there as something subjective.

The same process through which the moral standpoint develops (see the Remark to the preceding Paragraph) takes the form, from this point of view, of the development of the *right* of the subjective will, or of the mode of its existence. In this process the subjective will further determines what it recognizes as its own in its object [*Gegenstand*], so that this becomes the will's own true concept, becomes objective [*objektiv*] in the sense of the will's own universality.*

Addition: This entire determination of the subjectivity of the will is once again a whole which, as subjectivity, must also have objectivity. It is in a subject that freedom can first be realized, since the subjective is the true material for this realization. But this existence of the will which we have called subjectivity is different from the will which is in and for itself. That is to say, the will must free itself from this second one-sidedness of pure subjectivity in order to become the will in and for itself. In morality, it is the human being's distinctive interest that comes into question, and the high worth of this interest consists precisely in the fact that the human being knows himself as absolute and determines himself. The uneducated person allows himself to be constrained in everything by brute force and natural factors; children have no moral will but leave their parents to decide things for them. The educated person, however, develops an inner life and wills that he himself shall be in everything he does.

108. The subjective will, as immediately for itself and distinguished from the will in itself (see Remark to § 106), is therefore abstract, restricted, and formal. But not merely is subjectivity itself formal; in addition, as the infinite self-determination of the will, it constitutes the formal aspect of the will. In this, its first appearance in the individual will, this formal aspect has not yet been posited as identical with the concept of the will, and therefore the moral point of view is that of *relation*, of the *ought-to-be*, or demand. And since the difference [*Differenz*] of subjectivity involves at the same time the character of being opposed to objectivity as external existence, it follows that the point of view of *consciousness* comes on the scene here too (see § 8). The general point of view here is that of the will's difference, *finitude*, and *appearance*.

The moral is not determined initially as that which is opposed to the immoral, just as right is not immediately the opposite of wrong. The point is rather that the general standpoint of morality and immorality alike rests on the subjectivity of the will.

Addition: In morality, self-determination is to be thought of as the pure restlessness and activity which can never arrive at anything that *is*. It is in the sphere of ethical life that the will is for the first time identical with the concept of the will and has this concept alone as its content. In the moral sphere the will still *relates itself* to what is in itself and consequently its standpoint is that of difference. The process through which this standpoint develops is that whereby the subjective will becomes identified with its concept. Therefore the 'ought-to-be' which is still present in the moral sphere is fulfilled only in ethical life. Further, this 'other' in relation to which the subjective will stands is two-sided: first, it is what is substantial, the concept; secondly, it is that which exists externally. Even if the good were posited in the subjective will, that still would not mean that it was achieved.

109. This formal aspect of the will initially involves, in accordance with its general determination, (*a*) the opposition of subjectivity and objectivity, and (*b*) the activity (see § 8) related to this opposition. Now existence [*Dasein*] and determinacy are identical in the concept of the will (see § 104), and the will as subjective is itself this concept. Hence the moments of this activity consist more precisely in (*a*) distinguishing between objectivity and subjectivity and even ascribing independence to them both, and (*b*) positing them as identical.* In the will which is self-determining, (α) its determinacy is in the first place posited *in the will* by the will itself as its inner particularization, as a *content* which it gives to itself. This is the first negation, and the formal limitation [*Grenze*] of this negation is that of being only something *posited*, something subjective. (β) As infinitely reflected into itself, this limitation exists *for* the will, and the will is the struggle to overcome this restriction [*Schranke*], i.e. it is the activity of translating this content in some way or other from subjectivity into objectivity, into an immediate existence. (γ) The simple identity of the will with itself in this opposition is the content or *purpose* [*Zweck*] which remains self-identical in both these opposites and indifferent to these differences of form.

110. But, at the standpoint of morality, where freedom—this identity of the will with itself—is *for* the will (see § 105), this identity of content acquires its more precise and distinctive determination.

(*a*) The content is determined for me as 'mine' in such a way that, in its identity, it contains my subjectivity *for me* not only as my inner purpose, but also inasmuch as it has acquired external objectivity.

Addition: The content of the subjective or moral will contains a determination of its own, i.e. even when it has acquired the form of objectivity, it must still continue to enshrine my subjectivity, and the deed is to count only if on its inward side it has been determined by me, if it was my purpose, my intention. Beyond what lay in my subjective will I recognize nothing in its expression as mine. What I wish to see in my deed is my subjective consciousness over again.

111. (*b*) Though the content does have in it something particular, whencesoever it may be derived, still it is the content of the will *reflected into itself* in its determinacy and thus of the self-identical and universal will; and therefore:

(α) the content has the inner determination of being adequate to the will in itself or of possessing the objectivity of the concept; but

(β) since the subjective will, insofar as it is for itself, is at the same time still formal (see § 108), the content's adequacy to the concept is still only something *demanded*, and hence this entails the possibility that the content may not be adequate to the concept.

112. (*c*) While I retain my subjectivity in carrying out my aims (see § 110), during this process of objectifying them I simultaneously supersede the *immediacy* of this subjectivity as well as its character as my individual subjectivity. But the external subjectivity which is

thus identical with me is the *will of others* (see § 73). The will's ground of existence [*Existenz*] is now subjectivity (see § 106) and the will of others is that existence which I give to my aim and which is at the same time other to me. The achievement of my aim, therefore, implies this identity of my will with the will of others, it has a positive relation to the will of others.

The objectivity of the aim achieved thus involves three meanings, or rather it has three moments present within it at once; it is:
    (α) something existing *externally* and immediately (see § 109);
    (β) adequate to the *concept* (see § 111); [51]
    (γ) *universal* subjectivity.
The subjectivity which maintains itself in this objectivity consists:
    (α) in the fact that the objective aim is *mine*, so that in it I maintain myself as *this* individual (see § 110);
    (β) and (γ), in moments which coincide with the moments (β) and (γ) of objectivity above.

At the standpoint of morality, subjectivity and objectivity are distinct from one another, or united only as contradictory. It is this fact more particularly which constitutes the *finitude* of this sphere or its character as *appearance* (see § 108), and the development of this standpoint is the development of these contradictions and their resolutions—resolutions, however, which within this field can be no more than relative.

Addition: In dealing with formal right, I said [see § 38] that it contained prohibitions only, that hence a right action, strictly so called, was purely negative in character in respect of the will of others. In morality, on the other hand, my will has a positive character in relation to the will of others, i.e. the will in itself is inwardly present within what the subjective will effects. To effect something is to produce something or to alter what already exists, and such changes have a relation to the will of others. The concept of morality is the inner relation of the will to itself. But here there is not only *one* will; on the contrary its objectification implies at the same time that the individual will supersedes itself. In addition therefore, since the determination of one-sidedness falls away, two wills with a positive relation to each other are posited. So far as right is concerned, it makes no difference whether someone else's will may want something relating to my will when I give my will an existence in property. In morality, however,

---

[51] All editions have '§ 112'.

the welfare of others too is in question, and this positive relation cannot come on the scene before this point.

113. The externalization of the subjective or moral will is *action*. Action contains the determinations here indicated:

(α) in its externality it must be known to me as *my* action;

(β) it has an essential relation to the concept as an 'ought' [see § 131];

(γ) it has an essential relation to the will of others.

Only with the externalization of the moral will do we come to action. The existence which the will gives to itself in the sphere of formal right is existence in an immediate thing and is itself immediate; to start with, it neither has in itself any express relation to the concept, which is at that point not yet contrasted with the subjective will and so is not distinguished from it, nor has it a positive relation to the will of others; in the sphere of right, command in its fundamental character is only *prohibition* (see § 38). In contract and wrong, there is the beginning of a relation to the will of others; but the correspondence established in contract between one will and another is grounded in arbitrariness, and the essential relation which the will has there to the will of the other is, as a matter of right, something negative, i.e. one party retains his property (the value of it) and allows the other to retain his. On the other hand, crime insofar as it issues from the *subjective will*, and the question of the mode of its existence in that will, come before us now for consideration for the first time.

The content of a legal [*gerichtlich*] action (*actio*), as something determined by regulations, is not imputable to me. Consequently, such an action contains only some of the moments of a moral action proper, and contains them only in an external manner. The aspect of an action in virtue of which it is properly moral is therefore distinct from its legal aspect.

114. The right of the moral will involves three aspects:

(*a*) The abstract or formal right of action, the right that the content of the action, as carried out in immediate existence, shall be entirely *mine*, that thus the action shall be the *purpose* [*Vorsatz*] of the subjective will.

(*b*) The particular aspect of the action is its inner content, (α) i.e. the way in which its general character is determined *for me*; this constitutes the *value* of the action and the reason I think it valid—in short my *intention* [*Absicht*]. (β) Its content as my particular aim, the aim of my particular, subjective existence, is *welfare* [*Wohl*].

(*c*) This content, as something which is inward and which yet at the same time is raised to its universality and thus to objectivity in and for itself, is the absolute end of the will, the *good*. In the sphere of reflection it is opposed to *subjective* universality, which is now evil and now conscience.

Addition: If an action is to be moral, it must in the first place correspond with my purpose, since the moral will has the right to recognize in the resulting state of affairs only what was present inwardly as purpose. Purpose concerns only the formal principle that the external will shall be within me as something inward. On the other hand, in the second moment of the moral sphere, questions may be asked about the intention behind the action, i.e. about the relative value of the action in relation to me. The third and last moment is not the relative value of the action but its universal value, the good.

In a moral action, then, there may be a breach first between what is purposed and what is really effected and achieved; secondly, between what is there externally as a universal will and the particular inner determination which I give to it. The third and last point is that the intention should be in addition the universal content of action. The good is the intention raised to the concept of the will.

SUB-SECTION I

PURPOSE AND RESPONSIBILITY

115. The *finitude* of the subjective will in the immediacy of acting consists immediately in the fact that its action *presupposes* an external object in manifold circumstances. The deed [*Tat*] posits an alteration in this existence confronting the will, and my will has responsibility [*schuld*] in general for its deed insofar as the abstract predicate 'mine' belongs to the existence so altered.

An event, a situation which has been produced, is a concrete external actuality which because of its concreteness has in it an indeterminable multiplicity of circumstances. Any and every individual element which appears as the condition, ground, or cause of one such circumstance, and so has contributed its share to the event in question, may be looked upon as responsible for the event, or at least as sharing the responsibility for it. Hence, in the case of a complex event (e.g. the French Revolution) it is open to the formal understanding to choose which of an endless number of circumstances it will maintain to be responsible for it.

Addition: I am chargeable with what lay in my purpose and this is the most important point in connection with crime. But responsibility contains only the quite external judgement whether I have or have not done some thing. It does not follow that, because I am responsible [*schuld*], the thing done may be imputed to me.

116. It is, admittedly, not my own doing if damage is caused to others by things whose owner I am and which as external objects stand and are effective in manifold connections with other things (as may also be the case with myself as a mechanical body or as a living thing). This damage, however, is *more* or *less* my fault because the things that cause it are, indeed, mine, although it is true that they are subject to my control, vigilance, etc., only to an extent varying with their distinctive nature.

117. The freely acting will, in directing its aim on the existence confronting it, has an *idea* [*Vorstellung*] of the attendant circumstances. But because the will is finite, since this existence is presupposed, the objective phenomenon is contingent so far as the will is concerned, and may contain something other than what is contained in the will's idea of it. The will's *right*, however, is to recognize as its *action* [*Handlung*], and to accept responsibility for, only those presuppositions of the deed of which it was conscious in its aim, those aspects of the deed which were contained in its *purpose*. The deed can be imputed to me only if my will is responsible for it—this is the *right to know*.

Addition: The will has confronting it an existence upon which it acts. But in order to know what this existence is I must have an idea of it, and the responsibility is truly mine only insofar as I had knowledge of the situation confronting me. Such a situation is a presupposition of my volition and my will is therefore finite, or rather, since my will is finite, it has a presupposition of this kind. Insofar as my thinking and willing is rational, I am no longer at this level of finitude, since the object on which I act is no longer an 'other' to me. Finitude, however, implies fixed limits and restrictions. I have confronting me an 'other' which is only contingent, something necessary in a purely external way; its path and mine may meet or diverge. Nevertheless, I am nothing except in relation to my freedom, and my will is responsible for the deed only insofar as I know what I am doing. Oedipus, who killed his father without knowing it,* cannot be accused of parricide. The ancient penal codes, however, attached less weight to the subjective side of action, to imputability, than we do nowadays. That is why sanctuaries were instituted in ancient times for harbouring and protecting the fugitive from vengeance.

118. Further, action is translated into external existence, and external existence has connections in the field of external necessity through which it develops itself in all directions. Hence action has a multitude of consequences. These consequences are the outward form whose inner soul is the *aim* of the action, and thus they are the consequences *of the action*, they belong to the action. At the same time, however, the action, as the aim posited in the external world, becomes the prey of external forces which attach to it something totally different from what it is for itself and drive it on into alien and distant consequences. Thus the will has the right to accept responsibility only for the first set of consequences, since they alone were purposed.

The distinction between consequences that are contingent and those that are necessary is indeterminate, because the necessity internal to the finite comes into determinate existence as an external necessity, as a relation of individual things to one another, things which as self-subsistent are conjoined in indifference to one another and externally. The maxim: 'Ignore the consequences of actions' and the other: 'Judge actions by their consequences and make these the criterion of right and good' are both alike maxims of the abstract understanding. The consequences, as the shape proper to the action and immanent within it, exhibit nothing but its nature and are simply the action itself; therefore the action can neither disavow nor ignore them. On the other hand, however, among the consequences there is also comprised something interposed from without and introduced by chance, and this is quite unrelated to the nature of the action itself.

The development in external existence of the contradiction involved in the *necessity* of the *finite* is just the conversion of necessity into contingency and vice versa. From this point of view, therefore, acting means *submitting oneself to this law*. It is because of this that it is to the advantage of the criminal if his action has comparatively few bad consequences (just as a good action must accept that it may have no consequences or very few), and that the fully developed consequences of a crime are counted as part of the crime.

The self-consciousness of heroes (like that of Oedipus and others in Greek tragedy) had not advanced out of its primitive simplicity either to reflection on the distinction between deed and action, between the external event and the purpose and knowledge of the circumstances, or to the subdivision of consequences. On the contrary, they accepted responsibility for the whole compass of the deed.

Addition: The transition to intention depends on the fact that I accept responsibility only for what I had an idea of. That is to say, there can be imputed to me only what I knew of the circumstances. On the other hand, there are inevitable consequences linked with every action, even if I am only bringing about some individual, immediate state of affairs. The consequences in such a case represent the universal contained within that state of affairs. Of course I cannot foresee the consequences that might be prevented, but I must be aware of the universal character of my individual deed. The important element here is not the individual aspect but the whole, and that concerns not the specificity of the particular action, but its universal nature. Now the transition from purpose to intention lies in the fact that I ought to be aware not simply of my individual action but also of the universal which is conjoined with it. The universal which comes on the scene here in this way is what I have willed, my *intention*.

SUB-SECTION 2

INTENTION AND WELFARE

119. The external existence of an action is a complex of connected parts which may be regarded as divided into individual units *ad infinitum*, and the action may be treated as having touched in the first instance only one of these units. The truth of the individual, however, is the *universal*; and what gives action its explicit determinate character is not an isolated content limited to an external unit, but a *universal* content, comprising in itself the complex of connected parts. Purpose, as issuing from a thinker, comprises more than the mere unit; essentially it comprises that *universal* side of the action, i.e. the intention.

Etymologically, *Absicht* [intention] implies *abstraction*,* either the form of universality or the extraction of a particular aspect of the concrete thing. The endeavour to justify an action by the intention behind it involves the isolation of one or other of its individual aspects which is alleged to be the essence of the action on its subjective side.

To judge an action as an external deed without yet determining its rightness or wrongness is simply to bestow on it a universal predicate, i.e. to describe it as arson, killing, etc.

The individuated character of external actuality shows what the nature of that actuality is, namely a chain of external relations. Actuality is touched in the first instance only at a single point (arson, for instance, *directly* concerns only a tiny section of the firewood, i.e. is describable in a proposition, not a judgement),* but the universal nature of this point entails its expansion. In a living thing, the individual part is there in its immediacy not as a mere part, but as an organ in which the universal is really present as the universal; hence in murder, it is not a piece of flesh, as something individual, which is injured, but life itself which is injured in that piece of flesh. On the one hand, it is subjective reflection, ignorant of the logical nature of the individual and the universal, which indulges in the subdivision of individual parts and consequences; on the other hand, it is the nature of the finite deed itself to contain such separable contingencies. The device of *dolus indirectus** has its basis in these considerations.

Addition: It happens, of course, that circumstances may intervene in an action to a greater or lesser degree. In a case of arson, for instance, the fire may not catch or alternatively it may take hold further than the incendiary intended. In spite of this, however, we must not distinguish here between good and ill fortune, since in acting a human being must engage with externality. The old proverb is correct: 'A flung stone is the devil's.' To act is to expose oneself to misfortune. Thus misfortune has a right over me and is an existence of my own volition.

120. The right of intention is that the universal quality of the action shall not merely be what it is in itself but shall be *known* by the agent, and so shall have lain from the start in his subjective will. Vice versa, what may be called the right of the *objectivity* of action is the right of the action to assert itself as known and willed by the subject as a *thinker*.

This right to insight of this kind entails the complete, or almost complete, lack of responsibility of children, imbeciles, lunatics, etc., for their actions.—But just as actions on their external side as events include contingent consequences, so there is involved in the subjective agent an indeterminacy whose degree depends on the power and strength of his self-consciousness and circumspection. This indeterminacy, however, may not be taken into account except in connection with childhood or imbecility, lunacy, etc., since it is only such well marked states of mind that nullify [*aufheben*] the trait of thought and freedom of will, and permit us to treat the agent as devoid of the dignity of being a thinker and a will.

121. The universal quality of the action is the manifold *content* of the action as such, reduced to the simple form of universality. But the subject, an entity reflected into himself and so *particular* in relation to objective particularity, has in his end his own particular content, and this content is the soul of the action and determines its character. The fact that this moment of the *particularity* of the agent is contained and realized in the action constitutes subjective freedom in its more concrete sense, the right of the subject to find his *satisfaction* in the action.

Addition: I, for myself, reflected into myself, am a particular in relation to the externality of my action. My end constitutes the content of the action, the content determinant of the action. Murder and arson, for example, are universals and so are not the positive content of my action *qua* the action of a subject. If one of these crimes has been committed, its perpetrator may be asked why he committed it. The murder was not done for the sake of murdering; the murderer had in view some particular positive end. But if we were to say that he murdered for the mere pleasure of murdering, then the purely positive content of the subject would surely be pleasure, and if that is the case then the deed is the satisfaction of the subject's will. Thus the motive [*Beweggrund*] of a deed is, more particularly, what is called the 'moral' factor, and this has in that case the double meaning of the *universal* inherent in the purpose and the *particular* aspect of the intention. It is a striking modern innovation to enquire continually about the motives of human actions. Formerly, the question was simply: 'Is he an upright man? Does he do his duty?' Nowadays we insist on looking into people's hearts and so we presuppose a gulf between the objectivity of actions and their inner side, the subjective motives. To be sure, the subject's determination must be considered: he wills something and the reason for what he wills lies within himself; he wills the satisfaction of his desire, the gratification of his passion. Nonetheless, the good and the right are also a content of action, a content not purely natural but put there by my rationality. To make my freedom the content of what I will is a pure determination of my freedom itself. Therefore the higher moral standpoint consists in finding satisfaction *in* the action and advancing beyond the gulf between the self-consciousness of a human being and the objectivity of his deed, even though to treat action as if it involved such a gulf is a way of looking at the matter characteristic of certain epochs in world history and in individual biography.

122. It is on the strength of this particular aspect that the action has subjective *value* or *interest* for me. In contrast with this end—*the content of the intention*—the immediate character of the action in its further content is reduced to a means. Insofar as such an end is something finite, it may in its turn be reduced to a means to some further intention and so on *ad infinitum*.

123. For the content of these ends nothing is available at this point except (α) formal activity itself, i.e. the activity present owing to the fact that the subject puts himself into whatever he is to look upon and promote as his end. People are willing to be *active* in pursuit of what interests them, or should interest them, as something which is their own. (β) The still abstract and formal freedom of subjectivity has a more determinate content, however, only in its *natural subjective existence*, i.e. in needs, inclinations, passions, opinions, fancies, etc. The satisfaction of these is *welfare* or *happiness*, both in general and in its particular determinations—the ends of finitude as such.

Here—the standpoint of *relation* (see § 108), when the subject is characterized by his differences and so counts as a *particular*—is the place where the content of the natural will (see § 11) comes on the scene. But the will here is not as it is in its immediacy; on the contrary, this content now belongs to a will reflected into itself and so is elevated to become a universal end, the end of *welfare* or *happiness*.[52] This happens at the level of thinking which does not yet apprehend the will in its freedom but reflects on its content as on something natural and given—the level, for example, of the time of Croesus and Solon.*

Addition: Insofar as the determinations of happiness are *given*, they are not true determinations of freedom, because freedom is not genuinely free in

---

[52] *Hegel's reference*: *Encyclopaedia*, §§ 395 ff. [3rd edn. §§ 478 ff.].

its own eyes except in the good, i.e. except when it is its own end. Consequently we may raise the question whether a human being has the right to set before himself ends not freely chosen but resting solely on the fact that the subject is a living being. The fact that a human being is a living being, however, is not contingent, but in conformity with reason, and to that extent he has a right to make his needs his end. There is nothing degrading in being alive, and there is no higher spirituality in which existence would be possible. It is only the raising of the given to something self-created which yields the higher orbit of the good, although this distinction implies no incompatibility between the two levels.

124. Since the *subjective* satisfaction of the individual himself (including the recognition which he receives by way of honour and fame) is also part and parcel of the achievement of ends that are *valid in and for themselves*, it follows that the demand that such an end alone shall appear as willed and attained, like the view that, in willing, objective and subjective ends are mutually exclusive, is an empty assertion of the abstract understanding. And this assertion is more than empty, it is pernicious if it passes into the assertion that because subjective satisfaction is present, as it always is when any task is brought to completion, it is what the agent intended in essence to secure and that the objective end was in his eyes only a means to that.—What the subject *is, is the series of his actions*. If these are a series of worthless productions, then the subjectivity of his willing is just as worthless. But if the series of his deeds is of a substantial nature, then the same is true also of the individual's inner will.

The right of the subject's *particularity*, his right to be satisfied, or in other words the right of subjective freedom, is the pivot and centre of the difference between antiquity and modern times. This right in its infinity is given expression in Christianity and it has become the universal effective principle of a new form of the world. Amongst the more specific shapes which this right assumes are love, romanticism, the quest for the eternal salvation of the individual, etc.; next come moral convictions and conscience; and, finally, the other forms, some of which come into prominence in what follows as the principle of civil society and as moments in the constitution of the state, while others appear in the course of history, particularly the history of art, science, and philosophy.

Now this principle of particularity is, to be sure, one moment of the antithesis, and in the first place at least it is just as much identical with the universal as distinct from it. Abstract reflection, however, fixes this moment in its distinction from and opposition to the universal and so produces a view of morality as nothing but a bitter, unending struggle against one's own satisfaction, as the command: 'Do with abhorrence what duty commands'* [*mit Abscheu zu tun, was die Pflicht gebeut*].

It is just this type of understanding which produces that familiar psychological view of history which knows how to belittle and disparage all great deeds and great individuals by transforming into the main intention and operative motive of actions the inclinations and passions which likewise found their satisfaction in the achievement of something substantial, along with fame and honour, etc., and other consequences, in a word their particular aspect, the aspect which it decreed in advance to be something in itself pernicious. Such understanding assures us that, while great actions and the activity which consisted in a series of such actions have produced greatness in the world and have had as their consequences for the individual agent power, honour, and fame, what belongs to the individual is not the greatness itself but only those particular and external consequences which accrued to him from it; since this particular aspect is a consequence, it is *therefore* supposed to have been the agent's end and even his sole end. Reflection of this sort stops short at the subjective side of great individuals, since it itself stands on purely subjective ground, and consequently it overlooks what is substantial in this emptiness of its own making. This is the view of those valet psychologists 'for whom there are no heroes, not because the latter are not heroes, but because these psychologists are only valets'.[53]

Addition: 'In great things, it is enough to have willed'* is right in the sense that we ought to will something great. But we must also be able to achieve it, otherwise the willing is nugatory. The laurels of mere willing are dry leaves that never were green.

125. The subjective element of the will with its particular content—welfare—is reflected into itself and infinite and so stands related to the universal element, to will in itself. This moment of universality, posited first of all within this particularity itself, is the *welfare of others also*, or, in its complete though quite empty

[53] *Hegel's reference: Phenomenology*, 616 [Miller trans., 404].

determination, the welfare of all. The welfare of many other particulars in general is thus also an essential end and right of subjectivity. But since the universal that is in and for itself, in distinction from such a particular content, has not so far been further determined than as 'right', it follows that these ends of particularity, differing as they do from the universal, may be in conformity with it, but they also may not.

126. My particularity, however, like that of others, is only a right at all insofar as I am *a free being* [*ein Freies*]. Therefore it may not make claims for itself in contradiction to this its substantial basis, and an intention to secure my welfare or that of others (and it is particularly in this latter case that such an intention is called 'moral') cannot justify an action which is wrong [*unrechtlich*].

It is one of the most prominent of the corrupt maxims of our time to enter a plea for the so-called 'moral' intention behind wrong actions and to imagine bad subjects with well-meaning hearts, i.e. hearts willing their own welfare and perhaps that of others also. This doctrine is rooted in the 'benevolence' [*guten Herzen*] of the pre-Kantian philosophers* and constitutes, e.g., the quintessence of well-known touching dramatic productions;* but today it has been resuscitated in a more extravagant form, and inner enthusiasm and the heart, i.e. the form of particularity as such, have been made the criterion of right, rationality, and excellence. The result is that crime and the thoughts that lead to it, be they fancies however trite and empty, or opinions however wild, are to be regarded as right, rational, and excellent, simply because they issue from people's hearts and enthusiasms. (See the Remark to § 140, where more details are given.)

Incidentally, however, attention must be paid to the point of view from which right and welfare are being treated here. We are considering right as formal right and welfare as the particular welfare of the individual. The so-called 'general good', the welfare of the state, i.e. the right of actual, concrete spirit, is quite a different sphere, a sphere in which formal right is a subordinate moment like particular welfare and the happiness of the individual. As was remarked above,[54] it is one of the commonest blunders of abstract

---

[54] This has not been said before, but it is implicit in what is said in the Remark to *PR* § 29.

thinking to make private rights and private welfare count as valid in and for themselves in opposition to the universality of the state.

Addition: The famous answer: 'I do not see the need for it,'* given to the libeller who excused himself with the words: 'But I have to live,' is apposite at this point. Life ceases to be necessary in face of the higher realm of freedom. When St Crispin stole leather to make shoes for the poor,* his action was moral but wrong and so invalid.

127. The particularity of the interests of the natural will, taken in their entirety as a simple whole, is personal existence or *life*. In *extreme danger* and in conflict with the rightful property of someone else, this life may claim (as a right, not a mercy) a *right of distress* [*Notrecht*], because in such a situation there is, on the one hand, an infinite injury to someone's existence and the consequent loss of rights altogether, and, on the other hand, an injury only to a single restricted existence of freedom, whereby both right as such and the injured person's capacity for rights continue to be recognized, since the injury affects only *this* property of his.

The right of distress is the basis of the 'benefit of competence' [*beneficium competentiae*]* whereby a debtor is allowed to retain of his tools, farming implements, clothes, or, in short, of his resources, i.e. of his creditor's property, so much as is regarded as indispensable if he is to continue to support life—to support it, of course, on his own social level.

Addition: Life as the totality of ends has a right against abstract right. If for example it is only by stealing bread that the wolf can be kept from the door, the action is of course an encroachment on someone's property, but it would be wrong to treat this action as an ordinary theft. To refuse to allow someone in jeopardy of his life to take such steps for self-preservation would be to regard him as being without rights, and since he would be deprived of his life, his freedom would be annulled altogether. Many diverse details have a bearing on the preservation of life, and when we have our eyes on the future we have to engage ourselves in these details. But the only thing that is necessary is to live *now*; the future is not absolute but ever exposed to contingency. Hence it is only the necessity of the immediate present which can justify a wrong action, because not to do the action would in turn be to commit an offence, indeed the most wrong of all offences, namely the complete negation of the existence of freedom. *Beneficium competentiae* is relevant here, because kinship and other close relationships imply the right to demand that no one shall be sacrificed altogether on the altar of right.

128. This distress reveals the finitude and therefore the contingency of both right and welfare—of right as the abstract existence of freedom without being the existence of the particular person, and of welfare as the sphere of the particular will without the universality of right. In this way they are *posited* as one-sided and ideal, the character which in their concept they already possessed. Right has already (see § 106) determined its existence as the particular will; and subjectivity, in its comprehensive particularity, is itself the existence of freedom (see § 127), while as the infinite relation of the will to itself, it is in itself the *universal* aspect of freedom. The two moments present in right and subjectivity, thus integrated and attaining their truth, their identity, though in the first instance still remaining *relative* to one another, are (*a*) the *good* (as the fulfilled universal that is determinate in and for itself), and (*b*) *conscience* (as infinite subjectivity inwardly knowing and inwardly determining its content).

SUB-SECTION 3
GOOD AND CONSCIENCE

129. The good is the Idea as the unity of the *concept* of the will with the *particular* will. In this unity, abstract right, welfare, the subjectivity of knowing and the contingency of external existence, have their independent self-subsistence superseded [*aufgehoben*], though at the same time they are still contained and retained within it in their essence. The good is thus *freedom realized*, the absolute end and aim of the world.

Addition: Every stage is really the Idea, but the earlier stages contain it only in more abstract form. Thus for example, even the I, as personality, is already the Idea, though in its most abstract shape. The good, therefore, is the Idea further determined, the unity of the concept of the will with the particular will. It is not something abstractly right, but something concrete whose content is made up of both right and welfare alike.

130. In this Idea, welfare has no validity for itself as the existence of the individual particular will but only as universal welfare and essentially as universal in itself, i.e. as according with freedom. Welfare without right is not a good. Similarly, right without welfare is not the good; *fiat justitia* should not be followed by *pereat mundus*.* Consequently, since the good must of necessity be actualized through the particular will and is at the same time its substance, it has absolute right in contrast with the abstract right of property and the particular aims of welfare. If either of these moments becomes distinguished from the good, it has validity only insofar as it accords with the good and is subordinated to it.

131. For the subjective will, the good and the good alone is the essential, and the subjective will has value and dignity only insofar as its insight and intention accord with the good. Inasmuch as the good is at this point still only this *abstract* Idea of good, the subjective will has not yet been posited as taken up into it and as in accordance with it. Consequently, it stands in a *relation* to the good, and the relation is that the good *ought* to be substantial for it, i.e. it ought to make the good its aim and realize it completely, while the good on its side has in the subjective will its only means of stepping into actuality.

Addition: The good is the truth of the particular will, but the will is only what it posits itself to be; it is not good by nature but can become what it is only by its own labour. On the other hand, the good itself, apart from the subjective will, is only an abstraction without that reality which it is to acquire for the first time through the efforts of that will. Accordingly, the development of the good has three stages: (i) The good should present itself to my volition as a particular will and I should know it. (ii) One should say what is good and develop its particular determinations. (iii) Finally, the good must be determined for itself and particularized as infinite subjectivity that is for itself. This inward determining [of the good] is conscience.

132. The right of the subjective will is that whatever it is to recognize as valid shall be seen by it as *good*, and that an action, as its aim entering upon external objectivity, shall be imputed to it as right or wrong, good or evil, legal or illegal, in accordance with its *knowledge* of the value which the action has in this objectivity.

The good is in general the essence of the will in its substantiality and universality, i.e. of the will in its truth, and therefore it exists simply and solely in thinking and by means of thinking. Hence assertions such as 'humanity cannot know the truth but has to do only with phenomena', or 'thinking injures the good will', are assertions depriving spirit not only of intellectual but also of all ethical worth and dignity.

The right of giving recognition only to what my insight sees as rational is the highest right of the subject, although owing to its subjective character it remains a formal right; against it the right which *reason* qua the objective possesses over the subject remains firmly established.

On account of its formal character, insight is capable equally of being true and of being mere opinion and error. The individual's acquisition of this right of insight is, from the standpoint of what is still the moral sphere, part and parcel of his particular subjective education. I may demand from myself, and regard it as one of my subjective rights, that my insight into an obligation shall be based on good reasons, that I shall be convinced of the obligation and even that I shall apprehend it from its concept and fundamental nature. But whatever I may demand for the satisfaction of my conviction that an action is good, permitted, or forbidden, and so in this respect imputable, this in no way detracts from the *right of objectivity*.

This right of insight into the good is distinct from the right of insight in respect of action as such (see § 117). The right of objectivity which corresponds to the latter has the following form: since action is an alteration which is to take place in an actual world and so seeks recognition in it, it must in general accord with what has validity there. Whoever wills to act in this world of actuality has *eo ipso* submitted himself to its laws and recognized the right of objectivity.

Similarly, in the state as the objectivity of the concept of reason, *legal responsibility* cannot stop at what an individual may hold to be or not to be in accordance with his reason, or at his subjective insight into what is right or wrong, good or evil, or at the demands which he makes for the satisfaction of his conviction. In this objective field, the right of insight applies to insight into what is legal or illegal, i.e. into what is *recognized* as right, and the term 'insight' is restricted to its elementary meaning, i.e. to knowledge in the sense of acquaintance with what is legal and to that extent obligatory. By means of the publicity of the laws and the universality of customs [*Sitten*], the state removes from the right of insight its formal aspect and the contingency which it still retains for the subject at the level of morality. The subject's right to know action in its specific character as good or evil, legal or illegal, has the result of diminishing or cancelling in this respect too the responsibility of children, imbeciles, and lunatics,[55] although it is impossible to

---

[55] See Remark to *PR* § 120.

delimit precisely either childhood, imbecility, etc., or their degree of responsibility. But to turn momentary blindness, the goad of passion, intoxication, or, in a word, what is called the strength of sensual impulse (excluding impulses which are the basis of the right of distress—see § 127)[56] into *reasons* when the imputation, specific character, and culpability of a crime are in question, and to look upon such circumstances as if they took away the criminal's guilt, again means (compare § 100 and the Remark to § 120)[57] failing to treat the criminal in accordance with the right and honour due to him as a human being; for the nature of human beings consists precisely in the fact that they are essentially something universal, not beings whose knowledge is an abstractly momentary and piecemeal affair.

Just as what the incendiary really sets on fire is not the isolated square inch of wooden surface to which he applies his torch, but the universal in that square inch, e.g. the house as a whole, so, as subject, he is neither the individual of *this* moment of time nor this isolated hot feeling of revenge. If he were, he would be an animal which would have to be knocked on the head as dangerous and unsafe because of its liability to fits of madness.

The claim is made that the criminal in the moment of his action must have had a 'clear idea' of the wrong and its culpability before it can be imputed to him as a crime. At first sight, this claim seems to preserve the right of his moral subjectivity, but the truth is that it deprives him of his indwelling nature as intelligent, a nature whose active presence is not confined to the 'clear ideas' [*deutliche Vorstellungen*] of Wolff's psychology* and only in cases of lunacy is so deranged as to be divorced from the knowing and doing of individual things.

The sphere in which these circumstances come into consideration as grounds for the mitigation of punishment is a sphere other than that of right, the sphere of pardon [*Gnade*] [see § 282].

133. The particular subject is related to the good as to the *essence* of his will, and hence his will's *obligation* arises directly in this relation.* Since particularity is distinct from the good and falls within the subjective will, the good is characterized to begin with only as the

---

[56] Most editions have '§ 120'.
[57] Most editions have '§ 119'.

universal abstract essentiality of the will, i.e. as *duty*. Since duty is thus abstract and universal in character, it should be done for duty's sake.

Addition: The essence of the will for me is duty. Now if my knowledge stops at the fact that the good is my duty, I am still going no further than the abstract character of duty. I should do my duty for duty's sake, and when I do my duty it is in a true sense my own objectivity which I am bringing to realization. In doing my duty, I am with myself and free. To have emphasized this meaning of duty constitutes the merit of Kant's practical philosophy and its loftiness of outlook.[58]

134. Since every action for itself requires a particular content and a definite end, while duty as an abstraction entails nothing of the kind, the question arises: what is my duty? As an answer nothing is so far available except: (a) to do right, and (b) to promote welfare, one's own welfare, and welfare in universal terms, the welfare of others (see § 119).

Addition: This is the same question as was put to Jesus when someone wished to learn from him what he should do to inherit eternal life.[59] Good as a universal is abstract and cannot be accomplished so long as it remains abstract. To be accomplished it must acquire in addition the character of particularity.

135. These determinations, however, are not contained in the definition of duty itself; but since both of them are conditioned and restricted, they *eo ipso* bring about the transition to the higher sphere of the *unconditioned*, the sphere of duty. All that is left to duty, therefore—insofar as in moral self-consciousness it is the essence or the universality of that consciousness, the way in which it is inwardly related to itself alone—is abstract universality, and for its determinate character it has *identity without content*, or the abstractly positive, the indeterminate.

However essential it is to give prominence to the pure unconditioned self-determination of the will as the root of duty, and to the way in which knowledge of the will, thanks to Kant's philosophy, has won its firm foundation and starting-point for the first time

---

[58] See I. Kant, *Groundwork of the Metaphysics of Morals* (1785), trans. M. J. Gregor, in I. Kant, *Practical Philosophy*, ed. M. J. Gregor (Cambridge: Cambridge University Press, 1996), 52–3. [S.H.]

[59] See Luke 10: 25.

through the thought of its infinite autonomy, still to adhere to the merely moral position, without making the transition to the concept of ethical life, is to reduce this gain to an *empty formalism*, and the science of morals to the preaching of duty for duty's sake. From this point of view, no immanent doctrine of duties is possible; of course, material may be brought in from outside and particular duties may be arrived at accordingly, but if the definition of duty is taken to be the absence of contradiction, formal correspondence with itself—which is nothing but the establishment of abstract indeterminacy—then no transition is possible to the specification of particular duties nor, if some such particular content for acting comes under consideration, is there any criterion in that principle for deciding whether it is or is not a duty. On the contrary, by this means any wrong or immoral mode of conduct may be justified.

The further Kantian formulation—the possibility of envisaging an action as a *universal* maxim*—does lead to the more concrete representation of a situation, but in itself it contains no principle beyond formal identity and the 'absence of contradiction' already mentioned.

The absence of property contains in itself just as little contradiction as the non-existence of this or that people, family, etc., or the death of the whole human race. But if it is already established on other grounds and presupposed that property and human life are to exist and be respected, then indeed it is a contradiction to commit theft or murder; a contradiction must be a contradiction of something, i.e. of some content presupposed from the start as a fixed principle. It is to a principle of that kind alone, therefore, that an action can be related either by correspondence or contradiction. But if duty is to be willed simply for duty's sake and not for the sake of some content, it is only a *formal identity* whose nature it is to exclude all content and determination.

The further antinomies and configurations of this never-ending ought-to-be, in which the merely moral standpoint—the standpoint of *relation*—just wanders to and fro without being able to resolve them and get beyond the ought-to-be, I have developed in my *Phenomenology of Spirit*, 550 ff. [Miller trans., 365 ff.].[60]

---

[60] *Hegel's reference*: Cf. *Encyclopaedia*, §§ 420 ff. [3rd edn. §§ 507 ff.].

Addition: While we laid emphasis above on the fact that the outlook of Kant's philosophy is a high one in that it propounds a correspondence between duty and rationality, still we must notice here that this point of view is defective in lacking all articulation. The proposition: 'Consider whether your maxim can be laid down as a universal principle,' would be very good if we already had determinate principles of conduct. That is to say, to demand of a principle that it shall be able to serve in addition as a determinant of universal legislation is to presuppose that it already possesses a content. Given the content, then of course the application of the principle would be a simple matter. In Kant's case, however, the principle itself is still not available and his criterion of non-contradiction is productive of nothing, since where there is nothing, there can be no contradiction either.

136. Because of the abstract constitution of the good, the other moment of the Idea—particularity in general—falls within subjectivity. Subjectivity in its universality reflected into itself is the subject's absolute inward certainty [*Gewißheit*] of himself, that which posits the particular and is the determining and decisive element in him, his *conscience* [*Gewissen*].

Addition: We may speak in a very lofty strain about duty, and talk of the kind is uplifting and broadens the human heart, but if it never comes to anything specific it ends in being wearisome. Spirit demands particularity and is entitled to it. But conscience is that deepest inward solitude with oneself where everything external and every restriction has disappeared—this complete withdrawal into oneself. As conscience, the human being is no longer shackled by the aims of particularity, and consequently in attaining that position he has risen to a higher standpoint, the standpoint of the modern world, which for the first time has attained this consciousness, achieved this descent into oneself. The more sensuous consciousness of earlier epochs had something external and given confronting it, either religion or right. But conscience knows itself as thinking and knows that what alone has obligatory force for me is this thinking of mine.

137. True conscience is the disposition to will what is good *in and for itself*. It therefore has fixed principles* and these are for it determinations and duties that are objective for themselves. In distinction from this its content (i.e. truth), conscience is only the *formal* side of the activity of the will, which as *this* will has no special content of its own. But the objective system of these principles and duties, and the union of subjective knowing with this system, is not present until we come to the standpoint of ethical life. Here at the formal standpoint of morality, conscience lacks this objective content and so its character for itself is that of infinite formal self-certainty, which at the same time is for this very reason the self-certainty of *this* subject.

Conscience is the expression of the absolute title of subjective self-consciousness to know in itself and from within itself what is right and obligatory, to give recognition only to what it thus knows as good, and at the same time to maintain that whatever in this way it knows and wills is in truth right and obligatory. Conscience as this unity of subjective knowing with what is in and for itself is a sanctuary which it would be sacrilege to violate. But whether the conscience of a specific individual corresponds with this Idea of conscience, whether what it takes or declares to be good is actually so, is ascertainable only from the *content* of the good it seeks to realize. What is right and obligatory is the element that is rational in and for itself in the will's volitions and therefore it is not in essence the particular property of an individual, and its form is not that of feeling or any other individual (i.e. sensuous) type of knowing, but essentially that of universal determinations of thought, i.e. the form of laws and principles. Conscience is therefore subject to the judgement of its *truth* or untruth, and when it appeals only *to itself* for a decision, it is directly at variance with what it wishes to be, namely the rule for a mode of conduct which is rational, valid in and for itself, and universal. For this reason, the state cannot give recognition to conscience in its distinctive form as *subjective knowing*, any more than science can grant validity to subjective opinion, assertion, and the appeal to a subjective opinion. In true conscience, its elements are not different, but they may become so, and it is the determining element, the subjectivity of willing and knowing, which can sever itself from the true content of conscience, establish its own independence, and reduce that content to a form and a semblance. The ambiguity in connection with conscience lies therefore in this: it is presupposed to mean the *identity* of subjective knowing and willing with the true good, and so is claimed and recognized to be something sacrosanct; and yet at the same time, as the mere subjective reflection of self-consciousness into itself, it still claims for *itself* the title due, solely on the strength of its rational content which is valid in and for itself, to that identity alone.

At the level of morality, distinguished as it is in this treatise from the level of ethics, it is only formal conscience that is to be found.

True conscience has been mentioned only to indicate its distinction from the other and to obviate the possible misunderstanding that here, where it is only formal conscience that is under consideration, the argument is about true conscience. The latter is part of the ethical disposition* which comes before us for the first time in the following section.—The religious conscience, however, does not belong to this sphere at all.

Addition: When we speak of conscience, it may easily be thought that, in virtue of its form, which is abstract inwardness, conscience is at this point already true conscience in and for itself. But true conscience determines itself to will what is in and for itself good and obligatory. So far, however, it is only with good in the abstract that we have to do and conscience is still without this objective content and is but the infinite certainty of oneself.

138. This subjectivity, *qua* abstract self-determination and pure certainty of oneself alone, as readily evaporates into itself the whole determinate character of right, duty, and existence, as it remains both the power to judge, to determine from within itself alone, what is good in respect of any content, and also the power to which the good, at first only an ideal [*vorgestellt*] and an ought-to-be, owes its actuality.

The self-consciousness which has attained this absolute reflection into itself knows itself in this reflection to be the kind of consciousness which is and should be beyond the reach of every existent and given determination. As one of the commoner features of history (e.g. in Socrates, the Stoics, and others),* the tendency to look deeper into oneself and to know and determine from within oneself what is right and good appears in ages when what is recognized as right and good in contemporary customs cannot satisfy the better will. When the existing world of freedom has become faithless to the better will, that will fails to find itself in the duties there recognized and must try to find in the ideal world of the inner life alone the harmony which actuality has lost. Once self-consciousness has grasped and secured its formal right in this way, everything depends on the character of the content which it gives to itself.

Addition: If we look more closely at this process of evaporation and see how all specific determinations disappear into this simple concept and then have to be condensed out of it again, what we find is that it is primarily due to the fact that everything recognized as right and duty may be proved by thought to be nugatory, restricted, and in all respects not absolute. On the other hand, just as subjectivity evaporates every content into itself, so it may develop it out of itself once more. Everything which arises in the ethical sphere is produced by this activity of spirit. The moral point of view, however, is defective because it is purely abstract. When I am aware of my freedom as the *substance* within me, I am inactive and do nothing. But if I proceed to act and look for principles on which to act, I reach for something determinate and there is then the requirement that this be deduced from the concept of the free will. While, therefore, it is right enough to evaporate right and duty into subjectivity, it is wrong if this abstract groundwork does not then in turn develop itself. It is only in times when the world of actuality is hollow, spiritless, and unstable, that an individual may be allowed to take refuge from actuality in his inner life. Socrates lived at the time of the ruin of the Athenian democracy. His thought vaporized the world around him and he withdrew into himself to search there for the right and the good. Even in our day there are cases in which, to a greater or lesser degree, reverence for the established order is lacking, and people insist that what is authoritative is their will, that to which they have granted recognition.

139. Once self-consciousness has reduced all otherwise valid determinations to emptiness and itself to the sheer inwardness of the will, it has become the potentiality of either making what is universal in and for itself into its principle, or equally well of elevating above the universal the *self-will* of its *own particularity*, taking that as its principle and realizing it through its actions, i.e. it has become potentially *evil* [*böse*].

To have a conscience, if conscience is only formal subjectivity, is simply to be on the verge of slipping into evil; in independent [*für sich seiend*] self-certainty, with its independence of knowledge and decision, both morality and evil have their common root.

The origin of evil in general is to be found in the mystery of freedom (i.e. in the speculative aspect of freedom), the mystery whereby freedom of necessity arises out of the natural level of the will and is something inward in comparison with that level.* It is this natural level of the will which comes into existence as a self-contradiction, as incompatible with itself in this opposition, and so it is just this particularity of the will which later makes itself evil. That is to say, particularity is always duality; here it is the opposition of the natural level and the inwardness of the will.

In this opposition, the latter is only a relative and formal subjectivity which can draw its content only from the determinate content of the natural will, from desire, impulse, inclination, etc. Now it is said of these desires, impulses, etc., that they *may* be either good *or* evil. But since the will here makes into a determinant of its content both these impulses in the contingent character which they possess as natural, and also, therefore, the form which it has at this point, the form of particularity itself, it follows that it is set in opposition to the *universal* as inner objectivity, to the good, which comes on the scene as the opposite extreme to immediate objectivity, the natural pure and simple, as soon as the will is reflected into itself and consciousness is a *knowing* consciousness. It is in this opposition that this inwardness of the will is evil. The human being is therefore evil both in himself or by nature and at the same time through reflection into himself; and therefore evil belongs neither to nature as such by itself—unless nature were supposed to be the natural character of the will which rests in its particular content—nor to introverted reflection by itself, i.e. cognition in general, unless this were to maintain itself in that opposition to the universal.

With this facet of evil, its necessity, there is inevitably combined the fact that this same evil is determined as that which of necessity *ought not to be*, i.e. the fact that evil ought to be annulled. It is not that there ought never to be a diremption of any sort in the will—on the contrary, it is just this level of diremption which distinguishes the human being from the unreasoning animal. The point is that the will should not rest at that level and cling to the particular as if that and not the universal were the essential thing; it should overcome the diremption as a nullity. Further, as to this necessity of evil, [one should note that] it is *subjectivity*, as infinite self-reflection, which is confronted by and present in this opposition of universal and particular. If it rests in this opposition, i.e. if it is evil, then it is *eo ipso for itself*, retains its separate individuality, and is itself this arbitrary will. Therefore if the individual subject as such does evil, the evil is purely and simply his own responsibility.

Addition: The abstract self-certainty which knows itself as the basis of everything has in it the potentiality either of willing the universality of the concept or alternatively of taking a particular content as a principle and realizing that. The second alternative is evil, which therefore always includes the abstraction of self-certainty. It is only the human being who is good, and he is good only because he can also be evil. Good and evil are inseparable, and their inseparability is rooted in the fact that the concept becomes an object to itself, and as object it *eo ipso* acquires the character of difference. The evil will wills something opposed to the universality of the will, while the good will acts in accordance with its true concept.

The difficulty of the question as to how the will can be evil as well as good usually arises because we think of the will as related to itself purely positively and because we represent its volition as something determinate confronting it, as the good. But the problem of the origin of evil may be more precisely put in the form: 'How does the negative come into the positive?' If we begin by presupposing that in the creation of the world God is the absolutely positive, then, turn where we will, we shall never discover the negative within that positive, since to talk of God's 'permitting' evil is to ascribe to him a passive relation to evil which is unsatisfactory and meaningless. In the representational thinking [*Vorstellung*] of religious mythology there is no comprehension of the origin of evil; i.e. the positive and the negative are not discovered in one another; there is only a representation of their succession and juxtaposition, so that it is from outside that the negative comes to the positive. But this cannot satisfy thought, which demands a reason and a necessity and insists on apprehending the negative as itself rooted in the positive. Now the solution of the problem, the way the concept treats the matter, is already contained in the concept, since the concept, or to speak more concretely, the Idea, has it in its essence to differentiate itself and to posit itself negatively. If we adhere simply to the positive, i.e. if we rest in the pure good which is supposed to be good at its source, then we are accepting an empty category of the understanding which clings to abstractions and one-sided categories of this kind and which, by the very asking of this question, makes it a difficult one. If we begin with the standpoint of the concept, however, we apprehend the positive as activity and as the distinguishing of itself from itself. Evil and good alike have their origin in the will and the will in its concept is both good and evil.

The natural will is in itself the contradiction of self-differentiation, of being inward and for itself. To maintain then that evil implies the further point that the human being is evil insofar as his will is natural would be to contradict the usual idea that it is just the natural will which is guiltless and good. But the natural will stands in opposition to the content of freedom, and the child and the uneducated person, whose wills are only natural, are for that very reason liable to be called to account for their actions only to a lesser degree. Now when we speak of the human being, we mean not the child but the self-conscious human being, and when we speak of the good, we mean the knowledge of it. It is doubtless true that the natural is in itself innocent, neither good nor bad, but when it is drawn into the orbit of the will which is free and knows that it is free, it acquires the character of not being free and is therefore evil. When the human being wills what is natural, it is no longer merely natural, but the negative opposed to the good, i.e. to the concept of the will.

On the other hand, if it is now objected that since evil is rooted in the concept and inevitable, a human being would be guiltless if he committed it, our reply must be that a person's decision is his own act, and his own act is freely chosen and his own responsibility. In the religious myth it is said that the human being is as God when he knows good and evil;[61] and this likeness to God is indeed present in such knowledge in that the necessity here is no natural necessity but the decision is precisely the superseding [*Aufhebung*] of this duality of good and evil. When both good and evil are placed before me, I have a choice between the two; I can decide between them and endow my subjective character with either. Thus the nature of evil is that human beings may will it but need not.

140. In every end of a self-conscious subject, there is a *positive* aspect (see § 135) necessarily present because the end is what is purposed in an actual concrete action. This aspect he knows how to highlight, and he may then proceed to regard it as *a duty or a fine intention*. By so interpreting it, he is able to pass off his action as good in the eyes both of himself and others, despite the fact that, owing to his reflection into himself and his consciousness of the universal aspect of the will, the essentially negative content of the action stands *within him* in contrast to this universal. To assert in this way that the action is good for *others* is hypocrisy; while to assert that it is good for *oneself* is to proceed to the even further extreme of subjectivity that claims to be absolute.

This final, most abstruse, form of evil, whereby evil is perverted into good and good into evil, and consciousness, in being aware of its power to effect this perversion, knows itself to be absolute, is the highwater mark of subjectivity at the level of morality; it is the form into which evil has blossomed in our present epoch, a result due to philosophy, i.e. to a shallowness of thought which has twisted a profound concept into this shape and usurped the name of philosophy, just as it has arrogated to evil the name of good.

[61] See Genesis 3: 5.

In this Remark I will indicate briefly the chief forms of this subjectivity which have become current.

(*a*) In *hypocrisy* the following moments are contained: (α) knowledge of the true universal, whether knowledge in the form merely of a feeling for right and duty, or of a more extensive acquaintance with and knowledge of them; (β) volition of the particular which conflicts with this universal; (γ) conscious comparison of both moments (α) and (β), so that the conscious subject is aware in willing that his particular volition is evil in character.

[Yet by themselves] these determinations characterize *acting with a bad conscience*, not yet hypocrisy as such.

At one time great importance was attached to the question whether an action was evil only insofar as it was done with a bad conscience, i.e. with the developed consciousness of the three moments just specified. The inference from an affirmative answer is admirably drawn by Pascal: 'They will all be damned, these half-sinners, who retain some love for virtue. But as for the frank and open sinners, the hardened sinners, the undiluted, complete and consummate sinners, hell cannot hold them: they have deceived the devil by surrendering to him.'* 62

The subjective right of self-consciousness to know whether an action is in and for itself good or evil in character must not be thought of as so colliding with the absolute right of the objectivity of this character that the two rights are represented as separable, indifferent to one another, and related only contingently. It was such a conception of their relation that lay in particular at the root of the old questions about efficacious grace* [*wirksame Gnade*].

---

62 *Hegel's note*: In the same context, Pascal also quotes Christ's intercession on the Cross for his enemies: 'Father, forgive them, for they know not what they do' [Luke 23: 34]—a superfluous prayer if the fact that they did not know what they did made their action innocent and so took away the need of forgiveness. Pascal quotes there too Aristotle's distinction* [*Nicomachean Ethics*, 1110b27] between the one who acts οὐκ εἰδώς and the one who acts ἀγνοῶν; in the former type of ignorance, the person's action is involuntary [*unfreiwillig*] (here the ignorance depends on external circumstances, see above, § 117) and his action is not imputable to him. But of the latter Aristotle says: 'Every wicked person is ignorant of what he ought to do and what he ought to refrain from doing; and it is this kind of failure (ἁμαρτία) which makes people unjust and in general bad. An ignorant choice between good and evil is the cause not of the action's being involuntary' (of its being non-imputable) 'but only of its being wicked'. Aristotle evidently had a deeper insight into the connection between knowing and willing than has become common in a superficial philosophy which teaches that ignorance, the heart and enthusiasm, are the true principles of ethical action.

On its formal side, evil is most peculiarly the individual's own, since it is precisely his subjectivity positing itself purely and simply for itself, and for that reason it is purely and simply the individual's own responsibility (see § 139 and the Remark thereto); on his objective side the human being accords with his concept inasmuch as he is spirit, in a word a rational being, and has in his own nature as such the character of self-knowing universality. Therefore it means failing to treat him with the respect due to his concept if his good side is divorced from him, so that the character of his evil action as evil is divorced from him too and is not imputed to him as evil. How determinate is the consciousness of these moments in distinction from one another, or to what extent it has developed or failed to develop in clarity so as to become a recognition of them, and to what degree an evil action has been done with a conscience more or less downright evil—all these questions are the less important aspect of the matter,* the aspect mainly concerned with the empirical.

(*b*) Evil and doing evil with a bad conscience, however, is not quite *hypocrisy*. Into hypocrisy there enters in addition the formal aspect of untruth, that is, of holding up evil in the first place as good in the eyes of *others*, of setting oneself up to all appearance as good, conscientious, pious, and so on—conduct which in these circumstances is only a trick to deceive others. Further, however, the evil person may find in his good conduct on other occasions, or in his piety, or, in a word, in *good reasons*, a justification in his *own* eyes for the evil he does, since he can use these reasons to pervert that evil into good. His ability to do this resides in the subjectivity which, as abstract negativity, knows that all determinations are subordinate to itself and issue from its own will.

(*c*) In this perversion of evil into good we must first of all include the shape known as *probabilism*.* Its guiding principle is that an action is permissible, and may be done with an easy conscience, if the agent can come up with *any* good reason for it, be it only the authority of one theologian, and even if other theologians are known by the agent to dissent ever so widely from that authority. Even in this idea there is still present the correct apprehension that authority and a reason based on authority gives *probability* only, although this is supposed to be enough to produce an easy conscience; it is granted in probabilism that a good reason is inevitably of such a character that there may exist along with it different reasons at least as good. Even here we must recognize a vestige of objectivity in the admission that it is a *reason* [*Grund*] which should be the determining factor. But since the discrimination between good and evil is made to depend on the various good reasons, including also theological authorities, despite the fact that they are so numerous and contradictory, the implication is that it is not this objectivity of the thing, but *subjectivity*, which has the last word. This means that caprice and arbitrary will are made the arbiters of good and evil, and the result is that ethical life, as well as religious feeling, is undermined. But the fact that it is one's own subjectivity to which the decision falls is one which probabilism does not openly avow as its principle; on the contrary, as has already been stated, it gives out that it is some reason or other which is decisive, and probabilism is to that extent still a form of hypocrisy.

(*d*) The next stage in ascending order is the view that the goodness of the will consists in *its willing the good*;* this willing of the abstract good is supposed to suffice, in fact to be the sole requisite, to make its action good. As the willing of something determinate, action has a content, but good in the abstract determines nothing, and hence it devolves on particular subjectivity to give this content its determination and constituents. Just as, in probabilism, anyone who is not himself a learned 'Reverend Father' [*Révérend Père*] may call on the authority of such a theologian in order to subsume a determinate content under the universal predicate 'good', so here every subject is immediately invested with this honour of giving a content to good in the abstract, or in other words subsuming a content under a universal. This content is only one of the many aspects of an action as a concrete whole, some of which may perhaps justify its description as 'criminal' and 'bad'. That determinate content which I, as subject, give to the good, however, is the good known to me in the action, i.e. it is my *good intention* (see § 114 [and § 120]). Thus there arises a contradiction between descriptions: according to one the action is good, according to the other it is criminal. Hence also there seems to arise, in connection with a concrete action, the question whether in such circumstances *the intention behind it is actually good*. It may not only be generally the case, however, that the good is what is actually intended;

it must in fact always be the case if it is held that good in the abstract is the subject's determining motive. Where wrong is done through an action which is well intentioned but in other respects criminal and evil, the wrong so done must, of course, also be good, and the important question would seem to be: which of these sides of the action is really the essential one? This objective question, however, is here out of place, or rather it is the subjective consciousness itself whose decision constitutes objectivity at this point. Besides, 'essential' and 'good' mean the same thing; one is just as much an abstraction as the other. Good is that which is essential in respect of the will; and the essential in this respect should be precisely this, that my action be characterized as good in my eyes. But the subsumption under the good of any content one pleases is the immediate and explicit result of the fact that this abstract good is totally devoid of content and so is simply reduced to meaning something *positive*, i.e. to something which is valid in some respect and which in its immediate character may even be valid as an essential end, as for example to do good to the poor, to take thought for myself, my life, my family, and so forth. Further, just as the good is the abstract, so the bad too must be without content and derive its specification from my subjectivity; and it is in this way also that there arises the moral end of hating and uprooting the bad, the nature of the bad being left unspecified.

Theft, cowardice, murder, and so forth, as actions, i.e. as achievements of a subjective will, have the immediate character of being satisfactions of such a will and therefore of being something *positive*. In order to make the action a good one, it is only a question of recognizing this positive aspect of the action as my *intention*. This positive aspect becomes the *essential* element in virtue of which the action is made good, because I know it to be what is good in my intention. Theft in order to do good to the poor, theft or flight from battle for the sake of fulfilling one's duty to care for one's life or one's family (a poor family perhaps into the bargain), murder out of hate or revenge (i.e. in order to satisfy one's sense of one's own right or of right in general, or one's sense of another's wickedness, of wrong done by him to oneself or to others or to the world or the nation at large, by extirpating this wicked individual who is wickedness incarnate, and thereby contributing at least one's quota to the project of uprooting the bad)—all these actions are made well intentioned and therefore good by taking account in this way of the positive aspect of their content. Only the bare minimum of intelligence is required to discover in any action, as those learned theologians can, a positive side and so a good reason for it and a good intention behind it. Hence it has been said that in the strict sense there are no evil people, since no one wills evil for the sake of evil, i.e. no one wills the purely negative as such. On the contrary, everyone always wills something positive, and therefore, on the view we are considering, something good. In this abstract good the distinction between good and evil has vanished together with all concrete duties; for this reason, simply to will the good and to have a good intention in acting is evil rather than good, because the good willed is only this abstract form of good and the task of giving it *determinacy* thus falls to the arbitrary will of the subject.

To this context there also belongs the notorious maxim: 'The end justifies the means.' In itself and prima facie this expression is trivial and vacuous. Quite so, one may retort in terms equally general, a just end of course justifies the means, while an unjust end does not. The phrase: 'If the end is right, so is the means' is a tautology, since the means is precisely that which is nothing in itself but is for the sake of something else, and therein, i.e. in the end, has its purpose and worth—provided of course it be truly a means.

But the meaning of the above proposition is not just its formal significance; something more determinate is to be understood, namely that to use as means to a good end something which in itself is simply not a means at all, to violate something in itself sacrosanct, in short to commit a crime as a means to a good end, is permissible and even one's bounden duty. (i) There floats before the minds of those who say that the end justifies the means a vague consciousness of the dialectic of the aforesaid *positive* element in isolated legal or ethical principles, or of such equally vague general maxims as: 'Thou shalt not kill,' or 'Take care for your welfare and the welfare of your family'. Courts of law and soldiers have not merely the right but the duty to kill people, though there it is precisely determined what kind of people and what circumstances make the killing permissible and obligatory. So also my welfare and the welfare of my family must be subordinated to higher ends and so reduced to a means. (ii) Yet what bears the mark of crime is not something general of that kind, left vague and still subject to a dialectic; on the contrary, its determinate character is already objectively delimited. What is now placed over against this determination—the sacred end that is supposed to deprive the crime of its criminal nature—is nothing other than a *subjective opinion* about what is good and better. What happens here is the same as what happens when the will stops at willing good in the abstract, namely that every determinate characteristic of good and evil, right and wrong, that has being and validity in and for itself, is entirely swept away and the determination of them is assigned instead to the individual's feeling, imagination, and caprice.

(*e*) *Subjective opinion* is at last expressly acknowledged to be the measuring-rod of right and duty, when it is supposed that *the conviction which holds something to be right* is to decide the ethical character of an action. Since the good we will to do is here still without content, the principle of conviction only adds the further specification that the subsumption of an action under the category of good is the responsibility of the *subject*. In this way, any semblance of ethical objectivity has totally disappeared. A doctrine like this is directly connected with the self-styled philosophy, often mentioned already, which denies that the truth is knowable.* (The truth of spirit *qua* will, the rationality of spirit in its self-actualizing process, is to be found in the commandments of ethical life.) Asserting, as such philosophizing does, that the knowledge of the true is an empty vanity, transcending the territory of knowledge (which is supposed to be mere appearance), it must in the matter of action at once find its principle also in appearance; the ethical is thereby reduced to the distinctive view of the world held by the individual and to his *particular conviction*. The degradation into which philosophy has thus sunk appears doubtless at a first glance to be only an affair of supreme indifference, an occurrence confined to the trivial field of academic futilities; but such a view necessarily makes itself at home in ethics, an essential part of philosophy; and it is then that the true meaning of these views makes its first appearance in and is apprehended by the world of actuality.

The result of the dissemination of the view that subjective conviction, and it alone, decides the ethical character of an action is that the charge of hypocrisy, once so frequent, is now rarely heard; you can qualify evil as hypocrisy only on the assumption that certain actions are *in and for themselves* misdeeds, vices, and crimes, and that the defaulter is necessarily aware of them as such, because he is aware of and recognizes the principles and outward acts of piety and honesty even in the pretence in which he misapplies them. In other words, it was generally assumed as regards evil that it is a duty to know the good and to be aware of its distinction from evil. At any rate, however, there was an absolute injunction which forbade the commission of vicious and criminal actions and which insisted on such actions being imputed to the agent, insofar as he was a human being and not a beast. But if a good heart, a good intention, a subjective conviction are declared to be the sources from which actions derive their worth, then there is no longer any hypocrisy or evil at all; for whatever someone does, he can always turn it into something good through reflecting on his good intentions and motives, and so the moment of his *conviction* renders it good.[63] Thus there is no longer anything absolutely vicious or criminal in and for itself; and instead of the above mentioned frank and free, hardened and unperturbed sinner,[64] we have the person who is conscious of being fully justified by intention and conviction. My good intention in my action and my conviction of its goodness *make it good*. We speak of judging and evaluating an action; but on this principle it is only the intention and conviction of the agent, his *faith* [*Glauben*], by which he ought to be judged. Not, however, his faith in the sense in which Christ requires faith in *objective* truth, so that on one who has a bad faith, i.e. a conviction evil in its content, the judgement to be pronounced must be condemnation, i.e. one in conformity with this content. On the contrary, faith here means fidelity to conviction, and the question to be asked about action is: 'Has the agent in his acting kept *true to his conviction*?' Formal subjective

---

[63] *Hegel's note*: 'That he feels completely *convinced* I have not the least doubt. But how many people are led by such feelings of conviction into the worst of misdeeds. Thus, if everything may be excused on this ground, then there can no longer be any rational judgement of good and evil, honourable and shameful, decisions. Lunacy in that case would have equal rights with reason; or in other words reason would have no rights whatever, it would no longer be held to be valid. Its voice would be an absurdity [*Unding*]; *truth would be the possession of the one with no doubts!* I tremble at the results of such toleration, for it would be exclusively to the advantage of unreason.' (F. H. Jacobi to Count Holmer, on Count Stolberg's change of faith,* Eutin, 5 Aug. 1800, in *Brennus* [Berlin, Aug. 1802].)

[64] See the quotation from Pascal in Remark (a) to this Paragraph [p. 139 above].

fidelity [to one's own conviction] is thus alone held to contain what accords with duty.

This principle, under which conviction is equally determined as something *subjective*, cannot but thrust upon us the thought of the possibility of *error*, with the further implied presupposition of a law that is in and for itself. But *the law does not act*; it is only the actual human being who acts. And, on the aforesaid principle, the only question, in estimating the worth of human actions, is how far he has taken up the law *into his conviction*. But if on this theory it is not actions which are to be judged, i.e. measured in any way, by that law, it is impossible to see what the law is for and what end it is to serve. Such a law is degraded to a mere external letter, in fact to an empty word, for it is only my conviction which *makes it a law* and a binding duty for me.

Such a law may have behind it the authority of God or the state, or even the authority of millennia during which it was the bond which gave people, with all their deeds and destiny, coherence and subsistence—authorities which enshrine the *convictions* of countless *individuals*. If *I* now set against these the *authority* of my individual conviction—as my subjective conviction its validity lies only in its authority—this at first seems to be a piece of monstrous self-conceit; but this appearance of self-conceit is removed by the very principle that subjective conviction is to be the measuring-rod.

Even if reason and conscience—which shallow science and bad sophistry can never altogether expel—admit with a noble illogicality that error is possible, by describing crime, and evil generally, as only an error, we minimize the fault. For *to err is human**—who has not been mistaken on one point or another, whether he had fresh or pickled cabbage for dinner yesterday, and about innumerable other things of greater or lesser importance? But the difference between what is important and unimportant vanishes if everything depends on the subjectivity of conviction and on adherence to it. The said noble illogicality which admits the possibility of error is inevitable then in the nature of the case, but when it comes round to say that a bad conviction is only an error, it only falls into a further illogicality, the illogicality of dishonesty. At one moment conviction is made the basis of ethics and of the supreme value of humanity, and is thus pronounced supreme and sacrosanct; at another, all we have to do with is error, and my conviction is something trivial and contingent, in fact something strictly external, which may turn out this way or that. Indeed, my being convinced is something supremely trivial if I cannot know the truth; for then it is a matter of indifference *how* I think, and all that is left to my thinking is that empty good, the abstraction to which the understanding reduces the good.

One other point. It follows further, on this principle of justification by conviction, that, in dealing with the way others act in relation to my action, logic requires me to admit that they are quite right to maintain in accordance with *their* faith and conviction that my actions are criminal. On such logic, not merely do I gain nothing, but I am reduced from a position of freedom and honour to a situation of slavery and dishonour. Justice, which in itself is also mine, I experience only as an alien subjective conviction, and when it is executed on me, I believe myself to be acted on only by an external force.

(*f*) Finally, the supreme form in which this subjectivity is completely comprehended and expressed is the phenomenon which has been called by a name borrowed from Plato—'irony'. Only the name, however, is taken from Plato. He used it to describe a way of speaking employed by *Socrates*, who applied it in conversation when defending the Idea of truth and justice against the conceit of the uneducated and the sophistical consciousness, but who treated ironically only this consciousness, not the Idea itself. Irony is only a manner of conversing with *people*. Without this personal direction, the essential movement of thought is dialectic, but Plato was so far from taking the dialectical by itself [*für sich*], still less irony, to be the last word in thought and to be the Idea itself, that on the contrary he put a stop to the toing and froing of thought, and especially of subjective opinion, by submerging it in the substantiality of the Idea.[65]

[65] *Hegel's note*: My colleague, the late Professor Solger,* adopted the word 'irony', which Friedrich von Schlegel brought into use at a comparatively early period of his literary career and extended to include the said principle of subjectivity knowing itself as supreme. But Solger's finer sense was far from such exaggeration; he had philosophical insight and so seized upon and retained only that part of Schlegel's view which was dialectic in the strict sense, i.e. dialectic as the animating pulse of speculative enquiry. His last publication, a solid piece of work, a thorough *Critique of August Wilhelm von Schlegel's Lectures on Dramatic Art and Literature** [*Kritik über die Vorlesungen des Herrn August Wilhelm von Schlegel über dramatische Kunst und Literatur*] (*Wiener Jahrbuch*, vol. VII, pp. 90 ff.), I find somewhat obscure, however, and I cannot agree with the argument

   The culminating form of this subjectivity which conceives itself
as the final court of appeal—our topic here—can be nothing except
what was already present in itself in its preceding forms, namely
subjectivity *knowing* itself as the arbiter and judge of truth, right,
and duty. It consists then in this, that it knows the objective
ethical principles, but fails to immerse itself in their seriousness in

which he develops. 'True irony', he says (p. 92), 'arises from the view that so long as
human beings live in this present world, it is only in this world that they can fulfil their
destiny, even in the highest sense of that word. Any hope we may have of transcending
finite ends is foolish and empty conceit. Even the highest exists for our action only in a
shape that is limited and finite.' Rightly understood, this is Platonic doctrine, and very
true as a rejection of what he referred to earlier, namely the empty striving towards the
(abstract) infinite. But to say that the highest exists in a limited and finite shape, like the
ethical order (and that order is in essence actual life and action), is very different from
saying that the highest thing is a *finite* end. The outward shape, the form of finitude, in
no way deprives the content of ethical life of its substantiality and the infinity inherent
within it. Solger continues: 'And just for this reason the highest is in *us* as negligible as
the lowest and perishes of necessity with us and our nugatory thoughts and feelings. The
highest is truly existent in God alone, and as it perishes in us it is transfigured into something divine, a divinity in which we would have no share but for its immediate presence
revealed in the very disappearance of our actuality; now the mood to which this process
immediately becomes clear in human affairs is tragic irony.' The arbitrary name 'irony'
would be of no importance, but there is an obscurity here when it is said that it is the
highest which *perishes* with our nothingness and that it is in the disappearance of our
actuality that the divine is first revealed. We find the same again on p. 91: 'We see heroes
beginning to wonder whether they have erred in the noblest and finest elements of their
feelings and sentiments, not only in regard to their successful issue, but also to their
source and their worth; indeed, we are elevated by the *destruction of the best* itself.' The
tragic destruction of figures whose ethical life is on the highest plane can interest and elevate us and reconcile us to its occurrence only insofar as they come on the scene in opposition to one another together with equally justified but different ethical powers which
have come into collision through misfortune, with the result that then these figures
acquire guilt through their opposition to an ethical law. (The just destruction of utter
scoundrels and criminals who flaunt their villainy—the hero of a modern tragedy, *Die
Schuld*,* is one—has an interest for criminal law, but none at all for art proper which is
what is in question here.) Out of this situation there arises the right and wrong of both
parties and therefore the true ethical Idea, which, purified and in triumph over this *one-
sidedness*, is thereby reconciled in us. Accordingly, it is not the highest in us which perishes; we are elevated not *by the destruction of the best* but by the triumph of the true. This
it is which constitutes the true, purely ethical, interest of ancient tragedy (in romantic
tragedy the character of the interest undergoes a certain modification).* All this I have
worked out in detail in my *Phenomenology of Spirit* (pp. 404 ff.; cf. pp. 683 ff. [Miller
trans., 279 ff.; cf. 443 ff.]). But the ethical Idea is actual and present in the ethical world
without the misfortune of tragic clashes and the destruction of individuals overcome by this
misfortune. And this Idea's (the highest's) revelation of itself in its actuality as anything
but a nullity is what the external existence of ethical life, the state, has as its aim and puts
into effect, and what the ethical self-consciousness possesses, intuits, and knows in the
state and what thinking cognition comprehends there.

self-forgetfulness and self-renunciation and to base action upon them. Although related to them, it holds itself aloof from them and knows *itself* as that which wills and decides thus, although it may equally well will and decide otherwise.—You actually accept a law, it says, and honestly respect it as absolute [*an und für sich seiend*]. So do I, but I go further than you, because I am beyond this law and can make it to suit myself. It is not the thing that is excellent, but I who am so; as the master of law and thing alike, I simply play with them as with my caprice, and in this ironic consciousness in which I let the highest things perish, I *enjoy only myself*. This type of subjectivism not only substitutes a void for the whole content of ethics, right, duties, and laws—and so is evil, indeed inherently and quite universally evil—but in addition its form is a *subjective* void [*Eitelkeit*], i.e. it knows itself as this contentless void and in this knowledge knows *itself* as absolute.

In my *Phenomenology of Spirit*, 605 ff. [Miller trans., pp. 397 ff.] I have shown how this absolute self-complacency does not rest in a solitary worship of itself but may form a community whose bond and substance consist in, e.g., mutual assurances of conscientiousness and good intentions, the enjoyment of this mutual purity, but above all the refreshment derived from the glory of this self-knowledge and self-expression, from the glory of fostering and cherishing this experience. I have shown also how what has been called a 'beautiful soul'[66]—that still nobler type of subjectivism which empties the objective of all content and fades away through its lack of actuality—is, like other shapes, a variety [of subjectivism] related to the stage we are considering here. What is said here may be compared with the entire section (C), 'Conscience', in the *Phenomenology*, especially the part dealing with the transition to a higher stage—a stage, however, there different in character.*

Addition: Representational thinking [*Vorstellung*] may go further and pervert the evil will into a semblance of goodness. Although it cannot alter the nature of evil, it can invest it with a semblance of goodness. Since every action has a positive aspect, and since the category of good as opposed to evil is likewise reduced to positivity, I may claim that my action in relation to my intention is good. Thus evil is linked with the good not only in my

[66] See first explanatory note to p. 37 [p. 333 below]. [S.H.]

consciousness but in its positive aspect. When self-consciousness pretends, to others only, that its action is good, this form is that of *hypocrisy*. But if it goes so far as to claim that the deed is good in its own eyes also, then we have a still higher peak of the subjectivity that knows itself as absolute. For this type of spirit good and evil in and for themselves have both vanished, and the subject is therefore at liberty to pass off as good or evil anything he likes. This is the position of the absolute sophistry which usurps the office of lawgiver and rests the distinction between good and evil on its own caprice. The chief hypocrites are the religious ones (the Tartuffes)* who submit themselves to all ceremony and may even be pious in their own eyes [*für sich*], while yet they do just as they please. There is little mention of hypocrites nowadays, partly because the accusation of hypocrisy seems to be too harsh; partly, however, because hypocrisy in its immediate form has more or less disappeared. This downright lie, this veneer of goodness, has now become too transparent not to be seen through, and the divorce between doing good with one hand and evil with the other no longer occurs, since advancing culture has weakened the opposition between these categories.

Instead, hypocrisy has now assumed the subtler form of *probabilism*, which involves the agent's attempt to represent a transgression as something good from the point of view of his own conscience. This doctrine can only arise when the moral and the good are determined by authority, with the result that there are as many reasons as there are authorities for supposing that evil is good. Casuist theologians, Jesuits especially, have worked up these cases of conscience and multiplied them *ad infinitum*.

These cases have now been elaborated to such a high degree of subtlety that numerous clashes have arisen between them, and the opposition between good and evil has become so weak that in individual instances they appear to turn into one another. The only desideratum now is *probability*, i.e. something approximately good, something which may be supported by any single reason or authority. Thus the special characteristic of this standpoint is that its content is purely abstract; it presents the concrete content as something inessential or rather abandons it to bare opinion. On this principle, anyone may have committed a crime and yet have willed the good. For example, if an evil character is murdered, the positive side of the action may be proclaimed to be the withstanding of evil and the will to diminish it.

Now the next step beyond probabilism is that it is no longer a question of someone else's statement or authority; it is a question only of the subject himself, i.e. of *his own* conviction—a conviction which alone is able to make a thing good. The defect here is that everything is supposed to fall within the orbit of conviction alone and that right in and for itself, for which this conviction should be only the form, no longer exists. It is certainly not a matter of indifference whether I do something by habit and custom or because I am actuated throughout by the truth which underlies these. But objective truth is also different from my conviction, because conviction lacks the distinction between good and evil. Conviction always remains conviction, and the bad could only be that of which I am not convinced.

Now while this standpoint is the highest example of the obliteration of good and evil, it entails the admission that it is subject to error, and to that extent it is brought down from its pedestal into mere contingency and seems undeserving of respect. This form is now *irony*, the consciousness that this principle of conviction is not worth much and that, highest criterion though it be, it is only caprice that governs it. This standpoint is really a product of Fichte's philosophy, which proclaims that the I is absolute, i.e. is absolute certainty, the universal selfhood [*Ichheit*] which advances through a course of further development to objectivity. Of Fichte himself it cannot properly be said that he made subjective caprice a guiding principle in the sphere of the practical, but, later on, this principle of the mere particular, in the sense of 'particular selfhood', was deified by Friedrich von Schlegel with reference to the good and the beautiful. As a result, he made objective goodness only an image produced by my conviction, receiving support from my efforts alone, and dependent for its appearance and disappearance on me as its lord and master. If I relate myself to something objective, it vanishes at the same moment before my eyes, and so I hover over an immense space, summoning shapes from the depths and annihilating them. This supreme standpoint of subjectivity can emerge only in a period of advanced culture when faith has lost its seriousness, and its essence is simply 'all is vanity'.

Transition from Morality to Ethical Life

141. For the *good* as the substantial universal of freedom, but as something still *abstract*, therefore, determinations of some sort and the principle for determining them are required (though a principle identical with the good itself). For *conscience* similarly, as the purely abstract principle of determination, it is required that its determinations shall be universal and objective. If good and conscience are each elevated to independent totalities, then both become the indeterminate which *ought* to be determined.—But the integration of these two relative totalities into an absolute identity has already been implicitly [*an sich*] achieved in that this very subjectivity of pure self-certainty, aware in its vacuity of its gradual evaporation, is identical with the abstract universality of the good. The *concrete* identity of the good with the subjective will, an identity which is therefore the truth of them, is *ethical life* [*Sittlichkeit*].

The details of such a transition of the concept are made intelligible in logic. Here, however, it need only be said that it is the nature of the restricted and the finite (i.e. here the abstract good which only *ought to be*, and the equally abstract subjectivity which only *ought to be good*) to have its opposite present within it, the good its actuality, and subjectivity (the moment in which ethical life is actual) the good; but since they are one-sided they are not yet *posited* as what they are in themselves. They become so posited in their negativity. That is to say, in their one-sidedness, when each is bent on declining to have in it what is *in itself* [*an sich*] present in it—when the good is without subjectivity and a determinate character, and the determining principle, subjectivity, is without that which has being-in-itself [*das Ansichseiende*]—and when both build themselves into independent totalities, they annul themselves and thereby reduce themselves to moments, to moments of the concept which becomes manifest as their unity and, having acquired reality precisely through this positing of its moments, is now present as Idea—as the concept which has developed its determinations to reality and at the same time is present in their identity as their essence in itself.

The existence of freedom which was (α) first of all immediate as *right*, is (β) determined in the reflection of self-consciousness as the *good*. (γ) The third stage, originating here, in its transition from (β) to ethical life, as the truth of the good and subjectivity, is therefore the truth both of subjectivity and right. Ethical life is a subjective disposition, but one imbued with what is right in itself. The fact that this Idea is the truth of the concept of freedom is something which, in philosophy, must be *proved*, not presupposed, not adopted from feeling or elsewhere. This demonstration is contained only in the fact that right and the moral self-consciousness both display in themselves their return to this Idea as their result. Those who hope to be able to dispense with proof and demonstration in philosophy show thereby that they are still far from knowing the first thing about what philosophy is. On other topics argue they may, but in philosophy they have no right to join in the argument if they wish to argue without the concept.

Addition: Each of the two principles hitherto discussed, namely good in the abstract and conscience, is defective in lacking its opposite. Good in the abstract evaporates into something completely powerless, into which I may introduce any and every content, while the subjectivity of spirit becomes just as empty because it lacks any objective significance. Thus a longing may arise for an objectivity in which the human being gladly degrades himself to servitude and total subjection, if only to escape the torment of vacuity and negativity. Many Protestants have recently gone over to the Roman Catholic Church,[67] and they have done so because they found their inner life empty and grasped at something fixed, at a support, an authority, even if it was not exactly the stability of thought which they caught.

The unity of the subjective with the objective good in and for itself is *ethical life*, and in it we find the reconciliation which accords with the concept. Morality is the form of the will in general on its subjective side. Ethical life is more than the subjective form and the self-determination of the will; in addition it has as its content the concept of the will, namely freedom. The spheres of right and morality cannot exist independently [*für sich*]; they must have the ethical as their support and foundation, for right lacks the moment of subjectivity, while morality in turn alone possesses that moment, and consequently both right and morality lack actuality by themselves. Only the infinite, the Idea, is actual. Right exists only as a branch of a whole or like the plant which twines itself round a tree that is firmly rooted in and for itself.

[67] See explanatory notes to pp. 145, 253 [pp. 347, 356 below]. [S.H.]

ETHICAL LIFE

142. Ethical life is the *Idea of freedom* in that, on the one hand, it is the living good—the good endowed in self-consciousness with knowing and willing and actualized by self-conscious action—while, on the other hand, self-consciousness has in the ethical realm its foundation in and for itself and its motivating end. Thus ethical life is the concept of freedom *developed into the existing world and the nature of self-consciousness.*

143. Since this unity of the concept of the will with its existence—i.e. the particular will—is knowing, consciousness of the distinction between these two moments of the Idea is present, but present in such a way that now each of these moments is for itself the totality of the Idea and has the latter as its foundation and content.

144. (α) The objective ethical order, which comes on the scene in place of good in the abstract, is substance made *concrete* by subjectivity as *infinite form*. Hence it posits within itself distinctions whose specific character is thereby determined by the concept,* and which endow the ethical order with a stable content which is necessary for itself and whose existence [*Bestehen*] is exalted above subjective opinion and caprice. These distinctions are *laws and institutions that have being in and for themselves.*

Addition: In the whole of ethical life the objective and subjective moments are alike present, but both of them are only its forms. Its substance is the good, i.e. the objective is filled with subjectivity. If we consider ethical life from the objective standpoint, we may say that in it we are ethical unselfconsciously. In this sense, Antigone proclaims that 'no one knows whence the laws come; they are everlasting',* i.e. they are the determination that is in and for itself and has its source in the nature of the thing. Nonetheless, however, the substance of ethical life has a consciousness also, though the status of this consciousness is never higher than that of being one moment.

145. It is the fact that the ethical order is the system of these specific determinations of the Idea which constitutes its *rationality*. Hence the ethical order is freedom or the will in and for itself as what is objective, a circle of necessity whose moments are the ethical powers which govern the life of individuals. To these powers individuals are related as accidents to substance, and it is in individuals that these powers are represented, have the shape of appearance, and become actualized.

Addition: Since the determinations [i.e. the laws and institutions] of the ethical order make up the concept of freedom, they are the substance or universal essence of individuals, who are thus related to them as accidents only. Whether the individual exists or not is all one to the objective ethical order. It alone is permanent and is the power governing the life of individuals. Thus the ethical order has been represented by peoples as eternal justice, as gods existing in and for themselves, in contrast with which the empty business of individuals is only a fluctuating play.

146. (β) The substantial order, in this its *actual self-consciousness*, knows itself and so is an object of knowledge. This ethical substance and its laws and powers are, on the one hand, an object over against the subject, and from the latter's point of view they *are*—'are' in the highest sense of self-subsistent being. This is an absolute authority and power infinitely more firmly established than the being of nature.

The sun, the moon, mountains, rivers, and the natural objects of all kinds by which we are surrounded, *are*. For consciousness they have the authority not only of mere being but also of possessing a particular nature which it accepts and to which it adjusts itself in dealing with them, using them, or in being otherwise concerned with them. The authority of ethical laws is infinitely higher, because natural objects conceal rationality under the cloak of contingency and exhibit it only in their utterly external and individuated way.

147. On the other hand, they are not something alien to the subject. On the contrary, his spirit bears witness to them as to *its own essence*, the essence in which he has a *feeling of his selfhood*, and in which he lives as in his own element which is not distinguished from himself. The subject is thus directly linked to the ethical order by a relation which is closer to identity than even the relation of faith or trust.

Faith and trust emerge along with reflection; they presuppose the power of forming ideas and making distinctions. For example, it is one thing to be a pagan, a different thing to believe in a pagan religion. That relation, or rather this relationless identity, in which the

ethical order is the actual life of self-consciousness, can no doubt
pass over into a relation of faith and conviction and into a relation
produced by means of further reflection, i.e. into an insight due
to reasoning starting perhaps from some particular purposes,
interests, and considerations, from fear or hope, or from historical
conditions. But *adequate knowledge* of this identity depends on
thinking in terms of the concept.

148. As substantial in character, these laws and institutions are
duties binding on the will of the individual, because as subjective, as
inherently undetermined, or determined as particular, he distinguishes himself from them and hence stands related to them as to the
substance of his own being.

The ethical 'doctrine of duties' (I mean the objective doctrine,
not that which is supposed to be contained in the empty principle
of moral subjectivity, because that principle determines nothing—
see § 134) is therefore comprised in the systematic development of
the circle of ethical necessity which follows in this Third Part. The
difference between the exposition in this book and the form of a
'doctrine of duties'* lies solely in the fact that, in what follows, the
specific types of ethical life emerge as necessary relationships, but
that there the exposition ends, without being supplemented in
each case by the addition that 'this determination is therefore a
duty for human beings'.

A 'doctrine of duties' which is other than a philosophical science takes its material from existing relationships and shows its
connection with one's own ideas or with commonly encountered
principles and thoughts, purposes, impulses, feelings, etc.; and as
reasons for accepting each duty in turn, it may tack on the further
consequences which this duty may have in reference to the other
ethical relationships or to welfare and opinion. But an immanent
and logical 'doctrine of duties' can be nothing except the development of the relationships which are necessitated by the Idea of
freedom and are therefore actual in their entirety, to wit in the
state.

149. The bond of duty can appear as a *restriction* only on indeterminate subjectivity or abstract freedom, and on the impulses
either of the natural will or of the moral will which determines its
indeterminate good arbitrarily. The truth is, however, that in duty

the individual finds his *liberation*; first, liberation from dependence on mere natural impulse and from the depression which as a particular subject he cannot escape in his moral reflections on what ought to be and what might be; secondly, liberation from the indeterminate subjectivity which, never reaching reality or the objective determinacy of action, remains self-enclosed [*in sich*] and devoid of actuality. In duty the individual liberates himself so as to acquire his substantial freedom.

Addition: Duty is a restriction only on the arbitrary will of subjectivity. It stands in the way only of that abstract good to which subjectivity adheres. When we say: 'We want to be free,' the primary meaning of the words is simply: 'We want abstract freedom,' and every institution and every organ of the state passes as a restriction on freedom of that kind. Thus duty is a restriction not on freedom, but only on freedom in the abstract, i.e. on unfreedom. Duty is the attainment of our essence, the winning of *affirmative* freedom.

150. Virtue [*Tugend*] is the ethical order reflected in the individual character so far as that character is determined by nature. When virtue displays itself solely as the individual's simple conformity with the duties of the circumstances to which he belongs, it is rectitude [*Rechtschaffenheit*].

In an *ethical* community, it is easy to say what someone must do, what are the duties he has to fulfil in order to be virtuous: he has simply to follow the well-known and explicit rules of his own situation. Rectitude is the general character which may be demanded of him by law or custom. But from the standpoint of *morality*, rectitude often seems to be something comparatively inferior, something beyond which still higher demands must be made on oneself and others, because the craving to be something special is not satisfied with what is universal and has being in and for itself; it finds consciousness of distinctiveness only in what is *exceptional*.

The various facets of rectitude may equally well be called *virtues*, since they are also properties of the individual, although not specially of him in contrast with others. Talk about virtue *as such*, however, readily borders on empty rhetoric, because it is only about something abstract and indeterminate; furthermore, such talk with its reasons and expositions is addressed to the individual as a being of caprice and subjective inclination. In an

existing ethical order in which a complete system of ethical relations has been developed and actualized, *virtue proper* is in place
and actually appears only in exceptional circumstances or when
one obligation clashes with another. The clash, however, must be
a genuine one, because moral reflection can manufacture clashes of
all sorts to suit its purpose and give itself a consciousness of being
something special and having made sacrifices. It is for this reason
that the phenomenon of virtue proper is commoner when societies
and communities are uncivilized, since in those circumstances
ethical conditions and their actualization are more a matter of individual preference or the distinctive natural genius of an individual.
For instance, it was especially to Hercules that the ancients
ascribed virtue. In the states of antiquity, ethical life had not grown
into this free system of an objective order self-subsistently developed, and consequently it was by the distinctive genius of individuals that this defect had to be made good. It follows that if a
'doctrine of virtues' is not a mere 'doctrine of duties', and if therefore it embraces the particular aspects of character that are
grounded in nature, it will be a *natural history of spirit*.

Since virtues are ethical principles applied to the particular, and
since in this their subjective aspect they are something indeterminate, there emerges here for determining them the quantitative
principle of 'more or less'. The result is that consideration of them
introduces their corresponding defects or vices, as in Aristotle,
who defined each particular virtue as strictly a mean between an
excess and a deficiency.[68]

The content which assumes the form of duties and then virtues
is the same as that which also has the form of *impulses* (see Remark
to § 19). Impulses have the same basic content as duties and virtues,
but in impulses this content still belongs to the immediate will
and to natural feeling; it has not been developed to the point of
becoming ethical. Consequently, impulses have in common with
the content of duties and virtues only the abstract object on
which they are directed, an object indeterminate in itself, and so
devoid of anything to discriminate them as good or evil. Or in
other words, impulses, considered abstractly in their positive

---

[68] See Aristotle, *Nicomachean Ethics*, 1106a24 ff. [S.H.]

aspect alone, are good, while, considered abstractly in their negative aspect alone, they are evil (see § 18).

Addition: If someone performs this or that ethical action, this does not make him virtuous; he is virtuous only when this mode of behaviour is a constant feature of his character. Virtue is rather like ethical virtuosity,* and the reason why we speak of virtue less nowadays than formerly is that ethical living is no longer so much the form of a particular individual. The French are *par excellence* the people who speak most of virtue, and the reason is that amongst them the individual is characterized more by his idiosyncrasies or by a natural mode of conduct. The Germans, on the other hand, are more thoughtful, and amongst them the same content acquires the form of universality.

151. But in simple identity with the actuality of individuals ethical life [*das Sittliche*] appears as their general mode of conduct, i.e. as *custom* [*Sitte*], while the habitual practice of ethical living appears as a *second nature* which, put in the place of the initial, purely natural will, is the soul of custom permeating it through and through, the significance and the actuality of its existence. It is spirit living and present as a world, and the substance of spirit thus exists now for the first time as spirit.

Addition: Just as nature has its laws, and as animals, trees, and the sun fulfil their law, so custom [*Sitte*] is that which belongs to the spirit of freedom. Right and morality are not yet what custom [*Sitte*] is, namely spirit. In right, particularity is still not the particularity of the concept, but only that of the natural will. So, too, at the standpoint of morality, self-consciousness is not yet spiritual consciousness. At that level it is only the worth of the subject in himself that is in question—that is to say, the subject who determines himself by reference to good in contrast with evil still has the arbitrary will as the form of his willing. Here, however, at the standpoint of ethical life, the will is the will of the spirit and it has a content which is substantial and in conformity with itself.

Education is the art of making people ethical. It considers them as natural beings and shows them the way to a second birth, the way to change their original nature into a second, spiritual, nature, and makes this spiritual level *habitual* to them. At this point the opposition between the natural and the subjective will disappears, the subject's internal struggle dies away. To this extent, habit is part of ethical life as it is of philosophical thought also, since such thought demands that mind be trained against capricious fancies, and that these be broken and overcome to leave the way clear for rational thinking. The human being also dies from habit, i.e. when he has once come to feel completely at home in life, when he has become spiritually and physically dull, and when the opposition between subjective consciousness and spiritual activity has disappeared; for the human being is active only insofar as he has not attained his end and wants to produce and assert himself in the effort to attain it. When this has been fully achieved, activity and vitality are at an end, and the result—loss of interest in life—is spiritual or physical death.

152. In this way ethical substantiality has attained its *right*, and its right its *validity*. That is to say, the self-will of the individual has vanished together with his personal conscience which would like to exist for itself and opposed itself to the ethical substance. For, when his character is ethical, he recognizes as the end which moves him to act the universal which is itself unmoved but is disclosed in its specific determinations as rationality actualized. He knows that his own dignity and the whole stability of his particular ends are grounded in this same universal, and it is therein that he actually attains these. Subjectivity is itself the absolute form and existent actuality of the substantial order, and the distinction between subject, on the one hand, and substance, on the other, as the object, end, and controlling power of the subject, is the same as, and has vanished directly along with, the distinction between them in form.

Subjectivity is the ground of the existence [*Existenz*] of the concept of freedom (see § 106). At the level of morality, subjectivity is still distinct from this its own concept; but at the level of ethical life it is the existence of the concept in a way that is adequate to the concept itself.

153. The *right of individuals* to be *subjectively determined* as free is fulfilled when they belong to an actual ethical order, because their certainty of their freedom finds its truth in such an objective order, and it is in an ethical order that they are actually in possession of their *own* essence or their own inner universality (see § 147).

When a father inquired about the best method of educating his son in ethical conduct, a Pythagorean replied: 'Make him a citizen of a state with good laws.'* (The phrase has also been attributed to others [e.g. Socrates].)

Addition: The educational experiments, advocated by Rousseau in *Émile*,* of withdrawing people from the common life of every day and bringing them up in the country, have turned out to be futile, since no success can attend an attempt to estrange people from the laws of the world. Even if the young have to be educated in solitude, one should still not imagine that the fragrance of the spiritual world will not ultimately permeate this solitude or that the power of the world spirit is too feeble to gain the mastery of those outlying regions. It is by becoming a citizen of a good state that the individual first comes into his right.

154. The right of individuals to their *particularity* is also contained in the ethical substantial order, since particularity is the outward appearance of the ethical order*—a mode in which that order exists.

155. Hence in this identity of the universal will with the particular will, *right* and *duty* coalesce, and by being in the ethical order a human being has rights insofar as he has duties, and duties insofar as he has rights. In the sphere of abstract right, I have the right and another has the corresponding duty. In the moral sphere, the right of my own knowledge and will, as well as of my welfare, has not, but only *ought* to have, coalesced with duties and become objective.

Addition: A slave can have no duties; only a free human being has them. If all rights were put on one side and all duties on the other, the whole would be dissolved, since their identity alone is the fundamental thing, and it is to this that we have here to hold fast.

156. The ethical substance, as containing self-consciousness that is for itself and united with its concept, is the *actual spirit* of a family and a people.

Addition: Ethical life is not abstract like the good, but is intensely actual. Spirit has actuality, and individuals are accidents of this actuality. Thus in dealing with ethical life, only two views are possible: either we start from the substantiality of the ethical order, or else we proceed atomistically and build on the basis of individuality. This second point of view lacks spirit because it leads only to an aggregation, whereas spirit is not something individual, but is the unity of the individual and the universal.

157. The concept of this Idea has being only as spirit, as something knowing itself and actual, because it is the objectification of itself, the movement running through the form of its moments. It is therefore

(A) ethical spirit in its natural or immediate phase—the *family*. This substantiality loses its unity, passes over into division, and into the phase of relation, i.e. into:

(B) *civil society*—an association of members as self-subsistent individuals in a universality which, because of their self-subsistence, is only formal. Their association is brought about by their needs, by the legal system—the means to security of person and property—and by an external organization for attaining their particular and common interests. This external state

(C) is brought back to and welded into unity in the *constitution of the state* which is the end and actuality of both the substantial universal order and the public life devoted thereto.

SUB-SECTION I

THE FAMILY

158. The family, as the *immediate substantiality* of spirit, is specifically characterized by *love*, which is spirit's feeling of its own unity. Hence in a family, one's disposition is to have self-consciousness of one's individuality within this unity as the essentiality that has being in and for itself, with the result that one is in it not as an independent person but as a *member*.

Addition: Love means in general terms the consciousness of my unity with another, so that I am not in isolation by myself but win my self-consciousness only through the renunciation of my independence [*Fürsichsein*] and through knowing myself as the unity of myself with another and of the other with me. Love, however, is feeling, i.e. ethical life in the form of something natural. In the state, feeling disappears; there we are conscious of unity as law; there the content must be rational and known to us. The first moment in love is that I do not wish to be a self-subsistent and independent person and that, if I were, then I would feel defective and incomplete. The second moment is that I find myself in another person, that I count for something in the other, while the other in turn comes to count for something in me. Love, therefore, is the most tremendous contradiction; the understanding cannot resolve it since there is nothing more stubborn than this point [*Punktualität*] of self-consciousness which is negated and which nevertheless I ought to possess as affirmative. Love is at once the producing and the resolving of this contradiction. As the resolving of it, love is unity of an ethical type.

159. The right which the individual enjoys thanks to the unity of the family, and which is in the first place simply the individual's life within this unity, takes on the *form of right* (as the abstract moment of determinate individuality) only when the family begins to dissolve.

At that point those who should be family members both in their disposition and in actuality begin to be self-subsistent persons, and whereas they formerly constituted one specific moment within the whole, they now receive their share separately and so only in an external fashion by way of money, food, educational expenses, and the like.

Addition: The right of the family properly consists in the fact that its substantiality should have determinate existence. Thus it is a right against externality and against secession from the family unity. On the other hand, to repeat, love is a feeling, something subjective, against which unity cannot make itself effective. The demand for unity can be sustained, then, only in relation to such things as are by nature external and not conditioned by feeling.

160. The family is completed in these three phases:

(a) *marriage*, the form assumed by the concept of the family in its immediate phase;

(b) *family property and assets* (the external existence of the concept) and attention to these;

(c) *the education of children and the dissolution of the family.*

A. *Marriage*

161. Marriage, as the *immediate ethical relationship*, contains first, the moment of *natural* life; and since marriage is a substantial relationship, the life involved in it is life in its totality, i.e. as the actuality of the species [*Gattung*] and its life-process.[69] But, secondly, in self-consciousness the natural sexual union—a union which is purely inward or in itself and whose existence [*Existenz*] is for that very reason purely external—is changed into a *spiritual* union, into self-conscious love.

Addition: Marriage is in essence an ethical relationship. Formerly, especially in most systems of natural law, attention was paid only to the physical side of marriage or to its natural character. Consequently, it was treated only as a sexual relationship, and this completely barred the way to its other characteristics. This is crude enough, but it is no less so to think of it as only a civil contract, and even Kant does this.* On this view,

---

[69] *Hegel's reference*: See *Encyclopaedia*, §§ 167 ff. and §§ 288 ff. [3rd edn. §§ 220 ff. and §§ 366 ff.].

the parties are bound by a contract of mutual caprice, and marriage is thus degraded to the level of reciprocal use governed by contract. A third view of marriage is that which bases it on love alone, but this must be rejected like the other two, since love is only a feeling and so is exposed in every respect to contingency, a shape which ethical life may not assume. Marriage, therefore, is to be more precisely characterized as rightfully ethical [*rechtlich sittliche*] love, and this eliminates from marriage the transient, fickle, and purely subjective aspects of love.

162. On the subjective side, marriage may have a more obvious source in the particular inclination of the two persons who are entering upon the marriage relationship, or in the foresight and contrivance of the parents, and so forth. But its objective source lies in the free consent of the persons, especially in their consent to make themselves *one person*, to renounce their natural and individual personality to this unity of one with the other. From this point of view, their union is a self-restriction, but in fact it is their liberation, because in it they attain their substantial self-consciousness.

Our objective determination and so our ethical duty is to enter the married state. The external origin of any particular marriage is in the nature of the case contingent, and it depends principally on the extent to which reflective thought has been developed. At one extreme, the first step is that the marriage is arranged by the contrivance of benevolent parents; the appointed end of the parties is a union of mutual love, and their inclination to marry arises from the fact that each grows acquainted with the other from the first as a destined partner. At the other extreme, it is the inclination of the parties which comes first, appearing in them as *these* two infinitely particularized individuals. The more ethical way to matrimony may be taken to be the former extreme or any way at all whereby the decision to marry comes first and the inclination to do so follows, so that in the actual wedding both decision and inclination coalesce. In the latter extreme, it is infinitely particular distinctiveness [*Eigentümlichkeit*] which makes good its claims in accordance with the subjective principle of the modern world (see Remark to § 124).

But those works of modern art, dramatic and other, in which the love of the sexes is the main interest, are pervaded by a chill despite the heat of passion they portray, for they associate the passion with contingency throughout and represent the entire dramatic interest as if it rested solely on the characters as *these individuals*; what rests on them may indeed be of infinite importance to *them*, but is of none whatever in itself.

Addition: Amongst peoples who hold the female sex in scant respect, marriages are arranged by the parents at will without consulting the individuals concerned. The latter raise no objection, since the particularity of feeling does not yet make any claims for itself. For the woman it is only a matter of getting a husband, for the man, of getting a wife. In other circumstances, considerations of wealth, connections, political ends, may be the determining factor. In such circumstances, great hardships may arise through making marriage a means to other ends. Nowadays, however, the subjective origin of marriage, the state of being in love, is regarded as the only important originating factor. Here the position is represented to be that each must wait until his hour has struck and that one can bestow one's love only on one specific individual.

163. The *ethical aspect* of marriage consists in the parties' consciousness of this unity as their substantial aim, and so in their love, trust, and common sharing of their entire existence as individuals. When the parties have this disposition and their union is actual, their natural drive sinks to the level of a natural moment, destined to be extinguished in its very satisfaction. On the other hand, the spiritual bond of union secures its rights as the substance of marriage and thus rises, as indissoluble in itself, to a plane above the contingency of passion and the transience of particular caprice.

It was noted above (in § 75) that marriage, so far as its essential basis is concerned, is not a contractual relation. On the contrary, though marriage begins in contract, it is precisely a contract to *supersede* [*aufheben*] the standpoint of contract, the standpoint from which persons are regarded in their individuality as self-subsistent units. The identification of personalities, whereby the family becomes *one person* and its members become its accidents (though substance is in essence the relation of accidents to itself),[70] is the ethical spirit. Taken by itself and stripped of the manifold externals of which it is possessed owing to its existence in *these* individuals and the interests of the phenomenal realm, interests determined in time and in numerous other ways, this spirit emerges as a shape for representational thinking [*Vorstellung*] and

---

[70] *Hegel's reference*: See *Encyclopaedia*, § 98 [3rd edn. § 150].

has been revered as the *Penates*, etc.; and in general it is in this spirit that the *religious* character of marriage and the family, or *pietas*,* is grounded. It is a further abstraction still to separate the divine, or the substantial, from its existence, and then to stamp it, together with the feeling and consciousness of spiritual unity, as what is falsely called 'Platonic' love. This separation is in keeping with the monastic doctrine which characterizes the moment of natural life as purely *negative* and which, precisely by thus separating the natural from the spiritual, endows the former by itself with infinite importance.

Addition: The distinction between marriage and concubinage is that the latter is chiefly a matter of satisfying natural desire, while this satisfaction is made secondary in the former. It is for this reason that natural occurrences may be mentioned in married life without a blush, although outside the marriage tie their mention would produce a sense of shame. But it is on this account, too, that marriage must be regarded as *in itself* indissoluble, for the end of marriage is the ethical end, an end so lofty that everything else is manifestly powerless against it and made subject to it. Marriage is not to be dissolved because of passion, since passion is subordinate to it. But it is only indissoluble *in itself*, since, as Christ says, divorce is permitted, though only 'for the hardness of your heart'. [71] Since marriage has feeling for one of its moments, it is not absolute but subject to fluctuations and potentially dissoluble. Legislators, however, must make its dissolution as difficult as possible and uphold the right of the ethical order against caprice.

164. By itself the stipulation of a contract contains the genuine transfer of the property in question (see § 79). Similarly, the solemn declaration by the parties of their consent to enter the ethical bond of marriage, and its corresponding recognition and confirmation by their family and community, constitutes the formal completion and actuality of marriage. (The fact that the church comes in in this connection is a further point, but not one for discussion here.) The knot is tied and made ethical only after this ceremony, whereby through the use of signs, i.e. of language (the most spiritual existence of spirit—see § 78), the substantial aspect of the marriage is brought completely into being. As a result, the sensuous moment, the one proper to natural life, is put into its ethical place as something only consequential and

---

[71] See Matthew 19: 8.

accidental, belonging to the external existence of the ethical bond, which indeed can subsist exclusively in reciprocal love and support.

If with a view to framing or criticizing legal determinations, the question is asked: what should be regarded as the chief end of marriage?, the question may be taken to mean: which single facet of marriage in its actuality is to be regarded as the most essential one? No one facet by itself, however, makes up the whole range of its content in and for itself, i.e. of its ethical character, and one or other of its facets may be lacking in an existing marriage without detriment to the essence of marriage itself.

It is in the actual conclusion of a marriage, i.e. in the ceremony, that the essence of the tie is expressed and established beyond dispute as something ethical, raised above the contingency of feeling and particular inclination. If this ceremony is taken as an external formality, a mere so-called 'civil requirement', it is thereby stripped of all significance except perhaps that of serving the purpose of edification and attesting the civil relation of the parties. It is reduced indeed to a mere *fiat* of a civil or ecclesiastical authority. As such it appears as something not merely indifferent to the true nature of marriage, but actually alien to it. The heart is constrained by the law to attach a value to the formal ceremony and the latter is looked upon merely as a condition which must precede the complete mutual surrender of the parties to one another. As such it appears to bring disunion into their loving disposition and, as an alien factor, to run counter to the inwardness of their union. Such a doctrine pretends to offer the highest conception of the freedom, inwardness, and perfection of love; but in fact it is a travesty of the ethical aspect of love, the higher aspect which restrains purely natural impulse and puts it in the background. Such restraint is already present at the natural level in *shame*, and it rises to chastity and modesty as consciousness becomes more specifically spiritual. In particular, the view just criticized casts aside marriage's specifically *ethical* character. This consists in the fact that the consciousness of the parties emerges from its natural and subjective mode to concentrate on what is substantial; instead of continually reserving to itself the contingency and caprice of sensuous inclination, it removes the marriage bond from the province of this caprice, surrenders to the substantial, and swears allegiance to the *Penates*; it subordinates the sensuous moment until the latter becomes something wholly conditioned by the true and ethical character of the marriage relation and by the recognition of the bond as an ethical one. It is effrontery and its buttress, the understanding, which cannot apprehend the speculative character of the substantial relationship; nevertheless, both ethical purity of heart and the legislation of Christian peoples are in accord with this speculative character.

Addition: Friedrich von Schlegel in his *Lucinde*, and a follower of his in the anonymous *Letters** (Lübeck and Leipzig, 1800), have put forward the view that the wedding ceremony is superfluous and a formality which might be discarded. Their reason is that love is, so they say, the substance of marriage and that the celebration therefore detracts from its worth. Surrender to sensual impulse is here represented as necessary to prove the freedom and inwardness of love—an argument not unknown to seducers.

It must be noticed in connection with relations between men and women that a girl in surrendering her body loses her honour. With a man, however, this is not so much the case, because he has a field for ethical activity outside the family. A girl is destined in essence only for the marriage relationship; it is therefore demanded of her that her love shall take the form of marriage and that the different moments in love shall attain their true rational relation to each other.

165. The difference in the natural characteristics of the two sexes has a rational basis[72] and consequently acquires an intellectual and ethical significance. This significance is determined by the difference into which the ethical substantiality, as the concept in itself, sunders itself in order that, through this difference, its vitality may become a concrete unity.

166. Thus one sex is spirit in its self-diremption into personal self-subsistence for itself and the knowledge and volition of *free universality*, i.e. the self-consciousness of conceptual thought and the volition of the objective final end. The other sex is spirit maintaining itself in unity as knowledge and volition of the substantial, but knowledge and volition in the form of *concrete individuality* and *feeling*. In relation to externality, the former is powerful and active, the latter passive and subjective. It follows that man has his actual substantial life in the state, in learning [*Wissenschaft*], and so forth, as well as in labour and struggle with the external world and with

---

[72] See *Encyclopaedia* (1830), §§ 369–70. [S.H.]

himself so that it is only out of his diremption that he fights his way to self-subsistent unity with himself. In the family he has a tranquil intuition of this unity, and there he lives a subjective ethical life on the plane of feeling. Woman, on the other hand, has her substantial vocation in the family, and her ethical disposition is to be imbued with family piety.

For this reason, family piety is declared in Sophocles' *Antigone*—one of the most sublime presentations of this virtue—to be principally the law of woman and the law of a substantiality at once subjective and on the plane of feeling, the law of the inward life, a life which has not yet attained its full actualization; it is declared to be the law of the ancient gods, the gods of the underworld, an everlasting law of which no one knows whence it appeared.[73] This law is there displayed as a law opposed to public law, to the law of the state. This is the supreme opposition in ethics and therefore in tragedy; and it is individualized in the same play in the opposing natures of man and woman.[74]

Addition: Women are capable of education, but they are not made for activities which demand a universal faculty such as the more advanced sciences, philosophy, and certain forms of artistic production. Women may have happy ideas [*Einfälle*], taste, and elegance, but they cannot attain to the ideal [*das Ideale*].* The difference between men and women is like that between animals and plants. Animals correspond more to the character of men, while plants correspond more to women because the latter's development is more peaceful and the principle that underlies it is the more indeterminate unity of feeling. When women hold the helm of government, the state is at once in jeopardy, because women regulate their actions not by the demands of universality but by contingent inclinations and opinions. Women are educated—one knows not how—by, as it were, breathing in ideas, by living rather than by acquiring knowledge. The status of manhood, on the other hand, is attained only through the achievement of thought and much technical exertion.

167. In essence marriage is *monogamy* because it is personality—immediate exclusive *individuality*—which enters into this relationship and surrenders itself to it; and hence the relationship's truth and inwardness (i.e. the subjective form of its substantiality) proceeds only from the mutual, *undivided*, surrender of this personality.

[73] See second explanatory note to p. 154 [p. 348 below]. [S.H.]
[74] *Hegel's reference*: See *Phenomenology*, 383 ff., 417 ff. [Miller trans., 267 ff., 286 ff.].

Personality attains its right of being conscious of itself in *another* only insofar as the other is in this identical relationship as a person, i.e. as an atomic individual.

Marriage, and especially monogamy, is one of the absolute principles on which the ethical life of a community depends. Hence marriage comes to be recorded as one of the moments in the founding of states by gods or heroes.

168. Further, marriage results from the *free surrender* by both sexes of their personality—a personality infinitely unique in each of the parties. Consequently, it ought not to be concluded within the *naturally* identical circle of people who are already acquainted and perfectly known to one another; for individuals in the same circle of relationship have no distinctive personality of their own in contrast with that of others in the same circle. On the contrary, the parties should be drawn from separate families and their personalities should be different in origin. Since the very concept of marriage is that it is a freely undertaken ethical action, not a bond grounded in immediate nature and its desires, it follows that the marriage of blood-relations runs counter to this concept and so also to genuine natural feeling.

Marriage itself is sometimes said to be grounded not in natural law but simply in natural sexual impulses; or again it is treated as a contract with an arbitrary basis. External arguments in support of monogamy have been drawn from physical considerations such as the number of men and women. Dark feelings are advanced as the sole ground for prohibiting consanguineous marriage. The basis of all these views is the fashionable idea of a state of nature and a natural origin for rights, and the lack of the concept of rationality and freedom.

Addition: A sense of shame is initially already a bar to consanguineous marriage. But this repugnance finds justification in the concept of the thing. For what is already united cannot be united for the first time by marriage. It is a commonplace of stock-breeding that the offspring are comparatively weak when animals of the same stock are mated, since if there is to be unification there must first be division. The force of generation, as of spirit, is all the greater, the greater the oppositions out of which it is reestablished. Familiarity, close acquaintance, the habit of common pursuits, should not precede marriage; they should be found only within it.

And the process of their discovery has all the more value, the richer it is and the more facets it has.

169. The family, as person, has its external reality in *property*; and only when this property takes the form of *resources* [*Vermögen*] does it become the existence of the substantial personality of the family.

B. *The Family's Resources*

170. It is not merely property which a family possesses; as a *universal* and *enduring* person, the family requires possessions specifically determined as *permanent* and *secure*, i.e. it requires *resources*. The arbitrariness of a mere individual's particular needs is one moment in property taken abstractly; but this moment, together with the selfishness of desire, is here transformed into something ethical, into care and acquisition for a *common purpose*.

In the sagas of the founding of states, or at least of a social and orderly life, the introduction of permanent property is linked with the introduction of marriage. The nature of these resources, however, and the proper means of their consolidation will appear in the section on civil society.[75]

171. The family as a legal [*rechtlich*] person in relation to others must be represented by the husband as its head. Further, it is his prerogative to go out and work for its living, to attend to its needs, and to control and administer its resources. These are common property so that, while no member of the family has property of his own, each has his right in the common stock. This right, however, may come into collision with the head of the family's right of administration owing to the fact that the ethical disposition of the family is still only at the level of immediacy (see § 158) and so is exposed to particularization and contingency.

172. A marriage brings into being a new family which is self-subsistent and independent of the clans or 'houses' from which its members have been drawn. The tie between these and the new family has a natural basis—consanguinity—but the new family is based on ethical love. Thus an individual's property too has an

[75] See *PR* §§ 199 ff. and 253.

essential connection with his marital relationship and only a comparatively remote one with his relation to his clan or 'house'.

The significance of marriage settlements which impose a restriction
on the couple's common ownership of their goods, of arrangements
to secure continued legal assistance for the woman, and so forth, lies
in their being provisions in case of the dissolution of the marriage,
either naturally by death, or by divorce, etc. They are also safe-
guards for securing that in such an eventuality the different members of the family shall secure their share of the common stock.

Addition: In many legal codes the wider circle of the clan is adhered to, and
this is regarded as the essential bond, while the other bond, that of each
particular family, appears less important in comparison. Thus in older
Roman law, the wife in the easily dissolved type of marriage* stood in a
closer relation to her kinsfolk than to her husband and children. Under
feudal law, again, the maintenance of the 'splendour of the family' [*splen-
dor familiae*] made it necessary for only the males of the family to be reckoned members and for the clan as a whole to count as the important thing,
while the newly founded family disappeared in comparison. Nevertheless,
each new family is the essential thing in contrast with the more remote
connections of clan-kinship, and parents and children form the nucleus
proper as opposed to the clan, which is also in a certain sense called a
'family'. Hence an individual's financial affairs must have a more essential
connection with his marriage than with the wider circle of his blood
relations.

C. *The Education of Children and the Dissolution of the Family*

173. In substance marriage is a unity, though only a unity of
inwardness or disposition; in outward existence, however, the unity
is sundered in the two parties. It is only in the children that the *unity*
itself exists for itself, objectively, and as a unity, because the parents
love the children as their love, as the existence of their own substance. From the natural point of view, the presupposition—persons
immediately existent (as parents)—here becomes a *result*,* a process
which runs away into the infinite series of generations, each producing the next and presupposing the one before. This is the mode in
which the simple spirit of the *Penates* reveals its existence as a species
in the finite sphere of nature.

Addition: The relation of love between husband and wife is not yet
objective, because even if their feeling is their substantial unity, still this

unity has no objectivity. Such an objectivity parents first acquire in their children, in whom they can see objectified the entirety of their union. In the child, a mother loves its father and he its mother. Both have their love objectified for them in the child. While in their resources their unity is embodied only in an external thing, in their children it is embodied in a spiritual one in which the parents are loved and which they love.

174. Children have the right to maintenance and education at the expense of the family's common resources. The right of the parents to their children's *services*, as services, is based upon and is restricted to the common task of looking after the family generally. Similarly, the right of the parents over the arbitrary will of their children is determined by the object in view—discipline and education. The punishment of children does not aim at justice as such; the aim is more subjective and moral in character, i.e. to deter them from exercising a freedom still in the toils of nature and to lift the universal into their consciousness and will.

Addition: A human being has to acquire for himself the position which he ought to attain; he is not already in possession of it through instinct. It is on this fact that the child's right to education is based. Peoples under patriarchal government are in the same position as children; they are fed from central stores and not regarded as self-subsistent and adults. The services which may be demanded from children should therefore have education as their sole end and be relevant thereto; they must not be ends in themselves, since a child in slavery is in the most unethical of all situations whatever. One of the chief factors in education is discipline, the purpose of which is to break the child's self-will and thereby eradicate what is merely sensuous and natural. We must not expect to achieve this by mere goodness, for the immediate will is precisely one that acts on immediate fancies and caprices, rather than on reasons and ideas [*Vorstellungen*]. If we advance reasons to children, we leave it open to them to decide whether the reasons are weighty or not, and thus we make everything depend on their whim. So far as children are concerned, universality and the substance of things reside in their parents, and this implies that children must be obedient. If the feeling of subordination, producing the longing to grow up, is not fostered in children, they become forward and impertinent.

175. Children are free *in themselves* and their life is only the immediate existence of this freedom. Consequently they are not things and cannot be the property either of their parents or others. In respect of his relation to the family, the child's education has the *positive* aim of instilling ethical principles into him in the form of an immediate feeling without opposition, so that thus equipped with the foundation of an ethical life, his heart may live its early years in love, trust, and obedience. In respect of the same relation, this education has the *negative* aim of raising children out of the natural immediacy in which they originally find themselves to self-subsistence and freedom of personality and so to the level at which they are able to leave the natural unity of the family.

One of the blackest marks against Roman legislation is the law whereby children were treated as slaves. This offence against the ethical order in its innermost and most tender life is one of the most important clues for understanding the place of the Romans in the history of the world and their tendency towards legal formalism.

The necessity for education is present in children as their own feeling of dissatisfaction with themselves as they are, as the desire to belong to the adult world whose superiority they sense, as the longing to grow up. The play theory of education* assumes that what is childish is itself already something of inherent worth and presents it as such to the children; in their eyes it lowers serious pursuits, and education itself, to a form of childishness for which the children themselves have scant respect. The advocates of this method represent the child, in the immaturity in which he feels himself to be, as really mature and they struggle to make him satisfied with himself as he is. But they corrupt and distort his genuine and proper need for something better, and create in him a blind indifference to the substantial relationships of the spiritual world, a contempt for people because they have presented themselves to him, a child, in a contemptible and childish fashion, and finally a vanity and conceit which feeds on the notion of its own superiority.

Addition: As a child, a human being must have lived with his parents encircled by their love and trust, and rationality must appear in him as his very own subjectivity. In the early years it is education by the mother especially which is important, since ethical principles must be implanted in the child in the form of feeling. It is noteworthy that on the whole children love their parents less than their parents love them. The reason for this is that they are gradually increasing in strength, and are learning to stand on their own feet, and so are leaving their parents behind them. The parents, on the other hand, possess in their children the objective embodiment of their union.

176. Marriage is but the ethical Idea in its *immediacy* and so has its objective actuality only in the inwardness of subjective feeling and disposition. In this fact is rooted the initial contingency of its existence. There can be no compulsion on people to marry; and, on the other hand, there is no merely legal or positive bond which can hold the parties together once their dispositions and actions have become hostile and contrary. A third ethical authority,* however, is called for to maintain the right of marriage—an ethical substantiality— against the mere whims of hostile disposition or the contingency of a purely passing mood, and so forth. Such an authority distinguishes these from the total estrangement of the two parties and may not grant divorce until it is satisfied that the estrangement is total.

Addition: It is because marriage rests only on subjective, contingent feeling that it may be dissolved. The state, on the other hand, is not subject to partition, because it rests on law. To be sure, marriage *ought* to be indissoluble, but this remains merely an 'ought'. Yet, since marriage is an ethical institution, it cannot be dissolved at will but only by an ethical authority, whether the church or the law-court. If the parties are completely estranged, e.g. owing to adultery, then even the religious authority must permit divorce.

177. The ethical dissolution of the family consists in this, that once the children have been educated to freedom of personality, and have come of age, they become recognized as persons in the eyes of the law and as capable of holding free property of their own and founding families of their own, the sons as heads of new families, the daughters as wives. They now have their substantial destiny in the new family; by contrast, the old family falls into the background as merely the initial ground and origin, while *a fortiori* the clan, as an abstraction, is devoid of rights.

178. The natural dissolution of the family by the death of the parents, particularly the father, has *inheritance* as its consequence so far as the family resources are concerned. The essence of inheritance is the transfer to individual ownership of what are in themselves common resources. When comparatively remote degrees of kinship are in question, and when persons and families are so dispersed in civil society that they have begun to gain self-subsistence, this transfer

becomes all the more indeterminate as the sense of family unity fades away and as every marriage leads to the renunciation of previous family relationships and the founding of a new self-subsistent family.

One might think that the basis of inheritance lies in the fact that, by a person's death, his property becomes wealth *without an owner* [*herrenloses Gut*], and as such falls to the first person who takes possession of it. Since of course it is the relatives who are normally closest to hand and so are generally the first to take possession, this customary occurrence might be made into a rule by positive legislation in the interests of orderliness.—This notion [*Einfall*], however, disregards the nature of the family relationship.

179. The result of this disintegration of the family is that an individual may at will either squander his resources altogether, mainly in accordance with his individual caprices, opinions, and ends, or else look upon a circle of friends and acquaintances, etc., as if they were his family and make a will embodying a declaration to that effect, with the result that they become his rightful heirs.

The ethical justification of the freedom to dispose of one's resources by will to a circle of friends would depend on the formation of such a circle; but there goes to its formation so much accident, arbitrariness, and shrewd self-seeking, etc.—especially since testamentary hopes played a role in that formation—that the ethical moment in it is something very vague. Further, the recognition of a person's entitlement to bequeath his property arbitrarily is much more likely to be an occasion for breach of ethical obligations and for base exertions and equally base subservience; and it also provides opportunity and justification for the folly, caprice, and malice of attaching to professed benefactions and gifts vain, tyrannical, and vexatious conditions operative after the testator's death and so in any case after his property ceases to be his.

180. The principle that the members of the family grow up to be self-subsistent persons in the eyes of the law (see § 177) lets into the circle of the family something of the same arbitrariness and discrimination among the natural heirs, though its exercise there must be restricted to a minimum in order to prevent injury to the basic family relationship.

The simple direct arbitrariness of the deceased cannot be made the principle underlying the *right to make a will*, especially if it runs counter to the substantial right of the family. For after all no respect would be forthcoming for his wishes after his death, if not from the family's love and veneration for its deceased fellow-member. Such arbitrariness by itself contains nothing worthy of higher respect than the right of the family as such—on the contrary.

The other ground for the validity of testamentary disposition would lie simply in its arbitrary recognition by others.* But such an argument may primarily be admitted only when family ties, to which testamentary disposition is intrinsic, become remoter and more ineffective. If they are actually present, however, without being effective, the situation is unethical; and to give extended validity to arbitrary dispositions at the expense of family ties *eo ipso* weakens the ethical character of the latter.

To make the arbitrary will within the family the main principle of inheritance was part of the harsh and unethical legal system of Rome to which reference has been made already. That system even gave a father power to sell his son, and if the son was given his freedom by others, he came under his father's authority once more. Not until he had been given his freedom for the third time was he actually and finally free. The son never attained his majority *de jure* nor did he become a person in law; the only property he could hold was booty won in war (*peculium castrense*). If he passed out of his father's authority after being thrice sold and set free, he did not inherit along with those who had continued in bondage to the head of the family, unless the will specifically so provided.* Similarly, a wife (i.e. a *matrona*, not a wife who *in manum conveniret, in mancipio esset** and whose marriage was a slavery to her husband) remained attached to her family of origin rather than to the new family which by her marriage she had helped to found, and which was now properly *her own*, and she was therefore precluded from inheriting any share of the resources of those who were actually her own family, just as the latter could not inherit from their wife and mother.

Later, with the growing feeling for rationality, the unethical provisions of laws [*Rechte*] such as these and others were evaded in the course of their administration, for example with the help of the expression *bonorum possessio* instead of *hereditas* [inheritance], and through the fiction of naming a daughter [*filia*] a son [*filius*].[76] (The fact that there is a further distinction between *bonorum*

[76] See explanatory note to p. 26 [p. 331 below]. [S.H.]

possessio and *possessio bonorum* belongs to the kind of erudition that makes one a legal expert.)* This was referred to above (see Remark to § 3 [p. 25]) as the sad necessity to which the judge was reduced in the face of bad laws—the necessity of smuggling reason into them on the sly, or at least into some of their consequences. Connected with this were the terrible instability of the chief political institutions and a riot of legislation to stem the outbreak of resulting evils.

From Roman history and the writings of Lucian and others,* we are sufficiently familiar with the unethical consequences which this right of arbitrariness in testamentary dispositions had among the Romans.

Marriage is ethical life at the level of immediacy; in the very nature of the case, therefore, it must be a mixture of a substantial relationship with natural contingency and inner arbitrariness. Now when by the slave-status of children, by legal provisions such as those mentioned above as well as others consequential upon them, and in addition by the ease of Roman divorce, pride of place is given to arbitrariness instead of to the right of the substantial (so that even Cicero—and what fine writing about *honestum* and *decorum* there is in his *On Duties** and in all sorts of other places!— even Cicero divorced his wife as a business speculation in order to pay his debts with his new wife's dowry), then a legal road is paved to the corruption of manners, or rather the laws themselves necessitate such corruption.

The institution of the law of inheritance with a view to preserving the family and its *splendour* by means of *fideicommissa* and *substitutiones** (in order to favour sons by excluding daughters from inheriting, or to favour the eldest son by excluding the other children) is an infringement of the principle of the freedom of property (see § 62), like the admission of any other inequality in the treatment of heirs. And besides, such an institution depends on an arbitrariness which in and for itself has no right to recognition, or more precisely on the thought of wishing to preserve intact not so much *this* family but rather *this* clan or 'house'. Yet it is not this clan or 'house', but the family *as such* which is the Idea and which therefore possesses the right to recognition, and both the ethical disposition and families are much more likely to be preserved by freedom of resources [*Freiheit des Vermögens*] and equality of inheritance than by their opposites.

Institutions of the kind just described, like the Roman, wholly ignore the right that belongs to marriage by virtue of the fact that the latter completes the foundation of a distinctive and actual family (see § 172), and that, in contrast with the new family, what is called the family in the wide sense, i.e. the *stirps* or *gens*, becomes only an abstraction (see § 177) growing less and less actual the further it recedes into the background as one generation succeeds another. Love, the ethical moment in marriage, is by its very nature a feeling for actual living individuals, not for an abstraction.—The abstraction of the understanding appears in history as the principle underlying the contribution of the Roman Empire to world history (see § 357).[77]—In the higher sphere of the state, a right of primogeniture arises together with resources rigidly entailed; it arises, however, not arbitrarily but as the inevitable outcome of the Idea of the state. On this point see below, § 306.

Addition: In earlier times, a Roman father had the right to disinherit his children and even kill them. Later he lost both these rights. Attempts were made to forge into a legal system this incoherence between unethical institutions and devices to render them ethical, and it is the retention of this incoherence which constitutes the deficiency and difficulty of the German law of inheritance. To be sure, the right to make a will must be conceded; but in conceding it our point of view must be that this right of arbitrariness arises or is magnified with the dispersion and remoteness of the members of the family. Further, the so-called 'family of friends' which testamentary disposition brings with it may be admitted only in the absence of members of the family proper, i.e. of spouse and children. To make a will at all entails something obnoxious and disagreeable, because in making it I reveal the names of my favourites. Favour, however, is arbitrary; it may be gained surreptitiously by a variety of expedients, it may depend on all sorts of foolish reasons, and as a condition of having his name included in a will, a beneficiary may be required to subject himself to the most abject servilities. In England, the home of all sorts of eccentricity, there is no end to the folly and whimsicality of bequests.

Transition of the Family into Civil Society

181. The family disintegrates (both essentially, through the working of the principle of personality, and also in the course of nature) into a *plurality* of families, each of which conducts itself as in

[77] All editions have '§ 356'.

principle a self-subsistent concrete person and therefore as externally related to its neighbours. In other words, the moments bound together in the unity of the family, since the family is the ethical Idea still in its concept, must be released from the concept to self-subsistent reality. This is the stage of *difference*. This gives us, to use abstract language initially, the determination of particularity which is related to universality but in such a way that *universality* is its basic principle, though still only an inward principle; for that reason, the universal merely *appears* in the particular as its form. Hence this relation of reflection initially represents the loss of ethical life or, since this life as the essence necessarily *appears*,[78] this relation constitutes the *world of appearance* [*Erscheinungswelt*] of the ethical—*civil society*.

The expansion of the family, as its transition into a new principle, is in existence [*Existenz*] sometimes its peaceful expansion until it becomes a people, i.e. a nation, which thus has a common natural origin, or sometimes the coming together of scattered groups of families under the influence of an overlord's power or as a result of a voluntary association produced by the tie of needs and the reciprocity of their satisfaction.

Addition: The starting-point for the universal here is the self-subsistence of the particular, and the ethical order seems therefore to be lost at this point, since it is precisely the identity of the family which consciousness takes to be the primary thing, the divine, and the source of obligation. Now, however, a situation arises in which the particular is to be my primary determining principle, and thus my ethical determination is superseded [*aufgehoben*]. But I am in fact mistaken about this, since, while I suppose that I am adhering to the particular, the universal and the necessity of the connection between particulars remains the primary and essential thing. I am thus altogether on the level of semblance [*Schein*], and while my particularity remains my determining principle, i.e. my end, I am for that very reason the servant of the universal which actually retains power over me in the last resort.

SUB-SECTION 2
CIVIL SOCIETY

182. The concrete person, who as a *particular person* is his own end, is, as a totality of needs and a mixture of caprice and natural

---

[78] *Hegel's reference: Encyclopaedia, §§ 64 ff., §§ 81 ff. [3rd edn. §§ 112 ff., §§ 131 ff.].*

necessity, one principle of civil society. But the particular person is essentially so related to other particular persons that each asserts himself and finds satisfaction by means of the others, and at the same time simply by means of the form of *universality*, the second principle here.

Addition: Civil society is the [stage of] difference which intervenes between the family and the state, even if its formation follows later in time than that of the state, because, as [the stage of] difference, it presupposes the state; to subsist itself, it must have the state before it as something self-subsistent. Moreover, the creation of civil society is the achievement of the modern world which has for the first time given all determinations of the Idea their due. If the state is represented as a unity of different persons, as a unity which is only a community, then what is really meant is only civil society. Many modern constitutional theorists have been able to attain no other view of the state but this. In civil society each individual is his own end, everything else is nothing to him. But except in contact with others he cannot attain the whole compass of his ends, and therefore these others are means to the end of the particular individual. A particular end, however, assumes the form of universality through this relation to other people, and it is attained in the simultaneous attainment of the welfare of others. Since particularity is inevitably conditioned by universality, the whole sphere of civil society is the territory of mediation where there is free play for every idiosyncrasy, every talent, every accident of birth and fortune, and where waves of every passion gush forth, regulated only by reason shining through them. Particularity, restricted by universality, is the only standard whereby each particular individual promotes his welfare.

183. In the course of the actual attainment of selfish ends—an attainment conditioned in this way by universality—there is formed a system of complete interdependence, wherein the livelihood, welfare, and rightful existence [*rechtliches Dasein*] of one individual are interwoven with the livelihood, welfare, and rights of all. On this system, individual welfare, etc., depend, and only in this connected system are they actualized and secured. This system may initially be regarded as the *external state*, the state based on need, the state as the understanding envisages it.

184. The Idea in this its stage of division grants to each of its moments a distinctive existence; to *particularity* it gives the right to develop and launch forth in all directions; and to *universality* the right to prove itself not only the ground and necessary form of particularity,

but also the power over it and its final end. It is the system of ethical life, split into its extremes and lost, which constitutes the Idea's abstract moment, its moment of *reality*. Here the Idea is present only as a *relative totality** and as the inner necessity behind this outward appearance.

Addition: Here ethical life is split into its extremes and lost; the immediate unity of the family has fallen apart into a plurality. Reality here is externality, the dissolution of the concept, the self-subsistence of its moments which have now won their freedom and their determinate existence. Though in civil society universal and particular have fallen apart, yet both are still reciprocally bound together and conditioned. While each of them seems to do just the opposite of the other and supposes that it can exist only by keeping the other at arm's length, nonetheless each still conditions the other. Thus, for example, most people regard the paying of taxes as injurious to their particular interest, as something inimical and obstructive of their own ends. Yet, however true this *seems*, particular ends cannot be attained without the help of the universal, and a country where no taxes were paid could not be singled out as strengthening particularity. Similarly, it might seem that universal ends would be more readily attainable if the universal absorbed the strength of the particular in the way described, for instance, in Plato's *Republic*. But this, too, is only an illusion, since both universal and particular turn into one another and exist only for and by means of one another. If I further my ends, I further the ends of the universal, and this in turn furthers my ends.

185. Particularity by itself [*für sich*], given free rein in every direction to satisfy its needs, contingent caprices, and subjective desires, destroys itself and its substantial concept in this process of gratification. At the same time, the satisfaction of need, necessary and contingent alike, is contingent because it arouses [new desires] without end, is in thoroughgoing dependence on arbitrariness and external contingency, and is held in check by the power of universality. In these contrasts and their complexity, civil society affords a spectacle of extravagance and want as well as of the physical and ethical degeneration common to them both.

The independent development of particularity (compare Remark to § 124) is the moment which appeared in the states of the ancient world as an invasion of ethical corruption and as the ultimate cause of that world's downfall. Some of these ancient states were built on the patriarchal and religious principle, others on the principle of an ethical order which was more explicitly spiritual, though still comparatively simple; in either case they rested on original natural intuition. Hence they could not withstand the division which arose in this state of mind when self-consciousness was infinitely reflected into itself; when this reflection began to emerge, they succumbed to it, first in disposition and then in actuality, because the simple principle underlying them lacked the truly infinite power to be found only in that unity which allows the opposition within reason to develop to its full strength and which has so overcome the opposition that it maintains itself in it and integrates it into itself.

In his *Republic*, Plato presents substantial ethical life in its ideal beauty and truth; but he could only cope with the principle of self-subsistent particularity, which in his day had forced its way into Greek ethical life, by setting up in opposition to it his purely substantial state. He completely excluded such particularity from his state, even in its very beginnings in private property[79] (see Remark to § 46) and the family, as well as in its more developed form as subjective will, the choice of a social position [*des Standes*], and so forth. It is this defect which is responsible both for the misunderstanding of the deep and substantial truth of Plato's state and also for the usual view of it as a dream of abstract thinking, as what is often called a 'mere ideal'. The principle of the self-subsistent inherently infinite personality of the individual, the principle of subjective freedom, is denied its right in the purely substantial form which Plato gave to spirit in its actuality. This principle dawned in an inward form in the Christian religion and in an external form (and therefore in one linked with abstract universality) in the Roman world. It is historically subsequent to the Greek world, and the philosophical reflection which descends to its depth is likewise subsequent to the substantial Idea of Greek philosophy.

Addition: Particularity by itself is measureless excess, and the forms of this excess are themselves measureless. By means of their ideas and reflections human beings expand their desires, which are not a closed circle like animal instinct, and extend them into a bad infinity.[80] At the other end of the scale, however, want and destitution are measureless too, and the

---

[79] See fifth explanatory note to p. 61 [p. 335 below]. [S.H.]

[80] See explanatory note to p. 89 [p. 339 below]. [S.H.]

confusion of this situation can be brought into a harmony only by the state which has powers over it. Plato wished to exclude particularity from his state, but this is no help, since help on these lines would contravene the infinite right of the Idea to allow freedom to the particular. It was in the Christian religion principally that the right of subjectivity arose, together with the infinity of being-for-self, and while granting this right, the whole order must at the same time retain strength enough to bring particularity into harmony with the unity of ethical life.

186. But in developing itself independently to totality, the principle of particularity passes over into *universality*, and only there does it attain its truth and the right to which its positive actuality is entitled. This unity is not that of ethical identity, because at this level, that of division (see § 184), both principles are self-subsistent. It follows that this unity is present here not as freedom but as the *necessity* whereby the particular must rise to the form of universality and seek and gain its stability in that form.

187. Individuals in their capacity as citizens [*Bürger*] of this state are *private persons* whose end is their own interest. This end is mediated through the universal which thus *appears* as a *means* to its realization. Consequently, individuals can attain their ends only in so far as they themselves determine their knowing, willing, and acting in a universal way and make themselves links in this chain of social connections. In these circumstances, the interest of the Idea—an interest of which these members of civil society are as such unconscious—lies in the process whereby their individuality and their natural condition are raised, both by the necessities of nature and by the arbitrariness of their needs, to formal freedom and the formal universality of knowing and willing—the process whereby subjectivity in its particularity is *educated*.

The idea that the state of nature is one of innocence, and that there is a simplicity of manners in uncivilized [*ungebildet*] peoples, implies treating education [*Bildung*] as something purely external, the ally of corruption. Similarly, the feeling that needs, their satisfaction, the pleasures and comforts of one's particular life, and so forth, are absolute ends, implies treating education as a mere means to these ends. Both these views display lack of acquaintance with the nature of spirit and the end of reason. Spirit attains its actuality only by creating a division within itself, by submitting itself to natural needs and the network of these external necessities, and so imposing on itself this limitation and this finitude, and finally by developing itself inwardly under these limitations until it overcomes them and attains its objective existence in them. The end of reason, therefore, is neither the natural simplicity of manners mentioned above, nor, as particularity develops, the pleasure for pleasure's sake which education procures. On the contrary, its end is to work to eliminate natural simplicity, whether the passivity which is the absence of the self, or the crude type of knowing and willing, i.e. immediacy and individuality, in which spirit is absorbed. It aims in the first instance at securing for this, its externality, the rationality of which it is capable, i.e. the form of *universality* or the *understanding* [*Verständigkeit*]. By this means alone does spirit come to be at home with itself in this pure externality. There, then, spirit's freedom has existence and spirit comes to be *for itself* in this element which *in itself* is alien to spirit's appointed end, freedom; it has to do there only with what it has itself produced and stamped with its seal. It is in this way then that the *form of universality* comes into existence for itself in thought, and this form is the only worthy element for the existence of the Idea. *Education* in its absolute determination is, therefore, liberation and work towards a higher liberation still; education is the absolute transition from an ethical substantiality which is immediate and natural to the one which is spiritual and infinitely subjective and which has been raised to the shape of universality. In the individual subject, this liberation is hard labour against the pure subjectivity of demeanour, against the immediacy of desire, against the empty subjectivity of feeling and the arbitrariness of inclination. The disfavour showered on education is due in part to its being this hard labour; but it is through this educational labour that the subjective will itself attains objectivity within itself, an objectivity in which alone it is for its part capable and worthy of being the actuality of the Idea.

Moreover, this form of universality—the understanding—to which particularity has worked its way and developed itself, brings it about at the same time that particularity comes to be the genuine being-for-itself [*Fürsichsein*] of individuality. And since it is from this particularity that the universal derives the content which fills it as well as its infinite self-determination, particularity itself is present in ethical life as subjectivity that is infinitely free and for itself. This is the position which reveals education as a moment immanent in the Absolute and which makes plain its infinite value.

Addition: By educated people, we may initially understand those who without the obtrusion of their particularity can do what others do. It is precisely this particularity, however, which uneducated people display, since their behaviour is not governed by the universal characteristics of the object. Similarly, an uneducated person is apt to hurt the feelings of others. He simply lets himself go and does not reflect on the sensitivities of others. It is not that he intends to hurt them, but his conduct is not consonant with his intention. Thus education rubs the edges off particular characteristics until a person conducts himself in accordance with the nature of the thing. Genuine originality, which produces the real thing, demands genuine education, while false originality shows the kind of bad taste that only enters the heads of the uneducated.

188. Civil society contains three moments:

(A) The mediation of need and the satisfaction of the individual through his work and through the work and satisfaction of the needs of all others—the *system of needs*.

(B) The actuality of the universal of freedom therein contained— the protection of property through the *administration of justice*.

(C) Provision against contingencies still lurking in systems (A) and (B), and care for the particular interest as a common interest, by means of the *police* and the *corporation*.

A. *The System of Needs*

189. Particularity is in the first instance characterized in general by its contrast with the universal of the will and thus is *subjective need* (see § 59).[81] This attains its objectivity, i.e. its satisfaction, by means of (α) external things, which at this stage are likewise the property and product of the needs and wills of others, and (β) the activity and work that mediate between the two sides. The aim here is the satisfaction of subjective *particularity*, but the universal asserts itself in the relation which this satisfaction has to the needs of others and their free arbitrary wills. The appearance [*Scheinen*] of rationality thus produced in this sphere of finitude is the *understanding*, and this

---

[81] All editions have '§ 60'.

is the aspect which is of most importance in considering this sphere and which itself constitutes the reconciling element within it.

Political economy is the science which starts from this view of needs and labour but then has the task of explaining mass-relationships and mass-movements in their complexity and their qualitative and quantitative character. This is one of the sciences which have arisen out of the conditions of the modern world. Its development affords the interesting spectacle (as in Smith, Say, and Ricardo)* of thought working upon the endless mass of details which confront it at the outset and extracting therefrom the simple principles of the thing, the understanding *effective* in the thing and directing it. It is to find reconciliation here to discover in the sphere of needs this appearance [*Scheinen*] of rationality lying in the thing and effective there; but if we look at it from the opposite point of view, this is the field in which the understanding with its subjective aims and moral opinions vents its discontent and moral frustration.

Addition: There are certain universal needs such as food, drink, clothing, etc., and it depends entirely on contingent circumstances how these are satisfied. The fertility of the soil varies from place to place, harvests vary from year to year, one person is industrious, another indolent. But this medley of arbitrariness generates universal determinations by its own working; and this apparently scattered and thoughtless sphere is upheld by a necessity which automatically enters it. To discover this necessary element here is the object of political economy, a science which is a credit to thought because it finds laws for a mass of contingencies. It is an interesting spectacle here to see all the connections acting on one another; particular spheres of action fall into groups, influence others, and are helped or hindered by others. The most remarkable thing here is this mutual interlocking of particulars, which is what one would least expect because at first sight everything seems to be given over to the arbitrariness of the individual, and it has a parallel in the solar system which displays to the eye only irregular movements, though its laws may nonetheless be ascertained.

(a) The Nature of Need and its Satisfaction

190. An animal's needs and its ways and means of satisfying them are both alike restricted in scope. Though the human being is subject to this restriction too, yet at the same time he evinces his transcendence of it and his universality, first by the multiplication of needs and means of satisfying them, and secondly by the differentiation and division of concrete need into individual parts and aspects which in turn become different needs, particularized and so more abstract.

In [abstract] right, what we had before us was the *person*; in the sphere of morality, the *subject*; in the family, the *family member*; in civil society as a whole, the *citizen* [*Bürger*] or *bourgeois*. Here at the standpoint of needs (compare Remark to § 123) what we have before us is the concrete idea [*Vorstellung*] which we call the *human being*. Thus this is the first time, and indeed properly the only time, to speak of the *human being* in this sense.

Addition: An animal is something particular. It has its instincts and means of satisfying them, means which are limited and which it cannot overstep. Some insects are parasitic on a certain kind of plant; some animals have a wider range and can live in different climates, but there is always a restriction preventing them from having the range open to human beings. The need for shelter and clothing, the necessity of no longer leaving food raw but making it fit to eat and of destroying its natural immediacy, both mean that the human being has less comfort than an animal, and indeed, as spirit, he ought to have less. Understanding, with its grasp of distinctions, multiplies these human needs, and since taste and utility become criteria of judgement, even the needs themselves are affected thereby. Finally, it is no longer need but opinion which has to be satisfied, and it is precisely the educated person who analyses the concrete into its particulars. The very multiplication of needs involves a check on desire, because when people use many things, the urge to obtain any one thing which might be needed is less strong, and this is a sign that want altogether is not so imperious.

191. Similarly, the *means* to particularized needs and all the various ways of satisfying these are themselves divided and multiplied and so in turn become relative ends and abstract needs. This multiplication goes on *ad infinitum*; taken as a whole, it is *refinement*, i.e. a discrimination between these multiplied needs, and judgement on the suitability of means to their ends.

Addition: What the English call 'comfortable' is something inexhaustible and infinitely extendable, for every comfort can be shown to have its discomforts, and these discoveries never come to an end. Hence a need is produced not so much by those who immediately experience it, but by those who hope to make a profit from its creation.

192. Needs and means, as really existing [*reelles Dasein*], become something which has being for others by whose needs and work satisfaction is reciprocally conditioned. When needs and means become abstract in quality (see § 191), abstraction also becomes a determination of the reciprocal relation of individuals to one another. This universality, as the quality of *being recognized*, is the moment which makes *concrete* and *social* the isolated and abstract needs and their ways and means of satisfaction.

Addition: The fact that I must direct my conduct by reference to others introduces here the form of universality. It is from others that I acquire the means of satisfaction and I must accordingly accept their views. At the same time, however, I am compelled to produce means for the satisfaction of others. We play into each other's hands and so hang together. To this extent everything particular becomes something social. In dress fashions and hours of meals, there are certain conventions which we have to accept because in these things it is not worth the trouble to insist on displaying one's own discernment. The wisest thing here is to do as others do.

193. This moment thus becomes a particular end-determinant for means in themselves and their acquisition, as well as for the manner in which needs are satisfied. Further, it directly involves the demand for *equality* of satisfaction with others. The need for this equality and for emulation [*Nachahmung*], which is the equalizing of oneself with others, as well as the other need also present here, the need of the particular to assert itself in some distinctive way, become themselves a fruitful source of the multiplication of needs and their expansion.

194. Since in social needs, as the conjunction of immediate or natural needs with spiritual needs arising from ideas, it is needs of the latter type which because of their universality make themselves preponderant, this social moment has in it the aspect of *liberation*, i.e. the strict natural necessity of need is obscured and the human being is concerned with his own opinion, indeed with an opinion which is universal, and with a necessity of his own making alone, instead of with an external necessity, an inner contingency, and mere arbitrariness.

The idea has been advanced that in respect of his needs the human being lived in freedom in the so-called 'state of nature' when his needs were supposed to be confined to what are known as the simple necessities of nature, and when he required for their satisfaction only the means which the contingencies of nature directly assured to him. This view takes no account of the moment of liberation intrinsic to work, on which see the following Paragraphs. And apart from this, it is untrue, because to be confined to mere natural needs as such and their immediate satisfaction would simply be the condition in which the spirit is submerged in nature and so would be one of savagery and unfreedom, while freedom itself is to be found only in the reflection of the spirit into itself, in the spirit's distinction from nature and its reflection upon the latter.

195. This liberation is *formal* since the particularity of the ends remains their basic content. When social conditions tend to multiply and subdivide needs, means, and enjoyments indefinitely—a process which, like the distinction between natural and refined* needs, has no limits—this is *luxury*. In this same process, however, dependence and want increase *ad infinitum*, and the material to meet these is permanently barred to the needy because it consists of external objects with the special character of being the property of the free will of others, and hence from their point of view its recalcitrance is absolute.

Addition: The entire Cynical mode of life adopted by Diogenes* was nothing more nor less than a product of Athenian social life, and what determined it was the way of thinking against which his whole manner protested. Hence it was not independent of social conditions but simply their result; it was itself a rude product of luxury. When luxury is at its height, distress and depravity are equally extreme, and in such circumstances Cynicism is the outcome of opposition to refinement.

(b) The Nature of Work

196. The means of acquiring and preparing the particularized means appropriate to our similarly particularized needs is *work*. Through work the raw material directly supplied by nature is specifically adapted to these numerous ends by all sorts of different processes. Now this formative change confers value on means and gives them their utility, and hence human beings in what they consume are mainly concerned with the products of human beings. It is the products of human effort which human beings consume.

Addition: There is hardly any raw material which does not need to be worked on before use. Even air has to be worked for because we have to warm it. Water is perhaps the only exception, because we can drink it as we find it. It is by the sweat of their brows and the toil of their hands that human beings obtain the means to satisfy their needs.

197. The multiplicity of objects and situations which excite interest is the stage on which *theoretical education* develops. This education consists in possessing not simply a multiplicity of ideas and bits of knowledge [*Kenntnisse*], but also a flexibility and rapidity of mind, an ability to pass from one idea to another, to grasp complex and general relations, and so on. It is the education of the understanding as such, and so also the building up of language.—*Practical education*, acquired through working, consists first in the self-perpetuating need for something to do and the habit of simply being busy; next, in the strict adaptation of one's activity according not only to the nature of the material worked on, but also, and especially, to the arbitrary will of others; and finally, in a habit, produced by this discipline, of objective activity and universally applicable skills.

Addition: The barbarian is lazy and is distinguished from the educated person by his dull brooding, because practical education is precisely education in the need and habit of being busy. A clumsy person always produces a result he does not intend; he is not master of his own activity. The skilled worker, on the other hand, may be said to be the person who produces the thing as it ought to be and who encounters in his subjective activity no resistance to the aim he is pursuing.

198. The universal and objective element in work, on the other hand, lies in the process of *abstraction* which effects the subdivision of needs and means and thereby *eo ipso* subdivides production and brings about the *division of labour*. By this division, the work of the individual becomes less complex, and consequently his skill at his abstract work increases, as does the volume of his output. At the same time, this abstraction of skill and means of production completes and makes necessary everywhere the *dependence* of people on one another and their reciprocal relation in the satisfaction of their other needs. Further, the abstraction of production makes work more and more mechanical, until finally the human being is able to step aside and let a machine take his place.

(c) Resources

199. When people are thus dependent on one another and reciprocally related to one another in their work and the satisfaction of their needs, subjective self-seeking turns into a contribution to the satisfaction of the needs of everyone else. That is to say, by a

dialectical advance, subjective self-seeking turns into the mediation
of the particular through the universal, with the result that each
person in earning, producing, and enjoying on his own account is *eo
ipso* producing and earning for the enjoyment of everyone else. This
necessity, which is rooted in the complex interdependence of each on
all, now presents itself to each individual as the *universal permanent
resources* (see § 170) which give each the opportunity, by the exercise
of his education and skill, to draw a share from it and so be assured
of his livelihood, while what he thus earns by means of his work
maintains and increases the general resources.

200. A particular person's resources, or in other words his opportunity of sharing in the general resources, are conditioned, however,
partly by his own immediate assets (his capital), and partly by his
skill; this in turn is itself dependent not only on his capital, but also
on contingent circumstances whose multiplicity introduces
differences in the development of natural, bodily, and spiritual aptitudes, which were already in themselves [*für sich*] unequal. In this
sphere of particularity, these differences are conspicuous in every
direction and on every level, and, together with the arbitrariness and
contingency which this sphere contains as well, they have as their
inevitable consequence *inequalities* in the resources and skills of
individuals.

The objective *right of the particularity* of spirit is contained in the
Idea. People are made unequal by nature, where inequality is in
its element, and in civil society the right of particularity is so
far from cancelling this natural inequality that it produces it out
of spirit and raises it to an inequality of skill and resources, and
even to one of moral and intellectual education. To oppose to this
right a demand for equality is a folly of the empty understanding
which takes as real and rational its abstract equality and its
'ought-to-be'.

This sphere of particularity, which fancies itself the universal,
is still only relatively identical with the universal, and consequently it still retains in itself both natural and arbitrary particularity, or in other words the remnants of the state of nature.
Further, it is reason, immanent in the restless system of human
needs, which articulates it into an organic whole comprising
different members (see the following Paragraph).

201. The infinitely complex, crisscross, movements of reciprocal production and exchange, and the equally infinite multiplicity of means therein employed, converge, owing to the universality inherent in their content, and become distinguished into *general groups*. As a result, the entire complex is built up into *particular systems* of needs, means, and types of work relative to these needs, modes of satisfaction and of theoretical and practical education, i.e. into systems, to one or other of which individuals are assigned—in other words, into different *estates* [*Stände*].

Addition: The ways and means of sharing in the resources of society are left to the particularity of individuals, but the subdivision of civil society into different general branches is a necessity. The family is the primary basis of the state, but the estates are the second. The importance of the latter is due to the fact that although private persons are self-seeking, they are compelled to direct their attention to others. Here then is the root which connects self-seeking to the universal, to the state, whose care it must be that this connection is solid and firm.

202. The estates are specifically determined in accordance with the concept* as (a) the *substantial* or immediate [or agricultural] estate; (b) the reflecting or *formal* [or business] estate; and finally, (c) the *universal* estate [the estate of civil servants].

203. (a) The substantial [or agricultural] estate has its resources in the natural products of the soil which it cultivates—soil which is capable of exclusively private ownership and which demands formation in an objective way and not mere haphazard exploitation. In face of the connection of [agricultural] work and its fruits with separate and fixed times of the year, and the dependence of harvests on the variability of natural processes, the aim of need in this estate turns into provision for the future; but owing to the conditions here, the agricultural mode of subsistence remains one which owes comparatively little to reflection and one's own will, and this mode of life is in general such that this estate has the substantial disposition of an ethical life which is immediate, resting on the family relationship and trust.

The real beginning and original foundation of states has been rightly ascribed to the introduction of *agriculture* along with *marriage*, because the principle of agriculture brings with it the formation of the land and in consequence exclusively private property (compare Remark to § 170); the nomadic life of savages, who seek their livelihood from place to place, it brings back to the tranquillity of private rights and the assured satisfaction of their needs. Along with these changes, sexual love is restricted to marriage, and this bond in turn grows into an enduring union, inherently universal, while needs expand into care for a family, and personal possessions into family goods. Security, consolidation, lasting satisfaction of needs, and so forth—things which are the most obvious recommendations of marriage and agriculture—are nothing but forms of universality, modes in which rationality, the final end and aim, asserts itself in these spheres.

In this matter, nothing is of more interest than the ingenious and learned explanations which my distinguished friend, Herr Creuzer,* has given (notably in the fourth volume of his *Mythology and Symbolism*) of the agrarian festivals, images, and sanctuaries of the ancients. He shows that it was because the ancients themselves had become conscious of the divine origin of agriculture and other institutions associated with it that they held them in such religious veneration. In course of time, the character of this estate as 'substantial' undergoes modifications through the working of the civil law, in particular the administration of justice, as well as through the working of education, instruction, and religion. These modifications, which occur in the other estates also, do not affect the substantial content of the estate but only its form and the development of its power of reflection.

Addition: In our day the [agricultural] economy is also conducted on methods devised by reflective thinking, i.e. like a factory. This has given it a character like that of industry and contrary to its natural one. Still, the agricultural estate will always retain a mode of life which is patriarchal and the substantial disposition proper to such a life. The human being here accepts with immediate feeling what is given him and takes what he gets, thanking God for it and living in faith and trust that this goodness will continue. What comes to him suffices him; once it is consumed, more comes again. This is the simple attitude of mind not directed towards the acquisition of riches. It may be described as the attitude of the *old nobility* which consumed just what there was. So far as this estate is concerned, nature does the major part, while individual effort is secondary. In the business estate, however, it is understanding which is the essential thing, and natural products can be treated only as raw materials.

204. (b) The business estate has the task of giving form to the products of nature, and for its means of livelihood it is thrown back on its work, on reflection and understanding, and essentially on the mediation of one person's needs and work with those of others. For what this estate produces and enjoys, it has mainly *itself*, its own activity, to thank. The task of this estate is subdivided into:

(α) work to satisfy individual needs in a comparatively concrete way and to supply individual orders—craftsmanship;

(β) work of a more abstract kind, mass-production to satisfy individual needs, but needs in more universal demand—manufacture;

(γ) the business of exchange, whereby separate commodities are exchanged the one for the other, principally through the use of the universal medium of exchange, money, in which the abstract value of all goods is actualized—trade.

Addition: In the business estate, the individual is thrown back on himself, and this feeling of self-hood is most intimately connected with the demand for a condition in which right is respected. The sense of freedom and order has therefore arisen above all in towns. The agricultural estate, on the other hand, has little occasion to think for itself;* what it obtains is the gift of a stranger, of nature. Its feeling of dependence is fundamental to it, and with this feeling there is readily associated a willingness to submit to whatever may befall it at other people's hands. The agricultural estate is thus more inclined to subservience, the business estate to freedom.

205. (c) The universal estate [the estate of civil servants] has for its task the *universal interests* of society. It must therefore be freed from direct labour to meet its needs, either by having private means or by receiving an allowance from the state which claims its industry, with the result that private interest finds its satisfaction in its work for the universal.

206. The estates, as particularity become objective to itself, are thus distinguished in this general way in accordance with the concept. But the question of the particular estate to which an individual is to belong is one on which natural capacity, birth, and other circumstances have their influence, though the essential and final determining factors are *subjective opinion* and one's *particular arbitrary will*, which win in this sphere their right, their merit, and their dignity. Hence what happens here by inner necessity occurs at the same time by the mediation of the arbitrary will, and to the conscious subject it has the shape of being the work of his own will.

In this respect too there is a conspicuous difference, in relation to the principle of particularity and the subject's arbitrary will, between the political life of the east and the west, and also between that of the ancient and the modern world. In the former, the division of the whole into estates came about objectively of its own accord, because it is rational in itself; but the principle of subjective particularity was at the same time denied its rights, in that, for example, the allotment of individuals to estates was left to the rulers, as in Plato's *Republic*, Book III [415a–d], or to the accident of birth, as in the Indian caste-system. Thus subjective particularity was not incorporated into the organization of society as a whole; it was not reconciled in the whole, and therefore—since as an essential moment it emerges there in any event—it shows itself there as something hostile, as a corruption of the social order (see Remark to § 185). Either it overthrows society, as happened in the Greek states and in the Roman Republic; or else, should society preserve itself in being as a force or as a religious authority, for instance, it appears as inner corruption and complete degeneration, as was the case to some extent in Sparta and is now altogether the case in India.

But when subjective particularity is upheld by the objective order in conformity with it and is at the same time allowed its rights, then it becomes the animating principle of the entire civil society, of the development alike of thoughtful activity, merit, and dignity. The recognition and the right that what is made necessary by reason in civil society and the state shall at the same time be effected by the mediation of the *arbitrary will* is the more precise definition of what is primarily meant by the general idea [*Vorstellung*] of freedom (see § 121).

207. An individual actualizes himself only by entering into existence [*Dasein*] as such and hence into *determinate particularity*; this means restricting himself exclusively to one of the particular spheres of need. In this system of estates, the ethical disposition therefore is that of *rectitude* and the *honour of one's estate*, i.e. the disposition to make oneself a member of one of the moments of civil society by one's own act, through one's energy, industry, and skill, to maintain

oneself in this position, and to provide for oneself only through this process of mediating oneself with the universal, while in this way gaining *recognition* both in one's own eyes and in the eyes of others.— *Morality* has its proper place in this sphere where reflection on one's doings, as well as the aims of particular need and of welfare, are paramount, and where the contingency in satisfying these also makes contingent and individual acts of assistance into a duty.

At first (i.e. especially in youth) an individual chafes at the idea of deciding upon a particular estate, and looks upon this as a restriction on his universal character and as a necessity imposed on him purely *ab extra*. This is because his thinking is still of that abstract kind which refuses to move beyond the universal and so never reaches the actual. It does not realize that if the concept is to be determinate, it must first of all proceed to the distinction between the concept and its reality and thereby into determinacy and particularity (see § 7). It is only thus that the concept can win actuality and ethical objectivity.

Addition: When we say that a human being must be 'somebody' [*etwas*], we mean that he should belong to a specific estate, since to be a somebody means to have substantial being. A person with no estate is a mere private person and does not enjoy actual universality. On the other hand, the individual in his particularity may take himself as the universal and presume that by entering an estate he is surrendering himself to an indignity. This is the false idea that in attaining a determinacy necessary to it, a thing is restricting and surrendering itself.

208. The principle of this system of needs, which is that of the personal particularity of knowledge and volition, contains universality in and for itself, the universality of freedom, only abstractly and therefore as the *right of property*. At this point, however, this right is no longer merely a right *in itself* but has attained its recognized actuality in the protection of property through the *administration of justice*.

B. *The Administration of Justice*

209. The relativity of the reciprocal relation between needs and the work to satisfy these is first of all reflected into itself in infinite personhood, in abstract right. But it is this very sphere of

relativity—as that of education—which gives abstract right determinate existence as something *universally recognized, known, and
willed*, and as having a validity and an objective actuality mediated by
this known and willed character.

It is part of education, of thinking as the consciousness of the individual in the form of universality, that the I comes to be apprehended as a universal person in which all are identical. A human
being counts as a human being in virtue of his *humanity*, not
because he is a Jew, Catholic, Protestant, German, Italian, etc.
This consciousness, for which *thought* is what is valid, is of infinite
importance. It is defective only when it becomes fixed—e.g. as
cosmopolitanism—in opposition to the concrete life of the state.

Addition: From one point of view, it is through the working of the system
of particularity that right comes to be externally necessary as protection
for particular interests. Even though its source is the concept, right nonetheless only becomes something existent because this is useful for people's
needs. To become conscious in thought of his right, one must be trained
to think and not remain attached to the merely sensuous. We must invest
objects with the form of universality and similarly we must direct our willing according to a universal principle. It is only after human beings have
devised numerous needs and after their acquisition has become inter-
twined with satisfaction, that laws can be framed.

210. The objective actuality of right consists, first, in its existence
for consciousness, in its being *known* in some way or other; secondly,
in its possessing the power which the actual possesses, in its being
valid, and so also in its becoming *known as universally valid*.

(*a*) Right as Law

211. What is right in itself [*an sich*] becomes law [*Gesetz*] when it
is posited [*gesetzt*] in its objective existence, i.e. when thinking makes
it determinate for consciousness and makes it *known* as what is right
and valid; and in acquiring this determinate character, right becomes
positive right as such.

To posit something as universal, i.e. to bring it before consciousness as universal, is, I need hardly say, to *think* (compare Remarks
to §§ 13 and 21). Thereby its content is reduced to its simplest
form and so is given its final determinacy. In becoming law, what
is right acquires for the first time not only the form proper to its

universality, but also its true determinacy. Hence making a law is not to be represented as merely the expression of a rule of behaviour valid for everyone, though that is one moment in legislation; the more important moment, the inner essence of the matter, is *knowledge of the content* in its *determinate universality*.

Since it is only animals which have their law as instinct, while human beings alone have law as custom, even *customary rights* contain the moment of being thoughts and being known. Their difference from law consists in the fact that they are known only in a subjective and contingent way, with the result that in themselves they are less determinate and the universality of thought is less clear in them; in addition, knowledge of this or that aspect of right, or of right as such, is the contingent property of the few. The supposition that customary right, on the strength of its character as *custom*, possesses the privilege of having become part of *life* is a delusion, since the valid laws of a nation do not cease to be its customs by being written and codified—and besides, it is as a rule precisely those versed in the deadest of topics and the deadest of thoughts who talk nowadays of 'life' and of 'becoming part of life'. When a people begins to acquire even a little education, its customary rights must soon come to be collected and put together. Such a collection is a *legal code*, but one which, as a mere collection, is markedly formless, indeterminate, and fragmentary. The main difference between it and a code properly so-called is that in the latter the principles of right in their *universality*, and so in their determinacy, have been apprehended in terms of thought and expressed. The law of the land, or common law, of England is contained, as is well known, in statutes (formal laws) and in so-called 'unwritten' laws. This unwritten law, however, is likewise written, and knowledge of it may, and indeed must, be acquired simply by reading the numerous quartos which it fills. The monstrous confusion, however, which prevails both in English law and its administration is graphically portrayed by those acquainted with the matter.* In particular, they comment on the fact that, since this unwritten law is contained in court verdicts and judgements, the judges are continually *legislators*. The authority of precedent is binding on them, since their predecessors have done nothing but give expression to the unwritten law; and yet they are just as much exempt from its authority, because they are themselves repositories of the unwritten law and so have the right to criticize previous judgements and pronounce whether they accorded with the unwritten law or not.

A similar confusion might have arisen in the legal system of the later Roman Empire owing to the different but authoritative judgements of all the famous jurists. An Emperor* met the situation, however, by an ingenious expedient when, by what was called the Law of Citations, he set up a kind of college of jurists who were long deceased. There was a President, and the majority vote was accepted.[82]

No greater insult* could be offered to a civilized people or to its lawyers than to deny them ability to codify their law; for such ability cannot be that of constructing a legal system with a *novel content*, but only that of apprehending, i.e. grasping in thought, the content of existing laws in its determinate universality and then applying them to particular cases.

Addition: The sun and the planets have their laws too, but they do not know them. Barbarians are governed by impulses, customs, and feelings, but they have no consciousness of this. When right is posited [as law] and is known, every contingency of feeling and opinion vanishes together with the form of revenge, sympathy, and selfishness, and in this way right attains for the first time its true determinacy and is given its due honour. Only through the discipline of being apprehended does right first become capable of universality. In the course of applying the laws, collisions occur, and in dealing with these the judge's understanding has its proper scope; this is quite inevitable, because otherwise carrying out the law would be something thoroughly mechanical. But to go so far as to get rid of collisions altogether by leaving much to the judge's discretion is a far worse solution, because collisions are also intrinsic to thought, to conscious thinking and its dialectic, while the mere decision of a judge would be arbitrary.

It is generally alleged in favour of customary right that it is 'living', but this vitality, i.e. the identity of the determination with the subject, is not the whole essence of the matter. Right must be known by thought, it must be a system in itself, and only as such can it be recognized in civilized nations. The recent denial that peoples have a vocation to codify their laws is not only an insult; it also implies the absurdity of supposing that not a single individual has been endowed with skill enough to bring into a

[82] *Hegel's reference*: See Hugo, *Textbook of the History of Roman Law* [1799 edn.], § 354.

coherent system the endless mass of existing laws. The truth is that it is just systematization, i.e. elevation to the universal, which our time is pressing for without any limit. A similar view is that collections of judgements, like those available in the *Corpus Juris*,* are far superior to a legal code worked out in the most general way. The reason alleged is that such judgements always retain a certain particularity and a certain reminiscence of history which people are unwilling to sacrifice. But the mischievousness of such collections is made clear enough by the practice of English law.

212. Due to this identity of *being-in-itself* [*Ansichsein*] and *posited being* [*Gesetztsein*], the only right that is binding is what is *law* [*Gesetz*]. In being posited [as law], right acquires determinate existence. Into such existence there may enter the contingency of self-will and other particular circumstances; hence there may be a discrepancy between the content of the law and what is right in itself.

In positive right, therefore, what is legal [*gesetzmäßig*] is the source of our knowledge of what is right, or, more exactly, of our legal rights [*Rechtens*]. Thus the science of positive right is to that extent a historical science with authority as its guiding principle. Anything over and above this historical study is matter for the understanding and concerns the collection of laws, their classification on external principles, deductions from them, their application to fresh details, etc. When the understanding meddles with the nature of the thing itself, its theories, e.g. of criminal law, show what its deductive argumentation can concoct.

The science of positive right has not only the right, but even the inescapable duty, to study given determinations of right, to deduce from their positive data their progress in history, their applications and subdivisions, down to the last detail, and to exhibit their implications. On the other hand, if, after all these deductions have been proved, the further question about the *rationality* of a specific determination of right is raised, those who busy themselves with these pursuits should at least not be absolutely astonished, even if the question may seem to them to be beside the point.

With this Remark, compare what was said in the Remark to § 3 about 'understanding' the law.

213. Right gains determinate existence [*Dasein*] in the first place when it has the form of being posited [as law]; it also becomes

determinate in content by being *applied* both to the material of civil
society (i.e. to the endlessly growing complexity and subdivision of
social relations and the different species of property and contract
within the society) and also to ethical relations based on the heart, on
love and trust, though only insofar as these involve abstract right as
one of their aspects (see § 159). Morality and moral commands concern the will in its most personal subjectivity and particularity, and
so cannot be a matter for positive legislation. Further material for the
determinate content of law is provided by the rights and duties
which have their source in the administration of justice itself, in the
state, and so forth.

Addition: In the higher relationships of marriage, love, religion, and the
state, the only aspects which can become the subject of legislation are
those whose nature is such that they are capable of having an external
dimension. Still, in this respect there is a wide difference between the laws
of different peoples. The Chinese, for instance, have a law requiring a husband to love his first wife more than his other wives. If he is convicted of
doing the opposite, corporal punishment follows. Similarly, the legislation
of the ancients in earlier times was full of precepts about loyalty and
integrity which are unsuited by nature to legal enactment because they fall
wholly within the field of the inner life. It is only in the case of the oath,
whereby things are left to conscience, that integrity and loyalty must be
taken into account as something substantial.

214. But apart from being applied to the particular, right by being
posited [as law] becomes applicable to the *individual* case. Hence
it enters the sphere where *quantity*, not the concept, is the principle
of determination. This is the sphere of the quantitative for itself or
of the quantitative as the determination of value in the exchange of
qualitative items. In this sphere, the concept merely lays down a general limit, within which vacillation is still possible. This vacillation
must be terminated, however, in the interest of getting something
done, and for this reason there is a place within that limit for contingent and arbitrary decisions.

The purely positive side of law lies chiefly in this focusing of the
universal not merely on the particular, but on the individual case,
i.e. in its *immediate* application. Reason cannot determine, nor can
the concept provide any principle whose application could decide,
whether justice requires for an offence (i) a corporal punishment
of forty lashes or thirty-nine, or (ii) a fine of five dollars [*Taler*] or

four dollars and twenty-three groschen, etc.,* or (iii) imprisonment of a year or three hundred and sixty-four, three, etc., days, or a year and one, two, or three days. And yet injustice is done at once if there is one lash too many, or one dollar or one cent, one week in prison or one day, too many or too few.

Reason itself requires us to recognize that contingency, contradiction, and semblance have a sphere and a right of their own, restricted though it be, and it is irrational to strive to resolve and rectify contradictions within that sphere. Here the only interest present is that something be actually done, that the matter be settled and decided somehow, no matter how (within a certain limit). This decision belongs to abstract subjectivity, to formal self-certainty, which may simply rely either on its ability to terminate deliberation and settle the matter so that it is thereby settled, or on such reasons for decision as keeping to round numbers or always adopting, say, thirty-nine.*

It makes no difference if the law does not provide the ultimate determinacy required by actual life but leaves this to the judge's discretion, while limiting him by a maximum and minimum: for each maximum and minimum is itself a round number of this kind and so does not exempt the judge from making a finite, purely positive, decision, but of necessity leaves such a decision to him.

Addition: There is one essential element in law and the administration of justice which contains a measure of contingency and which arises from the fact that the law is a universal determination which has to be applied to the individual case. If you wished to declare yourself against this contingency, you would be talking in abstractions. The magnitude of a person's punishment, for example, cannot be made to correspond to any determination of the concept [of punishment], and the decision made, whatever it be, is from this point of view always arbitrary. But this contingency is itself necessary, and if you argue against having a code at all on the ground that any code is incomplete, you are overlooking just that element of law in which completion is not to be achieved and which therefore must just be accepted as it stands.

(b) The Existence [*Dasein*] of the Law

215. If laws are to have a binding force, it follows that, in view of the right of self-consciousness (see § 132 and the Remark thereto) they must be made *universally known*.

To hang the laws so high that no citizen could read them (as Dionysius the Tyrant did)* is injustice of one and the same kind as to bury them in row upon row of learned tomes, collections of dissenting judgements and opinions, records of customs, etc., and in a dead language too, so that knowledge of the law of the land is accessible only to those who have made it their professional study. Rulers who have given a law of the land to their peoples in the form of a well-arranged and clear-cut legal code—or even a mere formless collection of laws, like Justinian's[83]—have been the greatest benefactors of their peoples and have received thanks and praise for their beneficence. But the truth is that their work was at the same time a great act of *justice*.

Addition: The legal profession, possessed of a special knowledge of the law, often claims this knowledge as its monopoly and refuses to allow any layman to discuss the subject. Physicists similarly have taken amiss Goethe's theory of colours* because he did not belong to their craft and was a poet into the bargain. But we do not need to be shoemakers to know if our shoes fit, and just as little have we any need to be professionals to acquire knowledge of matters of universal interest. Right is concerned with freedom, the worthiest and holiest thing in humanity, the thing a human being must know if it is to have obligatory force for him.

216. For a public legal code, simple universal determinations are required, and yet the nature of the *finite* material to which law is applied leads to further determinations *ad infinitum*. On the one hand, the law ought to be a comprehensive whole, closed and complete; and yet, on the other hand, the need for further determinations is continual. But since this antinomy arises only through the *specialization* of universal principles, which remain fixed and unchanged, the right to a complete legal code remains unimpaired, like the right that these simple general principles should be capable of being laid down and understood apart and in distinction from their specialization.

A principal source of complexity in legislation is the gradual intrusion of reason, of what is rightful in and for itself, into primitive institutions which contain unjust features and so are purely historical survivals. This occurred in Roman law, as was remarked above

[83] See explanatory notes to pp. 20, 201 [pp. 329, 352 below]. [S.H.]

(see Remark to § 180), in medieval feudal law, etc. It is essential to notice, however, that the very nature of the finite material to which law is applied entails that the application to it even of inherently universal determinations that are rational in and for themselves entails an infinite progression.[84]

It is misunderstanding which has given rise alike to the demand— one that is chiefly a German sickness—that a legal code should be something absolutely complete, incapable of any further determination, and also to the argument that because a code is incapable of such completion, therefore we ought not to produce something 'incomplete', i.e. we ought not to produce a code at all. The misunderstanding rests in both cases on a misconception of the nature of a finite subject-matter like civil law [*Privatrecht*], whose so-called 'completeness' is a perennial approximation to completeness, on a misconception of the difference between the universal of reason and the universal of the understanding, and also on the application of the latter to the material of finitude and individuality which goes on for ever.—'The greatest enemy of the good is the better'* is the utterance of healthy common sense [*Menschenverstand*] against the common sense of vain argumentation and abstract reflection.

Addition: Completeness means the exhaustive collection of every single thing pertaining to a given field, and no science or branch of knowledge can be complete in this sense. Now if we say that philosophy or any one of the sciences is incomplete, we are not far from holding that we must wait until the deficiency is made up, since the best part may still be wanting. But take up this attitude and advance is impossible, either in geometry, which seems to be a closed science although new propositions do arise, or in philosophy, which is always capable of further specialization even though its subject is the universal Idea. In the past, the universal law always consisted of the Ten Commandments; now we can see at once that not to lay down the law 'Thou shalt not kill', on the ground that a legal code cannot be complete, is an obvious absurdity. Any code could be still better—no effort of reflection is required to justify this affirmation; we can think of the best, finest, and noblest as still better, finer, and nobler. But a big old tree puts forth more and more branches without thereby becoming a new tree; though it would be silly to refuse to plant a tree at all simply because it might produce new branches.

[84] See explanatory note to p. 89 [p. 339 below]. [S.H.]

217. Right in itself passes over in civil society into law. My individual right, whose existence has hitherto been immediate and abstract, now acquires the significance of being recognized, of having its existence in the existent will and knowledge of everyone. Hence property acquisitions and transfers must thus be undertaken and concluded only in the form which that existence gives to them. In civil society, property rests on contract and on the formalities which make ownership capable of proof and valid in law.

Original, i.e. immediate, titles and means of acquisition (see § 54 ff.) are in fact discarded in civil society and appear only as individual contingencies or as limited moments. It is either feeling, refusing to move beyond the subjective, or reflection, clinging to its abstract essences, which casts formalities aside, while the dead understanding may for its part cling to formalities instead of the real thing and multiply them indefinitely.

Moreover, the course of education is the long and hard labour to free a content from its sensuous and immediate form, endow it with its appropriate form of thought, and thereby give it simple and adequate expression. It is because this is the case that when the development of right is just beginning, ceremonies and formalities are highly elaborate and count rather as the thing itself than as its symbol. Thus even in Roman law, a number of determinations and especially phrases were retained from old-fashioned ceremonial usages, instead of being replaced by determinations of thought and phrases adequately expressing them.*

Addition: Law is right posited as what it is in itself. I possess something, own a property, which I occupied when it was ownerless. This possession must now further be recognized and posited as mine. Hence in civil society *formalities* arise in connection with property. Boundary stones are erected as a sign for others to recognize. Entries are made in mortgage and property registers. Most property in civil society is held on contract, and contractual forms are fixed and determinate. Now we may have an antipathy to formalities of this kind and we may suppose that they only exist to bring in money to the authorities; we may even regard them as something offensive and a sign of mistrust because they impair the validity of the saying: 'A man is as good as his word.' But the formality is essential because what is right in itself must also be *posited* as right. My will is a rational will; it has validity, and its validity should be recognized by others. At this point, then, my subjectivity and that of others must be set aside and the will must achieve the security, stability, and objectivity which can be attained only through such formalities.

218. Since property and personality have legal recognition and validity in civil society, wrongdoing now becomes an infringement, not merely of what is subjectively infinite, but of the *universal* thing [*Sache*] whose existence is inherently stable and strong. Hence a new attitude arises: the action is seen as a *danger* to society and thereby the magnitude of the wrongdoing is increased.[85] On the other hand, however, the fact that society has become strong and sure of itself diminishes the external importance of the injury and so leads to a greater leniency in its punishment.

The fact that an injury to one member of society is an injury to all others does not alter the nature of the crime according to its concept, but it does alter it in respect of its outward existence as an injury done, an injury which now affects the ideas [*Vorstellung*] and consciousness of civil society as a whole, not merely the existence of the person who is immediately injured. In heroic times, as we see in the tragedy of the ancients,* the citizens did not feel themselves injured by wrongs which members of the royal houses did to one another.

In itself, crime is an infinite injury [see § 95]; but as an existence [*Dasein*] it must be measured in quantity and quality (see § 96), and since its existence is determined as affecting the idea and consciousness of the validity of the laws, its danger to civil society is a determinant of the magnitude of a crime, or even one of its qualitative characteristics.

Now this quality or magnitude varies with the state of civil society; and this is the justification for sometimes attaching the penalty of death to a theft of a few pence or a turnip, and at other times a light penalty to a theft of a hundred or more times that amount. If we consider its danger to society, this seems at first sight to aggravate the crime; but in fact it is just this which has been the prime cause of the lessening of its punishment. A penal code, then, is primarily the child of its age and the state of civil society at the time.

Addition: It seems to be a contradiction that a crime committed in society appears more heinous and yet is punished more leniently. But while it

---

[85] Compare Remarks to *PR* §§ 96 and 319.

would be impossible for society to leave a crime unpunished, since that would be to posit it as right, still since society is sure of itself, a crime must always be something singular in comparison, something unstable and exceptional. The very stability of society gives a crime the status of something purely subjective which seems to be the product rather of natural impulse than of a deliberate will. In this light, crime acquires a milder status, and for this reason its punishment too becomes milder. If society is still unstable in itself, then an example must be made by inflicting punishments, since punishment is itself an example over against the example of crime. But in a society which is internally strong, the commission of crime is something so feeble that its annulment must be commensurable with its feebleness. Harsh punishments, therefore, are not unjust in and for themselves but are related to contemporary conditions. A criminal code cannot hold good for all time, and crimes are only semblances of reality [*Scheinexistenzen*] which may draw on themselves a greater or lesser degree of repudiation.

(c) The Court of Law

219. By taking the form of law, right steps into existence [*Dasein*]. It is then something on its own account [*für sich*], and in contrast with particular willing and opinion about what is right, it is self-subsistent and has to assert itself as something universal. The task of knowing and actualizing what is right in particular cases without the subjective feeling of particular interest falls to a public authority—the *court of law*.

The historical origin of the judge and his court may have had the form of a patriarchal relationship or of force or free choice; but this makes no difference to the concept of the thing. To regard the introduction of a legal system as no more than an optional act of grace or favour on the part of monarchs and governments (as Herr von Haller does in his *Restoration of Political Science*)* is a piece of the mere thoughtlessness which has no inkling of the point at issue in a discussion of law and the state. The point is that legal and political institutions are rational and therefore necessary in and for themselves, and the question of the form in which they arose or were introduced is irrelevant to a consideration of their rational basis.

At the other extreme from this view is the crude notion that the administration of justice is now, as it was in the days when might was right, an improper exercise of force, a suppression of freedom, and a despotism. The administration of justice must be regarded as a duty, just as much as a right, of the public authority; and as a right, it does not depend at all on whether or not individuals choose to entrust it to an authority.

220. When the right against crime has the form of *revenge* (see § 102), it is only right *in itself*, not right in the form of what is lawful [*Rechtens*], i.e. it is not just [*gerecht*] in its existence. Instead of the injured party, the injured *universal* now comes on the scene, and this has its proper actuality in the court of law. It takes over the pursuit and the penalizing of crime, and this pursuit consequently ceases to be the subjective and contingent retribution of revenge and is transformed into the genuine reconciliation of right with itself, i.e. into *punishment*. Objectively, this is the reconciliation of the law with itself; through the annulment [*Aufheben*] of the crime, the law restores itself and thereby actualizes its authority. Subjectively, it is the reconciliation of the criminal with himself, i.e. with the law known by him as his own and as valid for him and his protection; when this law is executed upon him, he himself finds in this process the satisfaction of justice and nothing save his *own* act.

221. A member of civil society has the right to stand in a court of law and, correspondingly, the duty to acknowledge the jurisdiction of the court and accept its decision as final when his own rights are in dispute.

Addition: Since any individual has the right to stand in court, he must also know what the law is or otherwise this privilege would be useless to him. But it is also his duty to stand trial. Under the feudal system, the powerful often refused to stand trial. They defied the court and alleged that the court was wrong to demand their appearance. These conditions, however, contravened the very idea of a court. Nowadays monarchs have to recognize the jurisdiction of the court in their private affairs, and in free states they commonly lose their case.

222. In court the specific character which rightness acquires is that it must be *demonstrable*. When parties go to law, they are put in the position of having to make good their evidence and their claims and to make the judge acquainted with the facts. These *steps in a legal process are themselves rights*, and their course must therefore be fixed by law. They also constitute an essential part of jurisprudence.

Addition: A person may be indignant if a right which he knows he has is refused him because he cannot prove it. But if I have a right, it must at the same time be a *posited* right. I must be able to explain and prove it, and its validity can only be recognized in society if its rightness in itself is also posited.

223. These steps in a legal process are subdivided continually within no fixed limits into more and more actions, each being distinct in itself and a right. Hence a legal process, in itself in any case a means, now begins to be something external to its end and contrasted with it. This long course of formalities is a right of the parties at law and they have the right to traverse it from beginning to end. Still, it may be turned into an evil, and even an instrument of injustice, and for this reason it must by law be made the duty of the parties to submit themselves to a simple court (a court of arbitration or court of the first instance* [*Schieds-, Friedensgericht*]) and to the attempt to reconcile their differences out of court, in order that they—and right itself, as the substance of the thing and so the thing really at issue— may be protected against legal processes and their misuse.

Equity involves a departure from formal rights owing to moral or other considerations and is concerned primarily with the content of the lawsuit. A court of equity, however, comes to mean a court which decides in an individual case without insisting on the formalities of a legal process or, in particular, on the objective evidence which the letter of the law may require. Further, it decides on the merits of the individual case as a unique one, not in the interest of making a legal disposition that would be universal.

224. Amongst the rights of the subjective consciousness are not only the publication of the laws (see § 215) but also the possibility of knowing that the law has been actualized in a particular case (of knowing the course of the proceedings, the legal argument, etc.). This is the right to the *public administration of justice*.* The reason for this is that a trial is in itself an event of universal validity, and although the particular content of the action affects the interests of the parties alone, its universal content, i.e. the right at issue and the judgement thereon, affects the interests of everybody.

If the members of the bench deliberate amongst themselves about the judgement which they are to deliver, such deliberations express particular opinions and views and so naturally are not public.

Addition: It is straightforward common sense to hold that the public administration of justice is right and just. A strong reason against such publicity has always been the elevated status of justices; they are unwilling to sit in public and they regard themselves as a sanctuary of right which laymen are not to enter. But an integral part of right and justice is the confidence which citizens have in them, and it is this which requires that legal proceedings shall be public. The right of publicity depends on the fact that (i) the aim of the court is justice, which *as* universal should come *before* the universal (i.e. before the public), and (ii) it is through publicity that the citizens become convinced that the judgement is actually just.

225. By the judgement of the court, the law is applied to an individual case, and the work of judgement has two distinct aspects: first, ascertainment of the nature of the case as an immediate individual occurrence (e.g. whether a contract, etc., has been made, whether an offence has been committed, and if so by whom) and, in criminal cases, reflection to determine the substantial, criminal, character of the deed (see Remark to § 119); secondly, the subsumption of the case under the law that right must be restored. Punishment in criminal cases falls under this law. Decisions on these two different aspects are different functions.*

In the Roman judicial system, this distinction of functions appeared in that the praetor pronounced judgement on the assumption that the facts were so and so, and then appointed a special *judex* to inquire into the facts.*

In English law, it is left to the insight or option of the prosecutor to determine the precise character of a criminal act (e.g. whether it is murder or manslaughter) and the court is powerless to alter the indictment if it finds the prosecutor's choice wrong.[86]

226. First, the conduct of the entire process of enquiry and of the legal actions between the parties (these themselves being rights—see § 222), and then also the second of the aspects of the work of judgement mentioned in the previous Paragraph, are tasks which properly belong to the judge at law. He is the organ of the law, and the case must be prepared for him in such a way as to make possible its subsumption under some principle; that is to say, it must be stripped of its apparent, empirical, character and raised to a recognized fact of a general type.

---

[86] See W. Blackstone, *Commentaries on the Laws of England* (1765-9), iv. 333.

227. The first aspect of the work of judgement, i.e. the knowledge of the facts of the case as an immediate individual occurrence, and the description of its general character, involves in itself no pronouncement on points of law. This is knowledge attainable by any educated person. In settling the character of an action, the subjective moment, i.e. the agent's insight and intention (see the Second Part [esp. § 119]), is the essential thing; and apart from this, the proof depends not on objects of reason or abstractions of the understanding, but only on individual details and circumstances, objects of sensuous intuition and subjective certainty, and therefore does not contain in itself any absolutely objective determination. It follows that judgement on the facts lies in the last resort with *subjective conviction* and conscience (*animi sententia*),* while the proof, resting as it does on the statements and assurances of others, receives its final though subjective verification from the *oath*.

In this matter it is of the first importance to fix our eyes on the type of proof here in question and to distinguish it from knowledge and proof of another sort. To establish by proof a determination of reason, like the concept of right itself, means to apprehend its necessity, and so demands a method other than that requisite for the proof of a geometrical theorem. Further, in this latter case, the figure is determined by the understanding and made abstract in advance according to a rule. But in the case of something empirical in content, such as a fact, the material of knowledge is a given sensuous intuition and subjective sense-certainty, and statements and assurances about such material. It is then a question of drawing conclusions and putting two and two together out of depositions of that kind, attestations and other details, etc. The objective truth which emerges from material of this kind and the method appropriate to it leads, when attempts are made to determine it objectively for itself, to half-proofs and then—as a perfectly logical consequence, which at the same time involves formal illogicality—to *extraordinary punishments*. But such objective truth means something quite different from the truth of a determination of reason or a proposition whose content the understanding has already determined abstractly for itself. To show that the strictly legal character of a court covers competence to ascertain this sort of truth about empirical events and thereby properly qualifies a court for this task and so both gives it an exclusive right *in itself* to perform it and lays on it the necessity of performing it—this was a principal factor in the consideration of how far decisions on points of fact, as well as on points of law, should be assigned to formal courts of law.

Addition: No grounds can be adduced for supposing that the judge, i.e. the legal expert, should be the only person to establish how the facts lie, for ability to do so depends on general, not on purely legal, education. Determination of the facts of the case depends on empirical details, on depositions about what happened, and on similar perceptions, or again on facts from which inferences can be drawn about the deed in question and which make it probable or improbable. Here then, it is a *certainty* which should be attained, not truth in the higher sense which is something utterly eternal. Here such certainty is subjective conviction, or conscience, and the problem is: What form should this certainty take in a court of law? The demand, commonly made in German law, that a criminal should confess his guilt, has this to be said for it, that the right of self-consciousness thereby attains a measure of satisfaction; consciousness must chime in with what the judges pronounce, and it is only when the criminal has confessed that the judgement loses its alien character so far as he is concerned. But a difficulty arises here, because the criminal may deny his guilt, and the interest of justice may be jeopardized. If, on the other hand, the subjective conviction of the judge is to hold good, some hardship is once more involved, because the accused is no longer being treated as a free human being. Now the middle term between these extremes is trial by jury, which meets the demand that the declaration of guilt or innocence shall spring from the soul of the criminal.*

228. When judgement is pronounced—so far as the function of judgement is the subsumption under the law of the qualified case—the right due to the parties on the score of their self-consciousness is preserved in relation to the *law* because the law is known and so is the law of the parties themselves, and in relation to the *subsumption*, because the trial is public. But when a decision is made concerning the particular, subjective, and external content of the case (knowledge of which falls under the first of the aspects described in § 225), this right is satisfied by the confidence which the parties feel in the subjectivity of those who make the decision. This confidence is based primarily on the equality between them and the parties in respect of their particularity, i.e. their social position [*Stand*], etc.

The right of self-consciousness, the moment of *subjective freedom*, may be regarded as the fundamental thing to keep before us in considering the necessity for publicity in legal proceedings and for the so-called *jury-courts** [*Geschworenengerichte*], and this in the last resort is the essence of what may be advanced in favour of these institutions on the score of their utility. Other points of view and reasoning about their several advantages and disadvantages may give rise to arguments and counter-arguments, but reasoning of this kind, like all reasoning from grounds, is either secondary and inconclusive, or else drawn from other and perhaps higher spheres. It may be the case that if the administration of justice were in the hands of purely professional courts, and there were no other institutions [such as juries], it would in theory be managed just as well, if not better. This may be so, but even if this possibility could be raised to probability, or even necessity, it still does not matter, for on the other side there is always the *right of self-consciousness*, which insists on its claims and would find that they are not satisfied.

Owing to the character of the entire body of the laws, knowledge both of what is right and also of the course of legal proceedings may become, together with the capacity to pursue one's rights, the property of a profession [*Stand*] which makes itself an exclusive clique by the use of a terminology like a foreign tongue to those whose rights are at issue. If this happens, the members of civil society, who depend for their livelihood on *their activity, on their own knowledge and will*, are kept strangers to the law, not only to those parts of it affecting their most personal and intimate affairs, but also to its substantial and rational basis, right itself, and the result is that they become the wards, or even in a sense the bondsmen, of the legal profession. They may indeed have the right to appear in court in person and to 'stand' there (*in judicio stare*), but their bodily presence is a trifle if their spirits are not to be there also, if they are not to follow the proceedings with their own knowledge, and if the justice they receive remains in their eyes a fate pronounced *ab extra*.

229. In civil society, the Idea is lost in particularity and has fallen asunder with the separation of inward and outward. In the administration of justice, however, civil society returns to its concept, to the unity of the universal in itself with subjective particularity, although here the latter is only the particularity of the individual case and the universality in question is that of *abstract right*. The actualization of this unity through its extension to the whole range of particularity is (i) the specific function of the *police*, though the unification which it effects is only relative; (ii) the *corporation* actualizes the unity as a limited but concrete totality.*

Addition: In civil society, universality is necessity only. When we are dealing with human needs, right as such is the only firm point. But this right—a merely restricted sphere—relates only to the protection of what I have; welfare is something external to right as such. This welfare, however, is an essential end in the system of needs. Hence the universal, which in the first instance is right only, has to be extended over the whole field of particularity. Justice is a big thing in civil society. Given good laws, a state can flourish, and freedom of property is a fundamental condition of its prosperity. Still, since I am inextricably involved in particularity, I have a right to claim that, in this association with other particulars, my particular welfare too shall be promoted. Regard should be paid to my welfare, to my particularity, and this is done through the police and the corporation.

C. *The Police and the Corporation*

230. In the system of needs, the livelihood and welfare of every individual is a *possibility* whose actual attainment is just as much conditioned by his arbitrary and particular nature as by the objective system of needs. Through the administration of justice, offences against property or personality are annulled. But the right actually present in the particular requires, first, that contingent hindrances to one aim or another be removed, and undisturbed safety of person and property be attained; and secondly, that the securing of every individual's livelihood and welfare be treated and actualized as a *right*, i.e. that *particular welfare* as such be so treated.

(*a*) Police [or the public authority]

231. Inasmuch as the particular will is still the principle governing the choice of this or that end, the universal authority by which security is ensured remains in the first instance, (a) restricted to the sphere of contingencies, and (b) an external organization.

232. Crime is contingency as the arbitrary willing of evil, and this is what the universal authority must prevent or bring to justice.

But, crime apart, the permissible arbitrary willing in actions that are rightful for themselves and in the private use of property also comes into external relation with other individuals, as well as with other public organizations established for realizing a common end. This universal aspect makes private actions a matter of contingency which escapes my control and which either does or may injure others and wrong them.

233. There is here only a *possibility* of injury; but the fact that no harm is done is, as a contingency, equally no more than a possibility. This is the aspect of *wrong* that is inherent in such actions; it is the ultimate reason for police control and penal justice.

234. The relations between external existents fall into the infinite of the understanding; there is, therefore, no intrinsic boundary between what is and what is not injurious, even where crime is concerned, or between what is and what is not suspicious, or between what is to be forbidden or subjected to supervision and what is to be exempt from prohibition, from surveillance and suspicion, from enquiry and the demand to render an account of itself. These details are determined by custom, the spirit of the rest of the constitution, contemporary conditions, the crisis of the hour, and so forth.

Addition: Here nothing hard and fast can be laid down and no absolute boundaries can be drawn. Everything here is personal; subjective opinion enters in, and the spirit of the constitution and the dangers of the time have to provide precision of detail. In time of war, for instance, many a thing, harmless at other times, has to be regarded as harmful. As a result of this presence of contingency, of personal arbitrariness, the public authority acquires a measure of odium. When reflective thinking is very highly developed, the public authority may tend to draw into its orbit everything it possibly can, for in everything some aspect may be found which might make it dangerous. In such circumstances, the public authority may set to work very pedantically and inconvenience the day-to-day life of people. But however great this annoyance, no objective line can be drawn here.

235. In the indefinite multiplication and interconnection of day-to-day needs, (*a*) the acquisition and exchange of the means to their satisfaction—on whose unhindered possibility everyone relies—and (*b*) the need to make the related enquiries and transactions as short as possible give rise to factors which are of common interest,

and when one person occupies himself with these his work is at the same time done for all. This situation also produces means and arrangements which may be of use to the community as a whole.* These universal activities and arrangements of common utility call for oversight and care on the part of the public authority.

236. The differing interests of producers and consumers may come into collision with each other; and although the right relation between them *on the whole* comes about automatically, still its adjustment also requires a control which stands above both and is consciously undertaken. The right to exercise such control in individual cases (e.g. in the fixing of the prices of the commonest necessaries of life) depends on the fact that, by being publicly offered for sale, goods in quite universal daily demand are offered not so much to an individual as such but rather to a universal purchaser, the public; and thus both the defence of the public's right not to be defrauded, and also the management of goods inspection, may lie, as a common concern, with a public authority. But public care and direction are most of all necessary in the case of the larger branches of industry, because these are dependent on conditions abroad and on combinations of distant circumstances which cannot be grasped as a whole by the individuals tied to these industries for their living.

At the other extreme to freedom of trade and commerce in civil society is public organization to provide for everything and determine everyone's labour—take, for example, in ancient times the labour on the pyramids and the other huge monuments in Egypt and Asia which were constructed for public ends, labour that was not mediated by the individual worker's particular arbitrary will and particular interest. Such particular interest invokes freedom of trade and commerce against control from above; but the more blindly it sinks into self-seeking aims, the more it requires such control to bring it back to the universal. Control is also necessary to diminish the danger of upheavals arising from clashing interests and to abbreviate the period in which their tension might be eased through the working of a necessity of which they themselves know nothing.

Addition: The oversight and care exercised by the public authority aims at being a middle term between an individual and the universal possibility [afforded by society] of attaining individual ends. It has to undertake street-lighting, bridge-building, the pricing of daily necessities, and the care of public health. In this connection, two main views predominate at the present time. One asserts that the superintendence of everything properly belongs to the public authority, the other that the public authority has nothing at all to settle here because everyone will direct his conduct according to the needs of others. The individual must have a right to work for his bread as he pleases, but the public also has a right to insist that essential tasks shall be properly done. Both points of view must be satisfied, and freedom of trade should not be such as to jeopardize the general good.

237. Now while the possibility of sharing in the general wealth is open to individuals and is assured to them by the public authority, still it is subject to contingencies on the subjective side (quite apart from the fact that this assurance must remain incomplete), and the more it presupposes skill, health, capital, and so forth as its conditions, the more is it so subject.

238. Initially, the family is the substantial whole whose function it is to provide for the individual on his particular side by giving him either the means and the skill necessary to enable him to earn his living out of the resources of society, or else subsistence and maintenance in the event of his incapacity. But civil society tears the individual from his family ties, estranges the members of the family from one another, and recognizes them as self-subsistent persons. Further, for the paternal soil and external inorganic nature from which the individual formerly derived his livelihood, it substitutes its own soil and subjects the permanent existence of the entire family itself to dependence on itself and to contingency. Thus the individual becomes a *son of civil society* which has as many claims upon him as he has rights against it.

Addition: To be sure, the family has to provide bread for its members, but in civil society the family is something subordinate and only lays the foundations; its effective range is no longer so comprehensive. Civil society is rather the tremendous power which draws people into itself and claims from them that they work for it, owe everything to it, and do everything by its means. If a human being is to be a member of civil society in this sense, he has rights and claims against it just as he had rights and claims in the family. Civil society must protect its members and defend their rights, while its rights impose duties on every one of its members.

239. In its character as a universal family, civil society has the right and duty of superintending and influencing *education*, inasmuch as education bears upon the child's capacity to become a member of society. Society's right here is paramount over the arbitrary and contingent preferences of parents, particularly in cases where education is to be completed not by the parents but by others. Likewise, society must make communal arrangements to this end so far as is practicable.

Addition: The line which demarcates the rights of parents from those of civil society is very hard to draw here. Parents usually suppose that in the matter of education they have complete freedom and may arrange everything as they like. The chief opposition to any form of public education usually comes from parents and it is they who talk and make an outcry about teachers and schools because they have a faddish dislike of them. Nonetheless, society has a right to act on tested principles and to compel parents to send their children to school, to have them vaccinated, and so forth. The disputes that have arisen in France* between the advocates of state supervision and those who demand that education shall be free, i.e. at the option of the parents, are relevant here.

240. Similarly, society has the right and duty of acting as trustee to those whose extravagance destroys the security of their own or their families' subsistence. It must substitute for extravagance the pursuit of the ends of society and the individuals concerned.

Addition: There was an Athenian law compelling every citizen to give an account of his source of livelihood.[87] Nowadays we take the view that this is nobody's business but one's own. Of course every individual is from one point of view independent [*für sich*], but he is also a member of the system of civil society, and while everyone has the right to demand subsistence from it, it must at the same time protect him from himself. It is not simply starvation which is at issue; the further end in view is to prevent the formation of a pauperized rabble [*Pöbel*]. Since civil society is responsible for feeding its members, it also has the right to press them to provide for their own livelihood.

241. Not only caprice, however, but also contingencies, physical conditions, and factors grounded in external circumstances (see § 200) may reduce people to *poverty*. The poor still have the needs common to civil society, and yet since society has withdrawn from

[87] See Herodotus, *Histories*, 2. 177.

them the natural means of acquisition (see § 217) and broken the bond of the family—in the wider sense of the clan (see § 181)—their poverty leaves them more or less deprived of all the advantages of society, the opportunity of acquiring skill or education of any kind, as well as the administration of justice, health-care, and often even the consolations of religion, and so forth. The public authority takes the place of the family where the poor are concerned in respect not only of their immediate want but also of laziness of disposition, malignity, and the other vices which arise out of their plight and their sense of injustice.

242. Poverty and, in general, the distress of every kind to which every individual is exposed, even in his natural environment, has a subjective side which demands similarly subjective aid, arising both from the special circumstances of a particular case and also from love and sympathy. This is the place where *morality* finds plenty to do despite all public organization. Subjective aid, however, both in itself and in its operation, is dependent on contingency and consequently society strives to make it less necessary, by discovering the general causes of penury and general means of its relief, and by organizing relief accordingly.

Casual almsgiving and casual endowments, e.g. for the burning of lamps before holy images, etc., are supplemented by public poor-houses, hospitals, street-lighting, and so forth. There is still quite enough left over and above these things for charity to do on its own account. A false view is implied both when charity insists on having this poor relief reserved solely to the particularity of feeling and the contingency of its knowledge and charitable disposition, and also when it feels injured or offended by universal regulations and ordinances which are obligatory. Public social conditions are on the contrary to be regarded as all the more perfect the less (in comparison with what is arranged publicly) is left for an individual to do by himself according to his particular opinion.

243. When civil society is in a state of unimpeded activity, it is engaged in expanding internally in population and industry. The amassing of wealth is intensified by *generalizing* (*a*) the linkage of people by their needs and (*b*) the methods of preparing and distributing the means to satisfy these needs, because it is from this double process of generalization that the largest profits are derived. That is one side of the picture. The other side is the subdivision and restriction of particular work. This results in the *dependence* and *distress* of the class [*Klasse*] tied to work of that sort, and these again entail the inability to feel and enjoy the broader freedoms and especially the spiritual benefits of civil society.

244. When the standard of living of a large mass of people falls below a certain subsistence level—a level regulated automatically as the one necessary for a member of the society—and when there is a consequent loss of the sense of right and wrong, of integrity and of honour in maintaining oneself by one's own activity and work, the result is the creation of a *rabble of paupers* [*Pöbel*]. At the same time this brings with it, at the other end of the social scale, conditions which greatly facilitate the concentration of disproportionate wealth in a few hands.

Addition: The lowest subsistence level, that of a rabble of paupers, is fixed automatically, but the minimum varies considerably in different countries. In England, even the very poorest believe that they have rights; this is different from what satisfies the poor in other countries. Poverty in itself does not turn people into a rabble; a rabble is created only when there is joined to poverty a disposition of mind, an inner indignation against the rich, against society, against the government, etc. A further consequence of this attitude is that through their dependence on chance people become frivolous and idle, like the Neapolitan *lazzaroni* for example.* In this way there is born in the rabble the evil of lacking sufficient honour to secure subsistence by its own labour and yet at the same time of claiming the right to receive subsistence. Against nature a human being can claim no right, but once society is established, poverty immediately takes the form of a wrong done to one class [*Klasse*] by another. The important question of how poverty is to be abolished is one that agitates and torments modern society in particular.

245. When the masses begin to decline into poverty, (*a*) the burden of maintaining them at their ordinary standard of living might be directly laid on the wealthier class, or they might receive the means of livelihood directly from other public sources of wealth (e.g. from rich hospitals, monasteries, and other foundations). In either case, however, the needy would receive subsistence directly, not by means of their work, and this would violate the principle of civil society and the feeling of individual independence and honour in its individual members. (*b*) As an alternative, they might be given subsistence indirectly through being given work, i.e. the opportunity to work. In this event the volume of production would be increased, but the evil consists precisely in an excess of production and in the lack of a proportionate number of consumers who are themselves also producers, and thus it is simply intensified by both of the methods (*a*) and (*b*) by which it is sought to alleviate it. It hence becomes apparent that despite an *excess of wealth* civil society is *not rich enough*, i.e. its own resources are insufficient, to check excessive poverty and the creation of a penurious rabble.

In the example of England we may study these phenomena on a large scale and also in particular the results of poor-rates, immense foundations, unlimited private beneficence, and above all the abolition [*Aufheben*] of the corporations. There, particularly in Scotland, the most direct measure against poverty and especially against the loss of shame and honour—the subjective bases of society—as well as against laziness and extravagance, etc., the begetters of the rabble, has turned out to be to leave the poor to their fate and instruct them to beg from the public.

246. This inner dialectic of civil society thus drives it—or at any rate drives a specific civil society—to push beyond its own limits and seek markets, and so its necessary means of subsistence, in other lands which are either deficient in the goods it has overproduced, or else generally backward in creative industry, etc.

247. The condition of the principle of family life is the earth, the firm and solid ground. Similarly, the natural element for industry, animating its outward movement, is the *sea*. In pursuit of gain, by exposing such gain to danger industry at the same time rises above it; instead of remaining rooted to the soil and the limited circles of civil life with its pleasures and desires, it embraces the element of fluidity, danger, and destruction. Further, the sea is the greatest means of communication, and trade by sea creates commercial connections between distant countries and so relations involving contractual rights. At the same time, commerce of this kind is the most potent instrument of education [*Bildung*], and through it trade acquires its world-historical significance.

Rivers are not natural boundaries, which is what they have been accounted to be in modern times. On the contrary, it is truer to say that they, and the sea likewise, link people together. Horace is wrong when he says: 'A prudent god has sundered the lands by the estranging sea.'* The proof of this is provided not merely by river basins which are inhabited by a tribe or people, but also, for example, by the earlier relations between Greece, Ionia, and Magna Graecia, between Brittany and Britain, between Denmark and Norway, Sweden, Finland, Livonia,* etc., relations, further, which are especially striking in contrast with the comparatively slight intercourse between the inhabitants of the coastal territories and those of the interior. To realize what an instrument of education lies in the link with the sea, consider countries where creative industry flourishes and contrast their relation to the sea with that of countries which have eschewed seafaring and which, like Egypt and India, have become stagnant and immersed in the most frightful and scandalous superstition. Notice also how all great and enterprising peoples press onward to the sea.

248. This far-flung connecting link affords the means for the colonizing activity—sporadic or systematic—to which the mature civil society is driven and by which it supplies to a part of its population a return to the family principle in a new land and so also supplies itself with a new demand and field for its industry.

Addition: Civil society is thus driven to found colonies. Increase of population alone has this effect, but it is due in particular to the appearance of a number of people who cannot secure the satisfaction of their needs by their own labour once production exceeds the needs of consumers. Sporadic colonization is particularly characteristic of Germany. The colonists move to America or Russia and remain there with no connections to their fatherland [*Vaterland*], to which therefore they afford no benefit. The second and entirely different type of colonization is the systematic; the state initiates it, is aware of the proper method of carrying it out and regulates it accordingly. This type was common amongst the ancients, particularly the Greeks. Hard work was not the business of the citizens in Greece, since their energy was directed rather to public affairs. So if the population increased to such an extent that there might be difficulty in providing for it, the young people would be sent away to a new district, sometimes specifically chosen, sometimes left to chance discovery. In modern times, colonists have not been allowed the same rights as the inhabitants of the motherland [*Mutterland*], and the result of this situation has been wars and finally independence, as may be seen in the history of the English and Spanish colonies. Colonial emancipation proves to be of the greatest advantage to the mother country [*Mutterstaat*], just as the emancipation of slaves turns out to the greatest advantage of the owners.

249. While the public authority must also undertake the higher directive function of providing for the interests which lead beyond the borders of its society (see § 246), its primary purpose is to actualize and maintain the universal contained within the particularity of civil society, and its control takes the form of an *external system and organization* for the protection and security of particular ends and interests *en masse*, inasmuch as these interests subsist only in this universal. In accordance with the Idea, particularity itself makes this universal, which is present in its immanent interests, the end and object of its own willing and activity. In this way the *ethical returns* to civil society as something immanent in it; this constitutes the specific character of the corporation [*Korporation*].

(b) The Corporation

250. In virtue of the substantiality of its natural and family life, the agricultural estate has immediately within itself the concrete universal in which it lives. The estate of civil servants is universal in character and so has the universal for itself as its ground and as the aim of its activity. The estate between them, the business estate, is essentially concentrated on the *particular*, and hence it is to it that corporations are specially appropriate.

251. Work in civil society is divided, in accordance with its particular nature, into different branches. The inherent [*an sich*] likeness of particulars to one another comes into existence in an *association*, as something common to its members. Hence a selfish purpose, directed towards its particular self-interest, apprehends and evinces itself at the same time as universal; and a member of civil society is in virtue of his own particular skill a member of a corporation, whose universal purpose is thus wholly concrete* and no wider in scope than the purpose involved in the [particular] trade, its distinctive business and interest.

252. In accordance with this determination, a corporation has the right, under the surveillance of the public authority, (*a*) to look after its own interests within its own sphere, (*b*) to admit members, qualified objectively by the requisite skill and rectitude, to a number determined by the general context, (*c*) to protect its members against particular contingencies, (*d*) to provide the education requisite to fit others to become members. In short, its right is to come on the scene as a second family for its members, while civil society can only be an indeterminate sort of family because it is universal and farther removed from individuals and their particular exigencies.

The corporation member is to be distinguished from a day labourer or from a person who is prepared to undertake casual employment on a single occasion. The former who is, or will become, master of his craft, is a member of the association not for casual gain on single occasions but for the whole range and universality of his particular livelihood.

Privileges [*Privilegien*], in the sense of the rights of a branch of civil society organized into a corporation, are distinct in meaning from privileges proper in the etymological sense.* The latter are contingent exceptions to the universal law; the former, however, are just legally established determinations that lie in the particular nature of an essential branch of society itself.

253. In the corporation, the family has its stable basis in the sense that its livelihood is assured there, conditionally upon capability, i.e. it has stable resources (see § 170). In addition, both the capability and livelihood are *recognized*, with the result that the corporation member needs no further *external evidence* to demonstrate his skill and his regular income and subsistence, i.e. the fact that he is *somebody*.[88] It is also recognized that he belongs to a whole which is itself an organ of society in general, and that he is interested and actively engaged in promoting the less selfish end of this whole. Thus he has *his honour in his estate* [*Stand*].

The institution of corporations corresponds, on account of its securing of resources, to the introduction of agriculture and private property in another sphere (see Remark to § 203).

When complaints are made about the luxury of the business classes [*Klassen*] and their passion for extravagance—which have as their concomitant the creation of a rabble of paupers (see § 244)—we must not forget that besides its other causes (e.g. increasing mechanization of labour) this phenomenon has an *ethical* ground,

---

[88] See Addition to *PR* § 207.

as was implied in what was said above. Unless he is a member of an authorized corporation (and it is only by being authorized that an association becomes a corporation), an individual is without the *honour of his estate* [*Standesehre*], his isolation reduces his business to mere self-seeking, and his livelihood and satisfaction become insecure. Consequently, he has to try to gain *recognition* for himself by giving external proofs of success in his business, and to these proofs no limits can be set. He cannot live in the manner of his estate, for no estate really exists for him, since in civil society that which is common to particular persons really *exists* only if it is legally constituted and recognized. Hence he cannot achieve for himself a way of life that is appropriate to his estate and more universal.

Within the corporation the help which poverty receives loses its contingent character and the unjust humiliation associated with it. The wealthy perform their duties to their fellow associates and thus riches cease to inspire either pride or envy, pride in their owners, envy in others. In these conditions rectitude obtains its proper recognition and honour.

254. The so-called 'natural' right of exercising one's skill and thereby earning what there is to be earned is restricted within the corporation only insofar as that skill is therein made rational. That is to say, it becomes freed from personal opinion and contingency, saved from endangering either oneself or others, recognized, guaranteed, and at the same time elevated to conscious activity for a common end.

255. As the family was the first, so the corporation is the second *ethical* root of the state, the one planted in civil society. The former contains the moments of subjective particularity and objective universality in a substantial unity. But these moments are sundered in civil society to begin with: on the one side there is the particularity of need and satisfaction, reflected into itself, and on the other side the universality of abstract right. In the corporation these moments are united in an inward fashion, so that in this union particular welfare is present as a right and is actualized.

The sanctity of marriage and the honour of corporation membership are the two moments around which the disorganization of civil society revolves.*

Addition: The consideration behind the abolition of corporations in recent times is that the individual should fend for himself. But we may grant this and still hold that corporation membership does not alter an individual's obligation to earn his living. In modern states, the citizens have only a restricted share in the universal business of the state, yet it is essential to provide ethical individuals with a universal activity over and above their private business. This universal activity, which the modern state does not always offer people, is found in the corporation. We saw earlier [§ 199] that in fending for himself a member of civil society is also working for others. But this unconscious necessity is not enough; it is in the corporation that it first changes into a known and thoughtful ethical mode of life. Of course corporations must fall under the higher surveillance of the state, because otherwise they would ossify, build themselves in, and decline into a miserable system of guilds. In and for itself, however, a corporation is not a closed guild; its purpose is rather to bring an isolated trade into the ethical order and elevate it to a sphere in which it gains strength and honour.

256. The end of the corporation is restricted and finite, while the public authority was an external organization involving a separation and merely relative identity [of universal and particular]. The end of the former and the externality and relative identity of the latter find their truth in the end which is *universal* in and for itself and its absolute actuality. Hence the sphere of civil society passes over into the *state*.

The town is the seat of the civil life of business. There reflection arises, turns in upon itself, and pursues its individuating task; each individual maintains himself in and through his relation to others who, like himself, are persons possessed of rights. The country, on the other hand, is the seat of an ethical life resting on nature and the family. Town and country thus constitute the two—still ideal [*ideell*]—moments from which the state *emerges* as their true *ground*. The scientific proof of the concept of the state is this development of ethical life from its immediacy through the divisions of civil society to the state, which then reveals itself as their true ground. A proof in philosophical science can only be a development of this kind.

Since the state appears as a *result* in the development of the scientific concept through displaying itself as the *true* ground [of the earlier phases], that mediation and semblance cancel themselves in favour of *immediacy*. In actuality, therefore, the state as such is rather what is first. It is within the state that the family is

first developed into civil society, and it is the Idea of the state itself
which divides itself into these two moments. Through the development of civil society, the substance of ethical life acquires
its infinite form, which contains in itself these two moments:
(1) infinite *differentiation* to the point at which the interiority
[*Insichsein*] of self-consciousness is for itself [*für sich*], and (2) the
form of *universality* involved in education, the form of thought
whereby spirit is objective and actual to itself as an organic totality in laws and institutions which are its will as *thought*.

SUB-SECTION 3

THE STATE

257. The state is the actuality of the ethical Idea. It is ethical spirit
as the substantial will manifest and clear to itself, knowing and thinking itself, accomplishing what it knows and insofar as it knows it.
The state exists immediately in *custom* [*Sitte*], mediately in individual
self-consciousness, knowledge, and activity, while self-consciousness in
virtue of its disposition finds in the state, as its essence and the end
and product of its activity, its substantial freedom.

The *Penates* are inward gods, gods of the underworld; the spirit of
a people [*Volksgeist*] (Athena for instance) is the divine, *knowing*
and *willing* itself. Family piety is feeling, ethical behaviour
directed by feeling; political virtue is the willing of the end that is
thought and that is in and for itself.

258. The state is rational in and for itself inasmuch as it is the
actuality of the substantial will which it possesses in the particular
self-consciousness that has been raised to its universality. This substantial unity is an absolute unmoved end in itself, in which freedom
comes into its supreme right. On the other hand, this final end has
supreme right against the individual, whose supreme duty is to be a
member of the state.

If the state is confused with civil society, and if its specific end is
laid down as the security and protection of property and personal
freedom, then *the interest of individuals as such* becomes the
ultimate end of their association, and it follows that membership
of the state is something optional. But the state's relation to the
individual is quite different from this. Since the state is objective

spirit, it is only as one of its members that the individual himself has objectivity, truth, and ethical life. Unification as such is itself the true content and aim, and the individual's destiny is to live a universal life. His further particular satisfaction, activity, and mode of conduct have this substantial and universally valid life as their starting point and their result.

Rationality, taken generally and in the abstract, consists in the thoroughgoing unity of the universal and the individual. Rationality, concrete in the state, consists (*a*) so far as its content is concerned, in the unity of objective freedom (i.e. freedom of the universal or substantial will) and subjective freedom (i.e. freedom of the individual in his knowing and in his volition of particular ends); and consequently, (*b*) so far as its form is concerned, in self-determining action in accordance with laws and principles which are *thoughts* and so *universal*. This Idea is the being of spirit that is eternal and necessary in and for itself.

But if we ask what is or has been the *historical* origin of the state in general, still more if we ask about the origin of any particular state, of its rights and institutions, or again if we enquire whether the state originally arose out of patriarchal conditions or out of fear or trust, or out of corporations, etc., or finally if we ask in what light the basis of the state's rights has been conceived and consciously established, whether this basis has been supposed to be positive divine right, or contract, custom, etc.—all these questions are no concern of the Idea of the state. We are here dealing exclusively with the philosophical science of the state, and from that point of view all these things are mere appearance and therefore matters for history. So far as the authority of any existing state has anything to do with reasons, these reasons are derived from the forms of right authoritative within it.

The philosophical treatment of these topics is concerned only with their inward side, with the *thought of their concept*. The merit of Rousseau's[89] contribution to the search for this concept is that, by adducing the *will* as the principle of the state, he is adducing a principle which has *thought* both for its form and its content, a principle which is indeed *thinking* itself, not a principle, like the social instinct, for instance, or divine authority, which has thought

---

[89] See first explanatory note to p. 47 [p. 334 below]. [S.H.]

as its form only. Unfortunately, however, as Fichte[90] did later, he takes the will only in the determinate form of the *individual* will, and he regards the universal will not as the will's rationality in and for itself, but only as a 'general' will which proceeds from this individual will as from a conscious will. The result is that he reduces the union of individuals in the state to a *contract* and therefore to something based on their arbitrary wills, their opinion, and their capriciously given express consent; and the understanding proceeds to draw further consequences which destroy the divine aspect of the state, which has being in and for itself, together with its majesty and absolute authority. For this reason, when these abstract conclusions came into power, they afforded for the first time in human history the prodigious spectacle of the overthrow of the constitution of an actual great state and its complete reconstruction *ab initio* on the basis of pure thought alone, after the overthrow of all existing and given conditions. The will of its re-founders was to give it what they intended to be a purely rational basis, but it was only abstractions that were being used, in which the Idea was lacking, and the experiment was turned into the most terrible and drastic event.*

Confronted with the principle of the individual will, we must remember the fundamental conception that the objective will is that which is rational in itself or in its concept, whether or not it is recognized by individuals and affirmed by their arbitrary wills. We must remember that its opposite, i.e. knowing and willing, or subjective freedom (the *only* thing contained in the principle of the individual will) comprises only one moment, and therefore a one-sided moment, of the Idea of the rational will, i.e. of the will which is rational solely because what it is in itself it also is for itself.

The opposite to thinking of the state as something to be known and apprehended as rational for itself is taking the externality of appearance—i.e. the contingencies of want, the need for protection, strength, riches, etc.—not as moments in the state's historical development, but as its substance. Here again what constitutes the principle of cognition is the individual in isolation—yet not the *thought* of this individuality, but instead only empirical individuals, with all their contingent characteristics, their strength and

---

[90] See Johann Gottlieb Fichte, *Foundations of Natural Right* (1796–7), trans. M. Baur (Cambridge: Cambridge University Press, 2000), § 17 [pp. 165–82]. [S.H.]

weakness, riches and poverty, etc. This notion of ignoring that which is infinite and rational in and for itself in the state and excluding thought from apprehension of its inward nature has assuredly never been put forward in such an unadulterated form as in Herr von Haller's *Restoration of Political Science*.[91] I say 'unadulterated' [*unvermischt*], because in all other attempts to grasp the essence of the state, no matter on what one-sided or superficial principles, this very intention of comprehending the state rationally has brought with it thoughts, i.e. universal determinations. Herr von Haller, however, has not only consciously renounced the rational content of the state, as well as the form of thought, but he has even gone on with passionate fervour to inveigh against the form and the content so set aside. Part of what Herr von Haller assures us is the 'widespread' effect of his principles, this *Restoration* undoubtedly owes to the fact that, in his exposition, he has deliberately dispensed with thought altogether, and has deliberately kept his whole book all of a piece with its lack of thought. For in this way he has eliminated the confusion and disorder which lessen the force of an exposition in which the contingent is treated along with hints of the substantial, in which the purely empirical and external are mixed with a reminiscence of the universal and rational, and in which in the midst of wretched inanities the reader is now and again reminded of the loftier sphere of the infinite. For the same reason again his exposition is consistent. He takes as the essence of the state, not what is substantial but the sphere of contingency, and consistency in dealing with a sphere of that kind amounts to the complete inconsistency of utter thoughtlessness which jogs along without heed, and is just as much at home now with the exact opposite of what it approved a moment ago.[92]

[91] See explanatory note to p. 208 [p. 353 below]. [S.H.]

[92] *Hegel's note*: I have described the book sufficiently to show that it is of an original kind. There might be something noble in the author's indignation taken by itself, since it was kindled by the false theories, mentioned above, emanating principally from Rousseau, and especially by the attempt to realize them in practice. But to save himself from these theories, Herr von Haller has gone to the other extreme by dispensing with thought altogether and consequently it cannot be said that there is anything of intrinsic value in his virulent hatred of all laws and legislation, of all formally and legally determined right. The hatred of law, of right made determinate in law, is the shibboleth whereby fanaticism, imbecility, and the hypocrisy of good intentions are clearly and infallibly recognized for what they are, disguise themselves as they may.

Addition: The state in and for itself is the ethical whole, the actualization of freedom; and it is an absolute end of reason that freedom should be actual. The state is spirit on earth and consciously realizing itself there. In nature, on the other hand, spirit actualizes itself only as its own other,

Originality like Herr von Haller's is always a curious phenomenon, and for those of my readers who are not yet acquainted with his book I will quote a few specimen passages. This is how he lays down (vol. I, pp. 342 ff.) his most important basic proposition: 'Just as, in the inorganic world, the greater dislodges the less and the mighty the weak, . . . so in the animal kingdom, and then amongst human beings, the same law recurs in nobler' (often, too, surely in ignobler?) 'forms', and 'this, therefore, is the eternal, unalterable, ordinance of God, that the mightier rules, must rule, and will always rule.' It is clear enough from this, let alone from what follows, in what sense 'might' [*Macht*] is taken here. It is not the might of justice and ethics, but only the contingent force of nature. Herr von Haller then goes on (vol. I, pp. 365 ff.) to support this doctrine on various grounds, amongst them that 'nature with amazing wisdom has so ordered it that the mere sense of personal superiority irresistibly ennobles the character and encourages the development of just those virtues which are most necessary for dealing with subordinates'. He asks with a great elaboration of scholastic rhetoric 'whether it is the strong or the weak in the kingdom of science who more misuse their trust and their authority in order to achieve their petty selfish ends and the ruin of the credulous; whether to be a past master in legal learning is not to be a pettifogger, a *leguleius*,* one who cheats the hopes of unsuspecting clients, who makes white black and black white, who misapplies the law and makes it a vehicle for wrongdoing, who brings to beggary those who need his assistance and rends them as the hungry vulture rends the innocent lamb', etc., etc. Herr von Haller forgets here that the point of this rhetoric is to support his proposition that the rule of the mightier is an everlasting ordinance of God; so presumably it is by the same ordinance that the vulture rends the innocent lamb, and that hence those who are mighty through knowledge of the law are quite right to treat the credulous people who need their protection as the weak and to empty their pockets. It would be too much, however, to ask that two thoughts should be put together where there is really not a single one.

It goes without saying that Herr von Haller is an enemy of codes of law. In his view, civil laws are, on the one hand, in principle 'unnecessary, because they follow self-evidently from the laws of nature'. If people had remained satisfied with 'self-evidence' as the basis of their thinking, then they would have been spared the endless labour devoted, since ever there were states, to legislation and legal codes, and which is still devoted thereto and to the study of legal right. 'On the other hand, laws are not exactly promulgated for private individuals, but as instructions to lower judges, acquainting them with the will of the high court.' Apart from that, the provision of law-courts is (vol. I, pp. 297 ff. and all over the place) not a state duty, but a favour, help rendered by the more powerful, and 'quite supererogatory'; it is not the most perfect method of guaranteeing people's rights; on the contrary, it is an insecure and uncertain method, 'the only one left to us by our modern lawyers. They have deprived us of the other three methods, of just those which lead most swiftly and surely to the goal, those which, unlike law-courts, friendly nature has given to humanity for the safeguarding of our rightful freedom.' And these three methods are—what do you suppose?—'(1) Personal acceptance and inculcation of the law of nature; (2) Resistance to injustice; (3) Flight, when there is no other remedy.' Lawyers are unfriendly indeed, it appears, in comparison with the friendliness of nature! 'But' (vol. I, p. 292) 'the natural, divine, law, given to everyone by nature the all-bountiful, is: Honour everyone as your equal' (on the author's principles this should read 'Honour not the person who is your equal, but the one who is as spirit asleep. Only when it is present in consciousness, when it knows itself as a really existent object, is it the state. In considering freedom, the starting-point must be not individuality, the individual self-consciousness, but only the essence of self-consciousness; for whether people know it or not, this essence realizes itself as a self-subsistent power in which single individuals are only moments. It is God's way in the world that the state

mightier'); 'offend no one who does not offend you; demand from him nothing but what he owes' (but what does he owe?); 'nay more, love your neighbour and serve him when you can'. The 'implanting of this law' is to make legislation and a constitution superfluous. It would be curious to see how Herr von Haller makes it intelligible why legislation and constitutions have appeared in the world despite this 'implanting'.

In vol. III, pp. 362 ff., the author comes to the 'so-called national liberties', by which he means the laws and constitutions of nations. Every legally constituted right is in this wide sense of the word a 'liberty'. Of these laws he says, *inter alia*, that 'their content is usually very insignificant, although in books a high value may be placed on documentary liberties of that kind'. When we then realize that the author is speaking here of the national liberties of the German Imperial Estates, of the English nation (e.g. Magna Carta 'which is little read, and on account of its archaic phraseology still less understood', the Bill of Rights,* and so forth), of the Hungarian nation, etc., we are surprised to find that these possessions, formerly so highly prized, are only insignificant; and no less surprised to learn that it is only in books that these nations place a value on laws whose cooperation has entered into every coat that is worn and every crust that is eaten, and still enters into every day and hour of the lives of everyone.

To carry quotation further, Herr von Haller speaks particularly ill (vol. I, pp. 185 ff.) of the Prussian General Legal Code,* because of the 'incredible' influence on it of unphilosophical errors (though in this instance at any rate the fault cannot be ascribed to Kant's philosophy, a topic on which Herr von Haller is at his most bitter), especially where it speaks of the state, the resources of the state, the end of the state, the head of the state, his duties, and those of civil servants, and so forth. Herr von Haller finds particularly mischievous 'the right of defraying the expenses of the state by levying taxes on the private wealth of individuals, on their businesses, on goods produced or consumed. Under those circumstances, neither the king himself (since the resources of the state belong to the state and are not the private property of the king), nor the Prussian citizens can call anything their own, neither their person nor their property; and all subjects are bondslaves to the law, since they may not withdraw themselves from the service of the state.'

In this welter of incredible crudity, what is perhaps most comical of all is the emotion with which Herr von Haller describes his unspeakable pleasure in his discoveries (vol. I, Preface)—'a joy such as only the friend of truth can feel when after honest searching he is certain that he has found as it were' (yes indeed: 'as it were' is right!) 'the voice of nature, the very word of God'. (The truth is that the word of God very clearly distinguishes its revelations from the voices of nature and natural humanity.) 'The author could have sunk to the ground in sheer wonderment, a stream of joyful tears burst from his eyes, and living religious feeling sprang up in him there and then.' Herr von Haller might have discovered by his 'religious feeling' that he should rather bewail his condition as the hardest chastisement of God. For the hardest thing which humanity can experience is to be so far excluded from thought and reason, from respect for the laws, and from knowing how infinitely important and divine it is that the duties of the state and the rights of the citizens, as well as the rights of the state and the duties of the citizens, should be defined by law—to be so far excluded from all this that absurdity can foist itself upon him as the word of God.

should exist. The basis of the state is the power of reason actualizing itself as will. In considering the Idea of the state, we must not have our eyes on particular states or on particular institutions. Instead we must consider the Idea, this actual God, by itself. On some principle or other, any state may be shown to be bad, this or that defect may be found in it; and yet, at any rate if one of the developed states of our epoch is in question, it has in it the moments essential to its existence. But since it is easier to find defects than to understand the affirmative, we may readily fall into the mistake of looking at individual aspects of the state and so forgetting its inward organic life. The state is no ideal work of art; it stands on earth and so in the sphere of caprice, chance, and error, and bad behaviour may disfigure it in many respects. But the ugliest person, or a criminal, or an invalid, or a cripple, is still always a living human being. The affirmative, life, subsists despite such defects, and it is this affirmative factor which is our theme here.

259. The Idea of the state

(*a*) has immediate actuality and is the individual state as a self-relating organism—the *constitution* or *right within the state* [*inneres Staatsrecht*];

(*b*) passes over into the relation of the individual state to other states—*right between states* [*äußeres Staatsrecht*];

(*c*) is the universal Idea as a genus and as an absolute power in relation to individual states—the spirit which gives itself its actuality in the process of *world-history*.

Addition: The state in its actuality is essentially an individual state, and beyond that a particular state. Individuality is to be distinguished from particularity. The former is a moment in the very Idea of the state, while the latter belongs to history. States as such are independent of one another, and therefore their relation to one another can only be an external one, so that there must be a third thing standing above them to bind them together. Now this third thing is the spirit which gives itself actuality in world-history and is the absolute judge of states. Several states may form an alliance to be a sort of court with jurisdiction over others, and there may be confederations of states, like the Holy Alliance* for example, but these are always relative only and restricted, like any 'perpetual peace'.* [93] The one and only absolute judge, which makes itself authoritative against the particular and at all times, is the spirit in and for itself which manifests itself in the history of the world as the universal and as the genus there operative.

---

[93] See Remark and Addition to *PR* § 324 and Remark to *PR* § 333.

A. *Right within the State*

260. The state is the actuality of concrete freedom. But *concrete freedom* consists in this, that personal individuality and its particular interests not only achieve their complete development and gain recognition of their right for itself (as they do in the sphere of the family and civil society) but, for one thing, they also pass over of their own accord into the interest of the universal, and, for another thing, they know and will the universal; they even recognize it as their own substantial spirit; they take it as their end and aim and are active in its pursuit. The result is that the universal does not prevail or achieve completion except along with particular interests and through the cooperation of particular knowing and willing; and individuals likewise do not live as private persons for their own ends alone, but in the very act of willing these they will the universal for the sake of the universal, and their activity is consciously aimed at the universal end. The principle of modern states has prodigious strength and depth because it allows the principle of subjectivity to progress to its culmination in the self-sufficient extreme of personal particularity, and yet at the same time brings it back to the substantial unity and so maintains this unity in the principle of subjectivity itself.

Addition: The Idea of the state in modern times has a special character in that the state is the actualization of freedom not in accordance with subjective whim but in accordance with the concept of the will, i.e. in accordance with its universality and divinity. Imperfect states are those in which the Idea of the state is still veiled and where its particular determinations have not yet attained free self-subsistence. In the states of classical antiquity, universality was indeed present, but particularity had not yet been released, given free scope, and brought back to universality, i.e. to the universal end of the whole. The essence of the modern state is that the universal be bound up with the complete freedom of particularity and with the well-being of individuals, that thus the interests of family and civil society must concentrate themselves on the state, although the universal end cannot be advanced without the personal knowledge and will of its particular members, whose own rights must be maintained. Thus the universal must be activated, but subjectivity on the other hand must attain its full and living development. It is only when both these moments subsist in their strength that the state can be regarded as articulated and genuinely organized.

261. In contrast with the spheres of private right and private welfare (the family and civil society), the state is from one point of view an *external* necessity and their higher authority; its nature is such that their laws and interests are subordinate to it and dependent on it. On the other hand, however, it is the end *immanent* within them, and its strength lies in the unity of its own universal end and aim with the particular interest of individuals, in the fact that individuals have duties to the state to the extent that they also have rights against it (see § 155).

In the Remark to § 3 above, reference was made to the fact that it was Montesquieu above all who, in his famous work *The Spirit of the Laws*,[94] kept in sight and tried to work out in detail both the thought of the dependence of laws—in particular, laws concerning the rights of persons—on the specific character of the state, and also the philosophical notion of always treating the part in its relation to the whole.

Duty is primarily a relation to something which from my point of view is substantial, universal in and for itself. A right, on the other hand, is simply the *existence* of this substance and thus is the particular aspect of it and enshrines my particular freedom. Hence at a formal level, right and duty appear as allocated to different sides or to different persons. In the state, as something ethical, as the interpenetration of the substantial and the particular, my obligation to what is substantial is at the same time the existence of my particular freedom. This means that in the state duty and right are *united in one and the same relation*. But further, since nonetheless the distinct moments acquire in the state the shape and reality peculiar to each, and since therefore the distinction between right and duty enters here once again, it follows that while they are in themselves, i.e. in form, identical, they at the same time *differ in content*. In the spheres of private right and morality, the relation of right and duty to one another lacks actual necessity; and hence there is at that point only an abstract equality of content between them, i.e. in those abstract spheres, what is one person's right ought also to be another's, and what is one person's duty ought also to be another's. That absolute identity of right and duty is present only as an identity of *content*, because in them this content is determined as quite universal and is simply the one principle of

---

[94] See third explanatory note to p. 20 [p. 329 below]. [S.H.]

both right and duty, i.e. the principle that human beings, as persons, are free. Slaves, therefore, have no duties because they have no rights, and vice versa. (Religious duties are not here under discussion.)

In the course of the inward development of the concrete Idea, however, its moments become distinguished and their specific determinacy becomes at the same time a difference of content. In the family, the content of a son's duties to his father differs from the content of his rights against him; the content of the rights of a member of civil society is not the same as the content of his duties to his prince and government.

This concept of the union of duty and right is a point of vital importance and in it the inner strength of states is contained.

The abstract aspect of duty goes no farther than the persistent neglect and proscription of particular interest, on the ground that it is the inessential, even unworthy, moment in life. But the concrete point of view—that of the Idea—reveals the moment of particularity as itself essential and so regards its satisfaction as indisputably necessary. In fulfilling his duty the individual must at the same time in some way attain his own interest and satisfaction or settle his account. Out of his position in the state, a right must accrue to him whereby the universal concern becomes his own particular concern. Particular interests should in truth not be set aside or, indeed, suppressed; instead, they should be harmonized with the universal, so that both they and the universal are upheld. The individual, so far as his duties are concerned, is a subject [*Untertan*]; but as a member of *civil society* he finds that in fulfilling his duties he gains protection of his person and property, regard for his particular welfare, the satisfaction of his substantial being, the consciousness and feeling of himself as a member of the whole; and, insofar as he fulfils his duties by performing tasks and services for the *state*, the state itself is upheld and preserved. Taken abstractly, the universal's interest would consist simply in the completion as duties of the tasks and services which it exacts.

Addition: In the state everything depends on the unity of universal and particular. In the states of antiquity, the subjective end simply coincided with the state's will. In modern times, however, we lay claim to our own views, our own willing and our own conscience. The ancients had none of these in the modern sense; the ultimate thing with them was the will of the state.

Whereas under the despots of Asia the individual had no inner life and no
justification in himself, in the modern world people insist on respect being
paid to their inner life. The conjunction of duty and right has a twofold
aspect: what the state demands from us as a duty is *eo ipso* our right as individuals, since the state is nothing but the organization of the concept of
freedom. The determinations of the individual will are given an objective
existence through the state and thereby they attain their truth and their
actualization for the first time. The state is the sole prerequisite of the
attainment of particular ends and welfare.

262. The actual Idea is spirit, which, sundering itself into the two
ideal spheres of its concept, family and civil society, enters into its
finitude, but it does so in order to emerge from its ideality as infinite
actual spirit for itself. It is therefore to these ideal spheres that the
actual Idea allocates the material of this its finite actuality, viz.
individuals as a mass, in such a way that in any individual case this
allocation appears as *mediated* by circumstances, the individual's
arbitrary will and his personal choice of vocation (see § 185 and the
Remark thereto).

Addition: In Plato's state, subjective freedom does not yet count, because
people have their occupations assigned to them by the Guardians.[95] In
many oriental states, this assignment is determined by birth. But subjective freedom, which must be respected, demands that individuals should
have free choice in this matter.

263. In these spheres in which its moments, particularity and
individuality, have their immediate and reflected reality, spirit is
present as their objective universality *appearing in them* as the power
of reason in necessity (see § 184), i.e. as the *institutions* considered
above.

Addition: The state, as spirit, sunders itself into the particular determinations of its concept, of its mode of being. We might use here an illustration drawn from nature. The nervous system is the sensitive system
proper; it is the abstract moment, the moment of being with oneself
[*bei sich*] and therein having identity with oneself. But analysis of sensation
reveals that it has two aspects and these are distinct in such a way that each
of them appears as a whole system. The first is feeling in the abstract,
keeping oneself self-contained, the dull movement which goes on internally, reproduction, internal self-nutrition, growth, and digestion. The
second moment is that this being-with-oneself has over against it the

---

[95] See Plato, *Republic*, 415a–d. [S.H.]

moment of difference, a movement outwards. This is irritability, sensation moving outwards. This constitutes a system of its own, and there are some of the lower types of animals which have developed this system alone, while they lack the soul-charged [*seelenvoll*] unity of inner sensation. If we compare these natural relations with those of spirit, then the family must be paralleled with sensibility and civil society with irritability. Now the third is the state, the nervous system itself, internally organized; but this lives only insofar as both moments (in this case family and civil society) are developed within it. The laws regulating family and civil society are the institutions of the rational order which appears in them. But the ground and ultimate truth of these institutions is spirit, their universal end and known object. The family too is ethical, only its end is not a known end, while it is the separation between individuals which makes civil society what it is.

264. Individuals *en masse* are themselves spiritual natures and therefore contain two moments: (i) at one extreme, individuality knowing and willing for itself, and (ii) at the other extreme, universality which knows and wills what is substantial. Hence they attain their right in both these respects only insofar as they are actual both as private and as substantial persons. Now in the family and civil society they acquire their right in the first of these respects directly, and in the second insofar as (i) they find their essential self-consciousness in institutions which are the universal aspect of their particular interests which has being in itself, and (ii) the corporation supplies them with an occupation and an activity directed towards a universal end.

265. These institutions form the *constitution* (i.e. developed and actualized rationality) in the sphere of particularity. They are, therefore, the firm foundation not only of the state but also of the citizen's trust in it and disposition towards it. They are the pillars of public freedom since in them particular freedom is realized and rational, and therefore in them the union of freedom and necessity is present *in itself*.

Addition: As was remarked earlier on [§ 255], the sanctity of marriage and the institutions in which civil society appears as ethical life constitute the stability of the whole, i.e. stability is secured when the universal is the concern of each individual in his particular capacity. What is of the utmost importance is that the laws of reason and of particular freedom should permeate one another, and that my particular end should become identified with the universal end, or otherwise the state is left in the air. The state is actual only when its individual members have a feeling of their own self-hood and it is stable only when the aims of the universal and of particular individuals are identical. It has often been said that the end of the state is the happiness of the citizens. That is perfectly true. If all is not well with them, if their subjective aims are not satisfied, if they do not find that the state as such is the means to their satisfaction, then the footing of the state itself is insecure.

266. But spirit is objective and actual to itself not merely as this necessity and as a realm of appearance, but also as the *ideality* and the inner nature of these. Only in this way is this substantial universality its own object and end, with the result that the necessity is for itself in the shape of freedom as well.

267. The necessity in ideality is the *development* of the Idea within itself. As subjective substantiality, it is [the individual's] political *disposition*; in distinction therefrom, as objective substantiality, it is the *organism* of the state, i.e. it is the properly *political* state and its *constitution*.

Addition: The unity of the freedom which knows and wills itself is present first of all as necessity. Here substance is present as the subjective existence of individuals. Necessity's other mode of being, however, is the organism, i.e. spirit is a process within itself, it articulates itself within, posits differences in itself, and thereby completes the cycle of its life.

268. The political *disposition*, patriotism pure and simple, is certainty based on *truth*—mere subjective certainty is not the outcome of truth but is only opinion—and volition which has become *habitual*. As such, it is simply a product of the institutions subsisting in the state, since rationality is *actually* present in the state, while action in conformity with these institutions gives rationality practical expression. This disposition is, in general, *trust* (which may pass over into a greater or lesser degree of educated insight), or the consciousness that my interest, both substantial and particular, is contained and preserved in another's (i.e. in the state's) interest and end, i.e. in the other's relation to me as an individual. In this way, this very other is immediately not an other in my eyes, and in being conscious of this fact, I am free.

Patriotism is often understood to mean only a readiness for *exceptional* sacrifices and actions. Essentially, however, it is the disposition which, in the relationships of our daily life and under ordinary conditions, habitually recognizes that the community is one's substantial basis and end. It is out of this consciousness, which during life's daily round stands the test in all circumstances, that there subsequently also arises the readiness for extraordinary exertions. But just as people would often rather be magnanimous than law-abiding, so do they readily persuade themselves that they possess this exceptional patriotism in order to exempt themselves from the genuine disposition or to excuse their lack of it. If again this disposition is looked upon as that which may begin of itself and arise from subjective ideas and thoughts, it is being confused with opinion, because so regarded it is deprived of its true ground, objective reality.

Addition: Uneducated people delight in argumentation and fault-finding, because it is easy enough to find fault, though hard to see the good and its inner necessity. The learner always begins by finding fault, but the educated person sees the positive in everything. In religion, this or that is quickly dismissed as superstitious, but it is infinitely harder to apprehend the truth contained therein. Hence the apparent disposition of people towards the state is to be distinguished from what they truly will; inwardly they really will the thing [*Sache*], but they cling to details and take delight in the vanity of pretending to know better. We trust that the state must subsist and that in it alone particular interests can be secured. But habit blinds us to that on which our whole existence depends. When we walk the streets at night in safety, it does not strike us that this might be otherwise. This habit of feeling safe has become second nature, and we do not reflect on just how this is due solely to the working of particular institutions. Representational thought [*Vorstellung*] often has the impression that force holds the state together, but in fact its only bond is the fundamental sense of order which everyone possesses.

269. The patriotic disposition acquires its specifically determined *content* from the various aspects of the organism of the state. This organism is the development of the Idea to its differences and their objective actuality. Hence these different aspects are the *various powers* of the state with their functions and spheres of action, by means of which the universal continually engenders itself, and engenders itself in a necessary way because their specific character is determined by the nature of the concept. Throughout this process the universal maintains its identity, since it is itself the presupposition of its own production. This organism is the *political constitution*.

Addition: The state is an organism, i.e. the development of the Idea into its differences. Thus these different sides of the state are its various powers with their functions and spheres of action, by means of which the universal continually engenders itself in a necessary way; in this process it maintains its identity since it is presupposed even in its own production. This organism is the political constitution; it is produced perpetually by the state, while it is through it that the state maintains itself. If the state and its constitution fall apart, if the different aspects of the organism break free, then the unity produced by the constitution is no longer established. This tallies with the fable about the belly* and the other members. The nature of an organism is such that unless each of its parts is brought into identity with the others, unless each of them is prevented from achieving independence, the whole must perish. By listing attributes, principles, etc., no progress can be made in assessing the nature of the state; it must be apprehended as an organism. One might as well try to understand the nature of God by listing his attributes, while the truth is that we must intuit God's life in that life itself.

270. (1) The *abstract actuality* or the substantiality of the state consists in the fact that its end is the universal interest as such and the conservation therein of particular interests since the universal interest is the substance of these. (2) But this substantiality of the state is also its *necessity*, since its substantiality divides itself into the distinct spheres of its activity which correspond to the moments of its concept, and these spheres, owing to this substantiality, are thus actually fixed determinations of the state, i.e. its powers. (3) But this very substantiality of the state is spirit knowing and willing itself after passing through the forming process of *education*. The state, therefore, knows what it wills and knows it in its universality, i.e. as something thought. Hence it works and acts in accordance with known ends, known principles, and laws which are laws not merely in themselves but also for consciousness; and further, it acts with determinate knowledge of existing conditions and circumstances, inasmuch as its actions have a bearing on these.

This is the place to touch on *the relation of the state to religion*, because it is often reiterated nowadays* that religion is the basis of the state, and because those who make this assertion even presume that, once it is made, political science has said its last word.

No doctrine is more fitted to produce so much confusion, more fitted indeed to exalt confusion itself to be the constitution of the state and the proper form of knowledge.

In the first place, it may seem suspicious that religion is principally sought and recommended for times of public misery, disorder, and oppression, and that people are referred to it as a solace in face of injustice or as a hope in compensation for loss. Furthermore, if religion is seen as commanding indifference to worldly interests, the march of events, and current affairs, while the state is spirit *that is present in the world*, the suggestion that people turn to religion does not seem to be the way to exalt the interest and business of the state into the fundamental and serious aim of life. On the contrary, this suggestion seems to assert that politics is wholly a matter of caprice and indifference, either because the way it is formulated implies that only the aims of passion and lawless force, etc., hold sway in the state, or because recommending religion is meant to be valid for itself and to be sufficient to determine and administer the law. It would seem to be a bitter jest to stifle all feeling against tyranny by asserting that the oppressed find their consolation in religion; it must equally not be forgotten that religion itself may take a form leading to the harshest bondage in the fetters of superstition and the degradation of human beings to a level below that of animals. (The Egyptians and the Hindus, for instance, revere animals as beings higher than themselves.) This phenomenon may at least make it evident that we ought not to speak of religion in wholly general terms and that we rather need a power to protect us from it in some of its forms and to espouse against them the rights of reason and self-consciousness.

The essence of the relation between religion and the state can be determined, however, only if we recall the *concept* of religion. The content of religion is absolute truth, and consequently the most elevated of all dispositions is to be found in religion. As intuition, feeling, representational knowledge [*vorstellende Erkenntnis*], its concern is with God as the unrestricted principle and cause on which everything hangs. It thus involves the demand that everything else shall be seen in this light and depend on it for corroboration, justification, and verification. It is in being thus related to religion that state, laws, and duties all alike acquire for consciousness their supreme confirmation and their supreme obligatoriness, because even the state, laws, and duties are in their actuality something determinate which passes over into a higher sphere and so into that on which it is grounded.[96] It is for this reason that in religion there lies the place where human beings are always assured of finding a consciousness of the unchangeable, of the highest freedom and satisfaction, even within all the mutability of the world and despite the frustration of their aims and the loss of their interests and possessions.[97] Now if religion is in this way the foundation which includes the ethical realm in general, and the nature of the state—the divine will—in particular, it is at the same time only a *foundation*; and it is at this point that state and religion begin to diverge. The state is the divine will, in the sense that it is spirit present on earth, unfolding itself to be the actual shape and organization of a world. Those who insist on stopping at the form of religion in opposition to the state are acting like those who, in cognition, think they are right if they continually stop at the essence and refuse to advance beyond that abstraction to existence [*Dasein*], or like those (see Remark to § 140) who will only good in the abstract and leave it to caprice to determine *what* is good. Religion is a relation to the Absolute, a relation which takes the form of *feeling, representation* [*Vorstellung*], *faith*, and brought within its all-embracing centre everything becomes only accidental and transient. Now if, in relation to the state, we cling to this form and make it the authority for the state and its essential determinant, the state as the organism in which enduring differences, laws, and institutions have been developed, must become a prey to instability, insecurity, and disorder. Set against the form of religion, which shrouds everything determinate and so comes to be

---

[96] *Hegel's reference*: See *Encyclopaedia*, § 453 [3rd edn. § 553].

[97] *Hegel's note*: Religion, knowledge, and science have as their principle a form peculiar to each and different from that of the state. They therefore enter the state partly as *means* to education and a [higher] disposition, partly insofar as they are in essence *ends* in themselves to the extent that they have an external existence. In both these respects the principles of the state have, in their application, a bearing on them. A comprehensive, concrete treatise on the state would also have to deal with those spheres of life as well as with art and merely natural conditions, and to consider their place in the state and their bearing on it. In this treatise, however, it is the principle of the state in its own special sphere which is being fully expounded in accordance with the Idea, and it is only in passing that reference can be made to the principles of religion, etc., and to the application of the right of the state to them.

something subjective, the objective and universal element in the state, i.e. the laws, acquires a negative instead of a stable and authoritative character, and the result is the production of maxims of conduct like the following: 'To the righteous person no law is given; only be pious, and for the rest, practise what you will; yield to your own caprice and passion, and if thereby others suffer injustice, commend them to the consolations and hopes of religion, or better still, call them irreligious and condemn them to perdition.' This negative attitude, however, may not confine itself to an inner disposition and attitude of mind; it may turn instead to actuality and assert its authority there, and thereby give rise to the religious *fanaticism* which, like fanaticism in politics, discards all political institutions and legal order as barriers cramping the inner life of the heart and incompatible with its infinity, and at the same time proscribes private property, marriage, the relations and work involved in civil society, etc., as degrading to love and the freedom of feeling. But since even then decisions must somehow be made for everyday life and practice, the same doctrine which we had before (see Remark to § 140, where we dealt generally with the subjectivity of the will which knows itself to be absolute) turns up again here, namely that subjective ideas, i.e. opinion and capricious inclination, are to do the deciding.

In contrast with the truth thus shrouded in subjective ideas and feelings, the genuine truth is the prodigious transfer of the inner into the outer, the building of reason into reality, and this has been the task of the world during the whole course of its history. It is by working at this task that civilized humanity has actually given reason an existence in laws and the institutions of the state and achieved consciousness of the fact. Those who 'seek guidance from the Lord' and are assured that the whole truth is immediately present in their unschooled opinions, fail to apply themselves to the task of raising their subjectivity to consciousness of the truth and to knowledge of duty and objective right. The only possible fruits of their attitude are folly, abomination, and the demolition of the whole ethical order, and these fruits must inevitably be reaped if the religious disposition holds firmly and *exclusively* to its own form and so turns against actuality and the truth present in it in the form of the universal, i.e. of laws. Yet, there is no necessity for this disposition to turn outward and actualize itself in this way. With its negative standpoint, it is of course also open to it to remain something inward, to accommodate itself to institutions and laws, and to acquiesce in these with sneers and idle longings, or with a sigh of resignation. It is not strength but weakness which has turned religious feeling nowadays into piety of a *polemical* kind, whether the polemic be connected with some genuine need or simply with unsatisfied vanity. Instead of subduing one's opinions through the labour of study, and subjecting one's will to discipline and so elevating it to free obedience, the line of least resistance is to renounce knowledge of objective truth. Along this line we may preserve a feeling of grievance and so also of self-conceit, and claim to have ready to hand in godliness everything requisite for seeing into the heart of the law and the institutions of the state, for passing judgement on them, and laying down what their character should and must be; and of course if we take this line, the source of our claims is a pious heart, and they are therefore infallible and unimpeachable, and the upshot is that since we make religion the basis of our intentions and assertions, they cannot be criticized on the score of their shallowness or their injustice.

But if religion be religion of a *genuine* kind, it does not run counter to the state in a negative or polemical way like the kind just described. It rather recognizes the state and upholds it, and furthermore it has a *position* and an *external expression* of its own. The practice of its worship consists in actions and in doctrinal instruction, and for this purpose possessions and property are required, as well as individuals dedicated to the service of the community. There thus arises a relation between the state and the church. To determine this relation is a simple matter. In the nature of the case, the state discharges a duty by affording every assistance and protection to the church in the furtherance of its religious ends; and, in addition, since religion is the moment that integrates the state at the deepest level of disposition, the state should even require all its citizens to belong to a church— *a* church is all that can be said, since the state cannot interfere with the content of faith insofar as it depends on the inner realm of representation [*Vorstellung*]. A state which is strong because its organization is mature may be all the more liberal in this matter; it may entirely overlook individual details [of religious practice] which affect it, and may even tolerate communities (though, of course, all depends on their numbers) which on religious grounds decline to recognize even their direct duties to the state. The state can do this because it hands over the members of such communities to civil society and its laws, and is content if they fulfil their direct duties to the state passively, for instance by such means as commutation or the performance of a different service.[98]

But since the church owns *property* and otherwise performs *acts* of worship, and since therefore it must have people in its service, it steps out of the inner realm into worldly life, and so enters the domain of the state and thereby *immediately* places itself under its laws. It is true that the oath and the ethical realm in general, like the marriage bond, entail that inner permeation and elevation of *disposition* which acquires its deepest confirmation through religion; [but] since ethical relations are in essence relations of *actual*

[98] *Hegel's note*: Quakers, Anabaptists, etc., may be said to be active members only of civil society, and they may be regarded as private persons standing in merely private relations to others. Even after this position has been allowed them, they have been exempted from taking the oath. They fulfil their direct duties to the state in a passive way; one of the most important of these duties, the defence of the state against its enemies, they refuse outright to fulfil, and their refusal may perhaps be admitted provided they perform some other service instead. To sects of this kind, the state's attitude is *toleration* [*Toleranz*] in the strict sense of the word,* because since they decline to recognize their duty to the state, they may not claim the rights of citizenship. On one occasion when the abolition of slavery* was being pressed with great vigour in the American Congress, a member from one of the Southern States made the striking retort: 'Give us our slaves, and you may keep your Quakers.' Only if the state is otherwise strong can it overlook and tolerate such anomalies, because it can then rely principally on the strength of custom and the inner rationality of its institutions to diminish and overcome the discrepancy if the state does not strictly assert its rights in this respect. Thus formally it may have been right to refuse a grant of even civil rights to the Jews on the ground that they should be regarded as belonging not merely to a particular religious group but to a foreign people. But the fierce outcry raised against the Jews, from that point of view and others, ignores the fact that they are, above all, *human beings*; and humanity, so far from being a mere superficial, abstract quality (see Remark to § 209), is on the contrary itself the basis of the fact that civil rights arouse in their possessors the *feeling of oneself* as counting in civil society as a person *with rights*. This feeling of selfhood, infinite and free from all restrictions, is in turn the root from which the desired similarity in disposition and ways of thinking comes into being. To exclude the Jews from civil rights, on the other hand, would rather be to confirm the isolation with which they have been reproached—a result for which the state that excludes them would rightly be blameable and reproachable, because by such exclusion, it would have misunderstood its own basic principle, its nature as an objective and powerful institution (compare the end of the Remark to § 268). The exclusion of the Jews from civil rights has been supposed to be a right of the highest kind and been demanded on that ground; but experience has shown that so to exclude them is the silliest folly, and the way in which governments now treat them has proved itself to be both wise and dignified.*

rationality, the first thing is to affirm within them the rights of this rationality. Confirmation of these rights by the church is secondary and is only the inward, comparatively abstract, side of the matter.

As for the other ways in which an ecclesiastical community gives expression to itself, so far as *doctrine* is concerned the inward preponderates over the outward to a greater extent than is the case with *acts* of worship and other lines of conduct connected with these, in which the legal side at least appears at once to be a matter for the state. (It is true, of course, that churches have managed to exempt their ministers and property from the power and jurisdiction of the state, and they have even arrogated to themselves jurisdiction over laymen in matters in which religion cooperates, such as divorce and the taking of the oath, etc.)—*Public control* of actions of this kind is indeterminate in extent, but this is due to the nature of public control itself and obtains similarly in purely civil transactions (see § 234). When individuals, holding religious views in common, form themselves into a community, a corporation, they fall under the general control and oversight of the state.— *Doctrine* as such, however, has its domain in conscience and falls within the right of the subjective freedom of self-consciousness, the sphere of the inner life, which as such is not the domain of the state. Yet the state, too, has a doctrine, since its institutions and whatever is authoritative in it with regard to rights and the constitution exist essentially in the form of *thought* as law. And since the state is not a mechanism but the rational life of self-conscious freedom, the system of the ethical world, it follows that an essential moment in the actual state is the *disposition* of the citizens and so also the consciousness of this disposition that is expressed in *principles*. Moreover, the doctrine of the church is in turn not purely and simply an inward concern of conscience. As doctrine it is rather the *expression* of something, in fact the expression of a content which is most closely linked, or even immediately concerned, with ethical principles and the laws of the state. Hence at this point the paths of church and state either *coincide* or *oppose one another*. The difference of their two domains may be pushed by the church into sheer antagonism since, by regarding itself as enshrining the content of religion—a content which is absolute— it may claim as its own the spiritual as such [*das Geistige überhaupt*] and so the whole ethical sphere, and conceive the state as a mere mechanical framework for the attainment of external, non-spiritual, ends. It may take itself to be the Kingdom of God, or at least the road to it or its vestibule, while it regards the state as the kingdom of this world, i.e. of the transient and the finite. In a word, it may think that it is an end in itself, while the state is a mere means. These claims produce the demand, in connection with doctrinal instruction, that the state should not only allow the church to do as it likes with complete freedom, but that it should pay unconditional respect to the church's doctrines as doctrines, whatever their character, because their determination is supposed to be the task of the church alone. The church bases this claim on the extended ground that the domain of spirit as such is its property. But science and knowledge in general also have a footing in that domain and, like a church, build themselves into a totality with a distinctive principle of its own, and they may, with even better justification, regard themselves as occupying the position which the church claims. Hence science also may in the same way demand to be independent of the state, which is then supposed to be a mere means with the task of providing for science as though science were an end in itself.

By the way, it makes no difference to this relationship between church and state whether the leaders of congregations or individuals ordained to the service of the church feel impelled to withdraw from the state and lead a sort of secluded life of their own, so that only the other church members are subject to the state's control, or whether they remain within the state except in their capacity as ecclesiastics, a capacity which they take to be but one side of their life. The most striking thing about such a conception of the church's relation to the state is that it implies the idea that the state's specific function consists in protecting and securing everyone's life, property, and arbitrary will, insofar as these do not encroach upon the life, property, and arbitrary will of others. The state from this point of view is treated simply as an organization to meet people's needs. In this way the element of truth in and for itself, of spirit in its higher development, is placed, as subjective religious feeling or theoretical science, beyond the reach of the state. The state, as the *laity* in and for itself, is confined to showing respect to this element and so is entirely deprived of any

properly ethical character. Now it is, of course, a matter of history
that in times and under conditions of barbarism, all higher forms
of spiritual life had their seat only in the church, while the state
was a mere secular regime of force, caprice, and passion. At such
times it was the abstract opposition of state and church which was
the main underlying principle of history (see § 359).[99] But it is a far
too blind and shallow way of proceeding to declare that this situation is the one which truly corresponds with the Idea. The development of this Idea has proved this rather to be the truth, that
spirit, as free and rational, is ethical in itself, while the Idea in its
truth is rationality *actualized*; and this it is which exists as the
state. Further, it has emerged no less clearly from this Idea that
the ethical truth in it is present to thinking consciousness as a content worked up into the form of universality, i.e. as *law*—in short,
that the state *knows* its aims, and apprehends and implements
them with determinate consciousness and in accordance with
principles. Now, as I said earlier, religion has the truth as its universal subject-matter, but it possesses it only as a *given* content
which has not been apprehended in its fundamental characteristics
through thought and the use of concepts. Similarly, the relation of
the individual to this subject-matter is an obligation grounded on
authority, while the witness of one's *own* spirit and heart, i.e. that
wherein the moment of freedom resides, is faith and feeling. It is
philosophical insight which sees that while church and state differ
in form, they do not stand opposed in *content*, for truth and rationality are the content of both. Thus when the church begins to teach
doctrines (though there are and have been some churches with a
ritual only, and others in which ritual is the chief thing, while doctrine and a more educated consciousness are only secondary), and
when these doctrines touch on *objective principles*, on thoughts of
the ethical and the rational, then their expression *eo ipso* brings the
church into the domain of the state. In contrast with the church's
faith and authority in matters affecting ethical life, right, laws,
institutions, in contrast with the church's *subjective conviction*, the
state is *the one that knows* [*das Wissende*]. Its principle is such that
its content is in essence no longer clothed with the form of feeling
and faith but belongs to determinate thought.

---

[99] All editions have '§ 358'.

If the content in and for itself appears in the form of religion as a particular content, i.e. as the doctrines peculiar to the church as a religious community, then these doctrines remain out of the reach of the state (in Protestantism there is no laity, so there is likewise no priesthood to be an exclusive depository of church doctrine). Since ethical principles and the organization of the state in general are drawn into the domain of religion and not only may, but also should, be established by reference thereto, this reference gives religious credentials to the state itself. On the other hand, however, the state retains the right and the form of self-conscious, objective, rationality, the right to make this form count and to maintain it against assertions springing from the *subjective* shape of truth, no matter how such truth may girdle itself with certitude and authority.

The state is universal in form, a form whose essential principle is thought. This explains why it was *in the state that freedom of thought and science* had their origin. It was a church, on the other hand, which burnt Giordano Bruno,* forced Galileo to recant on his knees his exposition of the Copernican view of the solar system,* and so forth.[100] Science too, therefore, has its place on the

---

[100] *Hegel's note*: 'When Galileo published the discoveries about the phases of Venus, etc., which he had made with the aid of the telescope, he showed that they incontestably proved the motion of the earth. But this idea of the motion of the earth was declared heretical by an assembly of Cardinals, and Galileo, its most famous advocate, was summoned before the Inquisition and compelled to recant it, under pain of severe imprisonment. One of the strongest of passions is the love of truth in a man of spirit. Convinced of the motion of the earth as a result of his own observations, Galileo meditated a long while on a new work in which he had resolved to develop all the proofs in its favour. But in order at the same time to escape from the persecution of which otherwise he would inevitably have been the victim, he hit upon the device of expounding them in the form of dialogues between three speakers. It is obvious enough in them that the advantage lies with the advocate of the Copernican system; but since Galileo did not decide between the speakers, and gave as much weight as possible to the objections raised by the partisans of Ptolemy, he might well have expected to be left to enjoy undisturbed the peace to which his advanced age and his labours had entitled him. In his seventieth year he was summoned once more before the tribunal of the Inquisition. He was imprisoned and required to recant his opinions a second time under threat of the penalty fixed for a relapse into heresy. He was made to sign an abjuration in the following terms: "I, Galileo, appearing in person before the court in my seventieth year, kneeling, and with my eyes on the holy Gospels which I hold in my hands, abjure, damn, and execrate with my whole heart and true belief the absurd, false, and heretical doctrine of the motion of the earth." What a spectacle! An aged, venerable man, famous throughout a long life exclusively devoted to the study of nature, abjuring on his knees, against the witness of his own conscience, the truth which he had demonstrated so convincingly! By the

side of the state since it has one element, its form, in common with the state, and its aim is *knowledge*, knowledge of *objective* truth and rationality in terms of thought. Such knowledge may, of course, fall from the heights of science into opinion and reasoning from grounds, and, turning its attention to ethical matters and the organization of the state, set itself against their basic principles. And it may perhaps do this while making the same claim as the church makes for its own distinctive sphere, namely that its opinion is rational and that it enjoys the right of subjective self-consciousness to freedom of opinion and conviction.

This principle of the subjectivity of knowing has been dealt with above (see Remark to § 140). It is here only necessary to add a note on the twofold attitude of the state towards opinion. On the one hand, insofar as opinion is mere opinion, a purely subjective matter, it is without any genuine inherent force or power, plume itself as it may; and from this point of view the state may be as totally indifferent to it as the painters who stick to the three primary colours on their palettes are indifferent to the academic wisdom which tells them there are seven. On the other hand, however, when this opinion based on bad principles gives itself a universal existence that corrodes the actual order, the state must protect objective truth and the principles of ethical life (and it must do the same in face of the formalism of unconditioned subjectivity, if the latter claims to be grounded in a scientific point of departure and seeks to turn state educational institutions against the state by encouraging them to make pretentious claims against it akin to those of a church). Equally, in face of a church claiming unrestricted and unconditional *authority*, the state has in general to make good the formal right of self-consciousness to its own insight, its own conviction, and, in short, its own thought of what is to hold good as objective truth.

Mention may also be made of the *unity of state and church*—a favourite topic of modern discussion and held up by some as the

judgement of the Inquisition he was condemned to perpetual imprisonment. A year later he was set at liberty through the intercession of the Grand Duke of Florence. He died in 1642. Europe mourned his loss. It had been enlightened by his labours and was exasperated by the judgement passed by a detested tribunal on a man of his greatness.' (Laplace, *Exposition of the System of the World** [*Exposition du système du monde*] [1796], Book V, chap. 4.)

highest of ideals.* While state and church are essentially united by the truth of their principles and disposition, it is no less essential that, despite this unity, the *distinction* between their forms of consciousness should be given particular existence. This often desired unity of church and state is found under oriental despotisms,[101] but an oriental despotism is not a state, or at any rate not the self-conscious form of state which is alone worthy of spirit, the form which is organically developed and where there are rights and a free ethical life. Further, if the state is to come into existence as the *self-knowing* ethical actuality of spirit, it is essential that its form should be distinct from that of authority and faith. But this distinction emerges only insofar as the church itself is subjected to inward division. It is only thereafter that the state, in contrast with the *particular* churches, attains *universality* of thought—its formal principle—and brings this universality into existence. (In order to understand this, it is necessary to know not only what universality is in itself, but also what its existence [*Existenz*] is.) Hence so far from its being or its having been a misfortune for the state that the church is divided, it is only as a result of that division that the state has been able to reach its appointed end as a self-consciously rational and ethical organization. Moreover, this division is the best piece of good fortune which could have befallen either the church or thought so far as the freedom and rationality of either is concerned.

Addition: The state is actual, and its actuality consists in this, that the interest of the whole is realized in and through particular ends. Actuality is always the unity of universal and particular, the universal articulated in the particulars which appear to be self-subsistent, although they really are upheld and contained only in the whole. Where this unity is not present, a thing is not *actual* even though it may have acquired *existence* [*Existenz*].[102] A bad state is one which merely exists; a sick body exists too, but it has no genuine reality. A hand which is cut off still looks like a hand, and it exists, but without being actual.[103] Genuine actuality is necessity; what is actual is inherently necessary. Necessity consists in this, that the whole is sundered into the differences of the concept and that this divided whole yields a fixed and permanent determinacy, though one which is not fossilized but perpetually recreates itself in its dissolution.

---

[101] See *PR* § 355. [S.H.]
[102] See first explanatory note to p. 14 [pp. 326–7 below]. [S.H.]
[103] See Aristotle, *Politics*, 1253a19.

To a mature state there essentially belong thought and consciousness. Therefore the state knows what it wills and knows it as something thought. Now since knowing has its seat in the state, the seat of science must be there too and not in the church. Despite this, it is often said nowadays that the state must grow out of religion. The state is developed spirit and it exhibits its moments in the daylight of consciousness. Now the fact that what is contained in the Idea steps forth into objectivity gives the state the appearance of something finite, and so the state reveals itself as a domain of worldliness, while religion displays itself as a domain of the infinite. If this be so, the state seems to be the subordinate, and since what is finite cannot stand on its own, the state is therefore said to need the church as its basis. As finite, it lacks justification, and it is only through religion that it can become sacrosanct and belong to the infinite. This view of the matter, however, is supremely one-sided. Of course the state is essentially worldly and finite; it has particular ends and particular powers; but its worldly character is only one of its aspects, and it is only to a spiritless perception that it is finite and nothing more. For the state has a life-giving soul, and the soul which animates it is subjectivity, which creates differences and yet at the same time holds them together in unity. In the realm of religion too there are distinctions and finitude. God, it is said, is three in one; thus there are three determinations whose unity alone is spirit. Therefore to apprehend the nature of God concretely is to apprehend it through distinctions alone. Hence in the kingdom of God there is finitude, just as there is in the world, and to hold that the worldly spirit, i.e. the state, is only a finite spirit, is a one-sided view, for actuality is not irrational. Of course a bad state is worldly and finite and nothing else, but the rational state is inherently infinite.

Secondly, it is averred that the state must derive its justification from religion. In religion, the Idea is spirit in the inwardness of the heart, but it is this same Idea which gives itself a worldly form as the state and fashions for itself an existence and an actuality in knowing and willing. Now if you say that the state must be grounded on religion, you may mean that it should rest on rationality and arise out of it; but your statement may also be misunderstood to mean that people are most adroitly schooled to obedience if their spirits are shackled by an unfree religion. (The Christian religion, however, is the religion of freedom, though it must be admitted that this religion may become changed in character and perverted from freedom to bondage when it is infected with superstition.) Now if you mean that people must have religion so that their spirits, already shackled, may the more easily be oppressed by the state, then the purport of your statement is bad. But if you mean that people ought to respect the state, this whole whose limbs they are, then of course the best means of effecting this is to give them philosophical insight into the essence of the state, though, in default of that, a religious frame of mind may lead to the same result. For this reason, the state may have need of religion and faith. But the state remains essentially distinct from religion, since whatever it claims, it claims in the form of a rightful duty, and it is a matter of indifference to it in what spirit that duty is performed. The field of religion, on the other hand, is inwardness, and just as the state would jeopardize the right of inwardness if it made demands in a religious manner, so also when the church acts like a state and imposes penalties, it degenerates into a religion of tyranny.

A third difference which is connected with the foregoing is that the content of religion is and remains shrouded [*eingehüllt*], and consequently religion's place is in the field of the heart, feeling, and representation. In this field everything has the form of *subjectivity*. The state, on the other hand, actualizes itself and gives its determinations a stable existence. Now if religious feeling wished to assert itself in the state in the same way as it is wont to do in its own field, it would overturn the organization of the state, because the different organs of the state have latitude to pursue their several distinct paths, while in religion everything is always referred back to the totality. If this totality, then, wished to embrace all the relations of the state, this would be fanaticism; the wish to have the whole in every particular could be fulfilled only by the destruction of the particular, and fanaticism is just the refusal to give scope to particular differences. Hence to say: 'To the pious no law is given' is nothing but an expression of this same fanaticism. Once piety usurps the place of the state, it cannot tolerate the determinate but simply destroys it. It is quite consistent with this if piety leaves decisions to conscience, to the inner life, and is not governed by *reasons*: for this inner life does not develop into reasoned argument or give an account of itself. Hence if piety is to pass for the actuality of the state, all laws are cast to the winds and subjective feeling is the legislator. This feeling may be pure caprice, and whether it is or not can only be learnt from its actions. But by becoming actions and precepts, its actions assume the guise of laws, and this is just the very opposite of the subjective feeling with which we started. This feeling has God for its object, and we might make him the determinant of everything. But God is the universal Idea and in feeling remains indeterminate and so is too immature to determine what is existent in the state in a developed form. It is precisely the fact that everything in the state is fixed and secure which is the bulwark against caprice and positive opinion. Religion as such, then, ought not to be the governor.

271. The political constitution is, in the first place, the organization of the state and the self-related process of its organic life, a process whereby it differentiates its moments within itself and develops them to self-subsistence. Secondly, the state is an individual, unique and exclusive, and therefore related to others. Thus it turns its differentiating activity outward and accordingly establishes within itself the *ideality* of its subsisting inward differences.

Addition: Just as irritability in the living organism is itself from one point of view something inward, something belonging to the organism as such, so here the outward reference is also an inner-directedness. The inner side of the state as such is the civil power, while its outward direction is the military power, although this has a determinate place inside the state itself. Now to have both these powers in equilibrium constitutes an important factor in the history [*Geschichte*] of the state.* Sometimes the civil power is wholly effaced and rests entirely on the military power, as was the case, for instance, in the time of the Roman Emperors and the Praetorians.* At other times, nowadays for example, the military power is solely the product of the civil power, as when all the citizens are eligible for conscription.

1. *The Internal Constitution for itself*

272. The constitution is rational insofar as the state inwardly differentiates and determines its activity in accordance with the *nature of the concept*. The result of this is that each of these powers is in itself the *totality*, because each contains the other moments and has them effective in itself, and because the moments, being expressions of the differentiation of the concept, remain utterly within its ideality and constitute nothing but a *single individual* whole.

In our day there has come before the public an endless amount of babble about the constitution, as about reason itself, and the stalest babble of all has been produced in Germany, thanks to those* who have persuaded themselves that they have the best understanding of what a constitution is, to the exclusion of everyone else and in particular of governments. These people are convinced that they have an unassailable justification for what they say because they claim that religion and piety are the basis of all this shallow thinking of theirs. It is no wonder that this babble has made reasonable men just as sick of the words 'reason', 'enlightenment', 'right', etc., as of the words 'constitution' and 'freedom', and one might well be ashamed now to go on discussing the constitution of the state at all! However, we may at least hope that this surfeit will be effective in producing the general conviction that philosophical *knowledge* of such topics cannot arise from argumentation, reasons [*Gründe*], and calculations of purpose and utility, still less from the heart, love, and inspiration, but only from the concept. We may also hope that those who hold that the divine is inconceivable* [*unbegreiflich*] and the knowledge of truth a wild-goose chase will feel themselves bound to refrain from taking part in the discussion. The products of their hearts and their inspirations are either undigested chatter or mere edification, and whatever the worth of these neither can lay claim to the attention of philosophy.

Amongst current ideas, mention may be made (in connection with § 269) of the necessity for a *division of powers within the state*.[104] This point is of the highest importance and, if taken in its true sense, may rightly be regarded as the guarantee of public freedom. It is an idea, however, with which the very people who pretend to talk out of their inspiration and love neither have, nor desire to have, any acquaintance, since it is precisely there that the moment of rational determinacy lies. That is to say, the principle of the division of powers contains the essential moment of *difference*, of rationality *realized*. But when the abstract understanding handles it, it reads into it the false doctrine of the *absolute self-subsistence* of each of the powers against the others, and then one-sidedly interprets their relation to each other as negative, as a mutual *restriction*. This view implies that the attitude adopted by each power to the others is hostile and apprehensive, as if the others were evils, and that their function is to oppose one another and as a result of this counterpoise to bring about a general equilibrium, but not a living unity. It is only the inner self-determination of the concept, not any other consideration, whether of purpose or advantage, that is the absolute source of the division of powers, and in virtue of this alone is the organization of the state something inherently rational and the image of eternal reason.

How the concept and then, more concretely, how the Idea, determine themselves inwardly and so posit their moments—universality, particularity, and individuality—in abstraction from one another, is discoverable from logic, though not of course from the logic commonly in vogue.[105] To take the merely negative as a

[104] See Charles Louis de Secondat, baron de Montesquieu, *The Spirit of the Laws* (1748), Part 2, Book II, chap. 6.

[105] See *Encyclopaedia* (1830), §§ 163 ff. [S.H.]

starting-point and to make the willing of evil and the mistrust of such willing the primary factor, and then on the basis of this presupposition slyly to construct dikes whose efficiency simply necessitates corresponding dikes over against them, is characteristic in thought of the negative understanding and in disposition of the outlook of the rabble (see § 244).

If the powers (e.g. what are called the 'executive' and the 'legislature') become self-subsistent, then as we have seen on a grand scale,* the destruction of the state is immediately posited; or, if the state is maintained in its essentials, it is strife which, through the subjection by one power of the others, initially produces unity of one form or another, and so alone secures what is essential, the maintenance of the state.

Addition: We should desire to have in the state nothing except what is an expression of rationality. The state is the world which spirit has made for itself; the course it follows, therefore, is one that is determinate and has being in and for itself. How often we talk of the wisdom of God in nature! But we are not to assume for that reason that the physical world of nature is a loftier thing than the world of spirit. As high as spirit stands above nature, so high does the state stand above physical life. One must therefore venerate the state as an earthly divinity [*Irdisch-Göttliches*], and observe that if it is difficult to comprehend nature, it is infinitely harder to understand the state. It is a fact of the highest importance that nowadays we have gained determinate intuitions about the state in general and have been so much engaged in discussing and making constitutions. But by getting so far we have not yet settled everything. In addition, it is necessary to bring to bear on a rational topic the reason of intuition [*Vernunft der Anschauung*], to know what the essence of the matter is and to realize that the obvious is not always the essential.

The powers of the state, then, must certainly be distinguished, but each of them must form a whole in itself and contain within itself the other moments. When we speak of the distinct activities of these powers, we must not slip into the monstrous error of so interpreting their distinction as to suppose that each power should subsist independently [*für sich*] in abstraction from the others. The truth is that the powers are to be distinguished only as moments of the concept. If instead they subsist independently in abstraction from one another, then it is as clear as day that two independent units cannot constitute a unity but must of course give rise to strife, whereby either the whole is destroyed or else unity is restored by force. Thus in the French Revolution, the legislative power sometimes engulfed the so-called 'executive', the executive sometimes engulfed the legislative, and in such a case it is absurd to formulate e.g. the moral demand for harmony.

Leave the thing to the heart if you like and be saved all trouble; but even if ethical feeling is indispensable, it has no right to determine the powers of the state by reference to itself alone. The vital point, then, is that since the determinations of the powers are in themselves the whole, so also all the powers in their existence constitute the concept as a whole. Mention is usually made of three powers: the legislative, the executive, and the judiciary. Of these the first corresponds to universality and the second to particularity, but the judiciary is not the third moment of the concept, since the individuality of the judiciary lies outside the above spheres.

273. The state as a political entity is thus divided into three substantial elements:

(*a*) the power to determine and establish the universal—the *legislative power*;

(*b*) the subsumption of individual cases and the spheres of particularity under the universal—the *executive power*;

(*c*) subjectivity, as the will with the power of ultimate decision—the *crown* [or princely power]. In the crown, the different powers are bound into an individual unity which is thus at once the apex and beginning of the whole, i.e. of a *constitutional monarchy*.

The development of the state to constitutional monarchy is the achievement of the modern world, a world in which the substantial Idea has gained infinite form. The history of this inner deepening of the spirit of the world—or in other words this free development in the course of which the Idea, realizing rationality [in the external], releases its moments (and they are only its moments) from itself as totalities, and in so doing retains them in the ideal unity of the concept—the history of this genuine formation of ethical life is the content of universal world-history.

The ancient division of constitutions into *monarchy*, *aristocracy*, and *democracy*, is based upon the notion of substantial, still undivided, unity, a unity which has not yet come to its inner differentiation (to a developed, internal organization) and which therefore has not yet attained depth or concrete rationality. From the standpoint of the ancient world, therefore, this division is the true and correct one, since for a unity of that still substantial type, a unity that has not achieved its absolute unfolding [*Entfaltung*] within itself, difference is essentially an *external* difference and appears at first as a difference in the *number*[106] of those in whom that substantial unity is supposed to be immanent.* These forms, which on this principle belong to different wholes, are reduced in constitutional monarchy to moments of the whole. The monarch is *one* person; the *few* come on the scene with the executive power, and the *many* in general with the legislative power. But, as has been indicated [§ 214], purely quantitative distinctions like these are only superficial and do not afford the concept of the thing. Equally inadequate is the mass of contemporary talk about the democratic and aristocratic elements in monarchy, because when the elements specified in such talk are found in *monarchy* they are no longer democratic or aristocratic in character.

There are notions [*Vorstellungen*] of constitutions in which the mere abstraction of the state is placed at the top to rule and command, and how many individuals are at the head of such a state, whether one or a few or all, is a question left undecided and regarded as a matter of indifference. 'All these forms', says Fichte, 'are justified, provided there be an ephorate [*Ephorat*]' (a scheme devised by Fichte to be a counterpoise to the chief power in the state), 'and may be the means of introducing universal rights into the state and maintaining them there.'* A view of this kind—and the device of the ephorate also—is begotten by the superficial conception of the state to which reference has just been made. It is true enough that in quite simple social conditions these differences of constitutional form have little or no meaning. For instance, in the course of his legislation Moses prescribed that, in the event of his people's desiring a king, its institutions should remain unchanged except for the new requirement that the king should not 'multiply horses to himself . . . nor wives . . . nor silver and gold'.[107] Furthermore, in a sense one may of course say that the Idea is also indifferent to these forms (including monarchy, but only when it is restricted in meaning by being defined as an *alternative* to aristocracy and democracy). But the Idea is indifferent to them, not in Fichte's but in the opposite sense, because all three are inadequate to it in its rational development (see § 272) and in none of them,

---

[106] *Hegel's reference:* See *Encyclopaedia* § 82 [3rd edn. § 132]. ['§ 82' is probably a misprint. It should read: '§ 52 [3rd edn. § 99]'. S.H.]

[107] Deuteronomy 17: 16–17.

taken singly, could the Idea attain its right and its actuality. Consequently, it is quite idle to enquire which of the three is most to be preferred. Such forms must be discussed historically or not at all.

Still, here again, as in so many other places, we must recognize the depth of Montesquieu's insight in his now famous treatment of the principles of these forms of government. To recognize the accuracy of his account, however, we must not misunderstand it. As is well known, he held that 'virtue'[108] was the principle of *democracy*, since it is indeed the case that that type of constitution rests on the disposition [of the citizens], i.e. on the purely substantial form in which the rationality of the will that is in and for itself still exists in democracy. Montesquieu goes on to say that in the seventeenth century England provided 'a fine spectacle of the way in which efforts to found a democracy were rendered ineffective by a lack of virtue in the leaders'. And again he adds: 'when virtue vanishes from the republic, ambition enters hearts which are capable of it and greed masters everyone . . . so that the state becomes everyone's booty and its strength now consists only in the power of a few individuals and the licence of all alike'. These quotations call for the comment that in more mature social conditions and when the powers of particularity have developed and become free, a form of rational law other than the form of disposition is required, because virtue in the heads of the state is not enough if the state as a whole is to gain the power to hold itself together and to bestow on the powers of developed particularity both their positive and their negative rights. Equally, we must remove the misunderstanding of supposing that because the disposition of virtue is the substantial form of a democratic republic, it is evidently superfluous in monarchy or even absent from it altogether; and, finally, we may not suppose that there is an opposition and an incompatibility between virtue and the legally determinate activity of a state whose organization is fully articulated.

The fact that 'moderation'[109] is cited as the principle of aristocracy implies the beginning at this point of a divorce between

---

[108] See Montesquieu, *The Spirit of the Laws*, Part 1, Book 3, chap. 3. The quotations which follow immediately are from the same chapter.
[109] See Ibid., chap. 4.

public authority and private interest. And yet at the same time these touch each other so immediately that this constitution by its very nature stands on the verge of lapsing forthwith into tyranny or anarchy—the harshest of political conditions—and so into self-annihilation. See Roman history, for example.*

The fact that Montesquieu discerns 'honour'[110] as the principle of monarchy at once makes it clear that by 'monarchy' he understands, not the patriarchal or any ancient type, nor, on the other hand, the type organized into an objective constitution,* but only *feudal monarchy*, the type in which the relationships of right within the state are crystallized into the rights of private property and the privileges of individuals and corporations. In this type of constitution, political life rests on privileged persons and a great part of what must be done for the maintenance of the state is settled at their pleasure. The result is that their services are the objects not of duty but only of ideas and opinions. Thus it is not duty but only *honour* which holds the state together.

Another question readily presents itself here: 'Who is to frame the constitution?' This question seems clear, but closer inspection shows at once that it is meaningless, for it presupposes that there is no constitution there, but only an atomistic *aggregate* of individuals. How an aggregate of individuals could acquire a constitution, whether through itself or through someone else's aid, whether through benevolence or through force or through thought, would have to be left to it to determine, since the concept has nothing to do with any aggregate. But if the question presupposes an already existent constitution, then it is not about framing, but only about altering the constitution, and the very presupposition of a constitution immediately implies that its alteration may come about only by constitutional means. In any case, however, it is absolutely essential that the constitution should not be regarded as *something made*, even though it has come into being in time. It must be treated rather as something simply existent in and for itself, as divine therefore, and constant, and so as exalted above the sphere of things that are made.

Addition: The principle of the modern world as such is freedom of subjectivity, the principle that all the essential aspects present in the spiritual

---

[110] See Ibid., chaps. 6—7.

totality are now coming into their right in the course of their development. Starting from this point of view, we can hardly raise the idle question: Which is the better form of government, monarchy or democracy? We may only say that all constitutional forms are one-sided unless they can sustain in themselves the principle of free subjectivity and know how to correspond with a developed rationality.

274. Spirit is actual only as that which it knows itself to be, and the state, as the spirit of a people, is both the law *permeating all relationships within the state* and also at the same time the customs and consciousness of its citizens. It follows, therefore, that the constitution of any given people depends in general on the character and development of its self-consciousness. In its self-consciousness its subjective freedom is rooted and so, therefore, is the actuality of its constitution.

The proposal to give a constitution—even one more or less rational in content—to a people *a priori* is an idea [*Einfall*] which overlooks precisely that moment through which a constitution is more than a product of thought. Hence every people has the constitution appropriate to it and suitable for it.

Addition: The state in its constitution must permeate all relationships within the state. Napoleon, for instance, wished to give the Spaniards a constitution *a priori*,* but the project turned out badly enough. A constitution is not just something manufactured; it is the work of centuries, it is the Idea, the consciousness of rationality so far as that consciousness is developed in a particular people. No constitution, therefore, is just the creation of its subjects. What Napoleon gave to the Spaniards was more rational than what they had before, and yet they recoiled from it as from something alien, because they were not yet educated up to its level. A people's constitution must embody its feeling for its rights and its condition, otherwise there may be a constitution there in an external way, but it is meaningless and valueless. Individuals may indeed often feel the need and the longing for a better constitution, but it is quite another thing, and one that does not arise till later, for the mass of the people to be animated by such an idea. The principle of morality, of Socratic inwardness, was a necessary product of his age, but time was required before it could become part and parcel of the general self-consciousness.

(a) The Crown

275. The power of the crown contains in itself the three moments of the totality (see § 272), viz. (α) the *universality* of the constitution

and the laws; (β) counsel, which refers the *particular* to the universal; and (γ) the moment of ultimate decision, as the *self-determination* to which everything else reverts and from which everything else derives the beginning of its actuality. This absolute self-determination constitutes the distinctive principle of the power of the crown as such, and this is the *first* thing to be expounded.

Addition: We begin with the power of the crown, i.e. with the moment of individuality, since this includes the state's three moments as a totality in itself. The I, that is to say, is at once the most individual thing and the most universal. In nature, there is also initially individuality, but reality— non-ideality and externality—is not being-with-itself [*das Beisichseiende*]. On the contrary, in nature the various individual things subsist alongside one another. In spirit, on the other hand, variety exists only as something ideal and as a unity. The state, then, as something spiritual, is the exposition of all its moments, but individuality is at the same time its inner soul and its life-giving principle, i.e. the sovereignty which contains all differences in itself.

276. (1) The fundamental determination of the political state is the substantial unity, i.e. the *ideality*,[111] of its moments. (α) In this unity, the particular powers and their activities are dissolved and yet retained. They are retained, however, only insofar as they have no independent justification but one whose nature and extent are determined by the Idea of the whole; from its authority [*Macht*] they originate, and they are its fluid members while it is their simple self.

Addition: Much the same thing as this ideality of the moments in the state occurs with life in the organic body. Life is present at every point. There is only one life at all points and nothing withstands it. Separated from that life, every point dies. This is also the ideality of all individual estates, powers, and corporations, however much they have the impulse to subsist and be independent [*für sich*]. It is with them as it is with the belly in the organism.[112] It, too, asserts its independence, but at the same time its independence is superseded and sacrificed and it passes over into the whole.

277. (β) The particular activities and agencies of the state are its essential moments and therefore are proper to *it*. The individual functionaries and agents are attached to their office not on the strength of their immediate personality, but only on the strength of their universal and objective qualities. Hence it is in an external and

---

[111] See third explanatory note to p. 31 [p. 331 below]. [S.H.]
[112] See first explanatory note to p. 242 [p. 355 below]. [S.H.]

contingent way that these offices are linked with particular persons, and therefore the functions and powers of the state cannot be *private property*.

Addition: The activity of the state is in the hands of individuals. But their authority to conduct its affairs is based not on nature but on their objective qualities. Ability, skill, character, all belong to an individual in his *particular* capacity. He must be educated and be trained to a particular task. Hence an office may not be saleable or hereditary. In France, seats in parliament were formerly saleable, and in the English army officers' commissions up to a certain rank are saleable to this day.* This saleability of office, however, was or is still connected with the medieval constitution of certain states, and such constitutions are nowadays gradually disappearing.

278. These two determinations (α) and (β) constitute the *sovereignty of the state*. That is to say, sovereignty depends on the fact that the particular functions and powers of the state are not self-subsistent or firmly grounded either on their own account or in the particular will of individuals, but have their roots ultimately in the unity of the state as their simple self.

This is the *internal* sovereignty of the state. Sovereignty has another side, i.e. *external* sovereignty, on which see below [§§ 321 ff.].

In the former feudal monarchy, the state was certainly sovereign vis-à-vis other states; internally, however, not only was the monarch not sovereign at all, but the state itself was not sovereign either. On the one hand, the particular functions and powers of the state and civil society were vested (compare Remark to § 273) in independent corporations and communities, so that the state as a whole was rather an aggregate than an organism; and, on the other hand, office was the private property of individuals, and hence what they were to do in relation to the whole was left to their own opinion and caprice.

The *idealism* which constitutes sovereignty is the same determination as that in accordance with which the so-called 'parts' of an animal organism are not parts but members, moments in an organic whole, whose isolation and independence spell disease.[113] The principle here is the same as that which came before us (see § 7) in the abstract concept of the will as self-relating negativity,

---

[113] *Hegel's reference*: See *Encyclopaedia*, § 293 [3rd edn. § 371].

and therefore as universality *determining itself to individuality* and so superseding all particularity and determinacy: it is that of the absolute self-determining ground (see Remark to § 279). To understand this, one must have mastered the whole concept of substance and of the genuine subjectivity of the concept.[114]

The fact that the sovereignty of the state is the ideality of all particular authorities within it gives rise to the easy and also very common misunderstanding that this ideality is mere power [*Macht*] and empty arbitrariness while 'sovereignty' is a synonym for 'despotism'. But despotism means any condition of lawlessness in which the particular will as such, whether of a monarch or the people (ochlocracy), counts as law or rather takes the place of law; while it is precisely under lawful, constitutional conditions that sovereignty is to be found as the moment of ideality—the ideality of the particular spheres and functions. That is to say, sovereignty brings it about that each of these spheres is not something independent, self-subsistent in its aims and modes of working, something immersed solely in itself, but that instead, even in these aims and modes of working, each is determined by and dependent on *the aim of the whole* (the aim which has been denominated in general terms by the rather vague expression 'welfare of the state').

This ideality manifests itself in a twofold way:

(i) In times of peace, the particular spheres and functions pursue the path of satisfying their particular functions and aims, and it is in part only by way of the unconscious necessity of the thing that their self-seeking is turned into a contribution to reciprocal support and to the support of the whole (see § 183). In part, however, it is by the *direct influence* of higher authority that they are not only continually brought back to the aim of the whole and restricted accordingly (see § 289), but are also constrained to perform direct services for the support of the whole.

(ii) In a situation of exigency [*Not*], however, whether in internal or external affairs, the organism of which these particular spheres are members fuses into the simple concept of sovereignty. The sovereign is entrusted with the salvation of the state at the sacrifice of these particular authorities whose powers are otherwise

---

[114] See *Encyclopaedia* (1830), §§ 150 ff. [S.H.]

valid, and it is then that that ideality comes into its proper actuality (see § 321).

279. (2) Sovereignty, at first simply the universal *thought* of this ideality, comes into *existence* only as subjectivity certain of itself, as the will's abstract and to that extent ungrounded self-determination in which finality of decision is rooted. This is the strictly individual aspect of the state, and in virtue of this alone is the state *one*. The truth of subjectivity, however, is attained only in a *subject*, and the truth of personality only in a *person*; and in a constitution which has progressed to real rationality, each of the three moments of the concept has its separate shape which is actual for itself. Hence this absolutely decisive moment of the whole is not individuality in general, but *one* individual, the *monarch*.

The immanent development of a science, the derivation of its entire content from the concept in its simplicity (a science otherwise derived, whatever its merit, does not deserve the name of a philosophical science), exhibits this peculiarity, that one and the same concept—the will in this instance—which begins by being abstract (because it is at the beginning) maintains itself even while it consolidates its specific determinations, and that too solely by its own activity, and in this way gains a concrete content. Hence it is the basic moment of personality, abstract at the start in immediate right, which has developed itself through its various forms of subjectivity, and now—at the stage of absolute right, of the state, of the completely concrete objectivity of the will—has become the *personality of the state*, its certainty of itself. This last reabsorbs [*aufhebt*] all particularity into its simple self, cuts short the weighing of pros and cons between which it lets itself oscillate perpetually now this way and now that, and by saying 'I will' makes its decision and so inaugurates all activity and actuality.

Further, however, personality, like subjectivity in general, as infinitely self-relating, has its truth (to be precise, its initial, immediate, truth) only in a person, in a subject existing for himself, and what exists for itself is also simply *one*. It is only as a *person*, the *monarch*, that the personality of the state is actual.—Personality expresses the concept as such; but the person enshrines the actuality of the concept, and only when the concept is determined as person is it the *Idea* or truth.—A so-called 'moral person', be it a society, a community, or a family, however inherently concrete it may be, contains personality only abstractly, as one moment of itself. In a 'moral person', personality has not achieved its true mode of existence. The state, however, is precisely this totality in which the moments of the concept have attained actuality in accordance with their distinctive truth. All these determinations, both for themselves and in the shapes they assume, have been discussed in the whole course of this treatise. They are repeated here, however, because while their existence in their particular shapes is readily granted, it does not follow at all that they are recognized and apprehended again when they appear in their true place, not isolated, but in their truth as moments of the Idea.

The concept of the monarch is therefore of all concepts the hardest for ratiocination [*Räsonnement*], i.e. for the method of reflection employed by the understanding. This method refuses to move beyond isolated determinations and hence here again knows only reasons [*Gründe*], finite points of view, and derivation from such reasons. Consequently it exhibits the dignity of the monarch as something *derived*, not only in its form, but in its determination. The truth is, however, that to be something not derived but *purely self-originating* is precisely the concept of monarchy. Closest to this concept, therefore, is the idea of treating the monarch's right as grounded in the authority of God, since the unconditional character of that right is contained in its divinity.* We are familiar, however, with the misunderstandings connected with this idea, and it is precisely this 'divine' element which it is the task of a philosophical treatment to comprehend.

We may speak of the 'sovereignty of the people' in the sense that a people is self-subsistent vis-à-vis other peoples, and constitutes a state of its own, like the British people for instance. But the peoples of England, Scotland, or Ireland, or the peoples of Venice, Genoa, Ceylon, etc., are no longer sovereign peoples now that they have ceased to have rulers or supreme governments of their own.

We may also speak of internal sovereignty residing in the people, provided that we are speaking generally about the *whole* and meaning only what was shown above (see §§ 277, 278), namely that it is to the *state* that sovereignty belongs.

The usual sense, however, in which one has recently begun to speak* of the 'sovereignty of the people' is that it is something opposed to the sovereignty existent in the monarch. So opposed to the sovereignty of the monarch, the sovereignty of the people is one of the confused notions based on the wild idea of the 'people'. Taken without its monarch and the articulation of the whole which is the necessary and immediate concomitant of monarchy, the people is a formless mass and no longer a state. It lacks every one of those determinations—sovereignty, government, courts of law, public authorities [*Obrigkeit*], estates, etc.—which are to be found only in a whole which is inwardly organized. By the very emergence into a people's life of moments of this kind which relate to an organization, to life in the state, a people ceases to be that indeterminate abstraction which, when represented in a quite general way, is called the 'people'.

If by 'sovereignty of the people' is understood a *republican* form [of government], or to speak more specifically (since under 'republic' are comprised all sorts of other empirical combinations which are in any case irrelevant in a philosophical treatise) a *democratic* form, then all that is needed in reply has been said already (in the Remark to § 273); and besides, such a notion cannot be further discussed in face of the Idea of the state in its full development.

If the 'people' is represented neither as a patriarchal clan, nor as living under the undeveloped conditions which make democracy or aristocracy possible as forms of government (see Remark to § 273), nor as living under some other unorganized and haphazard conditions, but instead as an inwardly developed, genuinely organic, totality, then sovereignty is there as the personality of the whole, and this personality is there, in the reality adequate to its concept, as the *person of the monarch*.

At the stage at which constitutions are divided, as above mentioned [in the Remark to § 273], into democracy, aristocracy, and monarchy, the point of view taken is that of a still substantial unity, abiding in itself, without having yet attained its infinite differentiation and immersion in itself. At that stage, the moment of the final, self-determining decision of the will does not come on the scene for itself in its own distinctive actuality as an organic moment immanent in the state. Nonetheless, even in those comparatively undeveloped shapes of the state, there must always be individuals at the head. Leaders must either be available already, as they are in monarchies of that type, or, as happens in aristocracies, but more particularly in democracies, they may rise to the top, as statesmen or generals, by chance and in accordance with the particular needs of the hour. This must happen, since all action and actuality has its beginning and completion in the decisive unity of a leader. But comprised in a union of powers which remains undifferentiated, this subjectivity of decision is inevitably either contingent in its origin and emergence, or else is in one way or another subordinate to something else. Hence in such states, the power of the leaders was conditioned, and only in something beyond them could there be found a pure unambiguous decision, a *fatum*, determining affairs from without. As a moment of the Idea, this decision had to come into existence, though rooted in something outside the circle of human freedom with which the state is concerned. Herein lies the origin of the need for deriving the last word on great events and important affairs of state from oracles, a 'daemon' (in the case of Socrates),* the entrails of animals, the feeding and flight of birds, etc. It was when people had not yet grasped the depths of self-consciousness or risen out of their undifferentiated unity of substance to their being-for-self [*Fürsichsein*] that they lacked strength to look *within* their own being for the final word.

In the 'daemon' of Socrates (compare Remark to § 138) we see the will which formerly had simply displaced itself beyond itself now beginning to turn in on itself and to recognize itself within itself. This is the beginning of a *self-knowing* and so genuine freedom. This real freedom of the Idea consists precisely in giving to each of the moments of rationality its own self-conscious, present actuality. Hence it is this freedom which makes the ultimate self-determining certainty—the culmination of the concept of the will—the function of a single consciousness. This ultimate self-determination, however, can fall within the sphere of human freedom only insofar as it has the position of a pinnacle, isolated for itself and raised above all that is particular and conditional, for only so is it actual in a way adequate to its concept.

Addition: In the organization of the state—which here means in constitutional monarchy—we must have nothing before our minds except the inherent necessity of the Idea. All other points of view must vanish. The state must be treated as a great architectonic structure, as a hieroglyph of the reason which reveals itself in actuality. Everything to do with mere utility, externality, and so forth, must be eliminated from the philosophical treatment of the subject. Now our ordinary ideas can quite well grasp the conception of the state as a self-determining and completely sovereign will, as the ultimate source of decision. What is more difficult is to apprehend this 'I will' as a person. To do so is not to say that the monarch may act capriciously. Rather, he is bound by the concrete content of the counsel he receives, and if the constitution is stable, he has often no more to do than sign his name. But this name is important. It is the point beyond which it is impossible to go. It might be said that an organic, articulated, constitution was present even in the beautiful democracy of Athens, and yet we cannot help noticing that the Greeks derived their final decisions from the observation of quite external phenomena such as oracles, the entrails of sacrificial animals, and the flight of birds. They treated nature as a power which in those ways revealed and expressed what was good for humanity. At that time, self-consciousness had not yet advanced to the abstraction of subjectivity, not even so far as to understand that, when a decision is to be made, an 'I will' must be pronounced by man himself. This 'I will' constitutes the great difference between the ancient world and the modern, and in the great edifice of the state it must therefore have its distinctive existence. Unfortunately, however, this determination is regarded as only external and optional.

280. (3) This ultimate self in which the will of the state is concentrated is, when thus taken in abstraction, a simple self and therefore is *immediate* individuality. Hence the determination of *naturalness* is contained in its very concept. The monarch, therefore, is essentially determined as *this* individual, in abstraction from all other content, and *this* individual is raised to the dignity of monarchy in an immediate, natural, fashion, i.e. through his natural *birth*.

This transition of the concept of pure self-determination into the immediacy of being and so into the realm of nature is of a purely speculative character, and cognition of it therefore belongs to logic.[115] Moreover, this transition is on the whole the same as that familiar to us in the nature of willing, and there the process is to translate something from subjectivity (i.e. some purpose held before the mind) into existence (see § 8). But the distinctive form of the Idea and of the transition here under consideration is the immediate conversion of the pure self-determination of the will (i.e. of the simple concept itself) into *this* natural existence with-

---

[115] See *Encyclopaedia* (1830), § 244. [S.H.]

out the mediation of a *particular* content (like a purpose in the case
of action).

In the so-called 'ontological' proof of the existence of God, we
have the same conversion of the absolute concept into being. This
conversion has constituted the depth of the Idea in the modern
world, although recently it has been declared inconceivable,* with
the result that knowledge of truth has been renounced, since truth
is simply the unity of concept and existence (see § 23). Since the
consciousness of the understanding does not have this unity
within itself and refuses to move beyond the separation of these
two moments of the truth, it may perhaps, so far as God is concerned, still permit a 'faith' in this unity. But since the idea of the
monarch is regarded as being quite familiar to ordinary consciousness, the understanding clings here all the more tenaciously to its
separation [of the two moments] and the conclusions which its
astute reasoning deduces therefrom. As a result, it denies that the
moment of ultimate decision in the state is linked in and for itself
(i.e. in the rational concept) with the immediate and natural.
Consequently it infers, first, that this link is a matter of contingency,
and further—since it has claimed that the absolute difference of
these moments is what is rational—that such a link is irrational,
and then there follow the other consequences that disrupt the Idea
of the state.*

Addition: It is often alleged against monarchy that it makes the welfare of
the state dependent on contingency, for, it is urged, the monarch may be
badly educated, he may perhaps be unworthy of the highest position in the
state, and it is senseless that such a state of affairs should be regarded as
rational. But all this rests on a presupposition which is nugatory, namely
that everything depends on the monarch's particular character. In a completely organized state, it is only a question of the culminating point of
formal decision (and a natural bulwark against passion. It is wrong therefore to demand objective qualities in a monarch);[116] he has only to say 'yes'
and dot the 'i'; for the pinnacle [of the state] should be such that its particular character is not what is significant. (This determination of the
monarch is rational because it corresponds with the concept, but since this
is hard to grasp, we often fail to see the rationality of monarchy. Monarchy
must be inherently stable and) whatever else the monarch may have in

---

[116] The bracketed passages in this Addition are translated from the second edition of
the *Philosophy of Right* (1840); they did not appear in the first.

addition to this power of final decision belongs to his particular character and should be of no consequence. Of course there may be circumstances in which this particular character alone has prominence, but in that event the state is either not fully developed, or else is badly constructed. In a well-organized monarchy, the objective aspect belongs to law alone, to which the monarch has only to add the subjective 'I will'.

281. Both moments in their undivided unity—(*a*) the will's ultimate ungrounded self, and (*b*) therefore its similarly ungrounded existence [*Existenz*] (as the determination that belongs to nature)—constitute the Idea of something *unmoved* by caprice:* the 'majesty' of the monarch. In this unity lies the actual unity of the state, and it is only through this, its inward and outward immediacy, that the unity of the state is saved from the risk of being drawn down into the sphere of particularity and its caprices, ends, and opinions, and saved too from the war of factions round the throne and from the enfeeblement and overthrow of the power of the state.

The rights of birth and inheritance constitute the basis of *legitimacy*, the basis of a right not purely positive but contained in the Idea.

If succession to the throne is rigidly determined, i.e. if it is natural [and hereditary], then faction is obviated when the throne falls vacant; this is one aspect of hereditary succession and it has long been rightly stressed as a point in its favour. This aspect, however, is only a consequence, and to make it the reason for hereditary succession is to drag down the majesty of the throne into the sphere of argumentation [*Räsonnement*], to ignore its true character as ungrounded immediacy and ultimate inwardness, and to base it not on the Idea of the state immanent within it, but on something external to itself, on some extraneous notion such as the 'welfare of the state' or the 'welfare of the people'. Once it has been so based, its hereditary character may of course be deduced by the use of middle terms [*medios terminos*]. But other middle terms are equally available, and so therefore are different consequences, and it is only too well known what consequences have in fact been drawn from this 'welfare of the people' (*salut du peuple*).* Hence the majesty of the monarch is a topic for thoughtful treatment by philosophy *alone*, since every method of enquiry, other than the speculative method of the infinite Idea which is purely self-grounded, annuls the nature of majesty in and for itself.

An elective monarchy seems of course to be the most natural idea, i.e. the idea which superficial thinking finds the handiest. Because it is the concerns and interests of his people for which a monarch has to provide, so the argument runs, it must be left to the people to entrust with its welfare whomsoever it chooses, and only with the grant of this trust does his right to rule arise. This view, like the notion of the monarch as the highest official in the state, or the notion of a contractual relation between him and his people, etc., is grounded on the will interpreted as the whim, opinion, and caprice of the *many*.[117] A will of this character counts as the first thing in civil society (as was pointed out some time ago)[118] or rather it tries to count as the only thing there, but it is not the guiding principle of the family, still less of the state, and in short it stands opposed to the Idea of ethical life.

It is truer to say that elective monarchy is the worst of institutions, and its consequences suffice to reveal this to ratiocination. To ratiocination, however, these consequences have the appearance of something merely possible and probable, though they are in fact inherent in the very essence of this institution. For in an elective monarchy the nature of the situation is such that the ultimate decision is left with the *particular* will, and hence the constitution becomes an *electoral contract** [*Wahlkapitulation*], i.e. a surrender of the power of the state to the discretion of the particular will. The result of this is that the particular powers of state turn into private property, the sovereignty of the state is enfeebled and lost, and finally the state disintegrates within and is overthrown from without.*

Addition: If we are to grasp the Idea of the monarch, we cannot be content with saying that God has appointed kings to rule over us, since God has made everything, even the worst of things. The point of view of utility does not get us very far either, and it is always possible to point out counterbalancing disadvantages. Still less does it help to regard monarchy as a positive right. That I should hold property is necessary, but my holding of this particular property is contingent; and, in the same way, the right that one person must stand at the head of the state seems contingent too if it is treated as abstract and positive. This right, however, is present both as a felt need and as a requirement of the matter in and for itself. Monarchs are not exactly distinguished by their bodily prowess or intellectual gifts,

---

[117] See Remark to *PR* § 301.
[118] In the section on civil society; see e.g. *PR* §§ 183 and 206.

and yet millions submit to their rule. Now to say that people allow themselves to be ruled counter to their own interests, ends, and intentions is preposterous. People are not so stupid. It is their need, it is the inner power of the Idea, which, even against their apparent consciousness, constrains them to accept this rule and keeps them in that relation.

The monarch comes on the scene as the head and a part of the constitution, but it has to be said that there is no constitutional identity between a *conquered* people and its prince. A rebellion in a province conquered in war is a different thing from a rising in a well-organized state. It is not against their prince that the conquered are in rebellion, and they are committing no crime against the state, because their connection with their master is not a connection within the Idea or one within the inner necessity of the constitution. In such a case, there is only a contract, no political tie. 'I am not your prince, I am your master,'* Napoleon retorted to the envoys at Erfurt.

282. The right to *pardon* criminals arises from the sovereignty of the monarch, since it alone is empowered to actualize spirit's power of making undone what has been done and wiping out a crime by forgiving and forgetting it.

The right of pardon is one of the highest acknowledgements of the majesty of spirit. Moreover it is one of those cases where a determination which belongs to a higher sphere is applied to or reflected in the sphere below.* Applications of higher determinations to a lower sphere, however, concern the particular science which has to handle its subject-matter in all its empirical details (see footnote [97] to the Remark to § 270). Another instance of the same kind of thing is the subsumption under the concept of crime (which came before us earlier—see §§ 95–102) of injuries against the state in general, or against the sovereignty, majesty, and person of the prince. In fact these acquire the character of crime of the highest order, requiring a special procedure, etc.

Addition: Pardon is the remission of punishment, but it does not cancel right. On the contrary, right stands and the one who is pardoned remains a criminal as before. Pardon does not mean that he has not committed a crime. This annulment of punishment may take place through religion, since something done may be made undone in spirit by spirit itself. But the power to accomplish this on earth resides in [the sovereign's] majesty alone and must belong solely to his groundless decision.

283. The *second* moment in the power of the crown is the moment of *particularity*, or the moment of a determinate content and its subsumption under the universal. Insofar as this acquires a particular existence, it does so in the highest advisory offices and the individuals who hold them. They bring before the monarch for his decision the content of current affairs of state or the legal provisions required to meet existing needs, together with their objective aspects, i.e. the grounds on which decision is to be based, the relevant laws, circumstances, etc. The individuals who discharge these duties are in immediate contact with the person of the monarch and therefore their choice and dismissal alike rest with his unrestricted arbitrary will.

284. It is only for the *objective* side of decision, i.e. for knowledge of the content and the attendant circumstances, and for the legal and other determining grounds, that people are answerable; in other words, it is these alone which are capable of objective proof. It is for this reason that these may fall within the province of advisory offices which are distinct from the personal will of the monarch as such. Hence it is only such advisory offices or their individual incumbents that are made answerable. The personal majesty of the monarch, on the other hand, as the ultimately decisive subjectivity, is above all answerability for acts of government.

285. The *third* moment in the power of the crown concerns the universal in and for itself which subsists subjectively in the conscience of the *monarch* and objectively in the whole of the *constitution* and the *laws*. Hence the power of the crown presupposes the other moments in the state just as it is presupposed by each of them.

286. The *objective* guarantee of the power of the crown, of the hereditary right of succession to the throne, and so forth, consists in the fact that just as monarchy has its own actuality in distinction from that of the other rationally determined moments in the state, so these others possess for themselves the rights and duties appropriate to their character. In the rational organism of the state, each member, by maintaining itself as itself, *eo ipso* maintains the others in their distinctive character.

One of the results of more recent history is the development of a monarchical constitution with succession to the throne firmly fixed on hereditary principles in accordance with primogeniture. With this development, monarchy has been brought back to the patriarchal principle in which it had its historical origin, but its determination is now higher, because the monarch is the absolute

apex of an organically developed state. This historical result is of
the utmost importance for public freedom and for rationality in
the constitution, but, as was remarked above,[119] it is often grossly
misunderstood despite the respect paid to it.

The history of despotisms, as of the former, purely feudal, monarchies, is a tale of the vicissitudes of revolt, monarchical tyranny,
civil war, the ruin of princes and of dynasties, and, consequentially,
the general devastation and overthrow of the state in both its internal and external affairs. This is all due to the fact that, in monarchies
of that type, the division of the business of the state is purely
mechanical, the various parts being merely handed over to pashas,
vassals, etc. The difference between the parts is simply one of greater
or lesser power instead of being one of form and specific character.
Hence each part maintains itself and in doing so is productive *only of
itself* and not of the others at the same time; each incorporates in itself
all the moments required for independence and autonomy. When
there is an *organic* relation subsisting between members, not parts,
then each member by fulfilling the functions of its own sphere is
eo ipso maintaining the others; what each fundamentally aims at and
achieves in maintaining *itself* is the maintenance of the *others*.

The guarantees in question here for the maintenance of the succession to the throne or for the power of the crown generally, or
for justice, public freedom, etc., are secured by means of *institutions*. For *subjective* guarantees we may look to the affection of the
people, to character, oaths of allegiance, power, and so forth, but,
when the constitution is being discussed, it is only *objective* guarantees that are at issue. And such guarantees are institutions, i.e.
mutually conditioning moments, organically interconnected.
Hence public freedom in general and a hereditary monarchy guarantee each other; their connection is absolute, because public
freedom means a rational constitution, while the hereditary character of the power of the crown is, as has been shown [see § 280],
a moment lying in the concept of that power.

(*b*) The Executive Power

287. There is a distinction between the monarch's decisions and
their execution and application, or in general between his decisions

---

[119] See Remarks to *PR* §§ 279 and 281.

and the continued execution or maintenance of past decisions, existing laws, regulations, organizations for the securing of common ends, and so forth. This task of subsumption in general is comprised in the *executive power*, which also includes the powers of the *judiciary* and the *police* [or public authority]. The latter have a more immediate bearing on the particular concerns of civil society and assert the universal interest in these particular aims.

288. There are particular interests common to everyone which fall within civil society and lie outside the universal interest in and for itself of the state proper (see § 256). The administration of these is in the hands of corporations (see § 251), which represent communities and various professions and estates, and their officials, directors, administrators, and the like. It is the business of these officials to manage the private property and interests of these particular spheres and, from that point of view, their authority rests on the confidence of their peers and fellow-citizens. On the other hand, however, these circles of particular interests must be subordinated to the higher interests of the state, and hence the filling of positions of responsibility in corporations, etc., will generally be effected by a mixture of popular election by those interested with confirmation and determination by a higher authority.

289. The maintenance of the state's universal interest, and of legality, in this sphere of particular rights, and the work of bringing these rights back to the universal, require to be superintended by delegates of the executive power, by (a) the executive civil servants, and (b) the higher advisory officials (who are organized into committees). These converge in their supreme heads who are in direct contact with the monarch.

Just as civil society is the battlefield where everyone's individual private interest meets everyone else's, so here we have the struggle (*a*) of private interests against particular matters of common concern and (*b*) of both of these together against the organization of the state and its higher outlook. At the same time the spirit of the corporation, engendered when the particular spheres gain their rightful recognition, is now inwardly converted into the spirit of the state, since it finds in the state the means of maintaining its particular ends. This is the secret of the patriotism of the citizens in the sense that they know the state as their substance, because it is the state that maintains their particular spheres of interest together with the justification, authority, and welfare of these. The spirit of the corporation immediately entails the rooting of the particular in the universal, and for this reason it is in this corporate spirit that the depth and strength of disposition which the state possesses resides.

The administration of a corporation's business by its own officials is frequently clumsy, because although they keep before their minds and are acquainted with its special interests and affairs, they have a far less complete appreciation of the connection of those affairs with more remote conditions and universal points of view. In addition, other circumstances contribute to the same result, e.g. close private relationships and other factors putting officials on a footing of equality with those who should be their subordinates, the rather numerous ways in which officials lack independence, and so on. This personal sphere, however, may be regarded as one left to the moment of formal freedom, one which affords a playground for personal knowledge, personal decisions and their execution, petty passions and conceits. This is all the more permissible, the more trivial, from the point of view of the more universal affairs of state, is the intrinsic worth of the business which in this way comes to ruin or is managed less well or more laboriously, etc. And further, it is all the more permissible, the more this laborious or foolish management of such trivial affairs stands in direct relation with the self-satisfaction and vanity derived therefrom.

290. *Division of labour* (see § 198) occurs in the business of the executive also. For this reason, the organization of official bodies has the formal though difficult task of so arranging things that (a) civil life shall be governed in a concrete manner from below where it is *concrete*, but that (b) nonetheless the business of government shall be divided into *abstract* branches managed by special bodies, and further that (c) the operations of these different centres of administration shall converge again at the lowest level and in concrete supervision by the supreme executive.*

Addition: The point of special importance in the executive is the division of functions. The executive is concerned with the transition from the universal to the particular and the individual, and its functions must be divided in accordance with the differences between its branches. The difficulty, however, is that these different branches meet again at both the top and the bottom. The police and the judiciary, for instance, diverge, but in any particular case they coincide again. The usual expedient adopted to meet this difficulty is to appoint a Chancellor, a Prime Minister, or a Ministerial Council to simplify the upper level of government. But the result of this is that once more everything may be controlled from above and have its source in the Minister's power, and the business of the state is, as we say, centralized. This entails the maximum of simplification, speed, and efficiency in fulfilling the universal interests of the state. A regime of this kind was introduced by the French revolutionaries, elaborated by Napoleon, and still exists in France today. On the other hand, France lacks corporations and communes, i.e. circles wherein particular and universal interests meet. It is true that these circles won too great a measure of independence in the Middle Ages, when they were states within states and obstinately congealed into independent corporate bodies. But while that should not be allowed to happen, we may nonetheless affirm that the proper strength of the state lies in its communities. In them the executive meets with legitimate interests which it must respect, and insofar as the administration can only further such interests, though it must also supervise them, the individual finds protection in the exercise of his rights and so links his particular interest with the maintenance of the whole. For some time past organizations have been framed with a view to controlling these particular spheres from above, and effort has chiefly been expended on organizations of that type, while the lower levels, the mass of the population, have been left more or less unorganized. And yet it is of the utmost importance that the masses should be organized, because only so do they become a power or force. Otherwise they are nothing but a heap, an aggregate of separate atoms. Only when the particular spheres are organized, are they possessed of legitimate power.

291. The nature of the executive functions is that they are *objective* and that in their substance they have been explicitly fixed by previous decisions (see § 287); these functions have to be fulfilled and carried out by *individuals*. Between an individual and his office there is no immediate natural link. Hence individuals are not appointed to office on account of their birth or natural personality. The objective factor in their appointment is knowledge and proof of ability. Such proof guarantees that the state will get what it requires; and since it is the sole condition of appointment, it also guarantees to every citizen the chance of joining the universal estate [or estate of civil servants].

292. Since the objective qualification for the civil service is not genius (as it is for work as an artist, for example), there is of necessity an indefinite plurality of eligible candidates whose relative excellence is not determinable with absolute precision. The selection of one of the candidates, his nomination to office, and the grant to him of full authority to transact public business—all this, as the linking of two things, an individual and his office, which in relation to each other must always be fortuitous—is the *subjective* aspect of election to office, and it must lie with the crown as the power in the state which is sovereign and has the last word.

293. The particular public functions which the monarch entrusts to official bodies constitute one part of the *objective* aspect of the sovereignty residing in the crown. Their specific differences are therefore given in the nature of the thing. And while the actions of the official bodies are the fulfilment of their duty, their office is also a right exempt from contingency.

294. Once an individual has been appointed to his official position by the sovereign's act (see § 292), the tenure of his post is conditional on his fulfilling its duties. Such fulfilment is the very substance of his appointment, and it is as a *consequence* of this that he finds in his office his resources and the assured satisfaction of his particular interests (see § 264), and further that his external circumstances and his official work are freed from other kinds of subjective dependence and influence.

The state does not count on optional, discretionary, services (e.g. on justice administered by knights errant). It is just because such services are optional and discretionary that the state cannot rely on them, for casual servants may fail for subjective reasons to fulfil their duties completely, or they may arbitrarily decide not to fulfil them at all but pursue their subjective ends instead. The opposite extreme to a knight errant, so far as the service of the state goes, would be an official who clung to his office purely out of necessity without any real sense of duty and so without any real right to go on holding it.

What the service of the state really requires is that officials shall forgo the selfish and capricious satisfaction of their subjective ends; by this very sacrifice, they acquire the right to find their satisfaction in, but only in, the dutiful discharge of their public functions. In this fact, so far as public business is concerned, there lies the link between universal and particular interests which constitutes both the concept of the state and its inner stability (see § 260).

It follows that tenure of a civil service post is not contractual (see § 75), although appointment involves a consent and an undertaking on both sides. A civil servant is not appointed, like an agent [*Mandatarius*], to perform a single casual act of service; on the contrary, he concentrates his main interests (not only his particular interests but his spiritual interests also) on his relation to his work. Similarly, the work imposed upon him and entrusted to him is not a purely particular thing, external in character. The *value* of such a thing is something inward and therefore distinct from its outward character, so that it is not impaired if what has been stipulated is not fulfilled (see § 77). The work of a civil servant, however, is in its immediacy a value in and for itself. Hence the wrong committed through its non-performance or positive infringement (i.e. through an action contrary to official duty, and both of these are of that type) is an infringement of the universal content itself (i.e. is a negatively infinite judgement—see § 95)[120] and so is a misdemeanour or even a crime.

The assured satisfaction of particular needs removes the external necessity [*Not*] which may tempt an individual to seek ways and means of satisfying them at the expense of his official duties. Those who are entrusted with affairs of state find in its universal power the protection they need against another subjective phenomenon, namely the personal passions of the governed, whose private interests, etc., suffer injury as the interest of the state is made to prevail against them.

295. The security of the state and its subjects against the misuse of power by official bodies and their members lies immediately in their hierarchical organization and their answerability; but it lies too in the authority given to communities and corporations, because in itself this is a barrier against the intrusion of subjective caprice into the power entrusted to a civil servant, and it completes from below the control from above which does not extend as far as the conduct of individuals.

The conduct and education of officials is the point at which the laws and the government's decisions come into contact with

---

[120] See explanatory notes to pp. 67, 98 [pp. 337, 342 below]. [S.H.]

individuals and are actually made good. Hence it is on the conduct of officials that there depend not only the contentment of citizens and their trust in the government, but also the execution—or alternatively the distortion and frustration—of state projects; at any rate, this is the case in the sense that feeling and disposition may easily rate the *manner* of execution as highly as the *content* of the command to be executed, even though the content may in fact be the imposition of a burden. Owing to the immediate and personal nature of this contact with individuals, control from above can attain its ends in this respect only to a rather incomplete extent. Moreover, its ends may also be hindered by interests common to officials who form a clique [*Stand*] over against their inferiors on one side and their superiors on the other. In states whose institutions may perhaps be imperfectly developed in other respects also, the removal of hindrances like these requires and justifies the higher intervention of the sovereign (as for example of Frederick the Great in the notorious affair of Arnold the miller).*

296. But the fact that a dispassionate, upright, and polite demeanour becomes customary [in civil servants] is (i) partly a result of direct education in thought and ethical conduct. Such an education is a spiritual counterpoise to the mechanical and semi-mechanical activity involved in acquiring the so-called 'sciences' of matters connected with administration, in the requisite business training, in the actual work done, etc. (ii) The size of the state, however, is an important factor in producing this result, since it diminishes the weight of family and other personal ties, and also makes less potent and so less keen such passions as hatred, revenge, etc. In those who are occupied with the important interests of a great state, these subjective aspects automatically disappear, and the habit is generated of adopting universal interests, points of view, and activities.

297. Civil servants and the members of the executive constitute the greater part of the *middle class* [*Mittelstand*], in which the consciousness of right and the developed intelligence of the mass of the people is found. Sovereignty working on the middle class from above, and rights of corporations working on it from below, are the institutions which effectually prevent it from acquiring the isolated position of an aristocracy and using its education and skill as means to arbitrary domination.

At one time the administration of justice, which is concerned with the proper interests of all members of the state, was in this way turned into an instrument of profit and domination, when the knowledge of the law was buried in scholarship and a foreign tongue, and knowledge of legal processes was similarly buried in involved formalities.

Addition: The middle class, to which civil servants belong, is politically conscious and the one in which education is most prominent. For this reason it is also the pillar of the state so far as integrity and intelligence are concerned. A state without a middle class must therefore remain on a low level. Russia, for instance, has a mass of serfs on the one hand and a mass of rulers on the other. It is a prime concern of the state that a middle class should be developed, but this can be done only if the state is an organic unity like the one described here, i.e. it can be done only by giving authority to particular spheres, which are relatively independent, and through a realm of civil servants whose personal arbitrariness breaks against such authorized bodies. Action in accordance with universal right, and the habit of such action, is a consequence of the counterpoise to officialdom which independent and self-subsistent circles create.

(c) The Legislative Power

298. The *legislative power* is concerned (*a*) with the laws as such in so far as they require fresh and extended determination; and (*b*) with those internal affairs whose content is wholly universal. The legislative power is itself a part of the *constitution* which is presupposed by it and to that extent lies in and for itself outside the sphere directly determined by it; nonetheless, the constitution undergoes further development in the course of the further elaboration of the laws and the advancing character of the universal business of government.

Addition: The constitution must be in and for itself the fixed and recognized ground on which the legislative power stands, and for this reason it must not first be constructed. Thus the constitution *is*, but just as essentially it *becomes*, i.e. it advances and matures. This advance is an alteration which is imperceptible and which lacks the form of alteration. For example, the wealth of the German princes and their families began by being private property but then without any struggle or opposition it was converted into crown lands, i.e. into resources of the state. This came about because the princes felt the need of integrating their possessions and demanded property guarantees from their country and its Estates; the latter thus became involved in the conservation of the resources so that they ceased to be at the sole disposal of the princes. An analogous case is that [in the Holy Roman Empire] the Emperor was formerly a judge and travelled the Empire dispensing justice, and then, owing to the purely superficial results of cultural progress, external reasons made it necessary for him to delegate more and more of his judicial functions to others, with the result that the judicial power was transferred from the person of the monarch to groups of judges. Hence the advance from one state of affairs to another is tranquil in appearance and unnoticed. In this way a constitution changes over a long period of time into something quite different from what it was originally.

299. These matters are more precisely determined, in relation to individuals, under these two heads: (α) provision by the state for their well-being and happiness, and (β) the exaction of services from them. The former comprises the laws dealing with all sorts of private rights, the rights of communities, corporations, and organizations of a wholly universal character, and further it indirectly (see § 298) comprises the whole of the constitution. As for the services to be exacted, it is only if these are reduced to terms of *money*, the really existent and universal *value* of both things and services, that they can be fixed justly and at the same time in such a way that any particular tasks and services which an individual may perform come to be mediated through his own arbitrary will.

The proper object of universal legislation may be distinguished in a general way from the proper function of administrative officials or of state regulation, in that the content of the former is wholly universal, i.e. legal determinations, while what is particular in content falls to the latter, together with ways and means of *implementing* the law. This distinction, however, is not a hard and fast one, because a law, in order to be a law and not just a mere commandment in general (such as 'Thou shalt not kill'—compare Remark (*d*) to § 140), must be *determinate* in itself; but the more determinate it is, the more readily are its terms capable of being carried out as they stand. At the same time, however, to give to laws such a fully detailed determinacy would give them empirical features subject inevitably to alteration in the course of their being actually carried out, and this would contravene their character as laws. The organic unity of the powers of the state itself implies that it is *one* spirit which both firmly establishes the universal and also brings it into its determinate actuality and carries it out.

In the state it may at first seem remarkable that the numerous aptitudes, possessions, pursuits, and talents of its citizens, together with the infinitely varied living resources intrinsic to these—all of which are at the same time linked with their owner's disposition—are not subject to direct levy by the state. It lays claim only to one resource, namely *money*. (Services requisitioned for the defence of the state against enemies arise for the first time in connection with the duty considered in the next subdivision of this book [see §§ 324–6].) In fact, however, money is not one particular type of resource amongst others, but the universal aspect of all of them so far as they are expressed in an external existence and so can be taken as 'things'. Only at this extreme point of externality can services exacted by the state be determined *quantitatively* and so justly and equitably.

In Plato's *Republic*, the Guardians are left to allot individuals to their particular estates and impose on them their particular services (compare Remark to § 185).[121] Under the feudal monarchies the services required from vassals were equally indeterminate, but they had also to serve in their particular capacity, e.g. as judges. The same particular character pertains to services imposed in the East and in Egypt in connection with colossal architectural undertakings,* and so forth. In these circumstances the principle of *subjective freedom* is lacking, i.e. the principle that the individual's substantial activity—which in any case is something particular in content in services like those mentioned—shall be mediated through his *particular volition*. This is a right which can be secured only when the demand for service takes the form of a demand for something of universal value, and it is this right which has brought with it this conversion [of the state's demands into demands for money].

Addition: The two sides of the constitution relate respectively to the rights and the services of individuals. Services are now almost entirely reduced to money payments, and military service is now almost the only personal one exacted. In the past, far more claims were made directly on individuals, and they used to be called upon for work according to their ability. In our day, the state purchases what it requires. This may at first sight seem an abstract, heartless, and dead state of affairs, and for the state to be satisfied with abstract services may also look like decadence in the state.

---

121 See Plato, *Republic*, 415a–d. [S.H.]

But the principle of the modern state requires that the whole of an individual's activity shall be mediated through his will. By means of money, however, the justice of equality can be achieved much more efficiently. Otherwise, if assessment depended on concrete ability, a talented person would be more heavily taxed than an untalented one. But nowadays respect for subjective freedom is publicly recognized precisely in the fact that the state lays hold of someone only by that which is capable of being taken hold of.

300. In the legislative power as a totality the other two moments are effective from the outset: (i) the *monarchy* as that to which ultimate decisions belong; (ii) the *executive* as the advisory body since it is the moment possessed of (α) a concrete knowledge and oversight of the whole in its numerous facets and the actual principles firmly established within it, and (β) a knowledge in particular of what the state's power needs. The last moment in the legislature is the *Estates* [*das ständische Element*].*

Addition: The proposal to exclude members of the executive from legislative bodies, as for instance the Constituent Assembly did,* is a consequence of false views of the state. In England, ministers must be members of parliament, and this is right, because executive officers should be linked with and not opposed to the legislature. The idea of the so-called 'independence of powers' [122] contains the fundamental error of supposing that the powers, though independent, are to check one another. This independence, however, destroys the unity of the state, which is the chief requirement.

301. The Estates have the function of bringing the universal interest into existence not only *in itself* [*an sich*], but also *for itself* [*für sich*], i.e. of bringing into existence the moment of subjective *formal freedom*, public consciousness as the empirical universality of the thoughts and opinions of the many.

The phrase 'the many' (οἱ πολλοί) denotes empirical universality more strictly than 'all', which is in current use. If it is said to be obvious that this 'all' prima facie excludes at least children, women, etc., then it is surely still more obvious that the quite definite word 'all' should not be used when something quite indefinite is meant.

[122] See *PR* § 272 and Remark and Addition. [S.H.]

Current opinion has put into general circulation such a host of perverse and false ideas and ways of speaking about the 'people', 'constitution', and 'Estates' that it would be a waste of energy to try to specify, expound, and correct them. The idea uppermost in people's minds when they speak about the necessity or the expediency of 'summoning the Estates' is generally something of this sort: (i) The deputies of the people, or even the people themselves, *must know best* what is in their best interest, and (ii) they undoubtedly have the will that is best suited to promote this best interest. So far as the first of these points is concerned, however, the truth is that if 'the people' means a particular section of the members of the state, then it means precisely that section *which does not know what it wills*. To know what one wills, and still more to know what the will in and for itself, reason, wills, is the fruit of profound cognition and insight, precisely the things which are *not* characteristic of 'the people'.

The Estates are a guarantee of the general welfare and public freedom. A little reflection will show, however, that this guarantee does not lie in their particular insights, because the highest civil servants necessarily have a deeper and more comprehensive insight into the nature of the state's organization and requirements. They are also more habituated to the business of government and have greater skill in it, so that even without the Estates they are *able* to do what is best, just as they also continually *have* to do while the Estates are in session. No, the guarantee lies on the contrary (α) in the *additional* insight of the deputies, insight in the first place into the activity of such officials as are not immediately under the eye of the higher functionaries of state, and in particular into the more pressing and more specialized needs and deficiencies which are directly in their view; (β) in the fact that the anticipation of criticism from the many, particularly of public criticism, has the effect of inducing officials to devote their best attention beforehand to their duties and the schemes under consideration, and to deal with these only in accordance with the purest motives. This same compulsion is effective also on the members of the Estates themselves.

As for the conspicuously good will for the general welfare which the Estates are supposed to possess, it has been pointed out already (in the Remark to § 272) that to presuppose that the will of the

executive is bad, or less good [than that of the ruled], is characteristic of the rabble or of the negative outlook generally. This presupposition might at once be answered on its own ground by the
countercharge that the Estates start from individuals, from a private point of view, from particular interests, and so are inclined to
devote their activities to these at the expense of the general interest, while on the other hand the other moments in the power of the
state by their very nature take up the standpoint of the state and
devote themselves to the universal end.

As for the general guarantee which is supposed to lie peculiarly
in the Estates, each of the other political institutions shares with
the Estates in being a guarantee of public welfare and rational freedom, and some of these institutions, as for instance the sovereignty of the monarch, hereditary succession to the throne, the
judicial system, etc., guarantee these things far more effectively
than the Estates can.

Hence the specific function which the concept assigns to the
Estates is to be sought in the fact that in them the subjective
moment in universal freedom—the personal insight and personal
will of the sphere called 'civil society' in this book—*comes into
existence in relation to the state*. This moment is a determination of
the Idea once the Idea has developed to totality, a moment arising
as a result of an inner necessity not to be confused with external
necessities and expediencies. The proof of this follows, like all the
rest of our account of the state, from adopting the philosophical
point of view.

Addition: The attitude of the executive to the Estates should not be essentially hostile, and a belief in the necessity of such hostility is a sad mistake.
The executive is not a party standing over against another party in such a
way that each has continually to steal a march on the other and wrest
something from the other. If such a situation arises in the state, that is a
misfortune and cannot be called health. The taxes approved by the
Estates, moreover, are not to be regarded as a present given to the state.
On the contrary, they are approved in the best interests of those who
approve them. The real significance of the Estates lies in the fact that it is
through them that the state enters the subjective consciousness of the
people and that the people begins to participate in the state.

302. Regarded as a mediating organ, the Estates stand between
the government in general, on the one hand, and the people broken

up into particular spheres and individuals on the other. Their function requires them to possess a sense for and disposition toward the state and government, as well as the interests of particular circles and of individuals. At the same time the significance of their position is that, in common with the organized executive, they are a middle term preventing both the extreme isolation of the power of the crown, which otherwise might seem a mere arbitrary tyranny, and also the isolation of the particular interests of communities, corporations and individuals. Further, and more important, they prevent individuals from having the appearance of a mass or an aggregate and so from acquiring an unorganized opinion and volition and from crystallizing into a powerful bloc in opposition to the organized state.

It is one of the most important insights of logic that a specific moment which, by standing in an opposition, has the position of an extreme, ceases to be such and is a moment in an organic whole by being at the same time a middle term.[123] In connection with our present topic it is all the more important to emphasize this aspect of the matter because of the frequent, but most dangerous, prejudice which regards the Estates principally from the point of view of their *opposition* to the executive, as if that were their essential attitude. The Estates prove themselves to be organic—that is, taken up into the totality—solely through their mediating function. In this way their opposition to the executive is reduced to a semblance. There may indeed be an appearance of opposition between them, but if they were opposed, not merely superficially, but actually and in substance, then the state would be in the throes of destruction. The sign that the conflict is not of this kind is evident from the nature of the thing, if the matters in dispute are not the essential elements in the organism of the state, but only more specialized and trifling matters, and if the passion which even these arouse spends itself in party cravings in connection with purely subjective interests such as appointments to the higher offices of state.

Addition: The constitution is essentially a system of mediation. In despotic states, where there are only rulers and people, the people is effective, if at all, only as a mass destructive of the organization of the state. When the

---

[123] For Hegel's theory of the syllogism (to which this remark refers), see *Encyclopaedia* (1830), §§ 181 ff. [S.H.]

multitude enters the state in an organic way, it achieves its interests by legal and orderly means. But if these means are lacking, the voice of the masses will always be wild. Hence, in despotic states, the despot always indulges the people and keeps his wrath for his entourage. For the same reason too the people in such states pay only a few taxes. Taxes rise in a constitutionally governed state simply owing to the people's own consciousness. In no country are so many taxes paid as in England.

303. The *universal* estate, or, more precisely, the estate that devotes itself to the *service of government*, must, purely in virtue of its character as universal, have the universal as the end of its essential activity. In the *Estates*, as an element in the legislative power, the private estate [*Privatstand*] acquires its *political* significance and efficacy; it appears, therefore, in the Estates neither as a mere undifferentiated multitude nor as an aggregate dispersed into its atoms, but as what it already is, namely as divided into two, one part [the agricultural estate] being based on the substantial relationship, and the other part [the business estate] on particular needs and the work whereby these are met (see § 201 ff.). It is only in this way that there is a genuine link between the *particular* which is effective in the state and the universal.

This runs counter to another prevalent idea, the idea that since it is in the legislature that the private estate rises to the level of participating in the universal interest, it must appear there in the form of *individuals*, be it that individuals are to choose representatives for this purpose, or indeed that every single individual is thereby to have a vote himself. This atomistic and abstract point of view vanishes at the stage of the family, as well as that of civil society where the individual is in evidence only as a member of a general group. The state, however, is essentially an organization whose members constitute circles in their own right [*für sich*], and hence no one of its moments should appear as an unorganized aggregate. The *many*, as individuals—a favourite interpretation of 'the people'—are of course something connected, but they are connected only as an *aggregate*, a formless mass whose commotion and activity can therefore only be elementary, irrational, wild, and frightful. When we hear speakers on the constitution expatiating about the 'people'—as this unorganized collection—we know from the start that we have nothing to expect but generalities and perverse declamations.

The circles of association in civil society are already communities. To picture these communities as once more breaking up into a mere conglomeration of individuals as soon as they enter the field of politics, i.e. the field of the highest concrete universality, is *eo ipso* to hold civil and political life apart from one another and as it were to hang the latter in the air, because its basis could then only be the abstract individuality of caprice and opinion, and hence it would be grounded on contingency and not on what is stable and justified in and for itself.

So-called 'theories' of this kind involve the idea that the estates [*Stände*] of civil society and the Estates [*Stände*] in the political sense stand far apart from each other. But the German language, by calling them both *Stände* has still maintained the unity which they certainly possessed in former times.

304. The Estates, as an element in political life, still retain within their very determination the distinctions between estates already present in the preceding spheres of civil life. The position of the Estates is initially abstract, i.e. in contrast with the principle of monarchy or the crown in general their position is that of the extreme of empirical universality. This position implies the possibility, though no more, of harmonization, and the equally likely possibility of hostile opposition. This abstract position changes into a rational relation (into a syllogism, see Remark to § 302) only if its *mediation* comes into existence. From the point of view of the crown, the executive already fulfils this function (see § 300). From the point of view of the estates, one moment in them must also be adapted to the task of existing as in essence the moment of mediation.

305. The principle of one of the estates of civil society is in itself capable of adaptation to this political position. The estate in question is the one whose ethical life is natural, whose basis is family life and, so far as its livelihood is concerned, the possession of land. So far as its particularity is concerned, this estate has in common with the crown a will that rests on itself alone and the moment of natural determinacy that is also contained in the crown.

306. This estate is more particularly fitted for political position and significance in that its resources are independent alike of the state's resources, the uncertainty of business, the quest for profit, and any sort of fluctuation in possessions. It is likewise independent of favour, whether from the executive or the masses. It is even fortified *against its own arbitrary will*, because those members of this estate who are called to political life are not entitled, as other citizens are, either to dispose of their entire property at will, or to the assurance that it will pass to their children in proportion to the equal degree of love they feel for them. Hence their wealth becomes *inalienable inherited property*, burdened with primogeniture.

Addition: This estate has a volition of a more independent character. On the whole, the estate of landed property-owners is divided into an educated section and a section of farmers. But over against both of these sorts of people there stands the business estate, which is dependent on needs and concentrated on their satisfaction, and the civil service estate, which is essentially dependent on the state. The security and stability of the agricultural estate may be still further increased by the institution of primogeniture, though this institution is desirable only from the political point of view, since it entails a sacrifice for the political end of giving the eldest son a life of independence. Primogeniture is grounded on the fact that the state should be able to count on a disposition [towards politics] not just as a bare possibility but as something necessary. Now such a disposition is of course not bound to wealth, but there is a relatively necessary connection between the two, because a person with independent means is not hemmed in by external circumstances and so there is nothing to prevent him from entering politics and working for the state. Where political institutions are lacking, however, the foundation and encouragement of primogeniture is nothing but a fetter on the freedom of private rights, and either political meaning must be given to it, or else it will in due course disappear.

307. The right of this section of the substantial [or agricultural] estate is thus indeed based on the natural principle of the family. But this principle is at the same time given a new twist by the hard sacrifices that are made for *political ends*, so the activity of this estate is essentially directed towards those ends. As a consequence of this, this estate is summoned and entitled to its *political* vocation by *birth* without the hazards of election. It therefore has the fixed, substantial position between the subjective arbitrariness or contingency of both extremes; and while it mirrors in itself (see § 305) the moment of monarchical power, it also shares the otherwise equal needs and rights of the other extreme [i.e. civil society] and hence it becomes a support at once of the throne and society.

308. The second section of the Estates comprises the mobile element in civil society. This element can enter politics only through its *deputies*; the multiplicity of its members is an external reason for this, but the essential reason is the nature of its determination and activity. Since these deputies are the deputies of civil society, it follows as an immediate consequence that their appointment is made by the society *as it is*. That is to say, in making the appointment, society is not dispersed into atomic individuals, collected to perform only a single and temporary act, and kept together for a moment and no longer. On the contrary, it makes the appointment as a society, articulated into associations, communities, and corporations, which although constituted already for other purposes, acquire in this way a connection with politics. The existence of the Estates and their assembly finds a distinctive constitutional guarantee in the fact that this estate is entitled to send deputies at the summons of the crown, while members of the first estate are entitled to present themselves in person in the Estates (see § 307).

To hold that *all* individuals should share in deliberating and deciding on the universal affairs of the state on the grounds that all are members of the state, that its concerns are their concerns, and that it is their *right* that what is done should be done with their knowledge and volition, is tantamount to a proposal to put the *democratic* element *without any rational form* into the organism of the state, although it is only in virtue of the possession of such a form that the state is an organism at all. This idea comes readily to mind because it does not go beyond the *abstraction* of 'being a member of the state', and it is superficial thinking which clings to abstractions. The rational consideration of a topic, the consciousness of the Idea, is concrete, and to that extent coincides with genuine practical sense. Such sense is itself nothing but the sense of rationality or the Idea, though it is not to be confused with mere business routine or the horizon of a restricted sphere. The concrete state is the whole, articulated into its particular groups. The member of a state is a member of such a group, i.e. of an estate, and only as determined in this objective way does he come into consideration in relation to the state. His universal determination as such implies that he is at one and the same time both a private person and also a thinking consciousness, a will which wills the universal. This consciousness and will, however, lose their emptiness and acquire a content and a living actuality only when they are filled with particularity, and this is to be found in the particular estate and vocation; or, to put the matter otherwise, the individual is a genus [*Gattung*], but it has its *immanent* universal *actuality* in the *next* genus.—Hence the individual fulfils his actual and living vocation for universality only when he becomes a member of a corporation, a community, etc. (see § 251), and thereby it becomes open to him, on the strength of his skill, to enter any estate for which he is qualified, including the universal estate.

Another presupposition of the idea that *all* should participate in the business of the state is that *everyone has an understanding of this business*—a ridiculous notion, however commonly we may hear it put forward. Yet in public opinion (see § 316) a field is open to everyone in which they can express and assert their subjective opinions concerning the universal.

309. Since deputies are selected to deliberate and decide on universal matters, the point is to select individuals who are trusted to have a better understanding of these matters than those who select them and who are also trusted to assert essentially the universal interest, not the particular interest of a community or a corporation in preference to that universal interest. Hence their relation to those that select them is not that of agents with a commission or specific instructions. A further bar to their being so is the fact that their assembly is meant to be a living body in which all members deliberate in common and reciprocally instruct and convince each other.

Addition: The introduction of representation [*Repräsentation*] means that consent is given not directly by all but only by authorized deputies, since under a representative system the individual, *qua* infinite person, no longer comes into the picture. Representation is grounded on trust, but trusting another is something different from giving my vote *in person*. Majority voting also runs counter to the principle that I should be personally present in anything which is to be obligatory for me. We have trust in someone when we take him to have the insight to treat my affairs as if they were his own and to treat them conscientiously and to the best of his knowledge. Thus the principle of the individual subjective will disappears, since trust is placed in a thing, in a person's principles, or his demeanour or his conduct or his concrete sense generally. The important thing, then, is that a member of the Estates shall have a character, insight, and will adequate to his task of concentrating on universal affairs. In other words, it is not important that an individual should have a say as abstract individual.

The point is rather that his interests are made good in an assembly whose business is with the general interest. The electors [*die Wählenden*] require a guarantee that their deputy will further and secure this general interest.

310. The guarantee that deputies will have the qualifications and disposition that accord with this end—since independent resources already demand their right in the first section of the Estates—is to be found so far as the second section is concerned—the section drawn from the mobile and changeable element in civil society—above all in the knowledge (of the organization and interests of the state and civil society), the disposition, and the skill which a deputy acquires as a result of the *actual* transaction of business in positions of authority or political office and then evinces in his actions. As a result, he also acquires and develops a sense of authority and a political sense, tested by his experience, and this is a further guarantee of his suitability as a deputy.

Subjective opinion, naturally enough, finds superfluous and even perhaps offensive the demand for such guarantees, if the demand is made with reference to what is called the 'people'. The state, however, is characterized by objectivity, not by subjective opinion and its self-confidence. Hence it can recognize in individuals only what is objectively recognizable and tested, and it must be all the more careful on this point in connection with the second section of the Estates, since this section is rooted in interests and activities directed towards the particular, i.e. in the sphere where chance, mutability, and caprice enjoy their right of free play.

The external condition of having certain resources appears, if taken merely by itself, to be just as one-sided in its externality as, at the other extreme, are purely subjective confidence and the opinion of the electorate. Both alike are abstractions in contrast with the concrete qualifications requisite for deliberation on affairs of state and comprised in the points indicated in § 302. Nonetheless, in the choice of individuals for positions of authority and other offices in associations and communities, a property qualification has a sphere where it may work effectively, especially if many of these posts are unpaid, and it is directly relevant to the business of the Estates if the members draw no salary.

311. Furthermore, since deputies are selected from within civil society, the deputies should themselves be familiar with and participate in its special needs, difficulties, and particular interests. Owing to the nature of civil society, its deputies are the deputies of the various *corporations* (see § 308), and this simple mode of appointment removes any confusion that may arise from conceiving the electorate abstractly and as an agglomeration of atoms. Hence it immediately fulfils the demand set out above, and elections are therefore either something wholly superfluous or else reduced to a trivial play of opinion and caprice.

It is obviously of advantage that the deputies should include representatives of each particular main branch of society (e.g. trade, manufacture, etc.)—representatives who are thoroughly conversant with it and who themselves belong to it. The idea of a free and indeterminate election leaves this important consideration entirely at the mercy of contingency. All such branches of society, however, have equal rights of representation. If deputies are regarded as 'representatives', they are this in an organic, rational sense only if they are representatives not of individuals or a conglomeration of them, but of one of the essential *spheres* of society and its large-scale interests. Hence representation cannot now be taken to mean simply the substitution of one person for another; the point is rather that the interest itself is *actually present* in its representative, while he himself is there to present the objective element of his own being.

As for mass elections, it may be further remarked that especially in large states it leads inevitably to electoral indifference, since the casting of a single vote is of no significance where there is a multitude of electors. Even if a voting qualification is highly valued and esteemed by those who are entitled to it, they still do not enter the polling booth. Thus the result of an institution of this kind is more likely to be the opposite of what was intended; election actually falls into the power of a few, of a faction [*Partei*], and so of the particular and contingent interest which is precisely what was to have been neutralized.

312. Each of the two sections of the Estates (see § 305 and 308) contributes something particular to the process of deliberation. Further, one of the moments concerned has the distinctive function of mediation in the sphere of politics,* mediation between two existing things. Hence this moment must likewise acquire a separate

existence of its own. For this reason the assembly of the Estates is divided into *two houses*.

313. This division, by providing more than one instance [*Instanz*], is a surer guarantee of mature decisions, and it removes the contingency which decisions made on the spur of the moment and decisions passed by majority vote may have. But the principal advantage of this arrangement is that there is less chance of the Estates being in direct opposition to the executive; or, if the mediating moment is at the same time on the side of the second Estate, i.e. the lower house, the weight of the lower house's opinion is all the stronger, because it appears less partisan and its opposition appears neutralized.

314. The purpose of the Estates as an institution is not to ensure that the business of the state *in itself* is considered and decided in the best way possible, since in this respect their role is merely supplementary (see § 301). Their distinctive purpose is that through their participation in knowledge, deliberations, and decisions concerning universal matters, the moment of *formal* freedom shall come into its right in respect of those members of civil society who are without any share in the executive. Consequently, knowledge of universal affairs is extended above all by the *publicity* of Estates debates.

315. The opening of this opportunity to know has a more universal aspect because by this means public opinion first reaches thoughts that are true and attains insight into the situation and concept of the state and its affairs, and so first acquires the *ability to judge these more rationally*. By this means also, it becomes acquainted with and learns to respect the work, abilities, virtues, and skills of official bodies and civil servants. While such publicity provides these abilities with a powerful opportunity to develop and a theatre in which to attain high honour, it is at the same time an antidote to the self-conceit of individuals and of the masses, and a means—indeed one of the chief means—of their education.

Addition: Estates assemblies, open to the public, are a great spectacle and an excellent education for the citizens, and it is from them that the people learn best how to recognize the true character of its interests. The idea usually dominant is that everyone knows from the start what is best for the state and that the assembly debate is a mere discussion of this knowledge. In fact, however, the precise contrary is the truth. It is here that there first begin to develop the virtues, abilities, skills, which have to serve as examples to the public. Of course such assemblies are irksome to ministers, who have to equip themselves with wit and eloquence to meet the criticisms there directed against them. Nonetheless, publicity here is the chief means of educating the public in the affairs of state. A people which has such public sittings is far more vitally related to the state than one which has no Estates assembly or one which meets in private. It is only because their every step is made known publicly in this way that the two Houses remain in touch with the range of public opinion, and it then becomes clear that a man's castle building at home with his wife and his friends is one thing, while what happens in a great assembly, where one shrewd idea devours another, is something quite different.

316. The formal subjective freedom of individuals consists in their having and expressing their *own* judgements, opinions, and recommendations on matters of universal concern. This freedom is collectively manifested as what is called 'public opinion', in which what is universal in and for itself, the substantial and the true, is linked with its opposite, the purely particular and distinctive opinions of the many. Public opinion as it exists is thus a standing self-contradiction, knowledge as appearance, the essential just as immediately present as the inessential.

Addition: Public opinion is the unorganized way in which a people's opinions and wishes are made known. Whatever gains authority in the state must operate in an organized manner, as the parts of the constitution do. But at all times public opinion has been a great power and it is particularly so in our day when the principle of subjective freedom has such importance and significance. What is to be authoritative nowadays derives its authority, no longer from force, only to a small extent from habit and custom, but really from insight and argument.

317. Public opinion, therefore, is a repository not only of the genuine needs and correct tendencies of actuality, but also—in the form of *common sense* (i.e. all-pervasive fundamental ethical principles in the shape of prejudices)—of the eternal, substantial principles of justice, the true content and result of legislation, the whole constitution, and the universal condition in general. At the same time, when this inner truth emerges into consciousness and, embodied in general maxims, enters representational thinking [*Vorstellung*]—whether it be there on its own account or in support of concrete arguments about events, arrangements and relations within the state, or felt needs—it becomes infected by all the contingencies of opinion, by its ignorance

and perversity, by its mistakes and falsity of judgement. Since what matters to people here is their consciousness of the *distinctive charac-ter* of their views and knowledge, the worse the content of an opinion is, the more distinctive it is, because the bad is that which is wholly particular and distinctive in its content; the rational, on the other hand, is that which is universal in and for itself, while it is on distinc-tiveness that opinion prides itself.

Hence it is not simply due to a subjective difference of view that we find it said, on the one hand, that 'the voice of the people is the voice of God'* and, on the other hand, as Ariosto has it, that 'the ignorant populace reproves everyone and talks most of what it understands least'.*[124] Both are true at one and the same time of public opinion, and since it is such a hotchpotch of truth and end-less error, it cannot be genuinely serious about either. What it *is* serious about can seem hard to determine; and indeed it will be hard if we cling simply to the words in which public opinion is immediately expressed. The substantial, however, is the heart of public opinion, and therefore it is with that alone that it is truly serious. What the substantial is, though, is not discoverable from public opinion, because its very substantiality implies that it is known in and from itself alone. The passion with which an opin-ion is urged or the seriousness with which it is maintained or attacked and disputed is no criterion indicating what it is really about; and yet the last thing which opinion could be made to see is that its seriousness is nothing serious.

A great spirit* propounded as a problem for a public essay com-petition the question 'whether it be permissible [*erlaubt*] to deceive a people'. The answer had to be that a people does not allow itself to be deceived about its substantial basis, the essence and specific character of its spirit. On the other hand, it *deceives itself* about the manner of its knowledge of these things and about its correspond-ing judgement of its actions, experiences, etc.

Addition: The principle of the modern world requires that what anyone is to recognize shall reveal itself to him as something entitled to recognition. Apart from that, however, everyone wishes to have some share in discussion and deliberation. Once he has had his say and so his share of

---

[124] *Hegel's note*: Or, as Goethe puts it, 'the masses can fight, they're respectable at that; *but their judgements are miserable*'.*

responsibility, his subjectivity has been satisfied and he puts up with a lot. In France freedom of speech has always seemed far less dangerous than silence, because with the latter the fear is that people bottle up their objections to a thing, whereas argument gives them an outlet and a measure of satisfaction, and this is in addition a means whereby the thing can be pushed ahead more easily.

318. Public opinion therefore deserves to be as much respected as despised—despised for its concrete expression and for the concrete consciousness it expresses, respected for its essential basis, a basis which only appears more or less dimly in that concrete expression. But in itself it has no criterion of discrimination, nor has it the ability to extract the substantial element it contains and raise it to precise knowledge. Thus to be independent of public opinion is the first formal condition of achieving anything great or rational whether in actuality or in science. Great achievement is assured, however, of subsequent recognition and grateful acceptance by public opinion, which in due course will make it one of its own prejudices.

Addition: Public opinion contains all kinds of falsity and truth, but it takes a great man to find the truth in it. The great man of the age is the one who can put into words the will of his age, tell his age what its will is, and accomplish it. What he does is the heart and the essence of his age, he actualizes his age. The person who lacks sense enough to despise public opinion as he encounters it here and there will never do anything great.

319. Freedom of public communication (of the two modes of communication, the press and the spoken word, the first exceeds the second in range of contact but lags behind it in vivacity), satisfaction of the goading desire to say one's say and to have said it, is directly assured by the laws and by laws, upheld by the public authority, which control or punish its excesses. But it is assured indirectly by the innocuous character which it acquires as a result principally of the rationality of the constitution, the stability of government, and also of the publicity of Estates assemblies. The reason why the latter makes free speech harmless is that what is voiced in these assemblies is a sound and mature insight into the concerns of the state, with the result that others are left with nothing of much importance to say, and above all are deprived of the opinion that what they say is of peculiar importance and efficacy. A further safeguard of free speech is the indifference and contempt speedily and necessarily visited on shallow and cantankerous talking.

To define freedom of the press as freedom to say and write *whatever we please* is parallel to the assertion that freedom as such means freedom to *do as we please*. Talk of this kind is due to wholly uneducated, crude, and superficial ideas. Moreover, it is in the very nature of the thing that formalistic thinking should nowhere be so stubborn, so unintelligent, as in this matter of free speech, because what it is considering is the most fleeting, the most contingent, and the most particular side of opinion in its infinite diversity of content and tergiversation. Beyond the direct incitation to theft, murder, rebellion, etc., there lies its artfully constructed expression—an expression which seems in itself quite general and indeterminate, while all the time it conceals a meaning anything but indeterminate or else is compatible with inferences which are not actually expressed and of which it is impossible to determine whether they rightly follow from it or whether they were meant to be inferred from it. This indeterminacy of matter and form precludes laws on these topics from attaining the requisite determinacy of law, and since any misdemeanour, wrong, and injury here assumes the most particular and subjective shape, judgement on it is reduced equally to a wholly subjective decision. Besides, such an injury is directed against the thoughts, opinions, and wills of others, and these form the element in which it is actually anything; but this element is the sphere of the freedom of others, and it therefore depends on them whether or not the injurious expression of opinion is an actual deed.

Laws then in this sphere may be criticized by exhibiting their indeterminacy as well as by arguing that they leave it open to the speaker or writer to devise turns of phrase or forms of expression to evade the laws or to claim that judicial decisions are mere subjective judgements. Further, however, against the view that the expression of opinion is an act with injurious effects, it may be maintained that it is not an act at all, but only opinion and thought, or only talk. And so we have before us a claim that mere opinion and talk are to go unpunished because they are purely subjective both in form and content, because they do not mean anything and are of no importance. And yet in the same breath we have the claim that this same opinion and talk should be held in high esteem and respect—the opinion because it is my property and indeed property of the most spiritual kind, the talk because it is only this same property being expressed and used.

But the substance of the matter is and remains that traducing the honour of anyone, slander, abuse, bringing government, its official bodies and civil servants, and in particular the person of the monarch into contempt, defiance of the laws, incitement to rebellion, etc., are crimes or misdemeanours with many gradations. The rather high degree of indeterminability which such actions acquire on account of the element in which they are expressed does not annul this substantial character of theirs. Its only effect is that the subjective field in which they are committed also determines the nature and form of the reaction to the offence. It is the field in which the offence was committed which itself necessitates subjectivity of view, contingency, etc., in the reaction to the offence, whether the reaction takes the form of punishment proper or of police action to prevent crimes. Here, as always, formalistic thinking sets itself to explain away the substantial and concrete nature of the thing by concentrating on *individual* aspects of its external appearance and on abstractions drawn therefrom.

The *sciences*, however, are not to be found anywhere in the field of opinion and subjective views, provided of course that they are indeed sciences. Their exposition [*Darstellung*] is not a matter of clever turns of phrase, allusiveness, half-utterances, and semi-reticences, but consists in the unambiguous, determinate, and open expression of their meaning and purport. It follows that they do not fall under the category of public opinion (see § 316).

As I said just now, the element in which views and their expression become completed actions and attain actual existence, consists of the intelligence, principles, and opinions of others. Hence this aspect of these actions, i.e. their proper effect and their danger to individuals, society, and the state (compare § 218), depends on the character of the ground on which they fall, just as a spark falling on a heap of gunpowder is more dangerous than if it falls on hard ground where it vanishes without trace. Thus, just as the right of science to express itself depends on and is safeguarded by its subject-matter and content, so an illegitimate expression may also acquire a measure of security, or at least sufferance, in the scorn which it has brought upon itself. Offences of this sort are legally punishable in themselves, but a part of them may be attributed to that kind of *nemesis* which inner impotence, feeling itself oppressed by the preponderating abilities and virtues of others, is impelled to exact in order to recover itself again in face of such superiority and to restore some self-consciousness to its own nullity. It was a nemesis of a more harmless type which Roman soldiers exacted against their generals when they sang scurrilous songs* about them in triumphal processions in order in a way to get even with them for all the hard service and discipline they had undergone, and especially for the omission of their names from the triumphal honours. The former type of nemesis, the bad and hateful type, is deprived of its effect by being treated with scorn, and hence, like the public that may provide a circle of spectators for such scurrility, it is restricted to futile malice and to the self-condemnation which it implicitly contains.

320. Subjectivity is manifested in its most *external* form as the dissolving of the established life of the state by opinion and ratiocination when they endeavour to assert the authority of their own contingent character and so bring about their own destruction. But its true actuality is attained in the opposite of this, i.e. in the subjectivity that is identical with the substantial will, the subjectivity which constitutes the concept of the power of the crown and which, as the *ideality* of the whole, has not up to this point attained its right or its existence.

Addition: Subjectivity has been treated once already [§§ 279 ff.] as the apex of the state, as the crown. Its other aspect is the manifestation of its arbitrariness in public opinion, its most external mode of appearance. The subjectivity of the monarch is abstract in itself, but it should be something concrete and so be the ideality which diffuses itself over the whole. The state at peace is that in which all branches of civil life subsist, but they possess their subsistence outside and alongside one another as something which issues from the Idea of the whole. This process of issuing must also come into *appearance* as the ideality of the whole.

2. *External Sovereignty*

321. Internal sovereignty (see § 278) is this ideality insofar as the moments of spirit and its actuality, the state, have been *developed* in their necessity and subsist as the organs of the state. Spirit in its freedom, however, is an infinitely negative relation to itself and hence its essential character is just as much being-for-self [*Fürsichsein*] which has incorporated these subsistent differences into itself and so is exclusive. So characterized, the state has *individuality*, and individuality is in essence an individual, and in the sovereign an actual, immediate individual (see § 279).

322. Individuality, as exclusive being-for-self, appears as a relation to other states, each of which is independent vis-à-vis the others. In this independence the being-for-self of the actual spirit has its existence; hence it is the primary freedom which a people possesses as well as its highest dignity.

Those who talk* of the 'wishes' of a collection of people constituting a more or less independent state with its own centre, of its 'wishes' to renounce this centre and its independence in order to unite with others to form a new whole, have very little knowledge of the nature of a collection or of the feeling of selfhood which a people possesses in its independence.

Thus the power which a state has at its first entry into history is this independence as such, even if it be quite abstract and without further inner development. For this reason, to have an individual at its head—a patriarch, a chieftain, etc.—is appropriate for this original appearance of the state.

323. This negative relation of the state to itself has its existence as the relation of *another* to *another*, as if the negative were something *external*. The existence of this negative relation, therefore, has the shape of a happening and an entanglement with contingent events that *come from without*. But in fact this negative relation is the state's *own* highest moment, the state's actual infinity as the ideality of everything finite within it. It is the moment wherein the substance of the state—i.e. its absolute power over everything individual and particular, over life, property, and their rights, even over societies and associations—brings the nullity of such things into existence and brings it home to consciousness.

324. This determination whereby the rights and interests of individuals are posited as a vanishing moment, is at the same time something *positive*, i.e. the positing not of their contingent, changing individuality, but of their individuality *in and for itself*. This relation and the recognition of it is therefore the individual's substantial duty,

the duty to maintain this substantial individuality, i.e. the independence and sovereignty of the state, at the risk and the sacrifice of property and life, as well as of opinion and everything else naturally comprised in the compass of life.

An entirely distorted account of the demand for this sacrifice results from regarding the state as a mere civil society and from regarding its final end as only the security of individual life and property. This security cannot possibly be obtained by the sacrifice of what is to be secured—on the contrary.

The ethical moment in *war* is implied in what has been said in this Paragraph. War is not to be regarded as an absolute evil and as a purely external contingency, which thus has a cause that is itself contingent, be it injustices, the passions of peoples or the holders of power, etc., or in short, something or other which ought not to be. What is by nature contingent is subject to contingencies, and this fate is therefore itself a necessity. Here, as elsewhere, the point of view from which things seem pure contingencies vanishes if we look at them in the light of the concept and philosophy, because philosophy knows contingency to be semblance and sees in it its essence, necessity. It is *necessary* that the finite—property and life—should be *posited* as contingent, because contingency is the concept of the finite. From one point of view this necessity appears in the form of the power of nature, and everything finite is mortal and transient. But in the ethical essence, the state, nature is robbed of this power, and necessity is elevated to the work of freedom, to something ethical. The transience of the finite becomes a *willed* passing away, and the negativity lying at the roots of the finite becomes the substantial individuality proper to the ethical essence.

War is the state of affairs in which the vanity of temporal goods and concerns is treated with all seriousness—a vanity at other times a common theme of edifying sermonizing. This is what makes it the moment in which the ideality of the particular *attains its right* and is actualized. War has the higher significance that by its agency, as I have remarked elsewhere,[125] 'the ethical health of

---

[125] See 'On the Scientific Ways of Treating Natural Law' (1802–3), in G. W. F. Hegel, *Political Writings*, ed. L. Dickey and H. B. Nisbet (Cambridge: Cambridge University Press, 1999), 141. [S.H.]

peoples is preserved in their indifference towards the stabilization of finite determinacies; just as the blowing of the winds preserves the sea from the stagnation which would be the result of a prolonged calm, so also stagnation in peoples would be the product of prolonged, let alone perpetual, peace.'[126] This, however, is said to be *only* a philosophical Idea, or, to use another common expression, a justification of providence, and it is maintained that actual wars require some other justification. On this point, see below [§§ 334–7 and 343].

The ideality which is in evidence in war, i.e. in a contingent external relationship, is the same as the ideality in accordance with which the domestic powers of the state are organic moments in a whole. This fact appears in history in various forms, e.g. successful wars have prevented domestic unrest and consolidated the internal power of the state. Other phenomena illustrate the same point: e.g. peoples unwilling or afraid to tolerate internal sovereignty have been subjugated from abroad, and they have struggled for their independence with the less glory and success the less they have been able previously to organize the internal powers of the state—their freedom has died from the fear of dying. Furthermore, states whose independence has been guaranteed not by their armed forces but in other ways (e.g. as with states that are disproportionately small in comparison with their neighbours) have been able to subsist with an internal constitution which by itself would not have assured peace in either internal or foreign affairs.

Addition: In peace civil life continually expands; all its spheres become firmly established, and in the long run people stagnate. Their idiosyncrasies become continually more fixed and ossified. But for health the unity of the body is required, and if its parts become hard within themselves, that is death. Perpetual peace is often advocated as an ideal towards which humanity should strive. With that end in view, Kant proposed a league of monarchs to settle differences between states,[127] and the Holy Alliance[128] was meant to be an institution of much the same kind. But the state is an individual, and individuality essentially implies negation. Hence even if a number of states make themselves into a family, this group as an individual must engender an opposite and create an enemy. As a result

---

[126] See second explanatory note to p. 234 [p. 355 below]. [S.H.]

[127] See Kant *Toward Perpetual Peace*, 'Second Definitive Article for Perpetual Peace'. [S.H.]

[128] See first explanatory note to p. 234 [p. 355 below]. [S.H.]

of war, peoples are strengthened, but nations involved in civil strife also acquire peace at home through making wars abroad. To be sure, war produces insecurity of property, but this *real* insecurity is nothing other than a necessary movement. We hear plenty of sermons from the pulpit about the insecurity, vanity, and instability of temporal things, but everyone thinks, however much he is moved by what he hears, that he at least will be able to retain his own. But if this insecurity now actually comes on the scene in all seriousness in the form of hussars with shining sabres, then the moving and edifying discourses which foretold all these events turn into curses against the invader. Be that as it may, the fact remains that wars occur when the nature of the case requires. The seeds burgeon once more, and talk is silenced by the solemn recurrences of history.

325. Sacrifice on behalf of the individuality of the state is the substantial relation of all its members and so is a *universal duty*. Since this relation is *one side* of the ideality (in contrast to the reality) of particular subsistence [*Bestehen*], it becomes at the same time a particular relation with an estate [*Stand*] of its own—the estate of courage—dedicated to it.*

326. The matter at issue in disputes between states may be only one particular aspect of their relation to each other, and it is for such disputes that the particular group devoted to the state's defence is principally appointed. But if the state as such, if its independence, is in jeopardy, all its citizens are in duty bound to answer the summons to its defence. If in such circumstances the entire state is under arms and is torn from its inner life within itself to fight abroad, the war of defence turns into a war of conquest.

The armed force of the state becomes a standing army, while its appointment to the particular task of state defence makes it an estate. This happens from the same necessity as compels other particular moments, interests, and activities in the state to crystallize into a given status or estate, e.g. into the status of marriage or the estates of trade and industry or the civil service. Ratiocination, running hither and thither from ground to consequent, launches forth into reflections about the relative advantages and disadvantages of standing armies. Opinion readily decides that the latter preponderate, partly because the concept of a thing is harder to grasp than its individual and external aspects, but also because particular interests and ends (the expense of a standing army, and its result, higher taxation, etc.) are rated in the consciousness of civil society more highly than what is necessary in and for itself. In this way the latter comes to count only as a means to particular ends.

327. In itself [*für sich*], courage is a *formal* virtue, because (i) it is the highest abstraction of freedom from all particular ends, possessions, pleasure, and life (though it negates them in a manner that is *external and actual*); and (ii) their alienation or abandonment [*Entäußerung*], the fulfilment of courage, is not intrinsically of a spiritual [*geistig*] character—the courageous person's inner disposition may be [the product of] this or that reason, and its actual result may only be there for others and not *for itself* [i.e. for the courageous person himself].*

Addition: The military estate is that universal estate which is charged with the defence of the state, and its duty is to give existence to the ideality within itself, i.e. to sacrifice itself. Courage, to be sure, takes different forms. The mettle of an animal or a brigand, courage for the sake of honour, the courage of a knight, these are not true forms of courage. The true courage of civilized peoples is readiness for sacrifice in the service of the state, so that the individual counts as only one amongst many. The important thing here is not personal mettle but aligning oneself with the universal. In India five hundred men conquered twenty thousand* who were not cowards, but who only lacked this disposition to work in close cooperation with others.

328. The worth of courage as a disposition is to be found in the genuine, absolute final end, the *sovereignty* of the state. The work of courage is to actualize this final end, and the means to this end is the sacrifice of personal actuality. This form of experience thus contains the harshness of extreme contradictions: alienation itself which yet is the existence [*Existenz*] of freedom; the highest independence of being-for-self, which at the same time exists only in serving the mechanism of an external organization; absolute obedience, renunciation of personal opinion and reasoning, in fact complete *absence* of spirit, coupled with the most intense and comprehensive *presence* of spirit and decision in the moment of acting; the most hostile and so most personal action against individuals, coupled with an attitude of complete indifference or even benevolence towards them as individuals.

To risk one's life is certainly superior to merely fearing death, but is still purely negative and so indeterminate and without value in itself.

It is the positive aspect, the end and content, which first gives significance to this spiritedness. Robbers and murderers bent on crime as their end, adventurers pursuing ends planned to suit their own whims, etc., these too have spirit [*Mut*] enough to risk their lives.

The principle of the modern world—thought and the universal—has given courage a higher form, because its expression now seems to be more mechanical, the act not of this particular person, but of a member of a whole. Moreover, it seems to be turned not against individual persons, but against a hostile group as such, and hence personal bravery appears impersonal. It is for this reason that thought has invented the gun, and the invention of this weapon, which has changed the purely personal form of courage into a more abstract one, is no accident.

329. The state's orientation towards the outside stems from the fact that it is an individual subject. Its relation to other states therefore falls to the *power of the crown*. Hence it directly devolves on the monarch, and on him alone, to command the armed forces, to conduct foreign affairs through ambassadors etc., to make war and peace, and to conclude treaties of all kinds.*

Addition: In almost all European countries the individual head of the state is the monarch, and external relations are his business. Where the Estates have constitutional powers, the question may arise whether they should not decide on war and peace, and in any case they have their influence on the question, particularly in connection with ways and means. In England, for example, no unpopular war can be waged. If, however, it is supposed that monarchs and cabinets are more subject to passion than parliaments are, and if for this reason an attempt is made to juggle the decision on war and peace into the hands of the latter, then we must point out that whole nations may often be prey to excitement or be carried away by passion to a greater extent than their leaders. In England the entire people has frequently pressed for war and to a certain extent compelled ministers to wage it. The popularity of Pitt* was due to his knowing how to fall in with what the nation wanted at the time. It was only later that the people cooled down and so began to reflect that the war was useless and unnecessary and had been undertaken without counting the cost. Moreover, a state stands in relation not with one other state only, but with many. And the complexities of their relations become so delicate that they can be handled only by the head of the state.

B. *Right between States*

330. Right between states [*das äußere Staatsrecht*] springs from the *relations* between independent states. It is for this reason that what is in and for itself in it retains the form of an ought-to-be [*Sollen*], since its actuality depends on different wills each of which is *sovereign*.

Addition: States are not private persons but completely independent totalities in themselves, and so the relation between them differs from a moral relation and a relation involving private rights. Attempts have often been made to regard the state as a person with the rights of persons and as a moral entity. But the position with private persons is that they are under the jurisdiction of a court which gives effect to what is right in itself. Now a relation between states ought also to be rightful in itself, but in worldly affairs that which has being in itself [*das Ansichseiende*] ought also to have power. Now since there is no power in existence which decides in face of the state what is right in itself and actualizes this decision, it follows that so far as international relations are concerned we can never get beyond an 'ought'. The relation between states is a relation between independent entities which make mutual stipulations but which at the same time are superior to these stipulations.

331. The people as a state is spirit in its substantial rationality and immediate actuality and is therefore the absolute power on *earth*. It follows that every state is sovereign and independent in relation to others. It is entitled in the first place and without qualification to be sovereign from their point of view, i.e. to be *recognized* by them as sovereign. At the same time, however, this title is purely formal, and the demand for this recognition of the state, merely on the ground that it is a state, is abstract. Whether a state in fact has being in and for itself depends on its content, i.e. on its constitution and condition; and recognition, implying as it does an identity of both form and content, is conditional on the neighbouring state's perception and will.

A state is as little an actual individual without relations to other states (see § 322) as an individual is actually a person without a relationship with other persons (see § 71 and elsewhere). The legitimacy of a state and, more particularly, so far as its external relations are concerned, of its monarch also, is partly a purely internal matter (one state should not meddle with the domestic affairs of another). On the other hand, however, it is no less essential that this legitimacy should be rendered complete through its recognition by other states, although this recognition requires a guarantee that where a state is to be recognized by others, it shall likewise recognize them, i.e. respect their independence; and so it comes about that they cannot be indifferent to each other's internal affairs.

The question arises how far a nomadic people, for instance, or any people on a low level of culture, can be regarded as a state. As once was the case with the Jews and the Muhammadan peoples, religious views may entail an opposition at a higher level [between one people and its neighbours] and so preclude the universal identity which is requisite for recognition.

Addition: When Napoleon said before the Peace of Campo Formio[129] that 'the French Republic needs recognition as little as the sun requires it', what his words implied was simply the strength of existence which carries with it, without any verbal expression, the guarantee of recognition.

332. The immediate actuality which any state possesses from the point of view of other states is particularized into a multiplicity of relations which are determined by the arbitrary will of both independent parties and which therefore possess the formal nature of *contracts* pure and simple. The subject-matter of these contracts, however, is infinitely less varied than it is in civil society, because in civil society individuals are reciprocally interdependent in the most numerous respects, while independent states are principally wholes which achieve satisfaction internally.

333. The principle of international law [*Völkerrecht*]—the universal right which ought to be valid in and for itself between states, as distinguished from the particular content of positive treaties—is that treaties, as the ground of obligations between states, ought to be kept. But since the sovereignty of a state is the principle of its relations to others, states are to that extent in a state of nature in relation to each other. Their rights are actualized only in their particular wills and not in a universal will constituted as a power over them. This universal determination of international law therefore does not go beyond an *ought-to-be*, and what really happens is that relations in

---

[129] See second explanatory note to p. 310 [p. 362 below]. [S.H.]

accordance with treaties alternate with the suspension [*Aufhebung*] of these relations.

There is no praetor[130] to judge between states; at best there may be arbitrators or mediators, and even these exercise their functions only contingently, i.e. in accordance with particular wills. Kant had an idea for securing 'perpetual peace' by a federation of states to adjudicate every dispute.[131] It was to be a power recognized by each individual state, and was to arbitrate in all cases of dissension in order to make it impossible for disputants to resort to war in order to settle them. This idea presupposes an *accord* between states; this would rest on moral or religious or other grounds and considerations, but in any case would always depend ultimately on particular sovereign wills and for that reason would remain infected with contingency.

334. It follows that if states disagree and their particular wills cannot be harmonized, the matter can only be settled by *war*. A state has an extensive range and, through its subjects, has many-sided relations, and these may be easily and considerably injured; but it remains inherently indeterminable which of these injuries is to be regarded as a specific breach of treaty or as an injury to the recognition and honour of the state. The reason for this is that a state may regard its infinity and honour as at stake in each of its individual concerns, and it is all the more inclined to take offence the more its strong individuality is impelled as a result of long internal peace to seek and create a sphere of activity abroad.

335. Apart from this, the state is something spiritual [*Geistiges*] and therefore cannot restrict itself to noting when an injury has *actually* occurred. On the contrary, there arises in addition as a cause of strife the *idea* [*Vorstellung*] of such an injury as the idea of a *danger* threatening from another state, together with calculations of degrees of probability on this side and that, guessing at intentions, etc.

336. Since states are related to one another as independent entities and so as *particular* wills on which the very validity of treaties depends, and since the particular will of the whole, as regards its

---

[130] See second explanatory note to p. 25 [pp. 330–1 below]. [S.H.]

[131] See Kant, *Toward Perpetual Peace*, 'Second Definitive Article for Perpetual Peace'. [S.H.]

content, is a will for its own *welfare* as such, it follows that welfare is the highest law governing the relation of one state to another. This is all the more the case since the Idea of the state is precisely the super-session of the opposition between right as abstract freedom and wel-fare as the particular content which fills it, and it is when states become *concrete* wholes that they first attain recognition (see § 331).

337. The substantial welfare of the state is its welfare as a *particu-lar* state in its specific interest and situation and its no less distinctive external circumstances, including its particular treaty relations. Its government therefore is a matter of *particular wisdom*, not of univer-sal providence (compare Remark to § 324). Similarly, its aim in rela-tion to other states and its principle for justifying wars and treaties is not a universal (philanthropic) thought but only its actually injured or threatened welfare in its determinate particularity.

At one time the opposition between morality and politics, and the demand that the latter should conform to the former, were much discussed. On this point only a general remark is required here. The welfare of a state has a justification that is totally different from that of the welfare of the individual. The determinate being [*Dasein*] of the ethical substance or the state—i.e. its right—is immediately embodied in an existence [*Existenz*] that is not abstract but concrete, and the principle of its conduct and behav-iour can only be this concrete existence and not one of the many universal thoughts supposed to be moral commands. When politics is alleged to clash with morals and so to be always wrong, the doctrine propounded rests on superficial ideas about morality, the nature of the state, and the state's relation to the moral point of view.

338. The fact that states reciprocally recognize each other as states remains *even in war*—the state of affairs in which rights disap-pear and force and contingency hold sway—a bond wherein each counts in the eyes of the others as something that has being in and for itself. Hence in war, war itself is characterized as something which ought to pass away. It entails therefore the determination of international law that the possibility of peace be retained (and so, for example, that envoys must be respected), and, in general, that war not be waged against internal institutions, against the peace of family and private life, or against private individuals.

Addition: Modern wars are therefore humanely waged, and person is not set over against person in hatred. At most, personal enmities appear in the vanguard, but in the main body of the army hostility is something indeterminate and gives way to each side's respect for the duty of the other.

339. Apart from this, the conduct of states towards one another in war (the fact that prisoners are taken), and in peacetime the concession of rights to subjects of other states for the purpose of private trade and intercourse, etc., depend principally upon the *customs* [*Sitten*] of nations, custom being the inner universality of behaviour maintained in all circumstances.

Addition: The European nations form a family in accordance with the universal principle underlying their legislation, their customs, and their civilization. Accordingly, this principle has modified their conduct under international law in a state of affairs [i.e. war] otherwise dominated by the mutual infliction of evils. The relations of state to state are uncertain, and there is no praetor available to adjust them. The only higher judge is the universal spirit in and for itself, the world spirit.

340. It is as *particular* entities that states enter into relations with one another. Hence their relations are on the largest scale a highly animated play of external contingency and the inner particularity of passions, interests and purposes, talents and virtues, vices, force, and wrong—a play wherein the ethical whole itself, the independence of the state, is exposed to contingency. The principles of the spirits of peoples [*Volksgeister*]* are in general restricted on account of their particularity, for it is in this particularity that, as *existent* individuals, they have their objective actuality and their self-consciousness. Their deeds and destinies in their relations to one another are the manifest [*erscheinende*] dialectic of the finitude of these spirits, and out of it arises the *universal spirit*, the *spirit of the world*, free from all restriction, producing itself as that which exercises its right—and its right is the highest right of all—over these finite spirits in world history as the *world's court of judgement*.*

C. *World History*

341. The element in which the universal spirit exists in art is intuition and imagery, in religion feeling and representation [*Vorstellung*], in philosophy pure, free thought. In world history this element is the actuality of spirit in its whole compass of inwardness and externality. World history is a court of judgement because in its universality in and for itself the particular—i.e. the *Penates,* civil society, and the spirits of peoples in their variegated actuality—is present as only *ideal* [*Ideelles*], and the movement of spirit in this element is the exhibition of that fact.*

342. Further, in world history it is not merely the *power* [*Macht*] of spirit that passes judgement, i.e. the abstract and non-rational necessity of a blind destiny. On the contrary, since spirit in and for itself is *reason*, and reason's being-for-self [*Für-sich-Sein*] in spirit is knowledge, world history is the necessary development, out of the concept of spirit's freedom alone, of the moments of reason and so of the self-consciousness and freedom of spirit. This development is the exposition [*Auslegung*] and *actualization of the universal spirit.*

343. The history of spirit is its own act. Spirit is only what it does, and its act is to make itself the object of its own consciousness. In history its act is to gain consciousness of itself as spirit, to apprehend itself in its exposition of itself. This apprehension is its being and its principle, and the completion of an act of apprehension is at the same time its alienation and transition. Expressed formally, spirit apprehending this apprehension anew, or in other words returning to itself out of its alienation, is the spirit of the stage higher than that on which it stood in its earlier apprehension.

The question of the perfectibility and *education of the human race* arises here. Those who have maintained this perfectibility* have divined something of the nature of spirit, something of the fact that its nature is to have 'Know thyself'* [Γνῶθι σεαυτόν] as the law of its being, and, since it apprehends that which it is, to have a form higher than that which constituted its mere being. But to those who reject this doctrine, spirit has remained an empty word, and history a superficial play of contingent, so-called 'merely human', strivings and passions. Even if, in connection with history, they speak of providence and the plan of providence, and so express a faith in a higher power, their ideas remain empty because they expressly declare that for them the plan of providence is inscrutable and incomprehensible.*

344. In the course of this activity [*Geschäft*] of the world spirit, states, peoples, and individuals arise animated by their particular determinate principle which has its exposition and actuality in their constitutions and in the whole range of their life and condition. While they are conscious of this actuality and are absorbed in its interests, they are all the time the unconscious tools and organs of this inner activity. The shapes which they take pass away, while the spirit in and for itself prepares and works out its transition to its next higher stage.

345. Justice and virtue, injustice, force and vice, talents and their deeds, passions strong and weak, guilt and innocence, grandeur in individual and national life, independence, fortune and misfortune of states and individuals, all these have their specific significance and worth in the field of conscious actuality; therein they are judged and justice— though only imperfect justice—is meted out to them. World-history, however, falls outside the point of view from which these things matter. Each of its stages is the presence of a necessary moment in the Idea of the world spirit, and that moment attains its *absolute right* in that stage. The people whose life embodies this moment secures its good fortune and fame, and its deeds are brought to fruition.

346. History is spirit giving itself the form of events or of immediate natural actuality. The stages of its development are therefore present as *immediate natural principles*. These, because they are natural, are a plurality external to one another, and they are present therefore in such a way that each of them is assigned to one people in the form of its geographical and anthropological existence.

347. The people to which is assigned a moment of the Idea in the form of a *natural* principle is entrusted with giving complete effect to it in the advance of the self-developing self-consciousness of the world spirit. This people is dominant in world history during this one epoch, and it is only once (see § 346) that it can play this epoch-making role. In contrast with this its absolute right of being the bearer of this present stage in the world spirit's development, the spirits of the other peoples are without rights, and they, along with those whose epoch has passed, no longer count in world history.

The particular history of a world-historical people contains (*a*) the development of its principle from its latent embryonic [*kindlich*] stage until it blossoms into the self-conscious freedom of ethical life and enters universal history; and (*b*) the period of its decline and fall, since it is its decline and fall that signals the emergence in it of a higher principle as simply the negative of its own. When this happens, spirit passes over into the new principle and so marks out another people for world-historical significance. After this period, the declining people has lost its absolute interest; it may indeed take up the higher principle positively and build it into itself, but—since the principle is something received from the out-side—the people's activity lacks immanent vitality and freshness. Perhaps it loses its independence, or perhaps it continues to exist (or to drag out its existence) as a particular state or a group of states and involves itself without rhyme or reason in manifold enterprises at home and battles abroad.

348. At the vanguard of all actions, including world-historical actions, stand *individuals* as subjectivities giving actuality to what is substantial (see Remark to § 279). They give life to the substantial deed of the world spirit and they are therefore immediately at one with that deed, though it is concealed from them and is not their aim and object (see § 344). For the deeds of the world spirit, therefore, they receive no honour or thanks either from their contemporaries (see § 344) or from public opinion in later ages. All that is vouchsafed to them by such opinion is *undying fame* as formal subjectivities.*

349. A people does not begin by being a state. The transition from a family, a horde, a clan, a multitude, etc., to political conditions is the *formal* realization of the Idea as such in that people. Without this form, a people, as an ethical substance—which is what it is in itself—lacks the objectivity of possessing for itself and for others a universal and universally valid existence in laws, i.e. in determinate thoughts, and as a result it fails to secure recognition from others. So long as it lacks objective law and a firm rationality for itself, its inde-pendence is formal only and is not sovereignty.

It would be contrary even to commonplace ideas to call patriarchal conditions a 'constitution' or a people under patriarchal govern-ment a 'state' or its independence 'sovereignty'. Hence, before his-tory actually begins, we have, on the one hand, dull innocence, devoid of interest, and, on the other, the courage of revenge and of the formal struggle for recognition (see § 331 and Remark to § 57).

350. It is the absolute right of the Idea to step into existence in legal determinations and objective institutions, beginning with marriage and agriculture (see Remark to § 203), whether the Idea be actualized in the form of divine legislation and favour, or in the form of force and wrong. This right is the *right of heroes* to found states.

351. The same consideration allows civilized nations to regard and treat as barbarians those who lag behind them in the substantial moments of the state. Thus a pastoral people may treat hunters as barbarians, and both of these are barbarians from the point of view of agricultural peoples, etc. The civilized nation is conscious that the rights of barbarians are unequal to its own and treats their independence as only a formality.

When wars and disputes arise in such circumstances, the trait which gives them a significance for world history is the fact that they are struggles for recognition in connection with something of determinate worth.

352. The concrete Ideas, the spirits of peoples, have their truth and their destiny in the concrete Idea which is *absolute universality*, i.e. in the world spirit. Around its throne they stand as the executors of its actualization and as witnesses to, and ornaments of, its grandeur. As spirit, it is nothing but its active movement towards absolute knowledge of itself and therefore towards freeing its consciousness from the form of natural immediacy and so coming to itself. Therefore the *principles* of the formations of this self-consciousness in the course of its liberation—the world-historical realms—are four in number.

353. In its *first* and immediate revelation, spirit has as its principle the shape of the *substantial* spirit as the identity in which individuality is absorbed in its essence and remains without justification for itself.

The *second* principle is knowledge on the part of the substantial spirit, so that the latter is both the positive content and filling of spirit and also the *being-for-self* which is the living *form* of spirit. This is the principle of *beautiful* ethical individuality.[132]

---

[132] On the close connection Hegel sees between the Greeks, beauty and art, see G. W. F. Hegel, *The Philosophy of History*, trans. J. Sibree (New York: Dover Publications, 1956), 241–50. [S.H.]

The *third* principle is the inward deepening of this knowing being-for-self until it reaches *abstract universality* and therefore infinite *opposition* to the objective world which in the same process has become forsaken by spirit.

The principle of the *fourth* formation is the conversion of this opposition so that spirit receives in its inner life its truth and concrete essence, while in objectivity it is at home and reconciled with itself. Since the spirit, which has thus reverted to the first substantiality, has *returned out of the infinite opposition*, it engenders and knows this its truth as thought and as a world of law-governed actuality.

354. In accordance with these four principles, the world-historical realms are the following: (1) the Oriental, (2) the Greek, (3) the Roman, (4) the Germanic.

355. (1) The Oriental realm.

The world-view of this first realm is substantial, without inward division, and it arises in natural communities patriarchically governed. According to this view, the secular government is theocratic, the ruler is also a high priest or God himself; constitution and legislation are at the same time religion, while religious and moral commands, or usages rather, are at the same time laws of the state and of right. In the magnificence of this whole, individual personality loses its rights and perishes; the external world of nature is either immediately divine or else God's ornament, and the history of actuality is poetry. Distinctions are developed in customs, government, and state on their many sides, and in default of laws and amidst the simplicity of manners, they become unwieldy, diffuse, and superstitious ceremonies, the accidents of personal power and arbitrary rule, and differences of estate become crystallized into natural castes. Hence in the Oriental state nothing is constant, and what is firm is fossilized; the state lives therefore only in an outward movement which becomes in the end an elemental fury and devastation. Its inner calm is merely the calm of private life and immersion in feebleness and exhaustion.

A still substantial, natural, spirituality is a moment in the development of the state, and the point at which any state takes this form is the absolute beginning of its history. This has been emphasized and demonstrated with learning and profound insight in connection with the history of particular states by Dr Stuhr* in his book *The Downfall of Natural States*—a work in which he leads the way to a rational treatment of constitutional history and of history generally. The principle of subjectivity and self-conscious freedom is there too shown to be the principle of the Germanic nation, but the book goes no further than the decline of natural states, and consequently the principle is only brought to the point where it appears either as a restless mobility, as human caprice and corruption, or in its particular form as emotion [*Gemüt*], and where it has not yet developed to the objectivity of *self-conscious* substantiality or to organized legality.

356. (2) The Greek realm.

This realm possesses this substantial unity of finite and infinite, but only as a mysterious foundation, suppressed in dim memory in the recesses [*Höhlen*] and images of tradition.* This foundation, reborn out of the spirit which differentiates itself into individual spirituality, emerges into the daylight of knowing and is tempered and transfigured into beauty and a free and serene [*heiter*] ethical life. Hence it is in a world of this character that the principle of personal individuality arises, though it is still not self-enclosed but kept in its ideal unity. The result is that the whole falls apart into a group of particular national spirits* [*Volksgeister*]; the ultimate decision is assigned not to the subjectivity of self-consciousness that is for itself, but to a power standing above and outside it (see Remark to § 279); on the other hand, the particularity associated with needs is not yet taken up into the sphere of freedom but is farmed out to a class of slaves [*Sklavenstand*].

357. (3) The Roman realm.

In this realm, differentiation is carried to its conclusion, and ethical life is sundered without end into the extremes of the private self-consciousness of *persons*, on the one hand, and *abstract universality*, on the other. This opposition begins in the clash* between the substantial intuition of an aristocracy and the principle of free personality in democratic form. As the opposition grows, the first of these opponents develops into superstition and the maintenance of cold, self-seeking power, while the second becomes more and more

corrupt until it sinks into a rabble [*Pöbel*]. Finally, the whole is dissolved and the result is universal misfortune and the death of ethical
life. The individualities of peoples [*Völkerindividualitäten*] perish in
the unity of a pantheon, all individuals [*Einzelnen*] are degraded to
the level of private persons equal with one another, possessed of
formal rights, and the only bond left to hold them together is an
abstract, monstrously insatiable self-will.

358. (4) The Germanic realm.

Spirit and its world are thus both alike lost and plunged in the
infinite pain of that loss for which a people, the Jewish people, was
held in readiness. Spirit is here pressed back upon itself in the
extreme of its absolute negativity. This is the *turning-point* in and for
itself. Spirit grasps the infinite positivity of this its inwardness, i.e. it
grasps the principle of the unity of the divine and human nature,*
the reconciliation of the objective truth and freedom which have
appeared within self-consciousness and subjectivity—a reconciliation, the fulfilment of which has been entrusted to the Nordic principle of the Germanic peoples.*

359. The inwardness of this principle is first of all abstract; it
exists in feeling as faith, love, and hope,[133] the reconciliation and resolution of all opposition. It then unfolds its content, raising it to
become actuality and self-conscious rationality, to become a *secular*
realm proceeding from the heart, fidelity, and comradeship of free
individuals, a realm which in this its subjectivity is equally a realm of
barbarous manners and crude arbitrariness that is for itself. This
realm is set over against a world beyond, an *intellectual* realm, whose
content is indeed the truth of its spirit, but a truth not yet thought
and so still veiled in the barbarism of imagery [*Vorstellung*]. This
world beyond, as the spiritual power over the actual heart, acts
against the latter as an unfree, frightful force.

360. These two realms* stand distinguished from one another
though at the same time they are rooted in *one* unity and Idea. Here
their distinction is intensified to absolute opposition and a hard struggle ensues in the course of which the spiritual realm [*das Geistliche*]
reduces the existence of its heaven to an earthly here and now, to the

---

[133] See 1 Corinthians 13: 13. [S.H.]

ordinary worldliness of actuality and representation [*Vorstellung*]. The secular realm, on the other hand, builds up its abstract being-for-self into thought and the principle of rational being and knowing, i.e. into the rationality of right and law. In this way their opposition *implicitly* [*an sich*] loses its strength and disappears. The present has discarded its barbarity and unjust arbitrariness, and truth has cast off its otherworldliness and contingent force, so that the true reconciliation which discloses the *state* as the image and actuality of reason has become objective. In the *state*, self-consciousness finds in an organic development the actuality of its substantial knowing and willing; in *religion*,* it finds the feeling and the representation of this its own truth as an ideal essentiality; while in [philosophical] *science*, it finds the free comprehension and knowledge of this truth as one and the same in its mutually complementary manifestations, i.e. in the *state*, in *nature*, and in the *ideal* [*ideell*] *world*.*

EXPLANATORY NOTES

Unless otherwise indicated all explanatory notes and footnotes are based on notes by T. M. Knox in the original edition (1952). Many of these notes have been extensively revised, and several have been supplemented with additional material. A few explanatory notes are based on notes by A. W. Wood (the editor), or H. B. Nisbet (the translator), in the Cambridge University Press edition of the *Elements of the Philosophy of Right* (1991). These have been indicated as follows: [S.H./A.W.W.] or [S.H./H.B.N.]. New explanatory notes and footnotes by the present editor are indicated by [S.H.].

PREFACE

3 *the Encyclopaedia of the Philosophical Sciences (Heidelberg, 1817)*: Hegel's references are always to this, the first edition of his *Encyclopaedia of the Philosophical Sciences*. For an English translation of this edition, see G. W. F. Hegel, *Encyclopedia of the Philosophical Sciences in Outline* [1817] *and Critical Writings*, ed. E. Behler (New York: Continuum, 1990). In the footnotes and Explanatory Notes reference will be made additionally (or sometimes exclusively) to the third edition published in 1830. For English translations of the three parts of the third edition, see G. W. F. Hegel, *The Encyclopaedia Logic*, trans. T. F. Geraets, W. A. Suchting, and H. S. Harris (Indianapolis: Hackett, 1991) [*Encyclopaedia* §§ 1–244]; *Hegel's Philosophy of Nature: Being Part Two of the Encyclopaedia of the Philosophical Sciences (1830)*, trans. A. V. Miller (Oxford: Clarendon Press, 1970) [*Encyclopaedia* §§ 245–376]; and *Hegel's Philosophy of Mind: Being Part Three of the Encyclopaedia of the Philosophical Sciences (1830)*, trans. W. Wallace, together with the *Zusätze* in Boumann's text (1845), trans. A. V. Miller (Oxford: Clarendon Press, 1971) [*Encyclopaedia* §§ 377–577]. [S.H.]

the Remarks: the Remarks are the indented passages that follow the main paragraphs of Hegel's text. They are to be distinguished from the Additions which were not included by Hegel himself, but compiled after his death by the editor of the first posthumous edition of the *Philosophy of Right*, Eduard Gans. [S.H.]

a work as ephemeral as Penelope's web: Penelope was the wife of Odysseus. During her husband's long absence from home, many suitors asked to marry her. She put them off by telling them they had to wait until she had finished weaving a shroud for her father-in-law and by secretly undoing each night the weaving she had done that day. See Homer, *Odyssey* 19. 137–55. [S.H.]

4 *I have fully expounded the nature of speculative knowing in my Science of Logic*: Hegel's *Science of Logic* was published in three volumes between 1812 and 1816. A second, expanded edition of the first part of the *Logic*—the Doctrine of Being—was published in 1832. See *Hegel's Science of Logic*, trans. A. V. Miller (Amherst, NY: Humanity Books, 1999). [S.H.]

7 *positive jurisprudence which often has to do only with contradictions*: Hegel has in mind here the inconsistencies in systems of positive law (see e.g. his comments on fictions in Roman law in the Remarks to *PR* §§ 3 and 180), as well as contradictory judgements (see e.g. Remark to *PR* § 211).

8 *contemporary philosophizing*: especially that of Immanuel Kant (1724–1804), Friedrich Heinrich Jacobi (1743–1819) and their respective followers. [S.H.]

philosophy of recent times: it is publications by the Romantics (e.g. Friedrich von Schlegel (1772–1829)) that Hegel has mainly in mind.

9 *He giveth to his own in sleep*: like many of Hegel's quotations (which are usually made from memory), this is inaccurate. Psalm 127: 2, in Luther's version, reads, literally translated, 'for to his friends he gives it [bread] in sleep'. The 'wares of sleep' are dreams.

Herr Fries: Jakob Friedrich Fries (1773–1843), professor at Heidelberg (where he was Hegel's predecessor) 1805–16, and thereafter at Jena.

a solemn public occasion: the Wartburg Festival of the German Student Fraternities on 18 October 1817.

Epicurus: Epicurus (341–270 BC), ancient Greek philosopher. He measured conduct by the standard of feeling and impulse, and truth by the standard of sense-perception.

a quotation I have used elsewhere: the lines (mis)quoted by Hegel are from *Faust. Part One* (1808) by Johann Wolfgang von Goethe (1749–1832). The lines to which Hegel refers are:

> *Verachte nur Vernunft und Wissenschaft*
> *Des Menschen allerhöchste Kraft. . . .*
> *Und hätt' er sich auch nicht dem Teufel übergeben,*
> *Er müsste doch zu Grunde gehn.*
> ('Studierzimmer', ll. 1851–5, 1866–7)

> Do but despise reason and knowledge,
> The highest strength in man! . . .
> And even if he had not given himself to the devil,
> He would still have to perish!

Hegel misquotes the lines both here and in the *Phenomenology*. See *Hegel's Phenomenology of Spirit*, trans. A. V. Miller (Oxford: Oxford University Press, 1977), 218.

10 *the subjective form of feeling*: the piety which Hegel attacks (Friedrich Schleiermacher (1768–1834) is sometimes in his mind) is that which regards the world as God-forsaken and which exalts the sanctities of inner conviction above the wickedness of the world. It forgets, Hegel holds, that God reveals himself *in* the world, in nature and history. Piety of the right sort worships God not as an abstract 'supreme being', but as a loving and self-revealing spirit. Such piety is at home in the world and is reconciled to it, because it has faith that, since the world is the revelation of God, reason must be immanent in it as its law and essential principle. Philosophy differs from such piety, in Hegel's view, only in substituting knowledge for faith.

11 *the service of the state*: there is nothing sinister in what Hegel says here. All that he means is that in Prussia philosophy was confined mainly or entirely to universities, i.e. to state institutions, whose professors were civil servants and so in 'the service of the state'. In Greece, on the other hand, philosophy was not a professional occupation.

outlined for us by Plato: see e.g. *Protagoras* and *Republic*, 493 ff., where the sophist is contrasted with the true philosopher. Plato is thought to have been born in 428 BC and to have died in 348 BC.

12 *numerous publications in the field of the positive sciences*: the reference is probably to the numerous attacks made by empirical scientists on the philosophy of nature of Friedrich Wilhelm Joseph von Schelling (1775–1854).

a letter of Johannes von Müller: Müller (1752–1809) was the most important Swiss historian of the eighteenth century. [S.H.]

They are tolerated, like brothels: 'On les tolère comme les bordels' (in French in Hegel's text). [S.H.]

13 *as I have said*: this has not been said before, but Hegel may be referring back to his earlier assertion that 'philosophy with us is not, as it was with the Greeks for instance, pursued as a private art, but has an existence in the open, in contact with the public' [p. 11 above]. [S.H.]

so I revert to what I have said before: this might be a reference back to Hegel's observation 'that nature is inherently rational, and that what knowledge has to investigate and grasp in concepts is this actual reason present in it' [p. 6 above]. [S.H.]

the pivot on which the impending world revolution turned: the principle breaking into the Greek world in Plato's time was the principle of 'subjective freedom', on which Hegel has a good deal to say in the third part of this book. The 'world revolution' then impending was the change in people's ideas due to the emergence of Christianity.

14 *What is rational is actual and what is actual is rational*: 'Was vernünftig ist, das ist wirklich; und was wirklich ist, das ist vernünftig.' Hegel's claim here is that reason is an actual [*wirklich*] power in the world, working to create the institutions of human freedom, but he is not saying that everything

that exists or is 'real' is rational. His famous statement is further explained and defended in *Encyclopaedia* (1830) § 6 [Geraets trans., 29–30]: 'But when I speak of actuality, one should, of course, think about the sense in which I use this expression, given the fact that I dealt with actuality too in a quite elaborate *Logic*, and I distinguished it quite clearly and directly, not just from what is contingent, even though it has existence too, but also, more precisely, from being-there [*Dasein*], from existence [*Existenz*], and from other determinations. [. . .] [Philosophical] science deals only with the Idea—which is not so impotent that it merely ought to be, and is not actual—and further with an actuality of which [. . .] objects, institutions and situations are only the superficial outer rind.' For Hegel's discussion of the concept of 'actuality', see *Science of Logic*, Miller trans., 541–53. [S.H.]

For since rationality . . . simultaneously with its actualization: reason at any stage does not attain full actuality until it passes over into existence and embodies itself in something objective; e.g. religious convictions are not genuinely actual until they are objectified in institutions, churches, etc. Similarly, the state, as an objectification in the external world of humanity's rational will, is that in which alone our freedom, the essence of our will, is fully actualized.

Plato might have omitted his recommendation: see Plato, *Laws* 789b–790a. Hegel's citation is not quite accurate, and he seems to have forgotten that Plato is saying that to make such a regulation is unnecessary and would be ridiculous.

And Fichte too: see Johann Gottlieb Fichte, *Foundations of Natural Right* (1796–7), trans. M. Baur (Cambridge: Cambridge University Press, 2000), § 21 [p. 257]. Fichte (1762–1814) limits this requirement to 'important persons (who therefore can afford it)'.

15 *Hic Rhodus, hic saltus*: 'Here is Rhodes; here's the jump [i.e. jump here!].' The proverb comes from one of Aesop's fables, in which an athlete boasts of the many feats he has performed in many countries and especially of a jump he once made in Rhodes. He says that he can prove this by the testimony of eyewitnesses 'if any of the people who were present ever come here'. At this, one of the bystanders tells the athlete that he doesn't need eyewitnesses since the place where he is standing will do just as well as Rhodes itself: 'Here is Rhodes; jump here!' See *Fables of Aesop*, trans. S. A. Handford (1954; Harmondsworth: Penguin Books, 1964), 185. [S.H.]

Here is the rose, dance here: Hegel is playing on words. 'Ρόδος means the island of Rhodes, but suggests 'Ρόδον, a rose. *Saltus* means a jump, but *salta* is the imperative of the verb 'to dance'. The rose is the symbol of joy, and the philosopher's task is to find joy in the present by discovering reason within it. In other words, philosophy may 'dance' for joy in this world; it need not postpone its 'dancing' until it builds an ideal world elsewhere.

15 *the rose in the cross of the present*: this metaphor was suggested to Hegel by the name and emblem of the Rosicrucians, a secret religious society established in the seventeenth century. [S.H.]

16 *What began with Luther*: the influence of Martin Luther (1483–1546) is marked in Hegel's work, and he declared himself to be a Lutheran; see *Hegel: The Letters*, trans. C. Butler and C. Seiler (Bloomington, Ind.: Indiana University Press, 1984), 520: 'I am a Lutheran, and through philosophy have been at once completely confirmed in Lutheranism.' In contrast to Luther, however, Hegel considers religion, especially Protestantism, and philosophy to have the same content. In Hegel's view, faith and feeling are the form of religion, while rationality is the form of philosophy (see Remark to *PR* § 270).

The saying has become famous: the phrase is from the English philosopher and statesman Francis Bacon (1561–1626), *The Advancement of Learning* (1605), Book I, I. 3: 'It is an assured truth, and a conclusion of experience, that a little or superficial knowledge of philosophy may incline the mind of man to atheism, but a further proceeding therein doth bring the mind back again to religion' (*Francis Bacon*, ed. A. Johnston (New York: Schocken Books, 1965), 24). There is a similar remark in Bacon's essay on Atheism.

the ideal [das Ideale]: here Hegel uses the word 'ideal' to refer not to what is beautiful, nor to what is a mere 'moment' of a whole, but to the realm of thought as such. See third explanatory note to p. 31 and second explanatory note to p. 60.

When philosophy paints its grey in grey: compare Hegel's remark with these words of Mephistopheles from Goethe's *Faust. Part One*: 'Grey, dear friend, is all theory, | And green life's golden tree' ('Studierzimmer', ll. 2038–9).

The owl of Minerva begins its flight only with the falling of dusk: Minerva was the Roman goddess of wisdom (and the equivalent of the Greek goddess Athena). Her sacred bird was the owl. [S.H.]

INTRODUCTION

18 *and its deduction is presupposed*: this deduction is provided in the *Encyclopaedia* (1830) §§ 469–86 and is summarized in *PR* §§ 5–32. [S.H.]

in civil law, all definition is hazardous: 'omnis definitio in jure civili periculosa' (Justinian, *Digest* [*Pandects*], 50. 17. 202) (in Latin in Hegel's text). The 'positive' science of right is the ordinary, *non-philosophical* study of right and law; see *PR* § 3 and Remark. [S.H.]

19 *immediate 'facts of consciousness'*: here and in other places where Hegel uses this phrase, his arrow is primarily aimed at J. F. Fries.

direct bearing on action and not simply on knowledge: see e.g. Remarks to *PR* §§ 126 and 140. If feeling or inspiration is made a substitute for law, then any crime may be justified by the convictions or 'moral intentions' of the criminal.

20 *the necessities of nature*: i.e. soil, climate, geographical position, etc. On the influence of these, see the section on the 'Geographical Basis of History' in G. W. F. Hegel, *The Philosophy of History*, trans. J. Sibree (New York: Dover Publications, 1956), 79–102.

much more like that between Institutes and Pandects: legal rights in any given system of law are regarded by Hegel as an embodiment of the legislator's conception of what is right in the nature of things. The illustration he chooses is not very happy. The *Institutes* of Justinian are an elementary textbook of law; the *Pandects* (or *Digest*) are a complete codex of case-law to which the *Institutes* are an introduction. Hegel takes the *Institutes* to lay down the general principles on which the detailed case-law collected in the *Pandects* is based, but that is not quite true of the books in question. (Justinian I (AD 482/3–565) was Eastern Roman Emperor from AD 527 until his death.)

Montesquieu proclaimed the true historical view: see Charles Louis de Secondat, baron de Montesquieu, *The Spirit of the Laws* (1748), trans. A. M. Cohler, B. C. Miller, and H. S. Stone (Cambridge: Cambridge University Press, 1989), Part 1, Book 1, chap. 3, pp. 8–9: 'Laws should be so appropriate to the people for whom they are made that it is very unlikely that the laws of one nation can suit another. [. . .] They should be related to the *physical aspect* of the country; to the climate, be it freezing, torrid, or temperate; to the properties of the terrain, its location and extent; to the way of life of the peoples, be they plowmen, hunters, or herdsmen; they should relate to the degree of liberty that the constitution can sustain, to the religion of the inhabitants, their inclinations, their wealth, their number, their commerce, their mores and their manners.' [S.H.]

21 *in order to comprehend law or an institution of right*: this is an allusion to the controversy started by the historical school of jurists—Friedrich Karl von Savigny (1779–1861) and his followers—in Hegel's day.

22 *Herr Hugo's Textbook of the History of Roman Law*: Gustav, Ritter von Hugo (1764–1844), was professor in Göttingen from 1788 and a member of the historical school of law. The first edition of his *Textbook of the History of Roman Law* [*Lehrbuch der Geschichte des römischen Rechts*] was published in 1790. The fifth edition appeared in 1815 and there were many subsequent editions.

Cicero praises the Twelve Tables: the reference to Cicero (106–43 BC) is to his *On the Orator* [*De Oratore*], 1. 44. The Twelve Tables was the early Roman legal code (*c*.450 BC).

23 *As far as the correction of the philosopher Favorinus . . . is concerned*: both Favorinus (AD 80–150), the philosopher from Arles, and Sextus Caecilius (d. *c*.AD 169/175), the African jurist, were historical figures, members of Hadrian's circle, but their conversation is rather imagined than reported by Aulus Gellius (*c*.AD 125–80). Gellius' *Attic Nights* [*Noctes Atticae*] is a collection of notes on grammar, geometry, philosophy, and

history which takes its name from the long winter nights Gellius spent in Attica, Greece.

23 *You must be aware . . .*: '*Non . . . ignoras legum* opportunitates *et medelas pro* temporum *moribus et pro rerum publicarum* generibus, *ac pro utilitatum* praesentium *rationibus, proque* vitiorum, *quibus medendum est,* fervoribus, mutari *ac* flecti, neque uno statu consistere, *quin, ut facies coeli et maris, ita* rerum *atque* fortunae *tempestatibus* varientur. *Quid salubrius visum est rogatione illa Stolonis . . ., quid utilius plebiscite Voconio . . . ? Quid tam necessarium existimatum est . . . quam Lex Licinia . . . ? Omnia tamen haec* obliterata *et* operta *sunt civitatis opulentia*' (in Latin in Hegel's text). Licinius Stolo was a tribune in the Roman Republic from 376 to 367 BC, during which time he proposed the Licinian law which required that a consul seat be given to a plebeian and restricted the amount of public land that could be owned by one individual. Voconius' decree (*c.*169 BC) regulated the inheritances of women. [S.H.]

24 *Shakespeare's Shylock in the Merchant of Venice*: Shylock lends 3,000 ducats to the young Bassanio to enable him to enter the competition for Portia's hand in marriage. The condition is that the merchant Antonio, who stands surety for Bassanio, must forfeit a pound of flesh if Bassanio fails to repay the loan within a specified time. When Shylock tries to enforce the contract, however, Portia (in disguise) discloses its flaw: while the contract permits Shylock to extract from Antonio his pound of flesh, it says nothing about any right to shed blood in the process. Shylock thus immediately loses his advantage, finds himself in the position of an alien who has threatened the life of a Venetian citizen, and so must plead for his own life. Shakespeare's *Merchant of Venice* was written in 1596–7. [S.H.]

not only a horse but also a carriage or wagon: by AD 100 *jumentum* meant a draught animal, but earlier it had meant a vehicle drawn by yoked animals. An *arcera* is a covered vehicle. [S.H./A.W.W.]

25 *a method commended by Leibniz*: Hegel is contrasting the method of mathematics, which lays down certain axioms, postulates, and hypotheses, and deduces what follows from them, with the method of philosophy, whose subject-matter is actuality and not hypotheses, and which develops by its own inner necessity, a necessity lacking, e.g., in the advance from one book of Euclid (fl. *c.*300 BC) to the next. Gottfried Wilhelm Leibniz (1646–1716) frequently uses the mathematical method in his philosophical work; e.g. in his *Principles of Nature and Grace* (1712–14) he lays down the supreme perfection of God, and then goes on, in §§ 10 ff., to deduce what follows therefrom, e.g. that this is the best of all possible worlds, that the perceptions and desires of each monad must be of a certain character, etc. (see *G. W. Leibniz: The Monadology and Other Philosophical Writings*, trans. R. Latta (Oxford: Oxford University Press, 1925), 417 ff.).

to call bonorum possessio what was nevertheless an inheritance: see Remark to *PR* § 180. The law of inheritance [*hereditas*], laid down by the Twelve Tables, led to much injustice, e.g. children emancipated from the authority of their fathers were *eo ipso* excluded from inheritance. Edicts by the praetors—Rome's magistrates—allowed parties so excluded to obtain their inheritance under another name—*bonorum possessio* ['the possession of goods']. Thus, by a legal fiction, the old law of inheritance was maintained unimpaired, while its unpalatable consequences were evaded. See e.g. Gaius, *Institutes*, 3. 25–8. (Gaius was a Roman jurist who is assumed to have lived AD 110–79.)

26 *by the fiction or pretence that a daughter [filia] was a son [filius]*: this example of a legal fiction was withdrawn, as a mistake, from later editions of the book in which Hegel finds it: J. G. Heineccius, *Illustrated Treatise on Ancient Roman Jurisprudence [Antiquitatum Romanarum jurisprudentiam illustrantium Syntagma]* (Frankfurt, 1771). What Heineccius says is that by a legal fiction the praetors in certain cases treated a daughter as a son in order to give her rights of inheritance from which in strict law she was excluded. Johann Gottlieb Heineccius (1681–1741) was a German jurist and professor of philosophy and jurisprudence at Halle.

28 *I hope by and by to be able to elaborate them still further*: the hope of producing an ampler exposition was not fulfilled. In the third edition (1830) of the *Encyclopaedia* this particular section (§§ 440–82) was not much enlarged, though some important changes were made.

29 *the annihilation of any organization which tries to rise anew from the ruins*: Hegel has in mind the ideas and actions of the French revolutionaries (especially during 1793–4). Compare the section on 'Absolute Freedom and Terror' in the *Phenomenology*, Miller trans., 355–63.

31 *appears (in the second proposition) merely as an addition*: Fichte published the first version of his *Science of Knowledge [Wissenschaftslehre]* in 1794–5. The first principle of Fichte's new science is that 'the self begins by an absolute positing of its own existence'. The second principle is that the self posits a 'not-self' in opposition to itself. Hegel's criticism here is that the second, 'negative', principle is not derived by Fichte immanently from the first, 'positive', principle, but is introduced as an *additional* principle. Unlike Hegel himself, therefore, Fichte does not apprehend the negativity that is *immanent* in the I itself. See J. G. Fichte, *Science of Knowledge*, trans. P. Heath and J. Lachs (Cambridge: Cambridge University Press, 1982), 93–105. [S.H.]

the I is this solitude and absolute negation: i.e. the pure I of *PR* § 5. As such, it is 'alone' and negative because it is the renunciation of everything determinate and is simply turned in upon itself.

something which is only ideal: by calling something 'ideal' [*ideell*] Hegel does not mean that it does not really exist or that it exists only in the mind; nor does he mean that it is 'ideal' in the sense of 'perfect' or 'beautiful'. He means that it is not something independent in its own right, but merely an aspect or 'moment' of some larger whole. In this sense, a part of the body, such as a hand, is 'ideal', since it is what it is only as a part *of the body*. See *Science of Logic*, Miller trans., 149–50: 'ideal being [*das Ideelle*] is the finite as it is in the true infinite—as a determination, a content, which is distinct but is not an *independent, self-subsistent* being, but only a *moment*.' [S.H.]

33 *which is not considered separately [für sich] any further here*: the will may be regarded as determinate in two different respects: (*a*) it may be determined as subjective only and not also as objective; i.e. it may be the self-consciousness which distinguishes itself from the external world. As *will*, this self-consciousness seeks to overcome its subjectivity and to give objectivity to itself, because to be only subjective is to be restricted, and the will's implicitly infinite nature struggles to overcome this restriction. This relation of consciousness to an object in which it finds not itself but only something other than itself is a mode in which the will *appears*, but it is only an appearance, not actuality. (Actuality is the synthesis of subjective and objective. A cleavage between these is only an appearance.) On this point see *PR* § 108. The first 'form' of the will which Hegel distinguishes here is thus the will determined in *form* as subjective. (b) The second form of the will is the will that is also determined in *content*—the will whose determinations are its *own* and thereby constitute its content. This form of will—the genuinely determinate will which supersedes (but also *includes*) the abstract or formal will of self-consciousness—Hegel proceeds to treat in the following Paragraphs.

34 *its purpose*: the second form of the will is the one whose determinations are its own and therefore *its content*; but since it also includes the first form of the will—and so is subjectivity in contrast to objectivity—this content is the will's *purpose* or aim.

as its object: that is, as its content and purpose.

the will is for itself what it is in itself: in itself or in its essential nature a child is a human being, a rational being. The child exemplifies the generic essence of humanity, and it is only if we know this that we can understand what a child is at all. But this generic essence is only implicit in the child; *in itself* the child is a man or woman, but it is not yet this for itself or in its own eyes. Childhood is the mode of *existence* that corresponds to the *concept* of humanity while that concept is still only *implicit*; or, to use Hegel's terminology, in the child, humanity is 'in its concept', or is 'as concept only', or is 'in accordance with its concept'. The potentialities of humanity are realized only when the child grows up, and then, as an adult, is *for* itself what it is *in* itself. Humanity explicit or for itself as the adult is a different thing, a different type of existent, from the child, despite the inner identity between child and adult in respect of their concept. A human being, however, is finite and may fail adequately to embody the concept of humanity: he may, for example, be a lunatic. Here again then there may be a discrepancy between the human being's implicit nature and what he explicitly is, and it is the occurrence of such a discrepancy which constitutes finitude. A lunatic exists, is a phenomenon, but because of this discrepancy, he lacks actuality and is a 'mere' existent or 'only' a phenomenon.

but for itself it is time: Hegel's point here is that in time the *negativity* inherent in space becomes explicit. Time, therefore, is nothing but the process whereby space negates *itself*. See *Encyclopaedia* (1830) §§ 254–9. For a detailed study of Hegel's understanding of space and time, see S. Houlgate, *An Introduction to Hegel: Freedom, Truth and History* (1991; Oxford: Blackwell, 2005), chap. 6. [S.H.]

35 *the immediate or natural will*: the natural or immediate will is treated in *PR* §§ 11–18. The will which is explicitly free and is the basis of formal rights is treated in *PR* §§ 21 ff. The concept of the will is freedom, but the natural will does not fully actualize that concept, since it is not free *for itself*. It is thus free only implicitly or in its *concept* alone. Such implicit freedom turns out to involve a fundamental *dependence* on natural desire (and caprice) and so is in fact a very restricted form of freedom.

36 *in this twofold indeterminacy*: the indeterminacy is twofold because (*a*) none of these desires is my *particular* desire (any more than any other), and (*b*) each of the desires is itself indeterminate (e.g. hunger, which all sorts of different foods might satisfy, is not hunger for anything specific).

the German language also contains the expression sich entschliessen: there is no precise parallel in English to the difference between *beschliessen* and *sich entschliessen*. Both expressions mean 'to decide'. Etymologically, the former implies simply 'closing the matter', while the latter implies that the decision is at the same time the 'disclosing' or 'opening' of the character of the person who makes it.

Thus they understand little of the nature of thinking: Hegel may have Kant and his followers in mind, but his remarks apply equally to René Descartes (1596–1650) who, in his Fourth *Meditation*, explains the phenomenon of human error by the fact that our will is unrestricted, whereas our understanding is finite and limited. [S.H.]

37 *However 'beautiful' such a disposition may be*: this is a reference to the ideal of the 'beautiful soul' described by Friedrich Schiller (1759–1805) in his essay *On Grace and Dignity* [*Über Anmut und Würde*] (1793), but associated by Hegel more with Romantics such as Novalis (1772–1801). See also *Phenomenology*, Miller trans., 400, 406. [S.H.]

'Whoever wills something great must be able to restrict himself': from Goethe's sonnet 'Nature and Art' ['Natur und Kunst'] (1800). Hegel quotes inaccurately. Goethe's actual words may be translated: 'Whoever wills something great must first collect his energies: it is in restriction that the master first shows himself.'

38 *at the time of Wolff's metaphysics*: Christian J. Wolff (1679–1754) was a rationalist metaphysician whose comprehensive system (indebted to Leibniz) dominated German philosophy until the 'critical' revolution inaugurated in the 1780s by Immanuel Kant (1724–1804). [S.H.]

39 *Pheidias has no mannerisms*: Pheidias was the greatest sculptor of the High Classical Period in ancient Athens. He was active from *c*.460 BC until

c.430 BC. His most famous works (both now lost) were the Athena Parthenos and the Olympian Zeus. [S.H.]

41 *or itself qua infinite form*: 'infinite' in the sense of 'purely self-related and free from all restriction'.

44 *the ethical will*: Hegel must have in mind here an undeveloped, 'childlike', form of ethical will, since he makes it clear later that ethical life is made *concrete* precisely by the 'infinite form' of subjectivity; see *PR* § 144. [S.H.]

46 *Kant's Doctrine of Right*: Hegel refers, quoting as usual from memory, to Kant's statement that one should 'so act externally that the free use of your choice can coexist with the freedom of everyone in accordance with a universal law' (I. Kant, *The Metaphysics of Morals* (1797), trans. M. Gregor (Cambridge: Cambridge University Press, 1991), 56 [*Metaphysical First Principles of the Doctrine of Right*, Introduction, § C]).

47 *especially popular since Rousseau*: Jean-Jacques Rousseau (1712–78), the author of *Discourse on the Origin of Inequality* (1755), *On the Social Contract* (1762), and *Émile* (1762). He is accused by Hegel of having understood freedom as primarily the freedom of the *individual*. [S.H.]

And the phenomena . . . on which they are based: Hegel is referring to the French Revolutionary Terror of 1793–4.

48 *even in Plato*: Hegel probably has in mind (among other dialogues) Plato's *Parmenides*. See *Science of Logic*, Miller trans., 55–6: 'Even the *Platonic* dialectic, in the *Parmenides* itself and elsewhere even more directly, on the one hand, aims only at abolishing and refuting limited assertions through themselves, and, on the other hand, has for result simple nothingness.' [S.H.]

49 *to endow its moments with this distinctively shaped existence*: a caution against the supposition that Hegel is writing a history of institutions. It is not until *PR* § 158 that he begins to deal with the family. The family thus logically presupposes all the 'determinations of the concept', or categories, dealt with in the earlier Paragraphs, but it does not follow that these logical presuppositions are always explicitly present in actual societies with families. In certain social conditions families may exist although private property does not.

51 *'Morality' [Moralität] and 'ethical life' [Sittlichkeit]*: for Hegel's distinction between these, see *PR* § 141. *Moralität* is abstract morality; it possesses the form of all genuinely moral action, i.e. conscientiousness, but it lacks a properly objective content to correspond with this form. *Sittlichkeit* is the concrete morality of a rational social order where rational institutions and laws provide the content of conscientious conviction.

ABSTRACT RIGHT

56 *The classification of the system of rights*: the classification adopted in Justinian, *Institutes*, 1. 2. 12. 'Every right exercised by us relates either to

persons, things, or actions.' The translator's authority for this and most of the other notes on Roman law is W. W. Buckland, *Text-book of Roman Law* (Cambridge: Cambridge University Press, 1921).

57 *capitis diminutio*: *caput* is a person's legal, political, and social status, his position in regard to family rights and consequently to freedom and citizenship. *Capitis diminutio* is a change in *caput*, amounting to its loss in the case of those sold as slaves, and suffered to some extent by those banished and by those adopted into new families. On the 'slave-status' of children, see Remarks to *PR* §§ 175, 180.

PROPERTY

58 *It is only these things*: i.e. the existences just referred to: (a) natural endowments, (b) external objects.

60 *The so-called 'philosophy' . . . the nature of the thing-in-itself*: it is (i) the philosophy of common sense, and (ii) the philosophy of Kant, which Hegel has in mind here.

the free will idealizes such actuality and so is its truth: the free will by using and destroying 'external' objects shows that these have no subsistence of their own but are only 'ideal' (see third explanatory note to p. 31), while the free will does subsist and is their truth because they exist only 'for' it.

61 *The nature of the elements*: i.e. the four elements of early Greek cosmology—earth, air, fire, water (see *Encyclopaedia* [1830] § 281).

In the Roman agrarian laws: especially the proposals of the Gracchi and their successors in the last century of the Roman Republic to distribute domain lands to individual colonists.

One factor in family testamentary trusts: a family testamentary trust (*fideicommissum*) requires those who inherit family property to pass it on to other specified family members at a later stage, and thus can be seen as a limitation on the right to dispose of property freely. [S.H.]

a so-called 'artificial' person [moralische Person] and into mortmain: an 'artificial' (or 'moral') person is a corporate body created for a specific purpose, such as a church or a corporation. 'Mortmain' is the transfer of property to a corporation that can never part with it again (and so has a 'dead hand'). [S.H.]

Plato's ideal state violates the right of personality . . . property: if Hegel has Plato's *Republic* in mind, then he fails to notice that it is the Guardians only who are there precluded from holding private property. But he may be thinking of *Laws* 739c.

62 *universal in content and undivided*: my body differs in form from other bodies and to that extent its form is particular; but its content is universal, since everything that is mine is grounded in it.

Diogenes Laertius: Diogenes Laertius (probably first half of 3rd cent. AD) was a biographer of ancient Greek philosophers. His *Lives and Sayings of*

Famous Philosophers, to which Hegel refers here, is an important source of information on the development of Greek philosophy. [S.H.]

64 *rationality developed into an organism*: an abstract universal has no organic connection with its particulars. Spirit, or reason, as a concrete universal, particularizes itself into differences which are interconnected by its universality in the same way in which the parts of an organism are held together by the single life which they all share. The parts depend on the whole for their life, but, on the other hand, the persistence of life necessitates the differentiation of the parts.

65 *the anticipated relation to others*: 'relation to others'—i.e. the recognition by others that the thing is mine. This recognition depends on my putting my will into the thing, and I cannot do this (except by infringing the rights of others) unless the thing is without an owner when I do so.

66 *Fichte has raised the question . . . a form on it*: see *Foundations of Natural Right*, § 19 [Baur trans., 189–91]. Fichte is there maintaining that the farmer has no right to his land as such but only to its products, to its 'accidents', not to its 'substance'; he may not prevent others from grazing cattle on it after harvest, unless, in addition to cultivation rights, he has grazing rights for cattle of his own.

67 *the positive, negative, and infinite judgements*: the relation between these three types of judgement is expounded in *Encyclopaedia* (1830) §§ 172–3. They represent progressive attempts to attach a predicate to a subject; e.g. (i) since the will is embodied in its property, we may say that 'the will is a particular thing, its property', 'this property is my will', 'this and my will are identical'. But the will is universal and the thing is particular, and so the thing is the negative of the universal or the will, and (ii) the will is therefore *not* the thing. By using it the will negates the thing in order to bring it into accordance with itself. Such negation, however, can never completely achieve its end, because the will, as universal, can never be adequately embodied in any one particular. Hence (iii) the will must be asserted to be the will, and the object must be altogether spurned or alienated. This is not a mere negative judgement, but a 'negatively infinite judgement' which asserts a total incongruity between the subject (the will) and the predicate (the thing).

68 *nothing further on this topic can be deduced from the concept*: this is one of the places in Hegel's work where he makes clear the *limits* of philosophical understanding. [S.H.]

72 *negated by the user*: when I mark a thing as mine, I attribute to it the universal predicate 'mine' and 'recognize' its particular characteristics in the sense that I do not interfere with them. But when I *use* it I 'negate' its particular characteristics in the sense that I change them to suit my purpose. To mark land as mine by fencing it does not change its character, but to use it, e.g. by planting it, does.

73 *Thus he who has the use of arable land*: i.e. the entire and enduring use of it—see *PR* § 62.

usufruct is the right . . . revert to the proper owner: '*ususfructus est jus* alienis *rebus utendifruendi salva rerum* substantia . . . . *Ne tamen in universum* inutiles *essent proprietates* semper *abscendente usufructu,* placuit, *certis modis extingui usumfructum et ad proprietatem reverti.*' (In Latin in Hegel's text.)

74 *res mancipi and nec mancipi, dominium quiritarium and bonitarium*: (*a*) things transferable by mancipation, a formal ceremony before witnesses, and things transferable by simple delivery. (*b*) Quiritarian ownership was originally the only type recognized in law; bonitarian ownership was that which was recognized by law even though there were formal defects in the owner's legal title to it.

in the relations of dominium directum and dominium utile, in the emphyteutic contract: the distinction Hegel is referring to is that between ownership in the abstract and usufruct. The landlord's ownership of land is *dominium directum* ['direct ownership'] whereas the tenant's is *dominium utile* ['useful ownership']. Emphyteutic contracts grant land in perpetuity or for a long term on condition of cultivating it properly and paying a stipulated rent.

dominium directum becomes at the same time a dominium utile: where burdens are attached to a tenancy, the tenant effectively has only *partial* use of the land with the result that the landlord also has partial use of it. [S.H.]

the utile [the usefulness of property] which here is the rational factor: lords of the manor are *eo ipso* nobility or gentry, whether their lands are being farmed or not. Use is a stage further on in the dialectic than mere abstract property, or the mere seizure of a possession, and, since it is further on, it is 'rational' in contrast with the lower stage of property in the abstract.

76 *prescription [Verjährung]*: positively, prescription is a title or right to the possession of property which has been uninterruptedly used or possessed either from time immemorial or for a period fixed by law. Negatively, it is a limitation of the time within which an action or a claim may be raised, e.g. to recover possession of property after it has been given to someone else to use.

the specific character of property as 'real': in Hegel's terminology, a thing has 'reality' [*Realität*] when it has objective existence in relation to something subjective. A plan is 'real' when it ceases to be merely subjective and becomes determinate in words or acts (see *Encyclopaedia* [1830] § 91 and Addition). Property is 'real' as embodying my will, and prescription in Hegel's view is a right because, when I use a thing, I embody my will in it and it becomes 'really' mine, while when I withdraw my will from it, it becomes ownerless. Hegel is not here speaking of 'real' property in the usual legal sense (of immovable property—land and the things affixed to it—as opposed to personal property).

such publications become ownerless . . . though in an opposite way: public memorials become private property through being disregarded and becoming objects of indifference. The content of books becomes public property by the opposite process, i.e. by being studied, assimilated, and used in the writing of new books.

77 *whose nature cannot be conceived except as existing*: 'cuius natura non potest concipi nisi existens' (in Latin in Hegel's text). In his *Ethics* (1677) Benedict de Spinoza (1632–77) defines a *causa sui* [cause of itself] as 'that whose nature cannot be conceived except as existing' (*Ethics*, Part 1, Definition 1) and he goes on in Proposition 7 to show that substance is such a cause. Hegel applies this definition to spirit, or, as he would say, to that which is both substance and subject as well. Spirit is actualized only when it passes over from mere abstract being into existence, i.e. into the actualization of its potentialities in a determinate way.

80 *is not to retain proprietorship without use [utile]*: in Hegel's view, therefore, it is *legitimate* (and not merely arbitrary) for an author to retain copyright over his works. [S.H.]

82 *Only an ethical Idea*: i.e. the state (see *PR* §§ 257 and 323 ff.).

83 *When Hercules destroyed himself . . . Brutus fell on his sword*: Hercules had himself burned to death on Mount Oeta in order to escape from a robe, poisoned with the blood of the hydra, which clung to him, tore his skin, and caused him agonizing and incurable suffering (see Ovid, *Metamorphoses*, Book IX). Marcus Junius Brutus (85–42 BC) was a senator in the late Roman Republic and one of the conspirators who in 44 BC assassinated Julius Caesar. Brutus took his own life by falling on his sword after his defeat at the second battle of Philippi in 42 BC. [S.H.]

CONTRACT

84 *my will as alienated is at the same time another's will*: to say that I am the rightful owner of a property implies that others recognize my right, i.e. they recognize that what I call mine is not merely a thing externally related to other things, but is my property, the external embodiment of my will. The 'thing' I can alienate on my own account, but the property I cannot alienate without the cooperation of someone else's will, because property (and therefore alienation) presupposes recognition. Hence in the social context of recognized rights, there is an equivalence between my will to alienate and another's will, and my will thus becomes objective to me in the will of the other (see *PR* § 71 and Remark).

85 *Just as at one time*: i.e. under feudalism (see *PR* §§ 277–8).

86 *excessive damage (laesio enormis)*: the principle that if you sell e.g. a farm for less than half its value, you have suffered excessive damage, and the contract is voidable, was enunciated in Roman law, though it is very exceptional and seems to apply only to land transactions, and there to sales only, not to purchases (see Justinian, *Codex*, 4. 44. 2).

87 *distinctions in Roman law between other types of contract*: Roman law recognized four main types of contract: contracts *re*, *verbis*, *litteris*, and *consensu*,

giving rise to real, verbal, literal, and consensual obligations. Obligations created by verbal and literal contracts are unilateral, those arising out of real and consensual contracts are bilateral or mutual (though sometimes imperfectly bilateral). *Real* obligations arise out of *traditio rei*, the handing over of things by way of loan, deposit, etc. *Verbal* obligations arise out of stipulations made by the parties in set terms by word of mouth to each other. *Literal* obligations arise out of a written entry made against a debtor (even in his absence, hence the 'unilateral' character of such a contract) by a creditor. *Consensual* obligations arise out of sales, purchases, etc.; they could be created by a common understanding without any formality and so could be contracted by letter, messenger, etc. In a verbal contract, the parties are liable only for what they have specifically promised in words to perform. In a consensual contract, they are reciprocally liable for what each in fairness and equity should do for the other (see Justinian, *Institutes*, 3. 13. 2). Kant uses the distinction between unilateral and bilateral contracts, and includes loans, deposits, and gifts in the former (*Doctrine of Right* § 31 [Gregor trans., 102–3]).

88 *The distinction in Roman law between pactum and contractus is a bad one*: *pactum* is the expression of an intention to make a *contractus* (or formal contract). The formula of a pact is 'I am prepared to sell'. Thus contract is enforceable at law, while pact is not. So Heineccius, *Illustrated Treatise on Ancient Roman Jurisprudence* [*Antiquitatum Romanarum jurisprudentiam illustrantium Syntagma*] (Frankfurt, 1841), 3. 14. 4, an earlier edition of which was probably Hegel's authority. More recent writers on Roman law give a different account of the matter.

89 *the progress ad infinitum*: for Hegel's distinction between the bad and the true infinite, see *Encyclopaedia* (1830) §§ 94–5 and the Addition to *PR* § 22. The true infinite returns from its other into itself and so is self-related and self-determined. The bad infinite, on the other hand, is the eternal sameness of an endless, 'infinite', progression; we lay down a limit, then we pass it and lay down another, and so on *ad infinitum*, but without ever leaving the finite behind or reaching true infinity. Hegel's point here is that the infinite divisibility of time, etc. makes it impossible to say at what precise point, in Fichte's view, the contract becomes legally, as distinct from morally, binding.

90 *formal and real [reell] contracts*: 'real' not in the legal sense mentioned in the Remark to *PR* § 79 (see explanatory note to p. 87), but in Hegel's sense defined in *PR* § 76.

nominate and innominate: transactions in the form: 'I am doing this for you now on the understanding that you will do this for me later,' were classed with 'real' contracts by Roman lawyers, but they have been called 'innominate' by modern writers in distinction from the four 'nominate' types enumerated in the explanatory note to p. 87.

mutuum and commodatum without . . . interest: Roman law distinguished four types of 'real' contract, namely *mutuum*, *commodatum*, *depositum*, and *pignus*. (*a*) *Mutuum* was a loan not for use but for consumption, i.e. a loan of *res fungibiles*, things returnable in kind. The borrower of a jar of oil would consume the oil and return other oil of the same kind. *Mutuum* was supposed to be a loan without charge. (*b*) *Commodatum* was a loan for use only, the thing itself being returned, a loan therefore of *res non fungibiles*. Again the loan was supposed to be without charge; if a fee was charged, the transaction became *locatio*, letting, hiring. (*c*) *Depositum* was deposit and (*d*) *pignus* was pledge.

91 *or even commodatum since rent is charged*: strictly speaking, *commodatum* (like *mutuum*) is a loan without charge (see previous note). Yet Hegel appears to suggest here that a loan of money in return for rent or interest (rather than, say, in return for some service) remains that of *commodatum*. Too little is said, however, to know precisely why he might think this. To be sure, *money* is loaned in return for *money*; but it is not the *same* money that is being returned in the rent, nor is its value normally equivalent to the value of the amount loaned. [S.H.]

92 *so far as the possession of the property is concerned*: i.e. the possession of the *value* of the property.

WRONG

93 *proceeds in wrong to become a semblance*: Hegel distinguishes between *Schein* (semblance) and *Erscheinung* (appearance) (see *Encyclopaedia* [1830] § 131). An appearance is a shining-forth of the reality or essence. A semblance is the inessential masquerading as the essential, the denial of the essence in its apparent assertion. Contract is an 'appearance' of right and no more than that, because the will in contract is not the universal will in its truth as self-mediating but only a *common* will, posited by the arbitrary wills of the parties. Since these wills are arbitrary, their correspondence with the rightness whose appearance they are is contingent on their arbitrary choice; and hence they may if they please make an arbitrary choice in defiance of the right. Although crime is a denial of right, it is only in a context of right that there can be a crime at all. Hence crime is a mere 'semblance', no genuine existence; what it denies is its own essential basis, *right*, on which the very being of crime depends.

95 *only the particular is negated*: if someone challenges my right to some particular thing, he does not deny my rights in general or my property as a whole; he denies only that I have rightly included this particular property amongst the things called 'mine'. Hence the judgement which he asserts is '*this* is not rightfully yours (although other things are)'. For the necessity of the advance from this type of negative judgement to the infinite judgement, see *Encyclopaedia* (1830) §§ 172–3.

96 *an infinite judgement expressed positively or as a tautology*: the 'positively infinite judgement' is the expression of a mere identity: the individual is the individual. This, though true, lacks the universality of thought.

The predicate should be a universal and tell us something about the subject, but in this case the subject is qualified by itself, and the judgement is bogus, a show, because it professes to be a judgement, to tell us something, and it does not. The same is true of fraud. Fraud as the sale of *this* article, e.g. this share certificate, which the purchaser voluntarily accepts, is prima facie a genuine transaction. But as a sale it should contain a universal element, i.e. value. The seller professes to sell this universality of which the printed paper is supposed to be only a symbol, and the transaction is fraudulent because the universality is absent.

Here again all there is, is the demand: a demand that remains unfulfilled because of the fraud. [S.H.]

98 *a negatively infinite judgement in its full sense*: the criminal by wronging someone is effectively denying that his victim is the bearer of right that should be respected, i.e. he asserts a total incompatibility between his victim and right. Hence 'you have no right' is a 'negatively infinite judgement'.

99 *The Stoic view*: 'The Stoics hold that the virtues accompany each other, and if a man has one, he has all' (Diogenes Laertius, 7. 125, 'Life of Zeno'). The single virtue is to live in accordance with nature, and vice is the converse.

the laws of Draco: in the early history of Athens, Draco (7th cent. BC) prescribed 'one penalty, death, for almost all offences' (see Plutarch, *Life of Solon*).

101 *The positive existence of the injury . . . the particular will of the criminal*: as a simple *event* a crime is not distinguished from other events such as accidents. What gives it positive existence as a *crime* (as opposed to an accident) is the presence in it of the criminal's will. In this sense, 'the *positive* existence of the injury consists solely in the *particular will of the criminal*'. To the person injured (and to onlookers), however, the crime is negative, a wilful attack on rights, a denial of them, and therefore something null and self-destructive.

[E. F.] Klein, Principles of Common German and Prussian Penal Law: Ernst Ferdinand Klein (1743–1810) was a prominent German jurist and co-author of the *Prussian General Legal Code* of 1794. [S.H.]

102 *Feuerbach bases his theory of punishment on threat*: Paul Johann Anselm Ritter von Feuerbach (1775–1833) was the father of the Young Hegelian philosopher Ludwig Feuerbach (1804–72), and the author of *Textbook of the Penal Law Commonly Valid in Germany* [*Lehrbuch des gemeinen, in Deutschland gültigen peinlichen Rechts*] (1801). He is regarded as the founder of the modern German theory of punishment. [S.H.]

103 *As is well known, Beccaria*: Cesare, marquis of Beccaria (1738–94), was an Italian philosopher and politician and the father of modern criminology. His best-known work (in which he set out his opposition to capital punishment) is *On Crimes and Punishments* [*Dei delitti e delle pene*] (1764). [S.H.]

103 *Even if neither Joseph II*: Emperor Joseph II of Austria was born in 1741 and reigned from 1765 to his death in 1790. [S.H.]

105 *In crime, whose basic determination is the infinite aspect*: a crime is a particular act with a particular character, e.g. it is a theft, and a theft of, say, £15. But it also has an infinite aspect because it is the negation of right by the free will and therefore it *deserves* to be punished, i.e. to be negated in its turn.

106 *The Eumenides sleep*: the Erinyes (or Furies) were female spirits of justice and vengeance in Greek (and Roman) mythology. They are known especially for pursuing Orestes, who murdered his mother Clytemnestra in revenge for her killing of his father Agamemnon. After Orestes was acquitted by a court in Athens on the deciding vote of Athena, the Erinyes were appeased and then welcomed into the city as the 'Eumenides' or 'kind-hearted ones'. See Aeschylus, *The Eumenides* (458 BC). [S.H.]

punished not as public crimes . . . but as private crimes: 'Private crimes' are those which are left to the injured party to prosecute, as opposed to those that are prosecuted by the state. In Roman law, for example, both theft and robbery were treated as private crimes (see Gaius, *Institutes*, 3. 182). [S.H.]

MORALITY

109 *posited as identical for itself with the will that is in itself*: at the start, there is an *implicit* identity between the universal will in itself and the will of the subject, because the latter does embody the former, though without fully realizing it. This identity becomes explicit only after the explicit individual will has sunk 'deeper and deeper into itself', i.e. estranged itself further from the universal, entrenched itself more and more deeply, plumbed the recesses of its own moralizing—a process which it may carry so far eventually as to defy the universal altogether and so be explicitly evil. The occurrence of evil is the transition to the higher stage of ethical life, just as the occurrence of wrong was the transition to morality.

110 *the right of the subjective will*: a right is the embodiment or 'existence' of the free will (see *PR* § 29). Abstract rights embody the freedom of personality, the abstract form of the will. We now come to more concrete rights, those of subjectivity, which itself is the higher ground in which the free will is now embodied. Just as personality in the process of becoming more and more determinate was embodied in a series of rights, so the development of subjectivity gives rise to a series of rights.

becomes objective [objektiv] in the sense of the will's own universality: the process which we are studying in the field of morality is two-sided: (*a*) the subject gradually comes to a realization of his own universality, i.e. of the objectivity of the universal will which his subjective will embodies. (*b*) The embodiment of the subject in his action—the right of the subject— changes in character as the character of subjectivity changes. To start with, the will recognizes its subjectivity in something which it has done;

the recognition is immediate and the action done is immediate too. Next, when the action is seen to embody the subject's *welfare*, the universality implicit in the subject begins to be explicit (*PR* § 125). Finally, the action is seen to embody the good, something explicitly universal. The whole process may be summed up by saying that the subject gradually determines the character of his action further and further until it expresses the universal nature, i.e. the concept, of the subject in concrete detail, and he does this in the course of discovering what this concept is.

111 *positing them as identical*: the will determined as subject is *eo ipso* an embodiment of the concept of the will. Implicitly, then, subjectivity is a unity of objective and subjective; but this unity cannot be made explicit until the *difference* of these moments is made explicit and the will overcomes that difference.

PURPOSE AND RESPONSIBILITY

117 *Oedipus, who killed his father without knowing it*: Oedipus, king of Thebes, unknowingly killed his father and married his mother and then blinded himself on discovering what he had done. In Sophocles' play, *Oedipus the King* (*c*.427 BC), Oedipus accepts responsibility for what he has done, even though he did it in ignorance [ll. 1310–35]. In Sophocles' *Oedipus at Colonus* (*c*.408 BC), however, Oedipus is more defensive and protests his innocence [ll. 265–75, 535–50]. [S.H.]

INTENTION AND WELFARE

119 *Etymologically, Absicht [intention] implies abstraction*: *Absicht* is derived from the word *absehen* (to 'look away').

describable in a proposition, not a judgement: in Hegel's terminology, a proposition [*Satz*] says something about the subject which does not stand to it in any universal relationship; it gives expression to some individual action or state of the subject. Hence 'gold is a metal' is a judgement [*Urteil*], but 'Caesar crossed the Rubicon' is a proposition (see *Encyclopaedia* [1830] § 167).

The device of dolus indirectus: 'The distinction between *dolus directus* and *indirectus*, in the sense that, in the latter case, the intention of the agent was not to commit the wrong which resulted, but only a slighter one, is now quite obsolete, although it still obtains in Austria' (F. J. W. P. von Holtzendorff, *Encyclopaedia of Jurisprudence Presented Systematically and Alphabetically* [*Enzyklopädie der Rechtswissenschaft in systematischer and alphabetischer Bearbeitung*] (Leipzig, 1875), 402).

121 *the time of Croesus and Solon*: Hegel refers to the conversation between the Lydian King Croesus (595–546 BC) and the Greek statesman and lawmaker Solon (638–558 BC), reported by the Greek historian Herodotus (*c*.484–425 BC). Croesus asked Solon: 'who is the happiest man you have

ever seen?', and received the reply: 'An Athenian called Tellus', because 'his city was prosperous, and he had fine sons [. . .]; he had wealth enough by our standards; and he had a glorious death'. When Croesus, somewhat irritated, pressed Solon further and asked: 'But what of my own happiness?', Solon replied that he would not answer this question 'until I know that you have died happily'. See Herodotus, *The Histories*, trans. A. de Sélincourt (1954; Harmondsworth: Penguin Books, 2003), 14–15 [1. 30–2]. [S.H.]

123 *Do with abhorrence what duty commands*: Hegel quotes from memory from Schiller, *Xenien* (published with Goethe), no. 389: 'Decision' [*Decisum*]:

> *Da ist kein andrer Rat, du mußt suchen, sie zu verachten,*
> *Und mit Abscheu alsdann thun, wie die Pflicht dir gebeut.*

> There is no alternative: you must seek to despise them
> And to do with abhorrence what duty commands you to do. [S.H.]

In great things, it is enough to have willed: 'In magnis voluisse sat est' (Propertius, *Elegies*, 2. 10. 6) (in Latin in the text).

124 *the 'benevolence' [guten Herzen] of the pre-Kantian philosophers*: for an analysis and criticism of the 'law of the heart' (the eighteenth-century doctrine exaggerated by Hegel's Romantic contemporaries), see *Phenomenology*, Miller trans., 221–8.

well-known touching dramatic productions: Hegel is apparently referring to certain *Sturm und Drang* dramas of the late eighteenth century, especially Schiller's *The Robbers* [*Die Räuber*] (1781), a play in which a young man with good intentions is expected to obtain the sympathy of the audience when he organizes a band of robbers to fight tyranny.

125 *The famous answer: 'I do not see the need for it'*: the libeller defends himself with the words: 'Il faut donc que je vive.' The famous answer—which is said to have been given by Cardinal Richelieu (1585–1642)—is: 'Je n'en vois pas la nécessité.' (Both statements are quoted in French by Hegel.) [S.H.]

When St Crispin stole leather to make shoes for the poor: St Crispin and St Crispinian were twin brothers born to a Roman family in the 3rd century AD. They evangelized Gaul, preaching in the streets by day and making shoes by night. They are the patron saints of cobblers and other leather-workers. [S.H.]

the 'benefit of competence' [beneficium competentiae]: the *beneficium competentiae* was the right of a debtor or an unsuccessful defendant in a civil action not to be condemned to pay more than his means would allow, i.e. not to have to forfeit the tools of his trade, and to be allowed to live honestly, according to his station in life.

GOOD AND CONSCIENCE

126 *fiat justitia should not be followed by pereat mundus*: 'fiat justitia pereat mundus' ('let justice be done, even if the world should perish'). [S.H.]

129 *the 'clear ideas' . . . of Wolff's psychology*: 'When we can recognize what it is that we perceive or when we can distinguish it from other perceivable things, then the perception which we have is a clear perception' (i.e. idea), 'e.g., when we look at a tree in daylight, we have a clear idea of the tree' (C. J. Wolff, *Empirical Psychology* [*Psychologia empirica*] [Frankfurt and Leipzig, 1732], § 31).

his will's obligation arises directly in this relation: the particular subject distinguishes between the essence of his will and the inessentiality of, e.g., particular desires, and endeavours to make the latter correspond with the former. He 'ought' to do what the essence of his will enjoins, but never gets beyond 'ought' to 'is' or 'does'.

131 *the possibility of envisaging an action as a universal maxim*: Hegel's citation of this formula is, to say the least, careless. The citation in the Addition to this Paragraph—'Consider whether your maxim can be laid down as a universal principle'—is more accurate (but still not completely so). See Kant, *Groundwork of the Metaphysics of Morals*, Gregor trans., 73: 'Act only in accordance with that maxim through which you can at the same time will that it become a universal law.' Full bibliographical details are given in footnote 58 [p. 130 above].

132 *It therefore has fixed principles*: what is good *in and for itself* is concrete and therefore systematically determinate and differentiated. Hence to will it is to will in accordance with determinate rational principles.

134 *The latter is part of the ethical disposition*: in the state, 'true' conscience takes the form of patriotism (see *PR* § 268). Note, however, that when Hegel says this, it is the state as Idea, the rational state, that he has in mind. Bad states exist, and patriotic acceptance, even if conscientious, of their bad laws would not in Hegel's view be the working of 'true' conscience, which is the conscientious acceptance of rational laws and institutions only. For the 'religious' conscience, see *Encyclopaedia* (1830) § 552.

in Socrates, the Stoics, and others: the keynote of the teaching of Socrates (*c*.470–399 BC) is the dictum of the Delphic oracle: 'Know thyself', and he described himself as a midwife, bringing to birth the ideas already present in embryo in people's minds (see *PR* §§ 279 and 343). The Stoic precept was 'live according to nature', i.e. in accordance with reason.

135 *something inward in comparison with that level*: we all begin life on the natural level; and at that level, i.e. in infancy, there is neither freedom nor morality. Freedom depends on the discovery of the self which is not natural but spiritual, i.e. the inner rational self present in germ, even in the infant, as the inner truth of its apparently purely impulsive life. It is by transcending that life that we attain to freedom, but since there is no breach of continuity, freedom may be said both to arise from the natural life and yet to be something opposed to that life, i.e. to be our inner— initially unrealized—essence.

139 *They will all be damned . . . surrendering to him*: 'Ils seront tous damnés ces demi-pécheurs, qui ont quelque amour pour la vertu. Mais pour ces francs pécheurs, pécheurs endurcis, pécheurs sans mélange, pleins et achevés, l'enfer ne les tient pas: ils ont trompé le diable à force de s'y abandonner'; see B. Pascal, *Lettres Provinciales* (1656–7), 4th letter (quotation in French in Hegel's text). Blaise Pascal (1623–62) was a French mathematician and philosopher. [S.H.]

the old questions about efficacious grace: the problem of the doctrine of grace is to reconcile a belief in our inability to attain salvation independently of God's grace with a belief in our individual freedom. In the seventeenth century the Jansenists, who tended to belittle human freedom, carried on a controversy with the Jesuits on this question; both parties believed in efficacious grace but differed as to how it was obtained. Hegel's point is that if grace—God's power, i.e. the objective—is regarded as given to some people and not others—as both parties to the controversy agreed that it was—then God's power and human freedom are being treated as if they were related only accidentally.

Pascal quotes there too Aristotle's distinction: Aristotle (384–322 BC) distinguishes between actions done '*through* ignorance' [δι᾽ ἄγνοιαν] (when the agent acts 'without idea' [οὐκ εἰδώς]), and actions done '*in* ignorance' (when the agent acts ἀγνοῶν). In the first case the ignorance is unavoidable; there are external circumstances which the agent (e.g. Oedipus) had no means of knowing. In the second case, the ignorance is due to circumstances within the control of the agent, e.g. to drunkenness. (Aristotle adds that every act done through ignorance is 'non-voluntary', but that, strictly speaking, such an act is 'involuntary' only when it causes the agent subsequent pain and repentance; see *Nicomachean Ethics* 1110b17–19.)

140 *all these questions are the less important aspect of the matter*: Hegel's position is this: evil consists in freely going against the content and (ethical) form of the good, the genuine universal (see Addition to *PR* § 139). This can be done in the explicit consciousness that it is evil—that is, with a 'bad conscience'—but also, as we see later in this Remark, in the belief that one is actually obeying a higher good oneself that only conscience can see. [S.H.]

probabilism: a doctrine of Jesuit moral theology which (in Hegel's interpretation) teaches that we incur no guilt if at least one reason can be found to make it *probable* that an action is permitted, even if most scholarly opinion judges the action to be wrong. Hegel's criticism of probabilism is indebted in part to Pascal. [S.H.]

141 *the goodness of the will consists in its willing the good*: Kant famously asserts that: 'It is impossible to think of anything at all in the world, or indeed even beyond it, that could be considered good without limitation except a *good will*' (*Groundwork of the Metaphysics of Morals*, Gregor trans., 49). Remark (*d*), however, is an attack not so much on Kant's doctrine itself, but on what Hegel regards as the perversion of that doctrine by the Romantics.

144 *which denies that the truth is knowable*: Hegel again has Kant's philosophy in mind, or rather the simplified Kantianism of some of Kant's followers. [S.H.]

145 *F. H. Jacobi to Count Holmer, on Count Stolberg's change of faith*: in the first twenty years of the nineteenth century there was a strong Roman Catholic revival in Germany. It began with the sensational conversion of the poet Count Friedrich Leopold zu Stolberg (1750–1819) in 1801, and gathered momentum by the accession of the leaders of the Romantic movement (such as Friedrich von Schlegel in 1808). Their change of faith antagonized Hegel the Lutheran as much as their elevation of emotion above reason disgusted Hegel the philosopher. Jacobi was a prominent critic of both Enlightenment and German Idealist rationalism and was often the target of Hegel's criticism. In this case, however, Hegel cites Jacobi's comments with approval. *Brennus* was a northern German periodical. Count Friedrich Levin Holmer (1741–1806) was first minister of the German Duchy of Oldenburg (after 1777 Holstein-Oldenburg) from 1774 to 1806.

146 *For to err is human*: see Alexander Pope: 'To err is human, to forgive divine' (*An Essay on Criticism* [1711], 2. 525). Hegel's source, however, is likely to be the Roman proverb, 'errare humanum est'. [S.H.]

147 *My colleague, the late Professor Solger*: Karl Wilhelm Ferdinand Solger (1780–1819) was a professor in Berlin from 1811 until his death and the author of *Erwin: Four Conversations about the Beautiful and Art* [*Erwin: Vier Gespräche über das Schöne und die Kunst*] (Berlin, 1815). He wrote a long review of Friedrich von Schlegel's thoughts on irony that was published in two parts (1809 and 1811). [S.H.]

Critique of August Wilhelm von Schlegel's Lectures on Dramatic Art and Literature: August Wilhelm von Schlegel (1767–1845) was a poet, translator, and critic and the brother of Friedrich von Schlegel. His lectures on dramatic art and literature were delivered in Vienna in 1808 and published 1809–11. [S.H.]

148 *the hero of a modern tragedy, Die Schuld*: Guilt [*Die Schuld*] is a play by Adolf Müllner (1774–1829). The play was an immediate success on its production in 1813. Hugo, a Norwegian, loves Elvira, the wife of Carlos, a Spaniard. He kills Carlos and marries Elvira. Carlos turns out to have been his brother, and he and Elvira commit suicide because of their guilt.

in romantic tragedy the character of the interest undergoes a certain modification: in 'romantic' tragedy (by which Hegel means tragedy produced since the Middle Ages by writers such as Shakespeare, Schiller, and Goethe), characters are motivated more by their own subjective drives, passions, and ambitions than by ethical concerns. For a detailed study of Hegel's understanding of tragedy, see S. Houlgate, 'Hegel's Theory of Tragedy', in id. (ed.), *Hegel and the Arts* (Evanston, Ill.: Northwestern University Press, 2007), 146–78. [S.H.]

149 *a stage, however, there different in character*: in the *Phenomenology* (1807) the transition is directly from conscience to religion, not as here and in the third edition of the *Encyclopaedia*, from subjective morality to a concrete, rational ethical order embodying both subjective convictions and objective institutions, and then later to religion.

150 *The chief hypocrites are the religious ones (the Tartuffes)*: *Tartuffe* (1664) is a comedy about religious hypocrisy by Molière (1622–73). [S.H.]

ETHICAL LIFE

154 *distinctions whose specific character is thereby determined by the concept*: what is concrete is self-determining and self-differentiating (see *PR* § 7). The substantiality which we are now considering is that of the spirit that is *free reason* and therefore of the *concept*. Hence the institutions and objective duties of the ethical order are the concept's differentiation of itself (see *PR* §§ 262, 269–70, 272).

no one knows whence the laws come; they are everlasting: in the modern translation by Elizabeth Wyckoff, Antigone's words to Creon are as follows:

> Nor did I think your orders were so strong
> that you, a mortal man, could over-run
> the gods' unwritten and unfailing laws.
> Not now, nor yesterday's, they always live,
> and no one knows their origin in time.

See Sophocles, *Antigone* (*c*.442 BC), *Greek Tragedies*, ed. D. Grene and R. Lattimore, 3 vols. (Chicago: University of Chicago Press, 1960), 196 [ll. 450–7]. Hegel refers to the same lines in *PR* § 166 Remark and *Phenomenology*, Miller trans., 261. [S.H.]

156 *the form of a 'doctrine of duties'*: Kant provides a doctrine of duties under the title 'Doctrine of the Elements of Ethics' in his *Metaphysics of Morals* (Gregor trans., 214 ff.), and Fichte's *System of Ethics* (1798) contains a 'Doctrine of Duties in the proper sense of the term' [§§ 19 ff.].

159 *Virtue is rather like ethical virtuosity*: heroes ('ethical virtuosi') lived in uncivilized conditions (see Addition to *PR* § 93) and there was no established ethical life in society as they found it; but since they introduced ethical institutions for the first time (see Remarks to *PR* §§ 167 and 203), they displayed virtue as a kind of virtuosity. Nowadays, ethical life is common to everyone and consists in conformity to the existing order, not in divergence from it.

160 *Make him a citizen of a state with good laws*: this answer is attributed to Xenophilus the Pythagorean by Diogenes Laertius (8. 1. 15), but emphasis on the educational value of good laws and institutions is a commonplace of Greek ethics and politics.

The educational experiments, advocated by Rousseau in Émile: in *Émile* (1762) Rousseau sets out his views on education by means of a semi-fictitious account of the upbringing of the young boy after whom the book is named. The boy is raised in the countryside in an attempt to keep him away from the corrupting influences of society. [S.H.]

161 *since particularity is the outward appearance of the ethical order*: the ethical order as appearance is civil society, and it is in that sphere that individuals attain their 'particular satisfaction', i.e. their livelihood through work.

THE FAMILY

163 *and even Kant does this*: 'The marriage contract [. . .] is a contract that is necessary by the principle of humanity, that is, if a man and a woman want to enjoy each other's sexual attributes they *must* necessarily marry, and this is necessary in accordance with pure reason's principles of right' (Kant, *Doctrine of Right*, § 24 [Gregor trans., 96]). [S.H.]

166 *the religious character of marriage and the family, or pietas*: *pietas*—dutiful conduct, especially to members of one's family, 'family piety'. *Penates*—the guardian deities of the Roman household, regarded here as representing the spirit of the family.

168 *Friedrich von Schlegel . . . and a follower of his in the anonymous Letters*: Friedrich von Schlegel's novel *Lucinde* was published in 1799, and the *Letters on Schlegel's 'Lucinde'* were published anonymously in 1800 by Friedrich Schleiermacher. [S.H.]

169 *the ideal [das Ideale]*: by this word Hegel means 'the beautiful and its associations' (*Science of Logic*, Miller trans., p. 149, Hegel's fn.). It is to be distinguished, therefore, from *das Ideelle*, for which see third explanatory note to p. 31 [p. 331 above]. [S.H.]

172 *the wife in the easily dissolved type of marriage*: if a wife stayed away from her husband for three nights in a year, she could avoid becoming effectively the property of her husband by remaining technically a part of her original family and under the authority of her father. Her husband then had no rights over her property and divorce was easier. Such a wife was called a *matrona* rather than a *materfamilias* (see Gaius, *Institutes*, 1. 136). [S.H./A.W.W.]

the presupposition . . . here becomes a result: i.e. persons immediately existent (as *children*).

174 *The play theory of education*: the play theory of education was popularized in Germany by Johann Bernhard Basedow (1724–90) in the years following the publication of Rousseau's *Émile* (1762). Friedrich Wilhelm August Fröbel (1782–1852), with whom the theory is now commonly associated (and who coined the term 'kindergarten'), did not publish his *On the Education of Man [Die Menschenerziehung]* until 1826.

175 *A third ethical authority*: a court of law (or the Church) (see Addition to this Paragraph). The married parties are the other two.

177 *its arbitrary recognition by others*: Hegel may have in mind Fichte's view in his *Foundations of Natural Right*, § 19 [Baur trans., 223–4], though Fichte's point is that any testamentary disposition requires recognition from the *state*. [S.H./A.W.W.]

unless the will specifically so provided: Hegel does not exaggerate the scope of a Roman father's authority. To allow to sons private possession even of *peculium castrense* was a revolutionary change, introduced by Augustus (63 BC–AD 14), and even then, if the son died intestate, this property passed to the father of the family.

a matrona, not a wife who in manum conveniret, in mancipio esset: on *matrona*, see first explanatory note to p. 172 [above]. *In manum convenire* means 'to come into the power [the hand] of a husband'; *in mancipio esse* means 'to have been taken by the hand [of another]' and so 'to be the *property* [of another]'. [S.H.]

178 *erudition that makes one a legal expert*: this titbit of legal lore is culled from Heineccius, *Illustrated Treatise on Ancient Roman Jurisprudence*.

the writings of Lucian and others: Lucian of Samosata (*c.* AD. 125–80) was a writer of satirical works, including a speech supposedly delivered in court by a man who was disinherited by his father and studied medicine. His father became insane, but the son cured him and was restored to his will. He was then disinherited a second time on his refusal to treat his stepmother's insanity. He appeals to the court against his father.—'And others': Hegel probably has in mind the *Controversiae* of Lucius Annaeus Seneca (54 BC–AD 39), known as 'Seneca the Elder' or 'Seneca the Rhetorician' and the father of the Roman philosopher and dramatist Seneca (*c.*4 BC–AD 65). The *Controversiae* was a collection of imaginary legal cases said to have been put together from memory in which the opinions of various Greek and Roman orators regarding each case were presented.

what fine writing about honestum and decorum there is in his On Duties: '*honestum* and *decorum*' are 'morality and propriety'. *On Duties* [*De Officiis*] was written in 44 BC. [S.H.]

fideicommissa and substitutiones: *Fideicommissa*—testamentary trusts; see third explanatory note to p. 61 [p. 335 above]. *Substitutiones*—nominations in a will of one or more heirs to inherit as substitutes in the event of the failure of the heir instituted to take possession of the inheritance, whether through death or otherwise.

CIVIL SOCIETY

182 *a relative totality*: i.e. the two sides of the Idea as a whole, universality and particularity, are merely *related* to one another, not integrated here in an organic unity.

187 *as in Smith, Say, and Ricardo*: Adam Smith (1723–90), Jean-Baptiste Say (1767–1832), and David Ricardo (1772–1823) are three of the most important 'classical' economists. Smith's *An Inquiry into the Nature and Causes of the Wealth of Nations* was published in 1776, Say's *Treatise on Political Economy* [*Traité d'économie politique*] in 1803, and Ricardo's *On the Principles of Political Economy and Taxation* in 1817.

190 *refined*: reading *gebildetem* for Hegel's *ungebildetem*.

The entire Cynical mode of life adopted by Diogenes: the Cynic school of philosophy was founded by Antisthenes (444–365 BC), a pupil of Socrates, and forms a link between Socrates and the Stoics. The Cynic Diogenes of Sinope (*c*.412–323 BC) showed contempt for civilization and contemporary ideas of human decency and made a virtue of extreme poverty. [S.H.]

193 *The estates are specifically determined in accordance with the concept*: the three estates correspond to the three main stages in the advance of the concept which is the animating principle of the whole of ethical life. At first we have the stage of immediacy, when thought is sunk in *substance*— the life of feeling for which difference is not explicit. This type of social life is therefore based on the family. Secondly, differences are made explicit; we have advanced from implicit universality to explicit particularity, from feeling to reflection, so that substance now has a particular content and a universal *form* apprehended by reflection. Social life here is based on reflection, i.e. it is the product of education and so is specially characteristic of civil society—the child of the modern world. Thirdly, the synthesis of these; the particular consciously finds himself in the universal; the original unity has been restored, but on a higher plane. Private satisfaction is secured by the deliberate pursuit of *universal* ends. This type of social life prefigures the life of the state. Hegel's point is that the distinction between agriculture, industry, and the civil service is not a matter of accident or convenience, but is based on logical necessities.

194 *my distinguished friend, Herr Creuzer*: Georg Friedrich Creuzer (1771–1858) was appointed professor at Heidelberg in 1804 and was Hegel's colleague there from 1816 to 1818. His *Symbolism and Mythology of Ancient Peoples, especially the Greeks* [*Symbolik und Mythologie der alten Völker, besonders der Griechen*] was published 1810–12. Further editions followed in 1819–23 and 1836–43.

195 *has little occasion to think for itself*: 'hat dagegen wenig selbst zu denken'. This may be a misreading by the compiler of the Additions, Eduard Gans, of the phrase 'hat wenig sich selbst zu danken' ('owes little to itself') from one of the transcripts of Hegel's lectures. [S.H./A.W.W.]

199 *graphically portrayed by those acquainted with the matter*: Hegel may be thinking of the eminent English jurist Sir William Blackstone (1723–80). Blackstone's *Commentaries on the Laws of England* were published in four volumes from 1765 to 1769.

200 *An Emperor*: Theodosius II, who was Eastern Roman emperor from AD 408 to 450. The law in question (the *lex citationum*) was created in

AD 426 and included in the Theodosian Code (AD 438), 1. 4. 3. The 'college' consisted of Papinianus, Paulus, Gaius, Ulpianus, and Modestinus. When the 'votes' cast on a given point were equal (as they might be, since judgements by all members were not available on all points), Papinianus, the 'president', had a 'casting-vote'. If Papinianus expressed no opinion on the matter, the judge would be free to use his own judgement. [S.H.]

200 *No greater insult*: precisely such an 'insult' constitutes the principal thesis of Karl von Savigny's *Of the Vocation of our Age for Legislation and Jurisprudence* [*Vom Beruf unsrer Zeit für Gesetzgebung and Rechtswissenschaft*] (1815).

201 *the Corpus Juris*: *Corpus Juris Civilis* [*The Body of Civil Law*] is the modern name (first used in 1583) for the collection of works in jurisprudence which was compiled by order of Justinian I from AD 529 to 534, and which comprises the *Digest* (or *Pandects*), the *Institutes*, and the *Codex Constitutionum* (see second explanatory note to p. 20 [p. 329 above]). [S.H.]

203 *four dollars and twenty-three groschen, etc.*: in Hegel's day there were 24 groschen in one dollar [Reichsthaler]. [S.H./A.W.W.]

or always adopting, say, thirty-nine: the Jamaica Consolidated Slave Law of 1816 provided that in no case was a slave to suffer more than thirty-nine lashes in one day. Thirty-nine lashes was a not uncommon statutory maximum in slavery legislation, and Hegel was a student of the English press, where such legislation was a good deal discussed. See also Deuteronomy 25: 3.

204 *as Dionysius the Tyrant did*: Dionysius I (430–367 BC) became tyrant of the Greek colony of Syracuse in Sicily in 405 BC. His son, Dionysius II (*c*.395–343 BC), succeeded him as tyrant in 367 and ruled until 357. It is not clear whether Hegel has the father or son in mind and, in any case, no such anecdote has been found about either of them. [S.H.]

Goethe's theory of colours:. Goethe's anti-Newtonian theory of colours [*Farbenlehre*] was published in 1810 and found favour with Hegel, as well as with Arthur Schopenhauer (1788–1860), though it was generally dismissed by the scientific community of the time. For Hegel's discussion of Goethe's theory, see *Encyclopaedia* (1830), § 320 and Addition. [S.H.]

205 *The greatest enemy of the good is the better*: 'Le plus grand ennemi du bien, c'est le mieux' (in French in Hegel's text). The first edition has 'meilleur' rather than 'mieux'. The proverb is best known from its use by Voltaire (1694–1778) in his poem, *La Bégueule* [*The Prude*] (1772), which begins with the lines:

> *Dans ses écrits un sage Italien*
> *Dit que le mieux est l'ennemi du bien*

> In his writings a wise Italian
> Says that the better is the enemy of the good.
> [S.H./A.W.W.]

206 *phrases adequately expressing them*: e.g. *mancipium*, a taking by the hand, originally meant the ceremonial transfer of something from one person to another. The ceremony involved an actual transfer by hand and the speaking of certain words. Later, when the ceremony was dropped, the word was used to mean not a transfer but the possession of something acquired by formal transfer. (See third explanatory note to p. 177 [p. 350 above].)

207 *in the tragedy of the ancients*: i.e. Greek tragedy.

208 *as Herr von Haller does in his Restoration of Political Science*: Karl Ludwig von Haller (1768–1854) was a Swiss jurist and Romantic reactionary. His *Restoration of Political Science* [*Restauration der Staatswissenschaft*] was published 1816–20. [S.H.]

210 *a court of arbitration or court of the first instance*: a *Friedensgericht* is sometimes a court of the first instance, competent in some of the German states to try actions where only small amounts are at issue, sometimes an arbitration tribunal. A *Schiedsgericht* is a court of arbitration. The details in Hegel's text apply to the judicial organization of only some of the German states in his day.

the public administration of justice: in the Prussia of Hegel's time trials were not held in public. Here, therefore, we see an example of the way in which Hegel's logical unfolding of the concept of freedom leads to a *critique* of contemporary conditions. [S.H.]

211 *Decisions on these two different aspects are different functions*: (*a*) A jury of laymen finds the facts, and (*b*) the judge declares the law and, in criminal cases, pronounces sentence.

and then appointed a special judex to inquire into the facts: under the *formula* system of trial, the praetor heard the parties informally and prepared an issue which he sent in writing to a panel of *judices* for trial, instructing them to give judgement for A or B in accordance with the evidence. *Judices* were laymen and not magistrates, though they often required and possessed legal knowledge. A. H. J. Greenidge (*The Legal Procedure of Cicero's Time* (Oxford, 1901), 150) says that it is a mistake to hold that the work of *judices* was limited to reaching conclusions on points of fact.

212 *animi sententia*: the words were used in the formula of the oath of the Roman *judex*: 'I swear to the best of my belief', or 'on my conscience' [*ex animi mei sententia*].

213 *spring from the soul of the criminal*: the verdict of his peers is the verdict of the criminal's own soul or reason because reason is universal and so common to them and to him alike. His crime is his subjective defiance of his own reason or his inner universality (see *PR* § 99).

214 *the so-called jury-courts*: jury trials were not part of the Prussian judicial system in Hegel's lifetime. They were established in Magdeburg, Hanover, and Westphalia under Napoleon's rule, but later abolished. [S.H./A.W.W.]

215 *the corporation actualizes the unity as a limited but concrete totality*: *Polizei*, translated 'police' here, has a wider sense than that conveyed by 'police' in English. Hence in what follows it is generally translated 'public authority'. The justification for this is that Hegel himself sometimes (e.g. in *PR* § 235) uses *öffentliche Macht* as a synonym for *Polizei*; but the disadvantage of this rendering is that it is less specific than Hegel's word.— 'Corporation' [*Korporation*] is a term which originates with the workmen's corporations in ancient Rome. Hegel is of course not thinking of what we know as trades unions, since his *Korporationen* are societies of which both employers and employed are members. Indeed, he is thinking not only of economic organizations but also of religious bodies, learned societies, and sometimes of town councils.

217 *means and arrangements which may be of use to the community as a whole*: i.e. public utility undertakings such as drainage, water supply, etc.

219 *The disputes that have arisen in France*: Rousseau's *Émile* (1762) is the classic demand for freedom in education. State supervision was advocated by Louis-René de Caradeuc de La Chalotais (1701–85) in his *Essay on National Education* [*Essai d'Éducation nationale*] (1763).

221 *the Neapolitan lazzaroni for example*: these were homeless people in Naples who lived by begging and occasional work. They were named after the Hospital of St Lazarus, which served as their refuge. [S.H.]

223 *A prudent god has sundered the lands by the estranging sea*: 'deus abscidit prudens Oceano dissociabili terras' (Horace, *Odes*, I. 3) (in Latin in Hegel's text). Quintus Horatius Flaccus (65–8 BC)—since known as Horace—was the leading Roman lyric poet during the time of Augustus (63 BC–AD 14). [S.H.]

Livonia: Livonia was located on the eastern coast of the Baltic in present-day Estonia and Latvia. [S.H.]

224 *whose universal purpose is thus wholly concrete*: because the universal purpose of the corporation is at the same time the particular purpose of its members. In the system of needs, the universal is abstract because the particular individual in pursuing his end is not clearly conscious of the universal which regulates his activity. In the corporation the case is otherwise. The difference between the corporation and the state is that the purpose of the corporation, though universal for its members, in the sense that it is the same for all of them, is still restricted; it is not the purpose of all the members of society but that of a section only.

225 *privileges proper in the etymological sense*: a *privilegium*—from *privus* ('particular', 'special') and *lex* ('law')—is a law affecting an individual only and hence is something exceptional. But the privileges of an order, for example, although peculiar to it, cannot rightly be regarded as exceptional or accidental. The order itself is there because it is a branch of society; as one particular branch it is like other branches in being a branch, but it is distinct from them in other respects, and its distinction from others is outwardly manifest in its privileges.

226 *the two moments around which the disorganization of civil society revolves*: the stability and organic unity of the state are foreshadowed in the family and the corporation. Civil society is characterized generally by its atomicity, and it is saved from complete disintegration only by these fixed and organic institutions. Hegel is here using a metaphor drawn from the solar system: the sun is a fixed point whose attractive power prevents the dissipation of the heavenly bodies which revolve around it and so confers a unity on the system as a whole.

THE STATE

230 *the most terrible and drastic event*: i.e. the French Revolution of 1789 (and especially the Terror of 1793–4). [S.H.]

232 *leguleius*: a lawyer who depends on legal technicalities for getting the better of his opponent.

233 *Magna Carta . . . the Bill of Rights*: Magna Carta was signed by King John at Runnymede in 1215 and guaranteed certain baronial privileges against royal incursion. John later repudiated the agreement. The English Bill of Rights was issued in 1689 under William and Mary. It recognized certain civil and political rights of British citizens and established the political supremacy of parliament. [S.H./A.W.W.]

the Prussian General Legal Code: the Prussian General Legal Code was begun during the reign of Frederick the Great (who ruled from 1740 to 1786) but not promulgated until 1794. It was regarded by Hegel and others as an important legacy of Frederick and of the Enlightenment. [S.H./A.W.W.]

234 *the Holy Alliance*: the Holy Alliance was concluded in 1815 by Austria, Russia, and Prussia (all opponents of Napoleonic France) to maintain peace in Europe after Napoleon's defeat and to protect against the influence of modern (and especially revolutionary) political ideas from France. [S.H.]

always relative only and restricted, like any 'perpetual peace': Hegel is alluding (critically) to Kant's famous essay *Toward Perpetual Peace* [*Zum Ewigen Frieden*] (1795). [S.H.]

242 *the fable about the belly*: the fable recounted by Menenius Agrippa (consul in 503 BC) to dissuade the Roman *plebs* from secession. See Livy, *History of Rome*, I. 2. 32, and Shakespeare, *Coriolanus*, I. i. 93–151.

it is often reiterated nowadays: by Friedrich von Schlegel and other Romantics.

247 *toleration [Toleranz] in the strict sense of the word*: i.e. the state bears or endures them (from Lat. *tolerare*—to 'bear', 'endure', 'sustain').

the abolition of slavery: Quaker petitions against the slave trade were presented to Congress in 1783 and 1790, and the retort in question may have been made then, or perhaps, if the date is not too late, in 1820 during the debates on the Missouri Compromise.

247 *proved itself to be both wise and dignified*: in Prussia Jews gained a measure of emancipation in 1812 under the Edict Concerning the Civil Condition of the Jews (see the editor's Introduction, p. xi above). [S.H.]

251 *Giordano Bruno*: Giordano Bruno (1548–1600) was an Italian philosopher, priest, and cosmologist. He was condemned by the Church for allegedly holding opinions contrary to the Catholic Faith and speaking against it and its ministers, believing in metempsychosis and in the transmigration of the human soul into brutes, and denying the virginity of Mary (among other things). He was declared a heretic and burned at the stake in Rome. [S.H.]

forced Galileo to recant . . . his exposition of the Copernican view of the solar system: Nicolaus Copernicus (1473–1543) set out his heliocentric view of the solar system in his work *On the Revolutions of the Celestial Spheres* (1543). Galileo Galilei (1564–1642) defended the Copernican theory in his *Dialogue Concerning the Two Chief World Systems* (1632), but was forced to recant his views in 1633. [S.H.]

252 *Laplace, Exposition of the System of the World*: Pierre-Simon, marquis de Laplace (1749–1827), was a French mathematician and astronomer who made significant contributions to mathematical astronomy and probability theory. [S.H.]

253 *held up by some as the highest of ideals*: wishes for the unity of church and state were characteristic of Romantics like Friedrich von Schlegel and Adam Müller (1779–1829). In conformity with these wishes, many of them became Roman Catholics (see Addition to *PR* § 141 and explanatory note to p. 145 [p. 347 above]) and longed for the days when an emperor owed his crown to a pope.

256 *the history [Geschichte] of the state*: reading *Geschichte* ('history') for *Gesinnung* ('disposition'). [S.H./H.B.N.]

in the time of the Roman Emperors and the Praetorians: under the reforms instituted by Diocletian (AD 245–312) and Constantine (c.AD 280–337), the Praetorian Prefects, who were originally exclusively military officials, had supreme authority, under the Emperor, in both civil and military affairs.

thanks to those: it is no doubt Fries and the Romantics whom Hegel has in mind, as well as von Haller.

257 *those who hold that the divine is inconceivable*: Hegel may have in mind Kant and his followers, though, if so, this is a distortion of Kant's views. Kant argues that God cannot be known in himself but not that he is beyond all conceiving. For Kant's conception of God, see his *Critique of Pure Reason* (1781), A 567 ff. ['The Ideal of Pure Reason']. [S.H.]

258 *as we have seen on a grand scale*: in the French Revolution.

260 *difference in the number . . . supposed to be immanent*: in Aristotle's *Politics*, for example, the three principal types of constitution identified by

Aristotle—monarchy, aristocracy, and 'polity' or 'constitutional government' (of which democracy is a 'perversion')—are distinguished on the basis of the number of those who govern; see *Politics*, 1279a30 ff. [S.H.]

All these forms . . . maintaining them there: see Fichte, *Foundations of Natural Right*, § 16 (vi) [Baur trans., 144]. The 'forms' to which Fichte refers are monarchy, aristocracy, and democracy. The name and the idea of the *ephorate* were derived by Fichte from the constitution of Sparta, where the power of the two kings, who held office for life, was checked by the five ephors ('overseers'), who were elected annually. Fichte distinguished his ephors from the Spartan, however, and likened them rather to the Roman tribunes, because his ephors were to have a veto only and no executive power.

262 *See Roman history, for example*: the constitution of the Roman Republic was still in essence aristocratic in the second century BC, and was tottering into anarchy or despotism in the first century BC. Hegel assumes that this was due to a defect in the character of aristocratic government as such, not to the inability of the particular form of Roman aristocratic government to adapt itself to the rule of an empire.

the type organized into an objective constitution: i.e. limited or 'constitutional' monarchy, where the moments of the concept are objectified in different institutions which yet so interlock as to form a single whole (see *PR* § 272).

263 *Napoleon . . . wished to give the Spaniards a constitution a priori*: Napoleon Bonaparte (1769–1821) expelled the Bourbons from Spain and put his brother Joseph Bonaparte on the throne under the Constitution of Bayonne in 1808. With the breakdown of the Napoleonic regime in 1812–13, the Bourbons were restored together with the old constitution. A liberal document, the Constitution of Cadiz, was drawn up in 1812, but it remained a dead letter.

265 *officers' commissions up to a certain rank are saleable to this day*: in Hegel's day all officers' commissions from an ensign's to a lieutenant-colonel's were on sale, but there were restrictions on both purchaser and price.

268 *the unconditional character of that right is contained in its divinity*: if a monarch derives his authority from God, he rules by divine right—a claim accompanied with disastrous results when interpreted, as in seventeenth-century England for example, as a 'divine right to govern wrong'. Hegel holds, however, that God's will is not inscrutable, but intelligible, and that it is the task of philosophy to understand it both in itself and in its results in the world. Hence, philosophy may admit that a monarch rules 'by divine right' in the sense that monarchy is a *rational* institution, the apex and basis of the state as a rational and so as a divine institution, and yet deny that a monarch may be absolute or defy the will of the people, because rationality requires a limited, *constitutional* and not an *absolute* monarchy.

268 *in which one has recently begun to speak*: i.e. at the end of the eighteenth century and the beginning of the nineteenth, largely as a result of Rousseau's work.

270 *a 'daemon' (in the case of Socrates)*: Socrates describes this 'daemon' as 'a sort of voice which comes to me' and 'dissuades me from what I am proposing to do'. See Plato, *Apology*, trans. H. Tredennick, in *The Last Days of Socrates* (1954; Harmondsworth: Penguin Books, 1969), 64 [31C ff.]. [S.H.]

272 *recently it has been declared inconceivable*: Hegel has in mind Kant's rejection of the ontological proof of God's existence. See Kant, *Critique of Pure Reason* A 592 ff., and Hegel, *Encyclopaedia* (1830) § 51.

the other consequences that disrupt the Idea of the state: as, for example, in the French Revolution. If kingship is irrational, then the king may be guillotined, and Terror, the breakdown of political life, may follow. See the reference to the *salut du peuple* ('welfare of the people') in the Remark to the next Paragraph.

273 *the Idea of something unmoved by caprice*: Hegel's point here is that the monarch is not (or should not be) moved by or 'grounded in' the *particular* contingent, changing—and that sense, 'capricious'—interests that move the members of civil society. The monarch does not (or should not) act on the basis of his own *particular* concerns, and he should not represent a *particular* faction or 'interest group', but should stand above such factions. Herein lies the *majesty* of the monarch—a majesty secured by the fact that he *inherits* his crown, and does not earn it by virtue of any particular talents he may possess. Yet precisely because the monarch's will is 'groundless', his decisions are in another sense *nothing but* the expression of his own arbitrary will (*Willkür*). The range of his arbitrary will is, however, strictly limited (see, for example, *PR* §§ 282–3, 291–2). For the most part 'he is bound by the concrete content of the counsel he receives, and if the constitution is stable, he has often no more to do than sign his name' (Addition to *PR* § 279). It remains the case, therefore, that Hegel's monarch is a constitutional, not an absolute monarch. [S.H.]

drawn from this 'welfare of the people' (salut du peuple): a reference to the French Revolution and the Committee of Public Safety (Comité de Salut Public). [S.H.]

274 *the constitution becomes an electoral contract*: in the sixteenth century, by compelling the man of their choice to accept such a compact as a condition of election, the Electors acquired a distinct preliminary control of both the internal government of the Holy Roman Empire and its foreign policy, and so circumscribed the Emperor's authority.

the state disintegrates within and is overthrown from without: In this treatment of elective monarchy, Hegel has in mind both the Holy Roman Empire (in which the Emperor was chosen by a college of six Electors whose positions were hereditary) and the elective monarchy in Poland.

275 *I am not your prince, I am your master*: 'Je ne suis pas votre prince, je suis votre maître' (in French in the text). When Napoleon met Tsar Alexander I at Erfurt in 1808, he was visited by envoys from many conquered German states who hoped to gain concessions from him by adopting the position of dutiful subjects petitioning their sovereign. This is one of the many stories of Napoleon's rudeness on that occasion.

applied to or reflected in the sphere below: pardon (forgiveness) belongs essentially to the sphere of religion. See the end of the Remark to *PR* § 137.

279 *in concrete supervision by the supreme executive*: the difficulty which Hegel finds in the construction of a civil service organization springs from the fact that he wishes to combine (*a*) administrative efficiency with (*b*) private freedom. To attain (*a*), he prescribes (*i*) the division of the civil service into distinct departments: Treasury, Ministry of Health, etc., and (*ii*) the unified control of these departments at the top in the person of the Prime Minister or other supreme official (see Addition to this Paragraph). To attain (*b*), he prescribes that civil life with its concrete business of buying and selling, and the concrete individuals who compose it, shall be governed 'from below', i.e. by officials elected at least partly by themselves. These are the corporations' officials (see Remark to *PR* § 289) and probably mayors also. These popularly elected officers are at the same time the lowest rung of the official hierarchy; it is they and not civil servants proper who directly oversee everyday life; in them again the different branches of the civil service converge, in the sense that the Treasury and other departments issue their orders not directly to private individuals, but to the mayor or corporation official who is thus at the same time the lowest of the treasury (or other departmental) officials (see *PR* § 295).

283 *the notorious affair of Arnold the miller*: the miller in question was sued for arrears of rent which he could not pay because a nobleman had cut off part of his water-power to construct a fishpond. This famous case dragged on for years until Frederick the Great overrode the magistrates and found in the miller's favour.

286 *colossal architectural undertakings*: such as the building of the pyramids. [S.H.]

287 *The last moment in the legislature is the Estates [das ständische Element]*: the Estates (or Estates assemblies) are the bodies in which the estates of civil society are given a political significance (see *PR* § 303).

as for instance the Constituent Assembly did: the French Constitution of 1791 laid down that 'ministers and other agents of the executive power [. . .] shall be obliged to choose between their offices and that of representative' (Title III, Chapter I, Section 3, § 4). This meant that no members of the executive could sit in the new Legislative Assembly that held its first session on 1 October 1791. The 'self-denying ordinance' of May 1791 further stipulated that no member of the outgoing Constituent Assembly would be eligible for election to the new Legislative Assembly. See J. H. Stewart, *A Documentary Survey of the French Revolution* (New York: Macmillan, 1951), 224, 237, 269. [S.H.]

297 *the distinctive function of mediation in the sphere of politics*: see *PR* § 304. If we consider in abstraction the monarch and the estates constitutive of civil society, then they are opposed to one another as the one and the many, or as the abstract individual and the abstract universal. The latter Hegel calls the universal of 'all-ness' [*Allheit*] (see Remark to *PR* § 24) or 'empirical universality' (*PR* §§ 301, 304). These opposites become fused into a unity only if some middle term comes into existence to mediate between them and so to produce the concrete unity of a syllogism. The executive is such a middle term from the point of view of the crown, because it carries out the crown's will and so particularizes it in the estates of civil society. But the estates do not feel their unity with the crown until they acquire political significance as the 'Estates' and until one of the Estates, in virtue of its likeness in certain respects to the crown, is able to mediate between the crown and civil society as a whole. The agricultural estate shares certain characteristics in common with the crown (see *PR* § 305) and is thus in a position to be such a mediator. But it can act as such in the constitution only if its political function is embodied in an institution separate both from the crown, on the one hand, and industry (or its embodiment in a lower house of parliament), on the other; i.e. it must be embodied in an upper house. The upper house then mediates between civil society and the crown; and if the upper house on any given issue sides with the lower house, this helps the lower house and obviates the impression that the latter is a mere faction against the crown and not genuinely devoted to the interest of the state (see *PR* § 313).

300 *the voice of the people is the voice of God*: 'vox populi, vox Dei' (in Latin in Hegel's text).

the ignorant populace reproves everyone and talks most of what it understands least: 'Che'l volgare ignorante ogn' un riprenda e parli più di quel che meno intenda' (in Italian in Hegel's text). Ludovico Ariosto (1474–1533) was an Italian poet and author of the epic poem *Orlando Furioso* [*Orlando Enraged*] (1516). The lines quoted by Hegel are from Canto XXVIII, Stanza I.

A great spirit: i.e. Frederick the Great, who set as a question for the Berlin Academy prize in 1778: 'Is it useful to deceive the people?' Both here and in the *Phenomenology* [Miller trans., 336] Hegel substitutes 'permissible' for 'useful'.

the masses can fight, they're respectable at that . . . miserable: Goethe's lines (from 'Proverbially' [*Sprichwörtlich*]) are:

> Zuschlagen muß die Masse,
> Dann ist sie respektabel;
> Urteilen gelingt ihr miserabel.

(Hegel substitutes *kann* for *muß* and *da* for *dann*.)

304 *when they sang scurrilous songs*: in his *Life of Julius Caesar* (the first part of his *On the Life of the Caesars* [AD 121]), Suetonius (*c*.AD 69/75–130) reports the irreverent songs sung by Caesar's soldiers during his triumphal procession after his victories over Gaul. See Suetonius, *Life of Caesar*, 49. [S.H./A.W.W.]

305 *Those who talk*: the allusion is to the wishes of some Prussians in Hegel's day to sacrifice the autonomy of Prussia and join with other German states to form a new whole called 'Germany'.

308 *an estate [Stand] of its own—the estate of courage—dedicated to it*: see Plato's *Republic*, 373e, where the warriors form a special class distinguished by their courage, as the Guardians are by their wisdom.—In war the state is, in Hegel's understanding, the 'ideality' of the real differences subsistent within it, and one aspect of this unity is that all individuals are bound to sacrifice themselves to it if need be. This aspect is realized objectively in an institution distinct from other institutions, i.e. in a standing army. Hegel is here criticizing Kant, who had proposed the abolition of standing armies (see *Toward Perpetual Peace*, preliminary article 3).

309 *not for itself [i.e. for the courageous person himself]*: this Paragraph must be taken with its successor. Courage is a virtue (*a*) because it is an expression of freedom, (*b*) because the courageous person insists on his freedom to such an extent that he evinces it by renouncing the achievement of particular aims. But 'in itself' (i.e. in abstraction from its intrinsic worth) it is a virtue only in form because (*a*) although it negates the material realm, it remains negative to the last; such a negation is the formal character of a virtue but there is no intrinsic value in mere negation, even negation of the material realm. Before we can know whether a given act of courage is merely physical or is of a 'spiritual' character, we must enquire into all the circumstances (see Remark to *PR* § 328). (*b*) The intrinsic worth of courage (see *PR* § 328) is derived from the end it subserves, i.e. from the sovereignty of the state. This sovereignty is both the animating principle and the goal of courageous action, but this may never be present to the courageous person's mind. A courageous person's motive may be not the defence of sovereignty but only devotion to a leader or even personal gain; and of what he achieves (the defence of sovereignty) he may be unconscious and think that he has only captured a particular fort.

In India five hundred men conquered twenty thousand: in 1751 Robert Clive (1725–74) 'led five hundred men to Arcot [. . .] and there held a crumbling fortress against ten thousand Indians with a stiffening of French troops for fifty days'. At Plassey 'he brought three thousand men into action, of whom nine hundred only were Europeans, against a force of forty thousand infantry and fifteen thousand cavalry, and with a loss of less than a hundred men routed his opponents' (H. A. L. Fisher, *A History of Europe* (London: Edward Arnold, 1936), 764).

310 *to make war and peace, and to conclude treaties of all kinds*: these are the powers which Blackstone ascribes to the King of England (see *Commentaries*, I. 252 ff.).

The popularity of Pitt: William Pitt the Younger (1759–1806) became prime minister of England in 1783. He was initially opposed to war with Revolutionary France but, after the execution of Louis XVI in 1793, he yielded to popular sentiment and joined the First Coalition against France (which also involved Prussia, Austria, Spain, and Portugal). The Treaty of Campo Formio (1797) marked the victorious conclusion of Napoleon's campaign in Italy and the collapse of the First Coalition. In 1799 a Second Coalition against France was formed (with Austria and Russia), but this again proved unsuccessful. Pitt resigned as prime minister over the issue of Catholic Emancipation in 1801—by which time his war policy had become extremely unpopular in England—but he returned to the premiership in 1804. [S.H.]

315 *the spirits of peoples [Volksgeister]*: the conception of the 'spirit of a people', which has appeared elsewhere in this book (see *PR* §§ 33, 257 Remark, 274), seems to be ultimately due to Montesquieu; see *The Spirit of the Laws*, Part 3, Book 19, chap. 5.

world history as the world's court of judgement: 'World history is the world's court of judgement' ['Die Weltgeschichte ist das Weltgericht'] is a phrase from Schiller's poem 'Resignation' (1784).

316 *the movement of spirit in this element is the exhibition of that fact*: *PR* §§ 341–60 are a very compressed summary of Hegel's philosophy of history, and, without the commentary which that work supplies, they are perhaps no less hard to understand in German than they are in English. See G. W. F. Hegel, *The Philosophy of History*, trans. J. Sibree (New York: Dover Publications, 1956).

Those who have maintained this perfectibility: Hegel has in mind above all Gotthold Ephraim Lessing (1729–81), whose essay *The Education of the Human Race* [*Die Erziehung des Menschengeschlechts*] was published in 1780.

Know thyself: the keynote of the teaching of Socrates.

for them the plan of providence is inscrutable and incomprehensible: the reference is probably to Kant, who says (in the 'First Supplement' to *Toward Perpetual Peace*) that we must understand the progress of humanity and the eventual arrival of perpetual peace to be guaranteed by nature, or rather by *providence*, even though we can have no knowledge of the designs of providence, nor even know that such providence actually exists. [S.H.]

318 *undying fame as formal subjectivities*: great individuals gain fame for the greatness of their own specific acts, but they are not honoured or thanked by their contemporaries or by succeeding generations for their contribution to fulfilling the aims of the 'world-spirit', of *humanity as such*.

Only speculative philosophy recognizes this contribution by showing how the deeds of such individuals further the historical development of human freedom. [S.H.]

321 *Dr Stuhr*: Peter Feddersen Stuhr (1787–1851) published *The Downfall of Natural States [Der Untergang der Naturstaaten]* (1812) under the pseudonym Feodor Eggo. The book was a discussion, in the form of letters, of the *History of Rome [Römische Geschichte]* (1811) by Barthold Georg Niebuhr (1776–1831).

the recesses [Höhlen] and images of tradition: the reference is presumably to the Eleusinian mysteries in ancient Greece, which are thought to have begun around 1500 BC. These were initiation ceremonies held every year for the cult—based at Eleusis—of Demeter (the goddess of grain and fertility) and her daughter Persephone.

the whole falls apart into a group of particular national spirits: Greece was divided into a plurality of city-states, each possessed of autonomy and so with a 'spirit' of its own.

This opposition begins in the clash: this is in part a reference to the conflict between the patricians and plebeians in the first two centuries of the Roman Republic. What Hegel is describing in this paragraph, however, is a conflict not just between two social groups but between two *principles* that inform the Roman world. [S.H.]

322 *the unity of the divine and human nature*: this unity is grasped in Christianity and in particular in its central doctrine of the Incarnation. [S.H.]

the Germanic peoples: 'Germanic' *[germanisch]* here does not mean 'German' *[deutsch]*. It refers to the whole range of Germanic peoples who would go on to form the core of modern European nations. [S.H.]

These two realms: the 'secular' realm (as described in the preceding Paragraph) is that of the medieval, feudal state, and the 'intellectual' or 'spiritual' realm is that of medieval Christianity and the medieval Church. In this Paragraph Hegel appears to describe the process whereby the Church becomes increasingly 'worldly' (prior to the Reformation), and the secular state then develops into an ordered realm of right and law (in the wake of the Reformation). In this process the opposition between the 'secular' and the 'spiritual' is implicitly dissolved and the *state* emerges as the objective embodiment of *reason* and *truth*. At the same time, religion (in the form of Protestantism) comprehends through *feeling* the truth that the secular and spiritual are reconciled, while philosophy comprehends this through *concepts*. [S.H.]

323 *in religion*: by which Hegel understands Lutheran Protestantism. [S.H.]

in the ideal [ideell] world: i.e. the world of art, religion, and philosophy itself.

INDEX

*The
Oxford
World's
Classics
Website*

www.worldsclassics.co.uk

- Browse the full range of Oxford World's Classics online
- Sign up for our monthly e-alert to receive information on new titles
- Read extracts from the Introductions
- Listen to our editors and translators talk about the world's greatest literature with our Oxford World's Classics audio guides
- Join the conversation, follow us on Twitter at OWC_Oxford
- Teachers and lecturers can order inspection copies quickly and simply via our website

www.worldsclassics.co.uk

American Literature

British and Irish Literature

Children's Literature

Classics and Ancient Literature

Colonial Literature

Eastern Literature

European Literature

Gothic Literature

History

Medieval Literature

Oxford English Drama

Poetry

Philosophy

Politics

Religion

The Oxford Shakespeare

A complete list of Oxford World's Classics, including Authors in Context, Oxford English Drama, and the Oxford Shakespeare, is available in the UK from the Marketing Services Department, Oxford University Press, Great Clarendon Street, Oxford OX2 6DP, or visit the website at www.oup.com/uk/worldsclassics.

In the USA, visit www.oup.com/us/owc for a complete title list.

Oxford World's Classics are available from all good bookshops. In case of difficulty, customers in the UK should contact Oxford University Press Bookshop, 116 High Street, Oxford OX1 4BR.

THOMAS AQUINAS	Selected Philosophical Writings
FRANCIS BACON	The Essays
WALTER BAGEHOT	The English Constitution
GEORGE BERKELEY	Principles of Human Knowledge and Three Dialogues
EDMUND BURKE	A Philosophical Enquiry into the Origin of Our Ideas of the Sublime and Beautiful Reflections on the Revolution in France
CONFUCIUS	The Analects
DESCARTES	A Discourse on the Method
ÉMILE DURKHEIM	The Elementary Forms of Religious Life
FRIEDRICH ENGELS	The Condition of the Working Class in England
JAMES GEORGE FRAZER	The Golden Bough
SIGMUND FREUD	The Interpretation of Dreams
THOMAS HOBBES	Human Nature and De Corpore Politico Leviathan
DAVID HUME	Selected Essays
NICCOLÒ MACHIAVELLI	The Prince
THOMAS MALTHUS	An Essay on the Principle of Population
KARL MARX	Capital The Communist Manifesto
J. S. MILL	On Liberty and Other Essays Principles of Political Economy and Chapters on Socialism
FRIEDRICH NIETZSCHE	Beyond Good and Evil The Birth of Tragedy On the Genealogy of Morals Thus Spoke Zarathustra Twilight of the Idols

Bhagavad Gita

The Bible Authorized King James Version
With Apocrypha

Dhammapada

Dharmasūtras

The Koran

The Pañcatantra

The Sauptikaparvan (from the
Mahabharata)

The Tale of Sinuhe and Other Ancient
Egyptian Poems

The Qur'an

Upaniṣads

ANSELM OF CANTERBURY   The Major Works

THOMAS AQUINAS   Selected Philosophical Writings

AUGUSTINE   The Confessions
On Christian Teaching

BEDE   The Ecclesiastical History

HEMACANDRA   The Lives of the Jain Elders

KĀLIDĀSA   The Recognition of Śakuntalā

MANJHAN   Madhumalati

ŚĀNTIDEVA   The Bodhicaryàvatàra

Travel Writing 1700–1830

Women's Writing 1778–1838

WILLIAM BECKFORD   Vathek

JAMES BOSWELL   Life of Johnson

FRANCES BURNEY   Camilla
Cecilia
Evelina
The Wanderer

LORD CHESTERFIELD   Lord Chesterfield's Letters

JOHN CLELAND   Memoirs of a Woman of Pleasure

DANIEL DEFOE   A Journal of the Plague Year
Moll Flanders
Robinson Crusoe
Roxana

HENRY FIELDING   Jonathan Wild
Joseph Andrews and Shamela
Tom Jones

WILLIAM GODWIN   Caleb Williams

OLIVER GOLDSMITH   The Vicar of Wakefield

MARY HAYS   Memoirs of Emma Courtney

ELIZABETH INCHBALD   A Simple Story

SAMUEL JOHNSON   The History of Rasselas
The Major Works

CHARLOTTE LENNOX   The Female Quixote

MATTHEW LEWIS   Journal of a West India Proprietor
The Monk

HENRY MACKENZIE   The Man of Feeling